THE ULTIMATE FOOD LOVER'S GUIDE TO HOUSTON

From the editors, writers and staff of
My Table: Houston's Dining Magazine

THE ULTIMATE FOOD LOVER'S GUIDE TO HOUSTON

Teresa Byrne-Dodge, editor & publisher
Jen Cooper, designer
Paula Murphy, director of marketing & special projects
Jane Kremer, associate publisher for distribution

THE ULTIMATE FOOD LOVER'S GUIDE TO HOUSTON
Copyright 2008
Lazywood Press

The Ultimate Food Lover's Guide to Houston is published by Lazywood Press, Houston, Texas. All rights reserved. Material may not be reproduced — mechanically, electronically or by any other means, including photocopying — without written permission of the publisher. Requests for permission should be made in writing to *My Table* magazine/Lazywood Press, 1908 Harold Street, Houston, TX 77098.

ISBN: 978-0-9665716-2-2

Manufactured in Houston, Texas
First edition

Copies of this book are available at special discounts when purchased in bulk for premiums and sales promotions as well as for fundraising or educational use. Special editions or book excerpts can also be created to specification. For details, contact Jane Kremer at jane.kremer@my-table.com.

WWW.MY-TABLE.COM

PHOTO CREDITS
Page 4 photo courtesy of Hotel ZaZa. Page 15 photo courtesy of Del Frisco's Double Eagle Steak House. Page 16 crab photo courtesy of Truluck's; other photos by Kim Park and Paula Murphy. Page 31, 32 and 35 photos by Paula Murphy. Page 36 photo by Ralph Smith. Page 42 photo courtesy of Fiesta. Page 47 photo by Paula Murphy. Page 59 photo courtesy of McCain's Market. Page 64 photo by Kim Park. Page 69 and 71 photos by Paula Murphy. Page 80 "Cork Woman" photo by Kenny Haner; model Maryann Murray; Hair/MUA by In Focus Makeup. Other page 80 photos by Kenny Haner, Kim Park and Paula Murphy. Page 83 photo by Kim Park. Page 84 photo by Paula Murphy. Page 91 photo by Kim Park. Page 93 photo courtesy of Christopher's. Page 109 photo by Paula Murphy. Page 120 photo courtesy of Rio Ranch. Page 122 photo courtesy of Saint Arnold Brewing Company. Page 128 photo by Kim Park. Page 133 photo by Paula Murphy. Page 136 photos by Paula Murphy, Shannon O'Hara and Kim Park, plus fireplace photo courtesy of Rainbow Lodge. Page 139 photo by Kim Park. Page 144 photo by Larry Fagala. Page 177 photo courtesy of Cantina Laredo. Page 196 photo courtesy of El Meson. Page 199 photo by Kim Coffman. Page 205 photo by Kim Park. Page 208 photo courtesy of Glass Wall. Page 235 photo courtesy of Houston Luxury Magazine. Page 248 photo by Kim Coffman. Page 259 photo by Kim Park. Page 264 photo by Paula Murphy. Page 273 photo courtesy of Omni Hotels. Page 277 photo by Jerry Hebert. Page 283 and 291 photos by Paula Murphy. Page 296 photo by Fred Rogers. Page 302 photo by Paula Murphy. Page 315 photo by Kim Coffman. Page 322 photo by Dave Mead Photography. Page 330 photo courtesy of Hotel Icon. Page 333 photo courtesy of Yatra Brasserie. Page 336 photos by Paula Murphy, plus photos of Palazzo's, Hotel Granduca and Gravitas. Page 341 photo by Paula Murphy. Page 347 photo by Sofia van de Dys. Page 352 photo by Tracy Vaught.

BACK COVER
Thank you, Houston Mayor Bill White, Texas Monthly *food editor Patricia Sharpe and entertainers Lisa Hartman and Clint Black for your nice words on the back cover.*

TABLE OF CONTENTS

Introduction: Forks Ready? 7
A Food Lover's Glossary 9
Acknowledgments 11
Preface: The Houston Stew Pot 13

LOCAL FLAVORS 16

We begin with a city-wide tour of ethnic grocers, farmers' markets, butchers, fishmongers, bakeries, chocolate shops, coffeehouses and teahouses, gelaterias, cupcake cafes and specialty shops.

SIDEBARS INCLUDE

Recommended
Houston's Top Food Festivals . . 24
Farmers' Markets 28
Barbecue Supplies 37
Pick-Your-Own Orchards 46
Weekend Foodie Diversions . . . 49
Bagels: Roll With It 53
Cooking Classes and Schools . . . 62
Kitchen Gadgets 66
Starbucks: Notes from the Coffee
    Grounds 76
    by M. Yvonne Taylor

Personal Favorites
Where I Buy Chiles 21
    by Sylvia Casares
The Coolest Party in Town 33
    by Jackson Hicks
Where I Buy Seafood 41
    by Bryan Caswell
Saturday Morning at the Bayou
    City Farmers' Market 43
    by Chris Shepherd
Tea Time 60
    by Lee Q. Garcia
Making & Giving Chocolates . . 71
    by Heidemarie Vukovic

SPIRITED HOUSTON 80

Raise a glass to Houston's wine bars, neighborhood icehouses, wine and spirits retailers, taverns, pubs, hotel bars and beloved dives. Pace yourself: We want you to visit Texas' oldest craft brewery and a nearby winery, too.

SIDEBARS INCLUDE

Recommended
Choice Bars for Grown-Ups . . . 91
Tasting Away in Margaritaville . . 97
Pub Food 104
Hoist a Pint 113
Wine Education 125
Drinking Up Clear Lake 130

Personal Favorites
Best Gay Bars 100
    by Johnny Hooks
Great Sports Bars 116
    by Brian Ching
Top BYOBs 121
    by Charles M. Bear Dalton

>>

RESTAURANTS & CAFES **136**
We spotlight more than 330 restaurants, everything from fine-dining establishments to quirky ethnic eateries off the eaten path.

SIDEBARS INCLUDE
Recommended
Great Architecture.......... 140
Brunch 154
Cheap & Greasy Burgers..... 159
Mexican Breakfasts 166
Al Fresco Dining........... 173
Soulful Houston 179
Dining Solo................ 192
Open Very Late............. 200
A Mess of Ribs 206
Boiled Crawfish............ 209
Pizza Palaces 216
Oyster Bars 227
Top Tortas................. 231
Fried Chicken 241
Houston Culinary Awards:
    The Houston "Oscars" 248
Haute Tamales.............. 254

My, Oh My, It's Pecan Pie 269
Old-Fashioned Texas Eats 278
Cajun Po'Boys de la Mer..... 289
Great Greek Salad 298
Enchiladas: Green With Envy.. 309
Upscale Burgers............. 327

Personal Favorites
Where I Go For Jewish Food.. 145
    by Ted Powers
Where I Go For Dim Sum ... 185
    by Dorothy Huang
Yes, Honey, We *Can* Take
    The Kids................ 213
    by Sarah Gish
Where One Politico Eats..... 262
    by Anne Clutterbuck

INDEXES **336**
Index by Cuisine Type..338
Index by Business Type 341
Index by Special Features....................................343
Alphabetical index...346

FOLD-OUT MAP .... **INSIDE BACK COVER**

Introduction

FORKS READY?

My Table magazine, Houston's authority on local food, wine, restaurants and more, is delighted to present the definitive "foodie" guidebook to Houston. Written for both out-of-town visitors and Houstonians who love to explore the ever-surprising food and drink available in our city, *The Ultimate Food Lover's Guide to Houston* offers a lively and delicious romp through the city.

The book is divided into three main sections. *Local Flavors* is a city-wide smorgasbord of bakeries, ethnic markets, butchers, fishmongers, chocolate shops, coffee and teahouses, pick-your-own orchards, specialty markets, gelato and ice cream shops, annual food festivals and much more. *Spirited Houston* includes wine bars, icehouses, wine and spirits retailers, taverns, pubs, hotel bars, even a nearby winery and a local microbrewery. *Restaurants & Cafes*, of course, covers everything from fine-dining establishments to walk-up burger and fried-chicken shacks to oddball eateries that bring a smile with the salad.

Besides the primary listings — more than 550 in all — *The Ultimate Food Lover's Guide to Houston* includes dozens of sidebars, with everything from a list of our favorite boiled-crawfish spots to area farmers' markets, from a round-up of local cooking schools to a chocolatier's secret sources for chocolate-making supplies, from our favorite BYOB restaurants to five spots that serve English-style afternoon tea. We even gathered up a dozen-plus recipes from local celebrity chefs to share with readers who *do* want to try this at home. In other words, this book is richer, deeper and more varied than the traditional restaurant guidebook.

The Ultimate Food Lover's Guide to Houston is also highly subjective. We don't list everything in town — only those places that are worthy, beloved, compelling, irresistible or simply cannot be ignored. Our over-riding editorial guideline: Where would we send our best foodie friend?

HELP US KEEP THIS GUIDEBOOK UP TO DATE

Every effort has been made by the researchers, fact-checkers and editors to make this guide as accurate and useful as possible. However, many things can change after a book is published — establishments close or relocate, phone numbers, hours and prices change, restaurants come under new management, etc. Avoid frustration and call before traveling.

We want to hear from you concerning your experiences with this guidebook and how you feel it could be improved and kept up to date. We especially welcome news of noteworthy openings and closings. While we may not be able to respond to all comments and suggestions, we will take them to heart and make certain they are shared with the editors. Please send your comments and suggestions to the following address:

> *My Table* magazine/Lazywood Press
> Reader Comments
> 1908 Harold Street
> Houston, TX 77098

Or simply email the editor at teresa.byrnedodge@my-table.com. Thank you for your input!

A NOTE ABOUT ADDRESSES

All the addresses in this guide are "web searchable," and we've included cross streets and other location details to help you on your foodie quest. For restaurants with more than two locations, we've listed the primary or original location only.

Keep in mind that the greater Houston area encompasses a huge sprawl of highways and thoroughfares, and some go by a variety of names. Below is a brief list of major highways and their alternate names.

Beltway 8	*Sam Houston Parkway, The Beltway*
Highway 59	*Southwest Freeway (southwest of downtown)*
	Eastex Freeway (northeast of downtown)
Highway 288	*South Freeway*
Highway 290	*Northwest Freeway*
Interstate 10 (I-10)	*Katy Freeway (west of downtown)*
	East Freeway (east of downtown)
Interstate 45 (I-45)	*North Freeway (north of downtown)*
	Gulf Freeway (south of downtown)
Loop 610	*The Loop*

A FOOD LOVER'S GLOSSARY

Not from Texas? Then you can be forgiven for perhaps not having heard of all of these Cajun, Creole, Mexican, South American, Vietnamese and other regional specialties, some of which are practically staples of the Houston dining scene. Here are brief descriptions of items not typically found at chain restaurants or major grocery stores elsewhere in the country:

AGUA FRESCA (Mexican) juice made from blended fruits or seeds, sugar and water

ANDOUILLE (Cajun) spicy pork sausage

BANH MI (Vietnamese) baguette sandwich with meat, cilantro, pickled carrots and daikon (radish)

BARBACOA (Mexican) slow-cooked meat, often steamed in a pit

BEIGNET (Creole) a holeless square doughnut dusted in powdered sugar

BOUDIN (Cajun) seasoned sausage typically stuffed with pork and rice (and blood, for *boudin noir*)

CAJETA (Mexican) a thick syrup of caramelized sweetened milk, similar to *dulce de leche*

CARNITAS (Mexican) small chunks of pork, usually braised, roasted or fried

CAMPECHANA (Mexican) shrimp and seafood cocktail, usually with diced tomatoes, onions, jalapeños and avocados

CHICHARRONES (Mexican) fried pork skin

CHILAQUILES (Mexican) casserole with scrambled eggs, tortilla strips and salsa

CHIMICHURRI (South American) marinade or sauce for grilled meat, typically made with parsley, garlic, paprika and other spices

CHURRASCO (South American) grilled beef, sausage and other meats, sometimes served on skewers

CHURRO (Mexican) ridged cylindrical doughnut sprinkled with powdered sugar and cinnamon

COCHINITA PIBIL (Mexican) slow-roasted pork marinated in citrus juice and colored with achiote (annatto)

DIRTY RICE (Cajun) white rice cooked with chicken liver or giblets, bell pepper, celery and onion

DULCE DE LECHE (South American) see *cajeta*, above; can be in syrup or candy form

EMPANADA (South American) baked or fried turnovers with savory or sweet fillings

>>

ÉTOUFFÉE (Creole) thick, stew-like sauce of butter and flour (roux), cayenne pepper, onions, bell peppers and celery, typically served with crawfish or shrimp

GORDITA (Mexican) thick corn or flour griddled tortilla, wrapped around a filling

HUEVOS RANCHEROS (Mexican) fried eggs covered in *ranchero* (spicy tomato) sauce, served on warm tortillas, often with refried beans

KING CAKE (Creole) Mardi Gras specialty made of sweet bread dough, frosting and colored sugars (yellow, green and purple), with a small plastic baby doll tucked inside — finding the doll in your slice is considered lucky

KING RANCH CHICKEN (Tex-Mex) casserole of chicken, corn tortillas, tomatoes, green chiles and cream of mushroom soup

KOLACHE (Czech) round baked yeast roll traditionally filled with savory, fruit or sweet filling

LICUADO (Mexican) milkshake-like drink of blended fruit, ice and milk (water or juice may be substituted)

MASA (Mexican) generally the cornmeal dough used to make tamales and corn tortillas

MIGAS (Tex-Mex) scrambled eggs with tortilla strips, tomatoes, chiles and cheese

MOLE (Mexican) thick sauce of tomatoes, chiles, seeds (pumpkin or sesame), nuts (almonds or peanuts), spices and, often, chocolate, traditionally served over chicken

RANCHERO (Mexican) "ranch style," often referring to a spicy tomato sauce (*salsa ranchera*)

TACOS AL PASTOR (Mexican) pork marinated with pineapple, onion red chile and other seasonings, then grilled with pineapple, sliced and served in tortillas

TAMALE (Mexican) corn dough (*masa*), usually with a meat or cheese filling, steamed inside a corn husk

TORTA (Mexican) hot or cold sandwich on a crusty white roll

TRES LECHES (Mexican) moist cake soaked in "three milks" — condensed, evaporated and whole milk (or cream)

TURDUCKEN (Cajun) a layered poultry dish of boned turkey stuffed with boned duck that is stuffed with a boned chicken

TURPORKEN (Cajun) similar to turducken, but with a pork loin between the turkey and the chicken

ACKNOWLEDGMENTS

A guidebook like this — especially the first edition — is composed of tens of thousands of details that must be tamed, organized and put to work. I can't imagine doing it alone. My deepest appreciation goes to the visionaries whose consultation, digging, hand-holding and enthusiasm made this project happen. Among the many, I must single out three, including graphic designer/cartographer/former English major Jen Cooper, who is as fussy as I am about the details; *My Table* director of special projects Paula Murphy, who also takes photos, writes cutlines, edits recipes and knows how to meet a deadline; and Jane Kremer, our associate publisher for distribution, who helped get this copy of the guidebook from the printing plant into your hands. We all learned from this project, and the ladies made it a true pleasure.

I'm indebted to the many writers, researchers, photographers, reviewers and contributors who wrote text, spent tedious hours setting up files, checked facts, took photos, proofread and scrambled every time we needed "just one more thing." Many of these folks are regular or occasional *My Table* magazine contributors, including Dennis Abrams, William Albright, George Igor Alexander, Rose Cahalan, Kim Coffman, Jeanne Cooper, Eric Gerber, Mark Hanna, Patricia Martin, Jim Sanders, James Sulak and Robin Barr Sussman.

Special thanks to *My Table* columnist Micki McClelland (see her regular *Food Lover's Quiz-ine* in the magazine) for her fun wordsmithing and Vickie Staff, *My Table*'s advertising director. I want to thank our Rice University intern Nikki Metzgar, who was tossed into this project and did an excellent job researching and writing between senior-year finals. Also, thanks to Mike Riccetti, a frequent *My Table* contributor who scours the city for the best small, inexpensive spots. Check out his book, *Houston Dining On the Cheap*, now in its third edition. And thank you, artist Brady Smith, for your "running man with fork" — and all your other *My Table* illustrations over the years.

Other folks joined us for the first time on this guidebook project, including Leigh Bell, Jordan Chan, Kenny Haner, Payman Khania, Jenny Rees, Sarah Rufca and Jessica West. I look forward to them becoming regulars for the magazine, too.

There were also a number of civilians who found themselves in the wrong place at the right time and were pressed into guidebook service, including Cameron Ansari (who must have eaten a thousand meals >>

"for research"), Dick Dace, Jacquie Miller, Kim Park, Stuart Rosenberg, Kelly Snow, Mark Sullivan and Andrew Yeh. Even my two kids worked on this book. Taylor Dodge wrote several of the listings, while Sam Dodge dialed every phone number and checked every website in the book.

Because we wanted *The Ultimate Food Lover's Guide to Houston* to be more than simply a directory of local restaurants, we asked a number of friends and acquaintances to contribute sidebars to enrich the book and take readers deeper into Houston's food scene. Thanks to all who provided sidebars to the book, including restaurateur Sylvia Casares, chef Bryan Caswell, Houston Dynamo player Brian Ching, City Council member Anne Clutterbuck, wine guru Bear Dalton, tea expert Lee Q. Garcia, writer Sarah Gish, caterer Jackson Hicks, writer Johnny Hooks, cookbook author Dorothy Huang, writer Ted Powers, chef Chris Shepherd, writer M. Yvonne Taylor and chocolatier Heidemarie Vukovic.

A big shout-out, too, to the local chefs, restaurateurs and mixologists who lent us their recipes: Sean Beck, Sara Brook, Bryan Caswell (again), Michael Cordúa, Mark Cox, Robert Del Grande, Levi Goode, Donnette Hansen, Mark Holley, Elouise "Ouisie" Adams Jones, Benjy Levit, Tony Mandola, John Sheely and Carl Walker.

At Rice University, an Action Learning Project team of students helped us set up our book-distribution network and and used the project to complete work toward their MBA. Our 2008 ALPies included Vickas Dangayach, Josh Gravenor, Katie Hilton, Jon Hook, Rick Kang and Kristen Wood. Thanks for all your research and well-written distribution plan.

Many, many thanks to the guidebook underwriters who believed in this project when it was still just an idea on paper. Very simply, we could not have done this without your support. They are Beirne, Maynard & Parsons, LLP, Chefs' Produce, Greater Houston Convention & Visitors Bureau, Houston Downtown Management District, KUHF-88.7 Houston Public Radio and Wells Fargo.

And if you bought a copy of *The Ultimate Food Lover's Guide to Houston*, thank you, too, dear reader.

Teresa Byrne-Dodge

editor & publisher

Preface

THE HOUSTON STEW POT

Every city has at least one icon that is the essence of its local restaurant culture. Dungeness crab stands on Fisherman's Wharf, for example, could only mean San Francisco; Miami conjures up mom-and-pop Cuban sandwich joints; New Orleans has its oyster bars. Houston is such a diverse melting pot that the city has spawned several "typical" kinds of restaurants, from inner-city barbecue joints with smoke-stained walls the color of tobacco to upscale Asian restaurants furnished with museum-quality *objets d'art* to a downtown aquarium-and-restaurant complex complete with Ferris wheel and albino tigers — the perfect emblem for all that is kooky and wonderful in this city.

Rising from its roots as a settlement on a swampy expanse to a thriving cosmopolitan tangle of freeways, skyscrapers, parks, malls, inner-city neighborhoods and a mass of suburban tentacles, Houston is dotted with amazing restaurants. It's a city where nearly every cuisine you can name is represented. Sardinian? Yes. Ethiopian? Sure, several. Pakistani? Guatemalan? Korean? Of course.

So how did Houston become such a foodie city?

The truth is such dining-out riches came fairly late to Houston. Unlike, say, Boston or Chicago, we had few settled ethnic neighborhoods where one could find family-run multi-generation restaurants. And let's be honest. Until liquor by the drink was ratified by local voters in 1972, the Houston restaurant scene was fairly dull.

This was a city where beef was king and its royal court included enormous Gulf shrimp and mild-flavored oysters from nearby Galveston Bay. But if the basic ingredients were luxurious, their preparation was, *uh*, predictable. The beef was mostly cut into thick steaks or smoked for hours in steel-drum barbecue pits, and the seafood was generally fried.

That changed in the 1980s, when Houston began to mature as an urban center. Part of the credit must go first to the oil boom, then the technology boom that brought so many Yankees and foreigners to this city and, likewise, took so many Houstonians to other countries. The result is that adventurous restaurateurs and chefs have found their efforts ever more welcome by a steadily more sophisticated dining-out public.

>>

Asians in particular have wrought a major influence on the local food scene, and we have countless Thai, Chinese, Japanese and Vietnamese restaurants as well as many fusion permutations, such as French-Japanese and Pacific Rim-Mexican hybrids. Many of these ethnic groups have clustered into distinctive neighborhoods. There's Little Saigon just south of downtown, Korea Town in Spring Branch and the sprawling Chinatown in the southwest part of the city. Such neighborhoods are not only well stocked with restaurants, there are also ethnic supermarkets, bakeries, liquor stores and fishmongers. Visiting these neighborhoods can easily turn into a daylong culinary adventure of dining, sampling and shopping.

Latin Americans, too, have greatly impacted Houston's dining scene over the past 25 years. We've never had a shortage of cheesy-greasy Tex-Mex cantinas around town, but now we find many other Latin cuisines, including elegant Mexico City-style Mexican dining. Hugo Ortega gratified (or confounded, depending upon your expectations) many when he opened his much-praised Hugo's restaurant a couple years ago. It's so authentically Mexican that the pastry chef even grinds his own cocoa beans for the chocolate. Nicaraguan native Michael Cordúa — who has Américas, Churrascos, Artista and the Amazon Grill — can pretty much take credit for single-handedly launching the Nuevo Latino culinary movement not just in Houston but in the United States.

Generally speaking, Houston has always been less trendy than either the East Coast or the West Coast. As food fads swept back and forth across the country, some took root here while others passed us by. When we find something we like, we stick with it. The Paul Prudhomme-fueled mania for blackened redfish and étouffée of the 1980s, for example, didn't make such big waves here because we've long eaten Cajun food. It was already part of the local potage, if you will, and it still is.

Indeed, when the late *New York Times* food critic Craig Claiborne once declared there are only five American regional cuisines worthy of serious attention — barbecue, Cajun, Creole, Tex-Mex and soul food — he probably didn't appreciate that all of those converge in Houston as nowhere else.

You might be asking, what *don't* they have in Houston? Well, we don't have a single Icelandic restaurant. Yet.

This essay is adapted from an article by Teresa Byrne-Dodge that originally appeared in the September 2005 issue of Texas Highways *magazine.*

local flavors

To begin the grazing tour of our abundant city, we've set out to explore Houston's local flavors.

Guided by this chapter, you will breeze into open-air farmers' markets where the produce, honey, meat and eggs on display come from bona fide farmers and are defined by "fresh and local." Linger over the spread laid out by our butchers, bakers and *cajeta latte* makers, by our fishmongers, chocolate shops and specialty grocery stores. Taste and take home everything from a *boule* to dragon fruit, from Taiwanese sno-cones to turducken, from candle-warmed Zen teas to burlap bags full of fresh oysters, from venison tamales to *babaganoush*, from Russian dumplings to Finnish licorice.

Use this chapter to find *chaat* corners that have nothing to do with small talk, visit a Latino *paleta* shop that offers its frozen fruit treats in 33 varieties or pick a class at an area cooking school. You'll discover that despite Starbucks' ubiquitous presence, independent coffeehouses have had a resurgence, and the charming revival of teahouses in the city is not limited to the August moon, but offers tea service year round. We have bagel shops, pick-your-own fruit orchards and fancy toys for >>

barbecue wizards.

Although many of these listings also dish up a counter or a few tables and chairs for eating in, the focus in *Local Flavors* is not sit-down dining (see chapter three, *Restaurants & Cafes*). Rather, the following pages are bursting with food resources unusual and playful, fanciful and unexpected. This is the chapter for the serious cook tracking down hard-to-find ingredients and kitchen wares. It's also the chapter for those who can't or don't want to cook, since it bulges with sumptuous prepared-food counters that aim to seduce the eye before you know what hit your wallet.

Houston's transformation from a meat-and-potatoes town to an international culinary city is a fairly recent phenomenon and owes much to the immigrants who have added their influence to the city's stock pot. The foods and cooking styles from Latin America, Asia, the Middle East and Europe have resulted in a local food tradition built layer upon delicious layer. That inspired stew makes Houston more than simply a city — it's one vast ethnic market. And *Local Flavors* is your guide.

An appreciation for all that is gloriously tasty guides this chapter. It's a heady ride on the street of gastronomic dreams. So start the hunger pangs, polish up your sweet tooth, put the palate in gear for fun, grab a shopping bag and let's indulge.

LOCAL FLAVORS

THE ACADIAN BAKERS

604 W. ALABAMA at Audubon
713-520-1484
www.acadianbakers.com
MAP E7

In lower Montrose, this neighborhood fixture (here since 1979) is justly famous for its custom cheesecakes and party cakes, many spiked with liqueur, such as amaretto. The wedding cakes — strawberry butter cream and Italian cream are popular favorites — and groom's cakes are gorgeous, and we also like this shop for traditional New Orleans-style king cakes. (They give you the tiny baby doll separately, for you to insert into the cake or not.) When ordering a custom cake, call for an appointment and allow at least 24 hours for preparation; wedding cakes, of course, should be ordered as far in advance as possible. For everyday snacks, try the fudge cake, carrot cake or, during the winter holidays, gingerbread men. Acadian Bakers also offers deli sandwiches and will deliver box lunches.

AIRLINE FARMERS MARKET

(aka FARMERS MARKETING ASSOCIATION) The official name is Farmers Marketing Association, but everyone calls this Mexican-style, mostly outdoor wonderland the Airline Farmers Market. Go on a weekend and meander through the narrow aisles.

2520 AIRLINE just inside Loop 610, behind Canino's Produce
713-862-8866
MAP E5

You will find mountains of chiles and produce (some totally unfamiliar, most artfully displayed), as well as dried fruits, grains in bulk, dried beans and spices at some of the cheapest prices in town. On a recent visit we bought excellent avocados and mangoes and a basket of gargantuan corn. Stuff your pocket with dollar bills, as most things are $1 or $2, and the vendors accept cash only. And come hungry: Numerous taco trucks are parked in back waiting to serve you a Mexican breakfast or fast lunch. If you don't speak Spanish, just point at what you want.

AIRLINE SEAFOOD MART

1841 RICHMOND between Hazard and Woodhead
713-526-2351
MAP E7

This unassuming shop, which is both a wholesale and retail operation, is easy to miss. But like all good things, Airline Seafood is worth the small effort it takes to locate and add to your regular food-shopping routine. The bare-bones shop has a large international selection of finfish and shellfish (from mahi mahi to enormous sea scallops to shark), but owner Steve Berreth has made a specialty of ultra-fresh Gulf Coast seafood: drum, flounder, croaker,

LOCAL FLAVORS

sheepshead, grouper, cobia, various snapper and much more. Aside from the raw fish selections, Airline also makes its own *campechana* rich with seafood and avocado, as well as smoked salmon, gumbo and crab cakes. We especially recommend the supremely retro stuffed crabs, which you bake in a 350-degree oven for 15 minutes.

ALAMO DRAFTHOUSE

1000 WEST OAKS MALL, Westheimer at Hwy. 6
281-920-9211
www.drafthouse.com
MAP A7

531 S. MASON at Merrymount, Katy
281-492-6900
MAP A6

Why does it seem like movies always start just when you're ready to sit down to dinner? For those tired of the age-old dilemma of early-bird dinner before the movie vs. waiting until the late screening and fighting off sleep, there's Alamo Drafthouse. This concept started in Austin: If all you want is dinner and a movie, why not combine the two? Each row of seats has a table in front of it, and before the movie begins you can make your order from the menu of standard American grill choices — burgers, pizza, salad, mozzarella sticks, you get the idea. The selection of draft and bottled beers, however, goes beyond the pale to include both local brews and a slew of quality imports, even a Drafthouse amber brewed in Austin. The waiters are surprisingly deft and unobtrusive once the feature begins, so you can eat, drink and be entertained. A word of warning to families and teens: All shows are 18 and up (unless accompanied by a parent), and children younger than six are not allowed except at shows designated all ages.

AMY'S ICE CREAM

3816 FARNHAM near Greenbriar
713-526-2697
www.amysicecreams.com
MAP E6

This Austin import is a local favorite, and for good reason. The vibe is casual, the people are friendly and the ice cream is addictively good. Seven varieties of chocolate and vanilla are standbys, and eight remaining flavors rotate onto the menu daily with the season and at the caprice of the staff. On a given day, they could include malted Belgian, cranberry muffin, campfire treat (graham cracker, marshmallow and chocolate chunks in vanilla) and a creation ambiguously named "The Dude." The atmosphere stays fun with a photo booth, graffiti on the walls and the occasional scoop tossed across the room. Staffers know exactly what mix-ins complement each flavor, and if a particular creation strikes your fancy you can put your name on the flavor call list and be notified every time it's on the menu.

ANTIDOTE COFFEE

Two young couples — Dawn Callaway and Scott Repass and Miriam Carrillo and Scott Walcott — own Antidote, where the low-slung furniture, records spinning and friendly staff make this Heights-area spot pure cure for all that frazzles. Regulars swear by the Velvet Tea made of chocolate, organic *rooibos* (South African red tea) and mint leaves. Adventurous types should try the *cajeta latte*, made with caramelized goat's milk. Snacks include German chocolate cake, quiche, fruit and cheese, red pepper hummus. As for those habit-forming brownies: Only the baker knows the precise ingredients. For people who want to unwind rather than wind up, beer and wine are stocked in the fridge. By the way, all the teas and coffees are fair trade. During happy hour 4 to 7 p.m. enjoy $2 Shiner and $1 double espresso shots. Free WiFi with purchase.

729 STUDEWOOD at 8th
713-861-7400
www.myspace.com/antidotecoffee
MAP E5

ARANDAS BAKERY

Arandas Bakery, an offshoot of the popular Taqueria Arandas, features Mexican-style breads, pastries and desserts. All the items are baked fresh and restocked throughout the day. To a pastry purist, the treats mostly feel like they could use a little more sugar and a little

8331-C BEECHNUT at S. Gessner, and other locations
713-771-3616
www.arandasbakery.com
MAP C8

Personal Favorites
WHERE I BUY CHILES

By Sylvia Casares

CANINO'S PRODUCE (*2520 Airline, 713-862-4027*) has great piles of fresh, dried and smoked chiles at excellent prices. Walking around here, especially in the back open-air market, is like being in a Mexican market.

In terms of grocery stores, I find the best chiles at **CENTRAL MARKET** (*3815 Westheimer, 713-386-1700*), **WHOLE FOODS** (*2955 Kirby, 713-520-1937, and other locations*) and **FIESTA** (*6200 Bellaire Blvd., 713-270-5889, and other locations*).

I only cook with fresh dried chiles; I never use powdered chiles. I don't recommend you buy chiles that are in plastic bags, because you can't tell how fresh they are. A good, dried chile is untorn, pliable and fragrant. If it crumbles in your hand, it is too old and too dry.

In 2008, Sylvia Casares, chef/owner of Sylvia's Enchilada Kitchen, was named one of the top 10 best Latino chefs in the USA by the Spanish language magazine, Siempre Mujer.

LOCAL FLAVORS

less flour, but the cinnamon-covered goodies don't disappoint, especially the crunchy *churros*. The standout of the bakery are the *tres leches* cakes and the just-sour-enough, football-shaped loaves of bread, continually replenished in their own bin. And the great thing about Arandas Bakery is that anyone who wants to try one of everything can do so for very little green.

> **1010 W. CAVALCADE**
> between Airline and N. Main
> **713-863-7074**
> www.asiamarket-hou.com
> **MAP** E5

ASIA MARKET & CONVENIENCE

This small Heights market has kept a low profile for years, catering to the Cambodian, Laotian and Thai communities. The shelves are stocked with canned goods, such as date palm, dried shrimp, chile pastes, coconut jelly and salted black beans, and the refrigerated section has produce (e.g. huge bags of mung bean sprouts), frozen ant eggs, fresh noodles and seafood. Not long ago, the owners renovated the store a little to take advantage of the growing reputation of their prepared-food counter, which serves up excellent Thai food. They added a sign out front, printed the menu in English and installed tables and chairs for dining in. The result is that Asia Market is now more accessible than before. But don't worry: It's lost none of its authenticity.

BALKAN MARKET

The second outpost by the Bosnian family who also own Cafe Pita+ just across the road, Balkan Market stocks mostly imports from the former Yugoslavia. One wall has goods for preparing a traditional Balkan meal, including pickles and Shokata sodas; toward the back of the shop, there is a refrigerated section that features dried meats and hard sausages, as well as dairy products (e.g. butter, thick creamy cheesy spreads, freshly made brined cheese). The reticent will be drawn to the aisle with prepackaged sweets, cookies and crackers. Wafer sandwiches with different flavors of nougat are popular, especially the Croatian Jadro brand. For Nutella fans, Eurokrem — which is similar and possibly better — is also stocked, as is a selection of buttery tea cookies. The two things not to miss: a loaf of the fresh, yeasty *lepinja* (it's baked at the restaurant and brought over to the shop a couple times a day) and a jar of the traditional red-pepper spread, *ajvar*.

> **10928 WESTHEIMER** at Lakeside Country Club Dr.
> **713-953-7237**
> **MAP** B7

In Matters of Food, as in Matters of Law, Getting One's Just Desserts is the Best Conclusion.

Here's to Houston, a City Where Great Dining and Great Lawyers Abound!

BEIRNE, MAYNARD & PARSONS, L.L.P.

STRATEGIC LITIGATION FOR A COMPLEX WORLD℠

HOUSTON • DALLAS
WWW.BMPLP.COM

LOCAL FLAVORS

Recommended
HOUSTON'S TOP FOOD FESTIVALS

The food-obsessed should mark their calendars for these Houston food festivals that celebrate our melting pot of cultures. Come with an empty stomach and wear comfortable shoes.

BEAUJOLAIS WINE AND FOOD FESTIVAL

At this French-accented event, you'll be among the first to uncork the year's just-arrived Beaujolais Nouveau vintage, plus sip the night away sampling Villages and the finest *cru* wines. Graze on the best Houston chefs have to offer too. Look for ticket sales beginning in September for this special French occasion celebrated around the world.
Takes place Downtown Hyatt Regency Hotel, 1200 Louisiana
Event date Third Thursday of November, or thereabout
Contact 713-960-0575 (French-American Chamber of Commerce)

CAESAR SALAD COMPETITION

For anyone who loves a great Caesar salad, Houston's annual Caesar Salad Competition is a must-see — or, make that, a must-taste. This popular toss-up, which is the oldest Caesar salad competition in the U.S., brings together some 20 Houston-area chefs from the city's best restaurants who compete in four categories. Guests are invited to sample every salad, washing them down with free-flowing wine or bottled water, and vote for the Consumers' Choice Award. You've never seen Caesar salad like this — Caesar salad lollipops, Caesar salad ice cream floats, Caesar salad martinis, inside-out Caesar salad, Caesar salad tacos, Caesar salad soup and beyond.
Takes place Doubletree Hotel Allen Center, 400 Dallas
Event date A Friday in mid-October
Contact 713-609-5510

GRAND WINE AND FOOD AFFAIR

This wine and food extravaganza presented by Central Market has become a local tradition garnering national attention. The affair features five days of wine and food from culinary influences worldwide. Pick your pleasure from the roster of events that might include winery luncheons at area restaurants, a vintner dinner at a Texas winery, celebrity cooking classes and demos, special guest speakers, a worldly bistro brunch and wine seminars. Saturday always features the Sienna Sip & Stroll with an outdoor walk-around wine tasting.
Takes place Marriott Sugar Land Town Square, 445 Commerce Green, Sugar Land, and other locations
Event date Last week in April
Contact 281-491-0216 (Fort Bend Chamber of Commerce)

THE ORIGINAL GREEK FESTIVAL

Be Greek for a day at this annual outdoor festival and you'll become an expert at Greek cuisine while enjoying Greek music. There are children's activities and an Athenian playground at the always-expanding festival that is a favorite for all ages.
Takes place Annunciation Greek

BELDEN'S

> **99 BRAESWOOD SQUARE** at Chimney Rock and N. Braeswood
> **713-723-5670**
> **MAP** D8

This is one beautiful little supermarket, with gleaming floors, plenty of space in the aisles and a friendly staff that almost makes this seem like a small-town grocery store. Even the entrance, where seasonal flowering plants and herbs are often sold, is kept manicured. Inside, you'll find an excellent meat department (including quite a range of organic meats), produce that is fresh and attractively displayed, smoked fish, gourmet goods (e.g. oils, vinegars and chips), an onsite bakery and a surprisingly large wine collection. The city's Jewish community comes here for the extensive selection of kosher products, including wine, meat and poultry (there is a full time *mashgiach* on the premises), cheeses, dry goods and candy.

BRASIL

> **2604 DUNLAVY** at Westheimer
> **713-528-1993**
> **MAP** E6

Long the artsy haunt for the stylish and smart, Brasil is the patriarch of Montrose-area coffee houses. Owned by Dan Fergus and Magda Sayeg, Brasil is a perennially popular meeting spot for an artsy-intellectual crowd.

Orthodox Cathedral, 3511 Yoakum
Event date First week in October
Contact 713-526-5377

RODEO UNCORKED! ROUNDUP AND BEST BITES COMPETITION

This annual charitable event features the announcement and tasting of award-winning wines from the Houston Livestock and Rodeo International Wine Competition and the signature dishes of regional restaurants. One ticket invites you to meander the huge ground-floor stadium visiting different winery stations to taste champion wines and restaurant kiosks for samples of their hot culinary creations. After giving your taste buds a workout with dozens of upscale restaurant bites and hundreds of wines, you'll either say, "yeehaw" or "pass the Tums."
Takes place Reliant Astrodome
Event date First week in February
Contact 832-667-1000

SOS TASTE OF THE NATION

A Houston tradition for two decades, this culinary extravaganza features food and wine from 50-plus of Houston's finest restaurants and chefs, live music and great silent auction. Spend a gala afternoon strolling, sampling, sipping and socializing on the lovely Meadow at The Houstonian, while raising money to fight hunger in Houston. If you like mingling with top chefs, this is one of their favorite events.
Takes place The Houstonian Hotel Club & Spa, on the Meadow
Event date Spring (usually May)
Contact www.houstontaste.org

Pluses include fresh-squeezed OJ and lemonade, about 40 beers and wines, and interesting sodas, as well as outdoor seating, good people watching and a rotating art exhibit. On the debit side: a self-conscious attitude that may strike some as pretentious. Since its opening in 1992, this has been one of our favorite places to hang out — does that make us pretentious, too? — and we recommend the sturdy coffees, plus a fine chicken salad and decent pizza. Every kind of person can be found here, from fresh-faced students to tattooed artists to neighborhood professionals. On Monday nights, Brasil screens movies on the patio after dark. There's no charge for the movie, as long as you eat or drink. And ask about the live music schedule. Over the years the owners have taken over adjacent buildings, including the space to the west that is now Domy, a subversive bookstore. (And we mean "subversive" in the best possible way.)

CANDYLICIOUS

Candylicious is a psychedelic retro-kitsch paean to the world of sweets. Brilliantly colorful candy adorns every surface from floor to ceiling: a wall of Haribo gummi snacks, licorices from Australia and Finland, a selection of gourmet chocolate bars (although if chocolate is your poison, you should really be next door at The Chocolate Bar), candy cigarettes, candy necklaces, wax lips, movie theater-style boxed candy and one of only two M&M colorworks stations in the state. Once your sweet tooth has been sated, there are tongue-in-cheek cards, Webkinz stuffed animals, retro candy-themed metal lunch boxes, a Hello Kitty corner and other fun surprises. Where else can you find astronaut ice cream and giant Pez dispensers? Candylicious is a treat for kids of all ages.

1837 W. ALABAMA between Woodhead and Hazard
713-529-6500
MAP E7

2515 UNIVERSITY BLVD. at Kirby
713-874-1988
MAP E7

CANINO'S PRODUCE MARKET

2520 AIRLINE just inside Loop 610
713-862-4027
MAP E5

Canino's is set up like a big semi-open shed and filled with produce and seasonal finds. Out front in the fall, nuts are freshly roasted and pecans are shelled on the spot. In the spring, you'll find carts full of tomato and chile plants and buckets of fresh strawberries. Inside, it's mostly produce — bins and bins of it — along with eggs, dried beans and jarred jams, salsas and honey. There's nothing terribly rare here, but the melons, particularly watermelons, are said to be the best in town, and you'll find an extensive selection of chiles. Plus, the prices can't be beat. Out behind is the Airline Farmer's Market, but you may not take your Canino's shopping cart with you. (Plan your shopping excursion accordingly.) Open daily at 6 a.m.

> **2201 WASHINGTON** at Studemont
> **713-861-8448**
> www.catalinacoffeeshop.com
> **MAP** E6

CATALINA COFFEE

You won't find 31 fanciful flavors at this serious coffee shop in an original 1928 A&P Trading Post building. You will find an espresso aficionado's paradise where owner Max Gonzalez's fundamental catechism seems to be, "Any schmuck can make coffee. It's the barista's skilled labor that real zealots appreciate." Gonzalez gets his beans from around the globe and promotes fair trade, and he disserts enthusiastically about aroma, body and acidity. Don't pass up the Cubano — strong espresso with sugar and half-and-half so beautifully foamed it's a feathery masterpiece. The hot chocolate, made with milk, chocolate syrup and a hint of vanilla, is a pleaser, too, and the dense rum cake, supplied by a small Cuban bakery, is intoxicating. Like its beverages, Catalina is simple and uncluttered. Black and white photographs of Guatemala adorn the exposed brick walls. "Cupping 101" courses are periodically offered, and there's occasional live music (check website). Free WiFi with purchase.

CENTRAL MARKET

Everything is bigger in Texas, and Central Market — Texas' gourmet superstore, now with eight locations around the state — is no exception. This is, quite simply, a food-lover's nirvana. Pyramids of a dozen types of everything line the maze-like aisles.

> **3815 WESTHEIMER** at Wesleyan
> **713-386-1700**
> www.centralmarket.com
> **MAP** D6

(In fact, if there's one recurring complaint about Central Market, it's the labyrinthine set-up. Just memorize the marked shortcuts, and you'll be fine.) Not only is there an overwhelming degree of selection, each item seems to have been carefully chosen for quality. Pricey? Yes. Worth it? Yes. If it is produce you're shopping for, this should be your first stop. On any given day, there are about 700 items in the sprawling produce section. Bulk-bin items such as fair-trade coffees, sea salts, organic grains, spices, dried beans and sweet and savory snacks are yours to scoop into plastic bags, weigh and tag yourself. The meat and fish counters are models of excellence in

LOCAL FLAVORS

Recommended
FARMERS' MARKETS

There are small farmers' markets and food co-ops all over the greater Houston area, if you know where to look. Most are open weekly, rain or shine, and feature producers-only foodstuffs — i.e. no re-selling allowed.

BAYOU CITY FARMERS' MARKET
3000 Richmond at Eastside (back lot)
Saturdays, 8 a.m. to noon
www.urbanharvest.org

Bayou City, under the umbrella of Urban Harvest, has transformed the asphalt behind a Richmond office building into a little patch of green that lures you to stroll, chat and linger. But go early. This is a popular market, and many things sell out. Somehow the combination of shaded stands for produce, umbrella-covered tables for gossip and coffee, friendly overall-clad farmers, artisan baskets replete with whatever is ripe today and cooking demos all add up to a sweet welcome. Live acoustic music draws a small crowd and a few dancing toddlers. Regulars include early morning exercisers, Rice students, hand-holding grown-ups with dogs on leashes, River Oaks and West U denizens as well as curious passers-by tempted by the bucolic bustle. We often spot local chefs stocking up.

Growers and Purveyors
Local organic produce from Gundermann's Peachland Farm, Wood Duck Farm, Animal Farm and others; prepared foods from Marian Bell's Healthy Kitchen, Words & Food, Angela's Oven with breads, Katz Coffee. You'll also find The Herbal Goat, pastured eggs from Hattermann Poultry Farm, free-range beef, Gulf shrimp, cheeses by Cheesy Girl, cut flowers, potted orchids and citrus trees, knife sharpening by 2Dull4You. There's an annual citrus festival, in December; order young trees and grow your own organic fruit.

HOUSTON FARMERS' MARKET
3106 White Oak, between Studewood and Heights Blvd., behind Onion Creek Coffee House
Saturdays, 8 a.m. to noon

Rice University parking lot at Entrance 9 off University Blvd.
Tuesdays 3:30 to 7 p.m.
www.houstonfarmersmarket.org

The market elder, this is the city's first Texas State Certified Farmers' Market. Each of these locations offers its signature setting and lighting effects — Saturday markets in morning sun or Tuesday evening markets in twilight (depending on time of year, of course).

ONION CREEK/Saturdays: Use the market as an appetizer and enjoy breakfast on the Onion Creek Coffee House patio after gathering produce. Parking is a tight, but worth the effort. Note: Demonstrations at 10:30. The audience is an assorted mix: families, artists, couples and serious produce aficionados.

Growers and Purveyors
Seasonal produce, micro greens and herbs from Gundermann Farms, Wood Duck Farm, Natural Urban

Gardener and others; bread from Kraftsmen Baking, meats from Jolie Vue Farms, chocolates, preserves, hot pepper jellies, soaps, honey products, plants, and cut and dried flowers.

RICE UNIVERSITY/Tuesdays: The Rice parking lot is magical when lit by candles after the sun sets. Happily, you are within walking distance of many places on Rice Blvd. for an after-market libation or light supper. The Rice market attracts an Eddie Bauer crowd: mommies with strollers, professionals heading home, Rice students on first dates.

Growers and Purveyors

Seasonal produce, micro greens and herbs from Gundermann Farms and others, bread from Angela's Oven, Houston Dairy Maids for cheese, handmade soaps, cut and dried flowers, honey and related products, Katz Coffee, Trentino Gelato, Georgia's Texas Grassfed Beef, free-range lamb, amazing sausages from Jolie Vue Farms, prepared foods from Words & Food, Ezee Indian Food and others.

MIDTOWN FARMERS MARKET

3701 Travis, just north of Alabama, around and inside T'afia restaurant
Saturdays, 8 a.m. to noon
www.tafia.com

Farmers' markets are an essential feature of any top-tier culinary city, according to chef Monica Pope. So, she created her own. At this indoor/outdoor market, she gathers her favorite food artisans and organic purveyors. Her motto: The best ingredients prepared the simplest way. It's hip, eclectic and the Zen/Provençal-style garden adds charm to the restaurant parking-lot-cum-outdoor-market where the locally grown is offered beneath tented stalls. Inside, T'afia shelters the more fragile hand-crafted foods and offers a place to admire your produce over a coffee. Lots of dedicated foodies shop here, and there's nice cross-pollination with next-door Breakfast Klub diners, kids, sub-teens, Midtown citizens and happy Mexican hairless dogs — all mingling, nibbling and looking like a real market audience. Bonus: The Metro train stops nearby.

Growers and Purveyors

Fresh produce from Animal Farm, Blue Marble Garden, Lola Daniel's Urban Farm and Gundermann's; container herbs from Semperflorens, Brown Paper Chocolates, Kraftsmen Baking's breads, Monica Pope's meals-to-go, Trentino Gelato (with unique flavors of gelato such as ginger, chile chocolate and sweet corn, and sorbets such as fig with walnuts and white wine), cut flowers, Katz Coffee and more.

In addition to the big three Houston markets noted, check out the **Katy Farmer's Market** (*23501 Cinco Ranch Blvd., Katy, www.katyfarmersmarket.com*) on Saturday mornings; the **Creekside Farmers Market** (*16628 Hwy. 36, Needville, www.creeksidefarmersmarket.com*) on Thursday afternoons in Fort Bend County; **Nassau Bay Farmer's Market** (*18045 Upper Bay Rd.*) on Saturday mornings in the Clear Lake area; and the **Central City Co-op** (*2115 Taft and a host of partner co-ops throughout the Houston-Galveston area, www.centralcityco-op.org*) on Wednesdays, Thursdays and Saturdays.

LOCAL FLAVORS

selection, cleanliness and helpfulness of the employees. It's all about the food here, and only the food, including charcuterie, cheese, wine, fresh juices, olive bar and bakery. If you need laundry detergent, pet food or Miss Clairol, plan on stopping at Target. In addition to groceries, Central Market has an outstanding prepared-foods section, as well as a deli where you can grab a hearty sandwich to enjoy on the outdoor patio. Central Market caters and also offers the city's best schedule of cooking classes, as well as an excellent floral department. A live band plays each weekend from noon until 4 p.m., and the party atmosphere draws the biggest crowds of the week. Parking is a fight with both determined errand-runners and free-sample mongers. It can be intense; you may prefer to shop during a quieter time of the week.

5302 MORNINGSIDE at Rice Blvd.
713-520-5600
www.chocolat-du-monde.com
MAP E7

CHOCOLAT DU MONDE

To walk into Chocolat du Monde is to leave Houston behind and enter a European confiserie. Candy sits in antique-looking armoires, soft music plays in the background, and nooks and crannies abound with delicious surprises. Belgian chocolate is the specialty: Chocolat du Monde is the exclusive seller of posh Neuhaus and Leonidas chocolates in Houston, as well as carrying Dagoba, Scharffenberger and Joseph Schmidt. David Heiland, the owner, can often be found behind the counter and will recommend a flavor or ganache based on your preferred percentage of cacao. Consider yourself warned: Once you've tasted the real stuff here, Hershey's will never be the same.

CHOCOLATA COCOA BAR

Perhaps the cutest sweets shop this side of Willy Wonka, it's easy to see why Chocolata Cocoa Bar has drawn crowds in The Woodlands. The pink and brown decor is fresh and modern, and the suede booths

25 WATERWAY AVE. at Lake Robbins Dr., The Woodlands
832-585-0595
www.chocolatacocoabar.com
MAP North of D1

are great for sharing with a date or group of friends. And, ah, the chocolate. Cookies, cake, ice cream, brownies, cupcakes — you'll want to order them all, but beware, portions are enormous. Packaged specialties include chocolate-covered marshmallows and dark chocolate tiramisu balls as well as chocolate bars in milk, white, dark and Mexican chocolate, each available with different goodies like toffee and s'mores mixed in. The coffee bar is excellent, and for those who want a harder beverage, Chocolata serves chocolate martinis and has a nicely varied wine list. Best of all? It's open until 1 a.m. on Friday and Saturday, so you've got all day and night to indulge your sweet tooth.

1835 W. ALABAMA between Woodhead and Hazard
713-520-8599
www.theoriginalchocolatebar.com
MAP E7

THE CHOCOLATE BAR
Chocoholics, this is your promised land. The one-of-a-kind shop is half candy store and half dessert cafe. An eclectic crowd perches on stools for brownies, cookies, cakes, frozen hot chocolate and ice cream (the chocolate ice creams are a local favorite). Specialty beverages beg trying, including Night and Day, made of espresso, steamed milk and dark and white chocolate. Owners Eric Shamban and Gilbert Johnson prepare the goodies daily on site, and lucky customers can watch through a window to the kitchen. Dessert is served until 10 p.m. on weekdays and midnight on Friday and Saturday, and there is live music on Tuesday and Thursday nights. The shop portion contains chocolate in myriad shapes, sizes and forms, including bricks, gourmet bars, popcorn and assorted dipped fruit. There are delicious gifts for every occasion and recipient, including your dog. Note: The Chocolate Bar is planning a second, much larger location in Rice Village to open fall 2008.

The Chocolate Bar makes most of its goodies onsite.

THE COFFEE GROUNDZ
There's something for every palate at this European-style cafe — espresso drinks, paninis, grilled wraps, 16 flavors of gelato, teas and pastries. The Caramella Crème and Buttered Toffee lattes are signature drinks, and there are freezes made with coffee or tea. Try a gelato *affogato* style, meaning it's topped with a shot of espresso or liqueur. This Midtown spot has an urban vibe with an ambience that is more fashion-forward than a typical coffee shop, almost like a wine bar. The Coffee Groundz is open to 3 a.m. on Friday and Saturday and features "Sangria Sundayz" all day. It's from brothers Jonathan and Segev Zadok (hence the "z" in the name) and partner Preetish Nijhawan. Free WiFi.

2503 BAGBY, one block north of McGowen
713-874-0082
MAP E6

CONNIE'S SEAFOOD MARKET

2525 AIRLINE at Aurora, and other locations

713-868-2144

MAP E5

One of many stores in the fresh market corridor down Airline, Connie's does not suffer from the competition. The hordes of customers, reaching peak volume at lunch, seek the relatively inexpensive seafood at this "you buy, we fry" spot. While Connie's functions as a fishmonger, most of the square footage is apportioned for the dining room where uncomplicated fried and garlicky grilled fish is served. There's a lot of buzz about the fried rice that can be ordered with the seafood, but we've never been particularly enchanted by it. (Still, it's better than the fries.) Buy either raw or cooked seafood by the pound: shrimp, frog legs, mussels, crawfish tails, squid, drum, snapper, trout, etc. The Airline location is good for families. A working knowledge of Spanish is useful.

THE COOKIE JAR BAKERY

1846 WESTHEIMER at Hazard

713-874-0877

www.thecookiejarbakery.com

MAP E6

Despite the noise level in the shop reaching the upper extremes of a child's vocal range during peak hours, the cupcakes and cookies are definitely not equivalent to the kid's menu chicken tender. The cupcake flavors change everyday, and they are all intriguing — peach Melba, Mexican chocolate, carrot, Coca-Cola and such — and in fact every one backs up the chic factor with excellence. The cake is moist and flavorful, never bland. Designer cupcakes are usually pricey and these are no exception, at almost $3 apiece. The cookies are also very good. A fun option is to design your own dozen by choosing the base dough (chocolate, vanilla, peanut butter or oatmeal) and any of the 15 add-ins (e.g. M&Ms, nuts, coconut, toffee pieces, cranberries). Give the staff about 20 minutes to mix up the dough and bake them off for you. The shop is minimally furnished, but board games and a mini kitchen are set out for the tykes. Closed Sundays and Mondays.

Drive, walk or peddle to this neighborhood spot for a sugar fix: cookies, cakes, cupcakes, truffles and more.

Personal Favorites
THE COOLEST PARTY IN TOWN

By Jackson Hicks, Houston's "Prince of Parties"

Here's where I look for the edgiest, trendiest, most fashion-forward ingredients for my parties:

DECOR
The Events Company, 7310 Old Katy Rd., 713-426-5800
Harry Rice, Galveston, 800-295-2253, www.harryrice.com

FAVORS
Events, 1966 W. Gray, 713-520-5700, www.eventsgifts.com

FLORAL DESIGNS
Bergner and Johnson, 519 Pecore, 713-662-3769, www.bergnerandjohnson.com
In Bloom, 814 Fairview, 713-523-3553, www.inbloominc.com

INVITATIONS
Embossed Graphics of Texas (many locations), www.embossedgraphics.com

LINENS
Linen House, 2505 River Oaks Blvd., 713-522-1711, and other location, www.linenhouse.com
Party Cloths, 1102 Autrey, 713-523-0853

MUSICIANS, DJS, ETC.
Gulf Coast Entertainment, 713-523-7004, www.gulfcoastentertainment.com

PHOTOGRAPHERS
Arthur Garcia, 713-961-2840, www.selectstudiosphoto.com
Phyllis Hand, 713-861-9327, www.phyllishand.com
Karen Sacher, 713-523-1150, www.ksacher.com

TABLETOPS
A Finer Event, 4617 Nett, 713-699-9911, www.afinerevent.com

VALETS, LIMOUSINES
Karr Limousine, 713-780-8300, www.karrlimousine.com
Sovereign Services, 713-777-0571, www.sovereignservices.com

VENUES
The Corinthian, 202 Fannin, 713-222-2002, www.thecorinthianhouston.com
Discovery Green, 1500 McKinney, 713-400-7336, www.discoverygreen.com
Gremillion Gallery, 2501 Sunset, 713-522-2701, www.gremillion.com
Jones Hall, 615 Louisiana, 713-237-1439, www.houstontx.gov/joneshall
The Parador, 2021 Binz, 713-529-3050, www.paradorhouston.com
Wortham Center Onstage, 500 Texas, 713-237-1439, www.houstontx.gov/worthamcenter

Besides being founder of the internationally renowned special-event production and catering firm, Jackson and Company, and proprietor of The Corinthian, Hicks is a widely sought-after speaker, writer and consultant on the subjects of entertaining, etiquette and fine service.

LOCAL FLAVORS

CRAWFISH & BEIGNETS

> **11201 #A-05 BELLAIRE BLVD.**
> between Wilcrest and S. Kirkwood
> **281-498-5044**
> **MAP** B7

Be sure to get the name right before trolling around the Hong Kong City Mall because Crawfish & Beignets is actually located next to another less-stellar crawfish stand. Crawfish connoisseurs from across the city gather here to get their hands messy peeling the boiled crawfish over a plastic food-court table and sucking down cheap beer. Taking a few pounds home for later is always an option. Obviously, given the year-round availability of crawfish here, these are imported, not local.

CROISSANT BRIOCHE

> **2435 RICE BLVD.**
> near Kelvin
> **713-526-9188**
> **MAP** E7

Pairing two of the most popular French baked goods in the shop's name may seem at first both simplistic and overreaching. The epitome of both croissant and brioche? But in actuality the mini brioche muffins and enormous croissants deserve placement on the storefront marquee. Tucked away in the Rice Village, this tiny bakery seems to be frequented mostly by ladies and couples with a sweet tooth. The lunch specials, available daily from 11 a.m. to 3 p.m., include an entree (such as quiche, ham and cheese croissant or chicken salad on a baguette), a side or pastry and a drink. Plenty of regulars opt for dessert only though, plus a cappuccino or espresso. Whole tarts are available to take home.

CUPCAKE CAFE

> **16525 LEXINGTON** at Austin Pkwy., Sugar Land
> **281-242-2744**
> www.cupcakecafeofsugarland.com
> **MAP** A9

Once the Los Angeles and Manhattan cupcake trend touched down in Houston, it quickly sidled down the freeway and into Sugar Land with Cupcake Cafe. Naturally the cupcakes were nurtured into enormous proportions, as Texas prefers, and the flavor is rather rich and sugary. The standard chocolate and vanilla cupcakes with buttercream icing are here alongside a rotating cast that includes Boston cream and Chocolate Lovers. The decor is like Salvador Dalí took his paintbrush to your little girl's room, the signature piece being a giant cupcake top hanging overhead. Our only request would be for a bit of a smile from the service to go with the treats, cheer being the reason anyone buys a cupcake in the first place.

RECIPE: JALAPEÑO JELLY

Recipe by chef/owner Bryan Caswell
Reef, 2600 Travis, 713-526-8282

Reef chef/owner Bryan Caswell began serving this jelly shortly after introducing the house yeast rolls as the restaurant's table bread. "Fresh yeast rolls, jalapeño jelly, collard greens, and chicken and dumplings take me back to my grandmother Birdie-Bea Caswell's farm. Some of the off-the-menu items belong to her, including the rolls and jalapeño jelly. We serve the jelly instead of butter and always have a couple of jars available if someone wants to take some home."

12 oz. jalapeño peppers, seeded and stemmed
  (you may use red, green or a combination)
2 cups Champagne vinegar, divided
6 oz. liquid pectin
6 cups sugar
2 Tbsp. unsalted butter

METHOD: Seed and stem the peppers and place in food processor. Add 1 cup of the vinegar and pulse until a small dice; pour into non-reactive saucepan (stainless steel is best). Add remaining vinegar, sugar and liquid pectin and cook over medium heat, stirring constantly. Once sugar is dissolved, whisk in butter (to help reduce foaming). Bring mixture to a boil, then remove from heat. Jelly may be canned or refrigerated for use as needed. If refrigerated, jelly will keep for about three weeks. Makes enough to fill five 8-oz. jars. Serve with biscuits or homemade yeast rolls.

For canning:
Remove jelly from the heat and skim any foam from the top. Immediately pour into hot, sterilized jars to ⅛-inch from the tops. Wipe the rims of jars with a clean cloth. Seal the jars with the flat lids and screw tops. Invert the jars for 5 minutes, then turn upright. After the jars are cool, check the seals by pressing the middle of the lid with your finger. If the lid springs up when your finger releases the lid, it is not properly sealed and should be used within a couple weeks.

LOCAL FLAVORS

DACAPO'S PASTRY CAFE

1141 E. 11TH at Studewood
713-869-9141
www.dacaposcafe.com
MAP E5

If your grandmother were to open her own bakery, it would probably be something like Dacapo's, where everything is both homemade and homey. Located in The Heights in an old commercial building, Tresa and Lisa Biggerstaff's little spot on the corner is a comfortable choice for a sweet treat or lunch. (The lunch menu includes salads, quiche and sandwiches built on the house-made bread.) The banana split cake is the most popular on the bakery side, and the Italian cream is perfection, while other desserts can veer into the territory of super-sweet or richly thick. One interesting specialty of Dacapo's is the cake top: Shaved off whole cakes during the icing process, the tops are made into small sweet sandwiches. Orders for wedding cakes are happily accepted.

THE DAILY GRIND

4115 WASHINGTON between Heights Blvd. and Shepherd
713-861-4558
MAP E6

Located on trendy Washington Avenue, the Daily Grind is a great place to sit back and relax. It's housed in a barely-modified old residence with lots of character. Locals stop in for the free WiFi, bottomless cups of coffee and laid-back service. The lattes and flavored iced tea are also particularly good. On a nice day, the back patio is one of the quietest in Houston so it's great for an iced coffee and a study session. If you stay so long you get hungry, there's good news: Daily Grind serves breakfast and lunch, and makes a mean frittata-style omelet with no limit on toppings.

DESSERT GALLERY

Sara Brook's whimsical purple and red bakery is an *Alice in Wonderland* surprise. Kids will love this place, popular for the brownies, lemon bars and dipped cookies. Classics like Jennifer's Birthday Cake and Mom's Chocolate Cake

Simplicity reigns supreme at Dessert Gallery — the yellow-cake-and-chocolate-icing "Diner Cake" is the runaway bestseller.

> **3200 KIRBY** at W. Main, and other locations
> **713-522-9999**
> www.dessertgallery.com
> **MAP** E7

are well-liked, and the lemon vacherin — a meringue shell filled with lemon mousse — makes for a yummy light alternative. Dessert Gallery specializes in adding graphics to baked goods: Order your company logo, for example, applied in icing to a couple dozen cookies (which actually taste good) for your next board meeting or to woo a potential customer. It also makes wedding cakes, chocolate-dipped long-stem strawberries and the intriguing 8-inch Texas-sized cupcake, plus sandwiches, salads, box lunches and dainty gifts.

Recommended
BARBECUE SUPPLIES

Our temperate winter makes grilling and barbecuing a year-round sport. Here are five suggestions for adding to your arsenal.

BBQ PITS BY KLOSE, *2216 W. 34th, 713-686-8720.* Since 1986 owner Dave Klose has been making, selling and delivering (sometimes across country) custom grills, smokers and catering rigs. Pits are made by hand, using only a welding machine. Caution: You can spend up to $50,000 on a single purchase here.

GATOR PIT, *11161 W. Little York, 713-896-0144.* All sorts and sizes of custom barbecue pits, smokers and grills are designed and fabricated using only new steel. There are even rental units for special events.

GOODE CO. HALL OF FLAME, online *(www.goodecompany.com) and phone orders (800-627-3502) only.* Since the Armadillo Palace assumed its quarters, the Hall of Flame resides only virtually, but it's still a cool shop for thoughtfully chosen barbecue and grilling supplies, plus Texana gifts.

PITTS AND SPITS, *14221 Eastex Fwy., 281-987-2474.* This nationally known maker of custom pits, grills and trailers also sells spices, sauces, cooking woods, accessories, cookbooks, etc. It even has its own video on YouTube, made with the Houston Texans band at a tailgating party.

TEXAS PIT CRAFTERS, *31909 Decker Industrial Dr., Pinehurst, 281-356-2168.* Located just a few miles north of Tomball, Texas Pit Crafters design and manufacture high-end stainless-steel grills, smokers, pits and outdoor kitchens.

LOCAL FLAVORS

8331 BEECHNUT
west of Hwy. 59
713-270-8501
MAP C7

13238 BELLAIRE BLVD. between Dairy Ashford and Eldridge
832-328-0761
MAP A8

DOÑA TERE TAMALES

These unassimilated bare-bones operations are essentially enclosed tamale stands selling excellent Mexico City-style versions of the masa pockets available with a variety of fillings, both savory (e.g. pork, chicken *mole*) and sweet. A great value, you'll probably only need to order one or two tamales per person, as these are about three times larger than typical Tex-Mex tamales. Larger yet is the Oaxaqueño, an enormous chicken tamale wrapped and steamed in a banana leaf. Most selections are perfectly complemented by a tangy and spicy green salsa, which, be sure to note, will have to be ordered separately.

DOSEY DOE COFFEE

If you like a little Merle Haggard with your macchiato, then away you go to this family hangout in The Woodlands. The dining hall is a 150-year-old barn from Kentucky that was disassembled and shipped to Texas. Children are welcome in the coffeehouse/restaurant/ live-music venue, where the staff is saintly patient with grits-slinging toddlers. The coffee is roasted on site, starting with green beans. To ease the morning commute, the drive-thru serves coffee, tea, pastries and box lunches. Inside are breakfasts, lunches and dinners of Southern comfort foods (e.g. Crockett meatloaf, chicken-fried steak) served with a twist. For a mid-morning break, share a Texas-sized chocolate-raspberry truffle torte or a piece of Granny Ruby's coffeecake and a cappuccino. There's a busy live-music schedule (check the website), plus open-guitar night every second and fourth Wednesday.

25911 I-45 NORTH between Sawdust and Woodlands Parkway, The Woodlands
281-367-3774
www.doseydoescoffeeshop.com
MAP North of E1

7333 HILLCROFT between Bellaire Blvd. and Bissonnet, and other locations
713-988-5897
MAP C7

DROUBI'S BAKERY & DELI

Long before there was Phoenicia Specialty, there was Droubi's. The Hillcroft store is admittedly getting on in years and a bit dimly lit inside, and parking is tight. But the falafel, fried to order, is crunchy and delicious. Droubi's pita bread is sold citywide — a testament to its quality — but at the source it's at its warmest and most fresh. There's a fair chance it will have run out by the end of the day, so go early. You should also try the cheese pita or the *zatar* bread made with wild thyme and other herbs. Besides the groceries (e.g. tea, jams, beans, spices), halal meat counter and corner kitchenware shop, there is a small cafe area serving up fresh hummus where some customers choose to sit and enjoy their shawarma or whole Cornish hens in the glow of foreign television programming. Encounters with the staff can be hit or miss. While some are very friendly, other are a bit frigid, like the deli lady who tends to keep her back to you even with your stomach rumbling. Depending on how serious you are about your falafel, you won't let this stand in your way.

2418 RICE BLVD. at Morningside, and other locations
713-529-8400
www.ediblearrangements.com
MAP E7

EDIBLE ARRANGEMENTS

When flowers seem wasteful and chocolates cliché, there's Edible Arrangements. Its beautiful fruit designs are made from fresh strawberries, pineapple (cut into adorable flower shapes), grapes, oranges, cantaloupe, honeydew, bananas and pears in a variety of shapes and sizes. Bouquets can be personalized by choosing to dip half or all of the strawberries, pineapples, oranges, apples or bananas in gourmet chocolate, and then adding a teddy bear, jar of dipping sauce or Mylar balloon to match the occasion. The fruit is fresh and delicious, and the result so beautiful you almost won't want to eat it (but you will). Making it even easier: Order online and arrange delivery.

EL TIEMPO MARKET

This Mexican market was founded in 1974 as a Matamoros Meat Market; in 2006 the Laurenzo family (of the El Tiempo restaurants) took it over and put their own brand on it. It remains a favorite source for carnitas, *barbacoa* and chorizo by the pound. The marinated fajita meat is excellent as well. A meat market first and taqueria second, customers often eat on barstools at the lunch counter. Food is very inexpensive at $1.69 a taco or $3.99 for a full lunch plate, all of which comes in a Styrofoam to-go container. The rest of the store offers a small amount of fresh produce, dry goods and Mexican dairy products.

5526 WASHINGTON at TC Jester
713-862-7792
MAP E6

EMPIRE CAFE

1732 WESTHEIMER at Elmen
713-528-5282
www.empirecafe.net
MAP E6

If this coffeehouse seeks imperial authority, then let us eat cake by the towering slice. Indeed, this Montrose spot, here since 1995, is famous for its big blowsy cakes displayed under glass on the counter. The coffee culture at Empire Cafe is more hectic than laid-back, but if you thrive on that kind of buzz, this is your spot. At breakfast, frittatas, oatmeal, a unique breakfast polenta and gingerbread waffles are nicely made, and the lunch menu offers soups, salad, paninis and pizza. In the evening, the menu is more ambitious yet, with grilled salmon, pasta and eggplant parmigiana. But given its streetside patio, we can't think of a more welcome funky-urban spot for a coffee break with a slice of cake, sticky bun or scone. Espressos and coffee drinks are expertly prepared. So take your coffee and cake outside, grab a chair flush up against Westheimer and feel like you're at the center of a world full of life in all its weirdness. Monday is Half-Price Cake Day.

EPICURE BAKERY

2005-C W. GRAY at McDuffie
713-520-6174
www.epicure-cafe.com
MAP E6

This roomy European-style cafe is popular with adults looking for a snack and a quiet place to relax after expanding their mental horizons with a foreign film at River Oaks Theatre next door. Epicure has an authentic bakery feel, which strikes you with the first smell of cinnamon buns at the door. There are many items to choose from, including éclairs and oversized pies, but the Linzer cookies and *alfajores* — an Argentinean *dulce de leche* cookie sandwich — are the most unique to Epicure. Breakfast and lunch items such as omelets and salads are available, and the freshly made berry lemonade makes the perfect accompaniment. On a fine day, you can dine on the sidewalk out front.

FIESTA MART

6200 BELLAIRE BLVD. at Hillcroft, and other locations
713-270-5889
www.fiestamart.com
MAP C7

Fiesta was founded back in 1972, catering to the working-class Hispanic market with the slogan "lower food prices." Now Fiesta is getting older and more conventional in some ways. (Affluent West Houston still mourns the loss of the bountiful Fiesta on the Katy

Freeway at Blalock, which closed in 2007 due to the freeway expansion.) In reality, Fiesta carries a selection of international foods that trumps most other grocery stores while still concentrating on staples from Mexico. It's an eclectic operation — some stores are

Personal Favorites
WHERE I BUY SEAFOOD

By Bryan Caswell

AIRLINE SEAFOOD, *1841 Richmond, 713-526-2351.* I use them daily. They have both a retail and wholesale side, and of all the fishmongers they have the largest variety of local product. I talk with owner Steve Berreth and Mark Musatto (who was my exec sous chef for two years at Bank/Hotel Icon) sometime three times a day. These guys live and breathe Gulf Coast seafood.

HONG KONG MARKET, *11205 Bellaire Blvd., 281-575-7886.* I get lost in this hangar-sized specialty store. If you're looking for anything Asian (from the Indian Ocean to the Sea of Japan), it's within their four walls, although finding it can prove maddening. They have a ton of live stuff for both the traditionalist and adventuresome: catfish, Dungeness crab, crawfish, lobster, blue crab, conger eel, sea cucumber.

LOUISIANA FOODS, *4410 W. 12th, 713-957-3476.* Here's another wholesaler that also has a retail counter. The cool thing is they have a lot more on the processed/halfway-there side: Prepared crab cakes, rémoulade, shrimp cocktail and jambalaya make it easier on the home cook.

WHOLE FOODS, *2955 Kirby, 713-520-1937, and other locations.* They don't have as much of a variety as the three above, but their quality is always pristine.

How about a road trip to Seadrift, Texas? During mid-spring (the soft-shell season) drive down Main Street to the water. Next to the public boat ramp is a Vietnamese crabbing shack. Outside there are crabbers in hammocks, smoking cigarettes, excitedly playing cards. Inside, the shallow water tanks are stacked like bunk beds each filled with molting blue crabs. Ms. An will usually be inside sorting crabs bare-handed, stretching the swimmer fin for that pin-size dot that tells her whether or not that crab has molted. Last time I was there she was selling them $2.25 each for "whalers," the largest size. It is a pretty unique place.

Bryan Caswell is the chef and co-owner of Reef restaurant, which readers of My Table *magazine voted Best New Restaurant in the 2007 Houston Culinary Awards.*

Each Fiesta store has a no-frills Mexico market feel, which keeps prices reasonable.

definitely nicer than others — but the chain continues to deliver on its original motto. Several dozen stores are spread across the city and beyond. Inside many of them customers will find a sno-cone stand, bakery (with empanadas, pita and bagels), prepared-foods section or deli, and a fair selection of beer and wine. In the larger Fiestas you will probably also come across men's work pants, religious candles, perhaps a travel agent. Produce is diverse and sometimes wilted — but sometimes brilliantly fresh and cheap. Stores can be very crowded at peak hours, but the immensity of the space allows wide berth for most everyone's cart.

FREDLYN NUT COMPANY

9350 WESTPARK
at Fondren
713-781-2710
www.fredlyn.com
MAP C7

Fredlyn Nut Company may look like any other wholesale storefront on its somewhat bland stretch of Westpark, but it would be a shame to pass by this hidden treasure. Once inside, the shop is strangely reminiscent of a Cracker Barrel, due to the wood paneling covering every surface. But never mind that, what you want are the endless bins of nuts. Sweet, salty, dipped in chocolate — the variety seems mind-boggling. Luckily everything can be tasted until you find your perfect snacking mix. The honey-glazed pecans and cranberry crunch are perfection, and the salty Sticks 'n' Stones mix would be a hit at any gathering. Best of all the prices are wholesale, so don't be afraid to, *ahem*, go nuts.

FRENCH GOURMET BAKERY

French Gourmet produces a solid baguette (but not the city's best — that would be found at French Riviera, below), as well as cinnamon buns, kolaches, coffeecake, Danishes and croissants. In addition, there are light lunches (salad plate, quiche, sandwiches piled on the house breads), cakes and cookies. (We'll take a chocolate thumbprint cookie anytime.) This is a convenient stop during the holidays for picking up bagged fresh rolls by the dozen, loaves of bread and the ever-important morning pastries and coffeecakes.

2250 WESTHEIMER
between S. Shepherd and Kirby
713-524-3744
www.fgbakery.com
MAP E6

12504 MEMORIAL
west of Gessner
713-973-6900
MAP C6

Personal Favorites

SATURDAY MORNING AT THE BAYOU CITY FARMERS' MARKET

By Chris Shepherd

Here are some of my favorite stops at Saturday morning's Bayou City Farmers' Market, located in the parking lot behind the office building at 3000 Richmond. Take a stroll. Say hello to the farmers and producers. Make a friend, and your dinner table will thank you.

ATKINSON FARMS Bobby Atkinson and family have been doing this since the 1950s, and they have everything. They grow it all up in Spring.

CUTS OF COLOR Rita Anders will take care of the teardrop tomatoes, lettuce heads and beautiful flowers.

GUNDERMANN'S PEACHLAND FARMS Joan Gundermann and family have been farming organically for a long time. They are bound to have tomatoes, greens, beets and just about everything else, depending on the season.

HATTERMANN'S POULTRY FARMS Leon Hattermann is the man! He has the best eggs on the planet. (Just don't take my duck eggs.)

KATZ COFFEE The coffee is certified fair-trade, organically grown and locally roasted in The Heights. Buy it by the bag or ask Mickey Morales for a cup of fresh-brewed.

OLDE WORLD FARMS John and Karla McLaughlin raise and sell grass-fed beef and lamb and free-range chickens. They are starting to do heritage pork, too.

WOOD DUCK FARMS Van Weldon grows those pretty little micro greens for all of the restaurants around town. You can have them at your house, too.

WORDS & FOOD Janice Schindeler makes what is possibly the best ready-to-eat food anywhere. I'm warning you about the pimiento salad and her mean cookies.

Chris Shepherd, the chef/partner at Catalan Food and Wine, is an avid supporter of all things local and seasonal.

LOCAL FLAVORS

FRENCH RIVIERA BAKERY & CAFE

3032 CHIMNEY ROCK
one block north of Richmond
713-783-3264
MAP D7

Sunshine-yellow walls create a pleasant atmosphere in which regulars mingle with the owners (who hail from Madagascar) and employees of this tiny shop. The baguettes, boasting a crust that shatters and a light interior, are contenders for best in class — no wonder many area restaurants use them — and are stacked alongside round *boules*, loaves of raisin walnut and other fresh breads. Chocolate-filled brioche, almond croissants and the chocolate croissants are standouts on the sweets side. At lunch, there are sandwiches (including a *croque monsieur* and *croque madame*) and salads that invite visitors to linger at one of the few inside or outside tables; alas, during the peak lunch hour the rush requires that most orders be take-out. We encourage customers to purchase the jumbo *boule*, if only for the giggles.

GELATO BLU

5710 MEMORIAL
just east of Birdsall
713-880-5900
www.gelatoblu.com
MAP E6

Owner Chuck Irwin spent a year in Tuscany immersing himself in the Italian language and culture in order to deeply understand gelato and sorbetto. His frozen results include both Italian inspirations (the Michelangelo combines fig, ricotta cheese and caramel and has engendered a local cult following) and good ol' American combos, such as Cookie Monster. The brisk little shop offers something for everyone. After choosing one of the many made-from-scratch flavors (when in doubt, the fruity concoctions seem to be especially tasty), you can watch the family-friendly movie playing up above on the flat-screen TV (helpful for keeping the kiddies seated as the sugar kicks in). Or break out the laptop and take advantage of the free WiFi. While some dessert places offer coffee as an afterthought, Gelato Blu really does coffee right, with top-of-the-line espresso machines and coffee. Even the cups and glasses are imported from Italy.

GOLDEN FOODS SUPERMARKET

9896 BELLAIRE BLVD.
just inside Beltway 8
713-772-7882
MAP B7

Go straight to the source, or as close as you can get in Houston, for traditional Chinese ingredients. This green-domed supermarket, located in the heart of Chinatown, serves as the centerpiece of the shopping center and hasn't yet enjoyed as much business as its clean and well-organized condition deserves. It is not so huge as Hong Kong Food Market #4 in the Hong Kong City Mall, but it's large and interesting. The seafood section doesn't even smell, a rarity among the local non-Japanese Asian markets. Live Dungeness crabs were only $5.99 a pound when we last visited. The fruit and vegetable selection were amazing in terms of bizarreness. There are at least a half-dozen types of pears alone, plus dragon fruit and piles of strange-looking melons and squashes. Exotic and inexpensive products can be found here, as well as extensive fresh fish and butcher counters. There's also a barbecue parlor where you can purchase freshly roasted ducks, chickens and *char siu* (barbecued pork) to take home. Bento boxes are available for a quick lunch or dinner.

HANK'S ICE CREAM PARLOR

9291 S. MAIN near Murworth
713-665-5103
www.hanksicecream.com
MAP E8

There's something about Hank's that makes you feel like a kid again — maybe music and sports stars, or maybe it's seeing Hank behind the counter, still serving up his award-winning ice cream after 20 years. Mostly, we think, it's the ice cream, which is simply yummy. Though Hank has more than 100 flavors in his recipe list, a typical day will have about 12, with lots of old favorites and a few curveballs (banana pudding and orange chocolate chip are popular choices). The ice cream is rich and creamy, and the waffle cones are equally tasty. It's a classic that's still served up right.

HEBERT'S SPECIALTY MEATS

4714 RICHMOND just inside Loop 610
713-621-6328
www.hebertshouston.com
MAP D7

1023 DAIRY ASHFORD between I-10 and Memorial
281-558-6328
MAP A6

A Houston outpost of Cajun cooking, Hebert's (pronounced "A-bears") offers marinated and seasoned meats as well as Louisiana favorites like boudin, étouffée, crawfish pie and a gumbo stock that sells faster than they can make it. The store is a simple tile-floor, wood-ceiling affair with friendly staff ready to recommend an item and tell you how to cook it. But what Hebert's is really known for is deboning and stuffing practically anything that walks, flies or swims. The lengthy

LOCAL FLAVORS

product list ranges from shrimp-stuffed chicken to stuffed rabbit, from stuffed bell peppers to stuffed brisket, from stuffed shrimp to the zenith of stuffed-ness, the turducken. Everything is prepared at the Dairy Ashford location, and the recipes are "straight from Louisiana," with the original store in Maurice, Louisiana.

HONG KONG FOOD MARKET

Walk into this Hong Kong Market and, wafting above the veritable forest of heavenly bamboo arrangements and orchids at the entrance, is the distinctive aroma of Asian groceries. This gargantuan

Recommended
PICK-YOUR-OWN ORCHARDS

Long before anyone coined the term "locavore" — New Oxford American Dictionary's 2007 word of the year — Houston had pick-your-own farms and orchards where urban dwellers harvest fruit grown just a few miles from the big city. Call for picking dates, since seasons and crops vary from year to year. Also, bring cash, since many farms and orchards don't accept credit cards.

CHMIELEWSKI'S BLUEBERRY FARM, *23810 Bauer Hockley Rd., Hockley, 281-304-0554.* A gift shop and picnic area complement orchards that have five varieties of blueberries, all grown using organic methods. Early summer is prime picking time.

E&B ORCHARDS, *28268 Clarke Bottom Rd., Hempstead, 979-826-6303.* Open daily from roughly mid-May through mid-July, you can come to pick peaches, nectarines and blackberries. Don't miss the house-made peach ice cream.

THE KING'S ORCHARDS, *11282 County Rd. 302, Plantersville, 936-894-2766.* Located adjacent to the Texas Renaissance Festival site, this large and varied orchard is open from about February to August. Cut your own flowers here, too. Call for crop availability.

MATT FAMILY ORCHARDS, *21110 Bauer Hockley Rd., Tomball, 281-351-7676.* On 145 acres and well-suited for groups, you can pick whatever is in season — blackberries, figs, pears, *jujubes* (Asian dates) or persimmons — from April to November. It also sells local honey and has a pumpkin patch in the fall.

TEXAS ORCHARDS, *42823 Old Houston Hwy., Waller, 936-931-2220.* Texas Orchards boast about 7,000 peach trees with seven different varieties to assure a ripe peach can be plucked from April through about mid-June.

| **11205 BELLAIRE BLVD.** |
| between Wilcrest and |
| S. Kirkwood, and other locations |
| **281-575-7886** |
| **MAP** B7 |

Chinatown landmark, which opened in 1999 with a vast selection of products, is the most popular grocery in the area and should not be missed. Despite its name, the groceries represent not only China but Thailand, Vietnam, Cambodia, Japan, Korea, India and the Philippines. A tour of the store is a cultural adventure for anyone not raised in the Far East. So pluck up your courage and plunge in. You may find yourself doing as our kids did, using their cell phones to photograph exotic seafood products (fish stomach, anyone?), preserved duck eggs, fresh pork blood and more. Working from the right side of the store to the left, the first department is the bakery, which features fresh cookies and buns as well as packages of bizarrely colored cookies and crackers. Produce is next — watch for great bargains here, especially mushrooms, greens and, in season, mangos — then tofu of every style. Within the market's 150,000 square feet are herbal remedies, frozen specialty items from all over Asia, dried herbs and roots, an excellent seafood counter, a butcher department with some mighty interesting cuts of meat and Asian cooking implements galore. Open seven days a week.

HOUSE OF COFFEE BEANS

The undeniable fact of gourmet coffee is that addicts don't have to pay as much for it as they do at the local Starbucks if they just grind and brew at home. While customers can purchase a fresh cup, House of Coffee Beans is first and foremost a whole bean purveyor. All roasting is done in small, hand-tended batches in a pre-WW II German coffee roaster that was acquired, rebuilt and ultimately renamed Madam Hasbean. Blended and unblended coffees, dark and espresso coffee, decaffeinated and flavored are all available.

| **2348 BISSONNET** near |
| Greenbriar |
| **713-524-0057** |
| www.houseofcoffeebeans.com |
| **MAP** E7 |

Don't let the simple brown bag fool you — there is a lot of flavor in the House of Coffee Beans' beans. Just brew it.

LOCAL FLAVORS

HOUSE OF PIES

3112 KIRBY at W. Main
713-528-3816
www.houseofpies.com
MAP E7

6142 WESTHEIMER between Fountain View and S. Voss
713-782-1290
MAP D6

Brown seating, a harsh fluorescent glow — House of Pies looks like a diner because it is one, and not the charming kind that strives for a nostalgic 1950s-era feel. This is the real deal, shabby and brusque, that is open 24 hours and is a mainstay for families in the daytime, students and a ravenous post-party clientele in the nighttime. (The Kirby location is popularly known as "House of Guys.") Breakfast is popular, the burgers are decent and of course there are the pies. The Bayou Goo, which involves a pecan crust with a layer of sweet cream cheese and a layer of vanilla custard swirled with chocolate chunks and is topped with whipped cream, is a signature flavor. Honestly, though, we prefer the lemon meringue and strawberry rhubarb. All pies may be purchased whole to take home (the week before Thanksgiving the lobby is filled with towers of boxed pecan pies). This is not the place to lounge with a cup of coffee and a laptop — there is a minimum table charge per hour.

HOUSTON PECAN COMPANY

7313 ASHCROFT, SUITE 212 at Evergreen
713-772-6216
www.houstonpecan.com
MAP D7

It's a culinary truism that good food requires good ingredients. Since 1942 a faithful Houston following has turned to Houston Pecan Company for the nuts and fruits they include in their baking and cooking. This small store creates its own mixes like Hawaiian and Cranberry Nut Crunch for good snacking as well as different sizes of gift tins and bags and a small selection of kosher items. You can order online, but the staff is so friendly and helpful it would be a shame to miss that and the toasty sweet smell of warm pecans.

INDIA GROCERS

6606 SOUTHWEST FWY. at Hillcroft
713-266-7717
MAP C7

This grocery store is a delight. It's clean, well-stocked with South Asian cooking supplies and fun to browse. Besides dried pulses, spices, herbs and seasonings of all kinds — available in half-pound and pound bags, well priced — there is a section of Indian grooming products where some of the packaging is so retro (e.g. Monkey Brand Black Tooth Powder) it will make you smile. Rice is sold in canvas bags with handles, and there's a *chaat* corner where you can order a heaping plate of Indian street treats, $3.50 each. We also like the aisle of incense, selection of *mukhwas* (the Indian after-meal digestive aid and mouth freshener), ready-to-use *ghee* and enormous many-fingered hunks of fresh ginger. The friendly staff is happy to answer questions.

Recommended
WEEKEND FOODIE DIVERSIONS

It's a gorgeous Saturday morning, and the wildflowers are at their most beautiful. So put down the ragtop, smear on some sunscreen and hit the road. Here are five easy day trips with good food waiting at the other end.

CAROL'S AT CAT SPRING, *10745 FM 949, Cat Spring, 979-865-1100.* Hearty Texas cooking gets an upscale twist at this rural outpost with such dishes as chicken-fried ribeye, cornmeal-crusted catfish, a bison tenderloin with port wine sauce and a filet mignon rubbed with coffee and sauced with red wine demi-glace.

HILLTOP HERB FARM RESTAURANT, *235 Chain-O-Lakes Resort, Cleveland, 832-397-4008.* Located in the East Texas woods, Hilltop's cuisine is inspired by the herbs grown onsite, which also find their way into jellies, chutneys, teas and other specialty items. Call for info on cooking classes and group demonstrations.

INN AT DOS BRISAS, *9400 Champion Dr. (FM 1155), Brenham, 979-277-7750.* This upscale bucolic retreat — it was recently admitted to Relais & Châteaux — boasts a fine-dining restaurant that serves dinner Thursday to Saturday as well as a five-course Sunday brunch. Most of the produce comes from the inn's own organic gardens.

MESSINA HOF, *4585 Old Reliance Rd., Bryan, 800-736-9436.* Not just an award-winning regional winery, but also a restaurant and B&B. You can make a weekend of it: Messina Hof has winery tours, tastings, cooking classes, specialty dinners and a wine bar.

ROYERS ROUND TOP, *105 Main, Round Top, 979-249-3611.* Beef, chicken, pork, quail, Gulf Coast seafood and pastas are featured at this always-crowded — you'll probably have to wait for a table — small-town cafe. And then there are the world-famous pies! Call for hours, which sometimes expand to accommodate nearby antique fairs.

INVERSION COFFEE HOUSE

1953 MONTROSE
near W. Gray
713-523-4866
www.inversioncoffee.com
MAP E6

Brush and brew meet in this newcomer (it opened in 2007) that has twisted the city's coffee and art scene upside down. Located at the Art League of Houston and the brainchild of Michael Terrazas, the shop displays work by local artists. The 30-foot ceilings, metal chairs and tables lend an industrial loft feel. Copious amounts of plain good joe are consumed here. But the lattes, like the Butterscotch Brouja made of coconut and half-and-half or the Chocolate Cherry Bomb, are masterpieces. Free WiFi with purchase.

JAVA JAVA

911 W. 11TH
four blocks east of N. Shepherd
713-880-5282
MAP E5

This quirky cafe near the western edge of The Heights was once a flower shop that served coffee, and it still retains that oddball synergy. The service can be sloppy or amateurish, but most regulars let it slide. It's open for breakfast and lunch, as well as for espresso and coffee drinks. It serves most of the standard American breakfasts and breakfast tacos during the week, many with a bit more panache than is expected, and the portions are good-sized. With a name like this, the coffee should be rich and flavorful. It is. Nice patio.

JERUSALEM HALAL MEAT MARKET

3330 HILLCROFT
south of Richmond
713-784-2525
MAP C7

Service is generally chaotic, and the high shelves are so cluttered and over-loaded that they are at risk of becoming a tumbling avalanche at this modest Arab grocery store where customers queue up for halal meat, permissible by Islamic law. Besides the butcher room, which you enter to have meat cut to order, there are tons of imported foods — snacks, herbs, dried legumes, cooking mixes, bakery goods, canned beans (*foul*) and fresh dates, as well as kettles, cooking pots and tableware. On a recent visit, we found 14 brands of pomegranate molasses alone, though some of the bottles looked a decade old. Warning: Hygiene at this grocery store leaves much to be desired. Even the packages of sweets and cookies are grimy. Still, if you care to eat in, you'll find kabobs, falafel and shawarma sandwiches served at the tiny counter tucked in the back. (A Persian friend claims the hummus here is the best in the city.) Western women may not feel comfortable eating here alone.

JUICE BOX

9889 BELLAIRE BLVD. at Beltway 8
713-484-8085
MAP B7

This is one of the best Taiwanese-style fruit-dessert shops in Houston, and it's often packed with Asian teens. The sterile yet cheery juice bar organizes its menu by fruit. Each "series" transforms the fruit into a number of options such as juice with yogurt or juice with Calpis, a milky Japanese soft drink. The item of note, however, is the milk shaved ice: A large bowl of shaved ice is topped with fruit — mango, melon, strawberry, lychee, red bean, kiwi, etc. — condensed milk and a quality scoop of ice cream. The shaved ice servings are huge and easy to share. Juice Box now features a list of traditional warm Chinese desserts as well. Everything is fairly inexpensive, which perhaps explains the insane traffic clogging the parking lot.

KEGG'S CANDIES

4844 BEECHNUT just outside Loop 610
713-664-4593
www.keggscandies.com
MAP D7

The Kegg family set up their first small shop in 1946, and Houstonians have been coming in droves to their various locations ever since. The delicious smell of melted chocolate is proof that all chocolates are made fresh on the premises. The counter spanning the shop has chocolates and truffles filled with pecans, almonds, caramel, creams and assorted other goodies in both milk and dark chocolate. A separate shelf contains non-chocolate sweets: Bing cherries, rock candy, jellybeans, English toffee, divinity and butterscotch. The true standout is the pecan crisp, a sweet, brittle-like dessert with less crunch and less sugar than regular versions.

KHO BO

11209 BELLAIRE BLVD. #C-8 west of Wilcrest, in the Hong Kong City Mall
281-988-6630
www.vnmetro.com
MAP B7

8388 W. SAM HOUSTON PKWY. #172 south of Beechnut
281-933-6630
MAP B8

Listen up, jerky lovers: We have found your Shangri-la. These two stores stock every kind of dried meat and fish we never even had the imagination to conjure. Prefer beef? We counted at least 15 varieties, including five-spice flavored, fruit flavored and curry flavored. There are also pork jerkies (including mildly spicy pork liver jerky) and deer jerkies. Then the offerings move offshore, with crispy cuttlefish jerky, barbecue-flavored dried shrimp, seasoned baked anchovies, baked baby crabs, fish jerky with sesame and much more. The two stores — tidy and attractively laid out — have even more in the way of dried fruits, nuts and confections. Among the more interesting snacks and culinary ingredients we spotted: shredded preserved green mango with chili, mixed fruit chips (jackfruit, banana, pineapple, taro and yam) and Japanese candied ginger. They even have Gummi Bears and Warheads sour candies.

2045 WESTHEIMER at S. Shepherd, and other locations
713-523-5567
www.kolachefactory.com
MAP E6

KOLACHE FACTORY

Kolaches — those slightly sweetish rolls stuffed with savory meat fillings, cheese or fruit — are a guilty pleasure that we take no pride in admitting to. However, the version made at Houston's many Kolache Factory locations are especially good and worth the diet sin. The regular menu includes bacon and cheese, potato, egg and cheese, sausage and cheese and many fruit (e.g. cherry, apple, peach) varieties; we're particularly fond of Philly cheesesteak kolaches. The same yeast dough is also fashioned into excellent cinnamon rolls and sticky buns.

KRAFTSMEN BAKING

Developed by chef Scott Tycer (who previously had the much-lauded Aries), Kraftsmen is an excellent place to study or chat while having a light breakfast or lunch on the patio under Montrose's lovely shade trees. The shop's location certainly adds to the draw, and sandwiches like the Green Gobbler, which incorporates apple butter, turkey and a brioche roll, are creative and tasty. Excellent soups as well, but we've found that the desserts are not always as delectable as they appear and the croissants are not as buttery and fragile as they might be. (The croissants seem to be sturdily made for sandwiches rather than as pastries.) Curiously, though this shop is run by a bakery, there are very few loaves on hand to choose from. In general, if you want a whole loaf of, say, organic

4100 MONTROSE
north of Richmond
713-524-3737
www.kraftsmenbaking.com
MAP E7

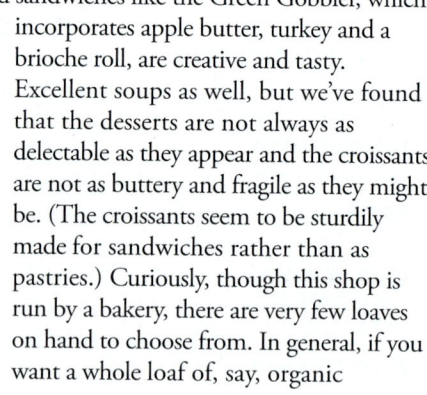

Kraftsmen's many artisan breads are sold in loaves or in made-to-order sandwiches.

multigrain, olive sourdough, Jewish rye, cranberry walnut or ciabatta, you need to order a day ahead.

KROGER SIGNATURE

5150 BUFFALO SPEEDWAY at Westpark, and other locations
713-661-8305
www.kroger.com
MAP D7

Kroger, a grocery chain founded in 1883 in Cincinnati, prides itself on its "Signature" stores that cater to the needs and tastes of the neighborhood. In our 'hood, this means a selection of ready-to-eat and heat-and-eat meals and a sushi bar that goes beyond the standard California roll and tuna offerings. The hand-made tortillas near the bakery are a great solution for people who want to have soft tacos and fajitas at home but hate bland factory-made tortillas. (It even has corn, wheat flour, white flour and buttered options.) We also love the regional food aisle. Though Kroger Signature

Recommended
ROLL WITH IT

Bagel, schmagel. Think they are all alike? Think again. "Bagels should be chewy on the inside, slightly crunchy on the outside and have no air holes," according to the late Houston jeweler I.W. Marks. Nada Chandler, president of the Houston chapter of Hadassah, says, "Forget about designer bagels — you can't put lox or herring on them!" Here's the hole situation.

EINSTEIN BROS. BAGELS, *5300 Kirby, and other locations, 713-528-1992.* Einstein's cornmeal-dusted bagels are compact with a snappy crust. Inside, the dough is fluffy and a tad sweet. Pack some patience for the line and peruse the vast, creative selection. Favorite: toasted sundried tomato bagel with lox, purple onion, capers and plain cream cheese.

HOT BAGEL SHOP, *2009 S. Shepherd, 713-520-0340.* Popular with Inner Loopers seeking a doughy carb fix. Excellent selection of hot bagels, plus great prices. Favorite: warm cinnamon raisin with cream cheese.

NEW YORK BAGEL & COFFEE SHOP, *9724 Hillcroft, 713-723-5897.* Large, crisp and chewy, these fresh-baked, aromatic bagel icons don't have many air holes — hence, perfect for spreads. (Check out the gorgeous braided challah loaves, too.) Favorite: black-and-white bagel straight from the oven.

THREE BROTHERS BAKERY, *4036 S. Braeswood, 713-522-2253.* Super fluffy and light, pretty (and tasty), the brothers' artisan bagels are so glossy and golden, they look artificial. Limited selection of the fruit variety. Favorite: toasted poppyseed.

can't compete with Central Market, it has a great selection of Middle Eastern and British specialties in addition to the standard Chinese and Mexican. The wine selection is decent and sorted by country of origin in addition to type of wine. It also offers a make-your-own-six-pack of Anheuser-Busch international beers: Grolsch, Harbin Lager, Tiger Beer, Kirin, Bass Ale and Boddingtons among them.

LA BOUCHERIE

3323 FM 1960 near TC Jester
281-583-8177
www.cajunmeats.com
MAP C2

Purveyors of such fascinating meat marvels as the turducken and the turporken as well as more traditional specialty meats, this butcher shop likes to tout its origins in Cajun country. Six different stuffing varieties, such as crawfish jambalaya and dirty rice, perk up everything from chicken to pork chops. Just ask and exceedingly specific cooking instructions will be given to you that make the preparation of your holiday poultry foolproof. They also sell *macque choux* (smothered corn), seafood gumbo, jalapeño cornbread, crawfish pie and tasso. Order online and get frozen meats shipped to you within two days.

LA MADELEINE

Taking the quaint boulangerie concept to a faux-rustic extreme, La Madeleine has been bringing French baked goods, breads and simple bistro food to the masses for decades. The legendary tomato-basil soup is sold in jars, and

6205 KIRBY at Amherst, and other locations
713-942-7081
www.lamadeleine.com
MAP E7

the zesty Caesar salad also has a dedicated following. Coffee and artful pastries like the strawberry Napoleon are reliable and we can't say we don't love the complimentary slices of freshly baked bread with jam. Watch out for those pigeons at the Kirby location, though: They'll take your finger off for a tidbit of food.

LA MICHOACANA MEAT MARKET

1348 N. SHEPHERD at W. 13th, and other locations
713-862-6129
www.lamichoacanameatmarket.com
MAP E5

La Michoacana is much more than a meat market today. This Mexican grocery chain was founded in 1986 by a Houston family before spreading its wings to other Texas cities. (It now has nearly 100 locations throughout Texas and beyond.) It's a safe bet for inexpensive cuts of

RECIPE: RED SAUCE & GREEN SAUCE

Created by Ninfa Laurenzo
Ninfa's, 2704 Navigation, 713-228-1175

The late Mama Ninfa Laurenzo, who opened her original restaurant east of downtown in 1973, was credited by many with coining the phrase "Tex-Mex" and for popularizing the fajita. Mama Ninfa's *salsa roja* (red sauce) and *salsa verde* (green sauce) are two of many original recipes that are still served.

RED SAUCE

- 4 Tbsp. oil
- ⅛ cup chopped onions
- ¼ oz. chile de árbol
- 5 lbs. ripe red tomatoes, sliced thickly
- 1¼ oz. cilantro
- 6 cloves garlic
- 3 jalapeños, sliced lengthwise, seeds removed
- salt & pepper to taste

METHOD: Place oil in sauté pan, add chopped onion and chile de árbol and sauté. In a separate pan, fry/grill tomatoes, turning frequently, until they are browned on both sides. Peel tomato skins (discard skins) and place tomatoes in blender. Add cilantro, garlic and jalapeños and blend for 6 seconds. Add sautéed onion and chile de árbol and blend for 3 more seconds. The consistency should be semi-thick, a little chunky. Add salt and pepper to taste. Refrigerate and serve.

GREEN SAUCE

- 3½ lbs. green tomatoes
- 1¾ lbs. tomatillos, husks removed
- ¾ lb. pulp of avocado
- 1¼ oz. cilantro, chopped
- 1 cup water
- salt & pepper to taste
- 3 whole jalapeños, sliced lengthwise, seeds removed
- 2 cloves garlic, chopped
- 10½ oz. sour cream
- pinch of cumin

METHOD: Boil green tomatoes in a pot of water for 15 to 20 minutes until tender, then remove and strain. Grill tomatillos until tender. Place all ingredients in blender or food processor and mix for 45 to 60 seconds. The green sauce should be smooth. Add salt and pepper to taste. Refrigerate and serve.

meat, baked goods, salsas, Mexican dairy products and cheeses, and cones of *piloncillo*, the hard dark sugar. Hungry? A take-out kitchen dishes up a respectable taco, as well as *chicharrones, barbacoa* and more. La Michoacana Meat Market is the largest independent Hispanic grocery store chain in the country.

LA PALETERA

1811 WIRT at Long Point
713-467-0005
www.lapaletera.com
MAP D5

It's great to see healthful options in a dessert shop, which is why La Paletera is such a refreshing place to indulge. If it's fruity and tasty, you can find it here. The specialty is the popsicles (*paletas* in Spanish, hence the name), which range from sugar-free to cream-based and come in no less than 33 varieties, with every fruit flavor you can think of and some you might not (tamarind, anyone?). The cream-based banana paleta was hands-down one of the best popsicles we've ever had. The fruit cups are also a popular choice, with strawberries, bananas or a mixture of both in a cup with sweet cream. Snow cones and smoothies are also on the menu, as is homemade ice cream, which may not be so healthful but sure is good.

LA VICTORIA BAKERY

7138 LAWNDALE at S. 75th St.
713-921-0861
MAP G7

This East End treasure, run by two sisters, produces Mexican-style breads, pastries, cakes and a variety of brightly hued sweets. Come here also for breakfast tortas or gorditas of egg, potato and bacon, grilled biscuits, crisp flautas and huevos rancheros — everyone else does. Parking at this converted service station is a battle well worth it. La Victoria is also well regarded for special-order cakes, finely decorated and flavorful.

LE PETIT PARIS BAKERY

7536 FM 1960 between Hwy. 249 and Cutten
281-970-5067
MAP B2

Le Petit Paris has the croissants, quiches, cakes and other treats ranging from bittersweet to rich to savory that make adults happy. But the secret delight of this Willowbrook shop are confections shaped like animals. From white meringue birds to almond pastry mice covered in chocolate butter cream, chocolate rum-ball penguins and frogs made of Grand Marnier-flavored butter cream, these extra-special treats are a favorite among kids and cost a fraction of what you might find (if you can find them) elsewhere.

LOCAL FLAVORS

14529 MEMORIAL
between Kirkwood and Dairy Ashford
281-493-3663
www.leibmans.com
MAP B6

LEIBMAN'S WINE & FINE FOODS

In the gourmet food and fine wine business since 1979, Ettienne Leibman's old location was destroyed by fire in 2003. Now she is back in this new and much larger location with 6,500 square feet of wonderful imported foodstuffs, wine (heavy on the South African, Australian, New Zealand bottles), hostess gifts, corporate gift baskets and doodads you'll find you must have for the kitchen. There's also a tasty deli where you should look for an expanded cheese section, its legendary housemade cheesesticks, Chicken Salad Afrique, sandwiches and lots of chocolate. The friendly staff will tell you about scheduled wine tastings. Party planners and homebodies take note, the store also caters.

LOUISIANA FOODS

This used to be strictly a wholesale operation known best for its quality oysters, but a small retail counter now welcomes home cooks who want to pick up fresh seafood and workers looking for a quick lunch. You can still buy oysters here, by the pound or by the burlap bag, as well as crawfish, shrimp, crab, flounder, various snappers, escolar, amberjack … basically, just about any cold-blooded water critter you can think of. Louisiana Foods was founded in 1972 by Jim Gossen, Billy Landry and Floyd Landry, in Morgan City, Louisiana, so it comes by its name honestly. The Landrys, of course, went on to operate a number of Houston restaurants. Gossen still runs the seafood facility, and he makes sure the seafood here is stellar, even going so far as to guarantee that the red snapper is, in fact, *Lutjanus campechanus*. The downside is that the retail shop is open just 25 hours a week, 10 a.m. to 3 p.m. Monday through Friday. Lagniappe: Louisiana Foods has an excellent website that details the various fish and scores of recipes for cooking them.

4410 W. 12TH east of N. Post Oak Rd.
713-957-3476
www.louisianafoods.com
MAP D5

550 HEIGHTS BLVD.
at White Oak
713-869-0011
www.mccainsmarket.com
MAP E6

McCAIN'S MARKET

This small specialty grocery in the historic Heights models itself after mid-size markets scattered throughout San Francisco and Manhattan. It doesn't stock toilet paper or even much fresh produce. Instead the focus is on local

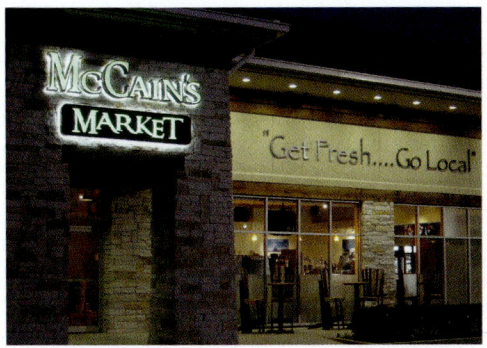

McCain's is a perfect fit for The Heights. Stop, shop and relax on the patio or in the coffee bar.

gourmet products. McCain's intention is to serve the neighborhood conveniently. However, the products are fairly specialized, and customers more often come for the coffee bar or a sandwich than they do for groceries. It's quiet and pleasantly decorated, which may be why so many loyal locals bring their laptops there. Still, people can find a huge variety of dangerous-looking hot sauces, chic baking kits and Katz coffee beans. The meat and fish is replaced every two days or as-needed, with specials everyday. The staff will be happy to answer your questions, give you tips on how to properly barbecue a chicken, or tell you how fabulous their neighborhood is. Essentially, McCain's is a good option if you are in The Heights exploring or only want a few things.

MI TIENDA

1630 SPENCER HWY. at S. Perez, Pasadena

713-941-7550

MAP H8

Mi Tienda is HEB's Latin-themed mega-market, aimed at immigrants from Mexico and Central America. A gringo may feel like an intruding tourist here, where pesos are accepted and employees approach you with rapid-fire Spanish. The signs, labels and magazines at checkout are all in Spanish, too, but once the staff realize you can't speak Spanish, they'll either switch to English or begin to pantomime indulgently. In some ways, Mi Tienda is like Fiesta. Groceries are significantly less expensive, and the focus is on Mexican specialties. At Mi Tienda, however, a simulated village, decorated festively with *papel picado* streamers, takes up half the store and serves hot food most customers enjoy in-store. Choose from ceviche, combo plates, tamales by the dozen and refreshing *aguas frescas*. Corn tortillas roll off a conveyor belt right onto a free sample tray or into 3-pound bags. There is a huge selection at the meat and cheese counter. It seems like a daunting journey for the non-fluent, but it's an interesting concept. Come on a weekday to avoid the weekend crowd, but know that the mariachi band is here only on Sundays.

LOCAL FLAVORS

> **1600 SHEPHERD**, three blocks south of I-10
> **713-426-1505**
> **MAP** E6

MOJO RISIN'

You say you want a revolution? The "Mom" and "Pop" aprons donned by owners Jack and Terri Mullen let you know there's nothing corporate about this hippie haven. Cappuccinos and the Instant Karma espresso are good, but try the White Rabbit macchiato and the

Personal Favorites
TEA TIME

By Lee Q. Garcia

You don't have to be English to love the custom of afternoon tea. In Houston especially, it provides a needed reprieve from our fast-paced agendas. Many local shops carry fine loose teas, scones, petit fours and savories that entice you to cherish this gentle custom. Here are five of my favorites:

GENERATIONS TEA ROOM Heading towards Galveston, stop off in League City (Route 518) where a historic building on Main Street is home to generations of Southern women who oversee a gracious tea service in quaint, old-fashioned rooms. Located at 1013 E. Main St., League City, 281-557-8336.

KIRAN'S Exceeding the convention of this popular event, Kiran Verma starts tea service with succulent Indian samosas and homemade chai. The service is impeccable, and Champagne is available. Located at 4100 Westheimer, 713-960-8472.

SERENITEA TEA ROOM Owner Archana Pyatt brings her New York tea knowledge to Sugar Land. This elegant tea shop serves elevenses, cream tea and full service all day. Located at 13889 Southwest Fwy., Sugar Land, 281-491-4588.

TÉ HOUSE OF TEA This teahouse boasts fair-trade teas from around the world, plus a creative menu of crêpes, sandwiches and desserts. It's a tranquil spot to visit during the day and more lively on weekends when the tango and swing dancers arrive. Located at 1927 Fairview, 713-522-8868.

TEA WITH CHARLES MARCEL Famed tea butler Charles Marcel creates an enchanting afternoon for his guests in an elegant setting with traditional service and even a harpist. Marcel is currently serving at the St. Regis Hotel, 1919 Briar Oaks Ln., 713-840-7600.

Lee Q. Garcia is the publisher of Tea in Texas Magazine, *which promotes tea and unique places in the Lone Star State and proves tea is more than a beverage — it's a state of mind. Visit www.teaintexas.com.*

Revolution, the shop's version of cafe mocha. The spinach feta quiche has a perfect consistency and is made from a family recipe. Posters cover the walls, and a regular customer's dog may be lazing out front in the sun. In our harried to-go times, this is a place of bottomless mellow — the anti-chain. Free WiFi with purchase.

MOO HIVE HONEY ICE CREAM

6285 BISSONNET
at Hillcroft
713-774-4200
MAP C7

A bright spot in an otherwise bleak corner, Moo Hive is a sweet surprise. Local owners Mark and Susan Hostetler make all the ice cream on location and sweeten with local honey in lieu of processed sugar. The result is truly delicious — cookies 'n' cream, coconut, lemon and banana rum are just a few of the standout flavors. The staff are friendly (and bilingual), prices are reasonable and even a small order gets two scoops of different flavors. Kids will also love the honeycombed walls and pint-sized seating. Moo Hive has a true neighborhood feel, attested to by the collage of customer photos alongside those of the owners and their daughter, Julia.

NIPPON DAIDO

Quick-knife Benihana-style chef aspirant or not, you too can enjoy authentic Japanese food in your own home. How? Shop at Nippon Daido, where all your sashimi-grade fish, containers of smelt roe and octopus tentacle dreams can come true. The store is impeccably clean with no errant fish smells wafting through the air. A small vegetable section is stocked with produce found in traditional Japanese cooking, and packaged goods like noodles, powdered wasabi, nori, miso, dashi and sushi rice are available as well. Sushi knives, sushi mats, hand-painted plates and tea mugs are also sold. A separate room houses intriguing Japanese-language magazines and videos.

11146 WESTHEIMER
at Wilcrest
713-785-0815
MAP B7

NUNDINI FOOD MART

500 N. SHEPHERD
between I-10 and W. 6th
713-861-6331
MAP E6

Driving past on Shepherd you'd likely mistake Nundini's for just another warehouse, which, technically, it is. The food mart is the retail portion of this Italian food importer, and what it lacks in atmosphere it makes up for in taste. Nundini stocks pastas, meats, cheeses, sweets and other Italian goodies at wholesale prices. Most significantly, Nundini is the source of most gelato found in Houston

LOCAL FLAVORS

Recommended
COOKING CLASSES AND SCHOOLS

Become a professional chef, sharpen your culinary skills, cut up with the foodie set or just make new friends. Houston cooking classes are peppered conveniently around town, each spiced with a unique personality and following.

BRENNAN'S, *3300 Smith, 713-522-9711. Date Night* cooking classes at venerable Brennan's restaurant with upbeat executive chef Randy Evans are a fun way for you and your beau or belle to get out of your cooking or dining routine. Classes include dinner, drinks and recipes for one price per couple. Evening classes start with drinks and appetizers on the lovely patio. Past classes have included Houston foods, seafood and "Mardi Gras Madness." Call for the seasonal schedule.

CENTRAL MARKET, *3815 Westheimer, 713-993-9860.* Anticipate a wide range of culinary classes with an exciting roster of visiting chef instructors from across the nation. Demonstration, hands-on and interactive classes, as well as a variety of wine classes, are available. Recipes and sample tastings are included, along with wine tastings for most evening classes. "Fine Foods from South Africa," "Gumbo Tales" and "Perfect Recipes for Eating Great" have been popular class topics.

L'AGLIO, *22100 Westheimer Pkwy., Katy, 281-579-7963.* Whether you are looking to spruce up your family weeknight dinners or seeking a "friends night out," these cooking classes offer useful and approachable step-by-step techniques with recipes and tastings included. Adults, teens and kids cooking classes are on the agenda with demonstration and hands-on classes guided by a staff of qualified instructors. No excuses to be a lame cook anymore! Check out the on-site gourmet shop.

LE LEED'S COOKING SCHOOL, *3001 Fondren #D, 713-339-4535.* Chef Tony Lee, former executive chef at Jones Hall and The Wortham Theater, founded his cooking school in 1998. Casual classes conducted by chef Lee cover the gamut from sushi, wok cooking, pizza and pasta-making from scratch to heart-healthy eating and divine desserts. The school also features kids' cooking classes and extensive cake-decorating segments. Buy a class membership and enjoy a discount on cake-decorating supplies. Team-building or business-to-business events are available for groups.

RICE EPICUREAN COOKING SCHOOL, *2020 Fountain View, 713-954-2152.* Cooking classes cover a delicious range of topics and feature local and visiting chefs or staff chefs of the Rice Cooking School. There are hands-on and demonstration classes, a Kids Summer Camp and a more advanced Cultivated Cooking School program for adults that includes 12 months of classes with a specialized curriculum. Go grocery shopping after you finish your class.

SUR LA TABLE, *1996 W. Gray, 713-533-0959.* Local and national celebrity chefs take the spotlight at these well-organized classes that cover everything from paella to petit fours. Learn about cooking with wine, how to make dumplings or perhaps the basics of wok cooking and steaming. Walk away with recipes for the "Perfect French Dinner," "International Appetizers" or a marvelous "Mexican Breakfast." There are morning and evening classes every month that feature both hands-on and demonstration styles, plus a Kids Spring Break Mini Camp.

Houston culinary schools that offer degree programs:

ART INSTITUTE OF HOUSTON, *1900 Yorktown #100, 713-623-2040.* Popular degree programs include culinary arts, restaurant management, culinary management and catering management. The modern facilities and personal instruction put most students at ease. Hungry? Students cook fabulous, beautifully presented gourmet meals at the on-site restaurant named Courses for an affordable price. The public is welcome.

CULINARY INSTITUTE LENOTRE, *7070 Allensby, 713-692-0077.* Founder Alain LeNotre created this international chef school in 1998, modeled after his former Parisian school. At least five full-time French instructors conduct the hands-on courses that start every 10 weeks. In addition to the three diplomas offered, there are two associate degrees in applied science (Culinary Arts or Pastry Arts) and eligible graduates are offered optional internships in France. Drop-in students can enjoy leisure classes that include summer camp for teens and adults.

HOUSTON COMMUNITY COLLEGE CENTRAL, *1300 Holman, 713-718-6000.* Internationally known instructors teach students in state-of-the-art facilities for professional chef positions in restaurants and other institutions. Students progress through a series of courses that emphasize sanitation in food handling, basic and advanced cooking and baking techniques, plus the latest trends in fine food production. Culinary Arts or Baking & Pastry Arts degree plans are available for students with a high school diploma.

THE CONRAD N. HILTON COLLEGE OF HOTEL AND RESTAURANT MANAGEMENT *at the University of Houston, 4800 Calhoun, 713-743-2255.* Get your ticket to culinary career success at one of the world's premier hospitality-education facilities. The graduate program that leads to a Master of Science in Hospitality Management is conducted in traditional classroom settings, online and in the extraordinary "living laboratory" offered by the Hilton University of Houston Hotel and Conference Center. Included in the 40,000-square-foot complex are banquet facilities, two restaurants, a cocktail lounge, three ballrooms and state-of-the-art facilities for quantity food production and culinary training.

LOCAL FLAVORS

restaurants, so naturally the dessert counter is where most people stop. While the gelato is good, though perhaps heavier and creamier than some, the sorbetto is by far the standout, with fruit flavors that burst in your mouth. They sell surplus custom-ordered flavors, so you never know what you'll find in the gelato cooler.

4791 WESTHEIMER inside Loop 610, and other locations
713-623-8681
www.omahasteaks.com
MAP D6

OMAHA STEAKS INC.

The not-quite-cozy-looking armchairs are the first indication that Omaha Steaks is not a typical meat market. The store actually specializes in flash-frozen, individually sealed foods, particularly beef, which are stored in neatly labeled cardboard boxes stuffing the refrigerators lining the walls. A pre-cooked "dinner tonight" section provides marinated meats with sides for the very busy among us. Bonus: Staff are very friendly and knowledgeable about the product.

OOH LA LA

This "dessert boutique" from owner/pastry chef Vanessa Newbill has an adorable old-fashioned display case filled with cookies, cupcakes, pies and towering cakes. One of the more unusual items we spotted is the bread pudding pie, available whole or by the slice. You can also have the signature jumbo cupcakes custom-designed with toppings at the Cupcake Bar. What else: dozens of wicked specialty coffee drinks, eye-catching coffee mugs and cookie cutters to use or just collect, and a cozy fireplace area with comfy overstuffed chairs. On a fine day, kick back on the outdoor patio or bring your laptop and use the free Wifi. Feeling lazy? It's got take-out, delivery and — ooh la la — a drive-thru. Closed Sundays.

23920 WESTHEIMER PKWY. west of the Grand Parkway, Katy
281-391-2253
www.oohlalasweets.com
MAP West of A7

The interior of Ooh La La is as comforting as the made-from-scratch desserts.

PANERA BREAD BAKERY CAFE

680 MEMORIAL CITY MALL near Gessner and I-10
713-465-2253
www.panerabread.com
MAP C6

Panera works towards "an era of bread," and Atkins diet proponents everywhere are cringing — because this St. Louis chain is actually pretty good. The bread is baked every morning, and the asiago and tomato basil are delicious. The Cobblestone — cinnamon raisin bread mixed with chunks of apples, topped with streusel and white icing — is a signature offering. Service is a little touch-and-go, due to the questionable custom of employing flirtatious and preoccupied teens. Panera deserves a pat on the back, however, because many locations donate their leftover baked goods to community kitchens at the end of the day.

THE PATH OF TEA

2340 W. ALABAMA near Kirby
713-252-4473
www.thepathoftea.com
MAP E7

Let your nose be your guide at this elegantly appointed, all-organic tea house, which includes a sniffing bar stocked with 120 organic teas. (It is Texas' only totally organic tea shop.) Staff at this Zen refuge serve tea in glass vessels warmed by candles. Try Organic Fire, with spicy notes of cinnamon, black pepper and orange zest. All desserts are tea-infused, including lemon bars. It's the brainchild of Thia and Chris McKann.

PENZEY'S SPICES

516 W. 19TH east of N. Shepherd
713-862-6777
www.penzeys.com
MAP E5

Although Penzey's is a nationwide establishment, it is a favorite stop for local restaurants and even NASA when fulfilling spice needs. Penzey's runs much of its business by catalogue and online, where spices can be bought in bulk and shipped freshly ground from Wisconsin, but the store itself is such an enjoyable experience and lets you experience the spices hands-on (nose-on?). The decor favors a faux-antique look, with never-used wooden crates and spice bags lining the walls. But there is generally little reason to look up, given what is on the shelves, which are sprinkled with cinnamon sticks and whole nutmeg. Penzey's stocks an enormous variety of spices and seasonings. Each bottle comes with helpful serving suggestions and recipes. The staff are very amenable to answering questions and almost pushy when it comes to having customers sniff-test sample jars. Feel free to take the kids because Penzey's has a coloring corner to keep them busy.

LOCAL FLAVORS

Recommended
KITCHEN GADGETS

No matter if you need to dash to the store to replace a Pyrex measuring cup or start from scratch in a brand new kitchen, Houston has the gadgets to get your culinary creations whipped up. Note: Besides the retailers, below, you'll find a large selection of dishes, linens, cookware and tools at Central Market, Hong Kong Market, Bed Bath & Beyond, Crate & Barrel, Target, Kitchen Collection, Pier 1 Imports, Linens & Things, World Market, Budget Restaurant Supply and Ace Mart.

BERING'S, *6102 Westheimer, 713-785-6400, and 3900 Bissonnet, 713-665-0500.* Expect a smart collection of cooking tools and a pleasant neighborhood feel at these popular Houston-born hardware stores that pack a surprising amount of great merchandise in their small sites. Cookbooks, aprons, basic to innovative kitchen and baking tools, cutlery, fine cutting boards and small appliances are a few of the staples. Also find chichi European ceramics, platters, cloth napkins and elegant glassware, ideal for gifts or an entertainment splurge.

BUFFALO HARDWARE, *2614 Westheimer, 713-524-1011.* In a pinch, River Oaks denizens rely on this tiny family-owned corner hardware store 60-plus years old packed with cool merchandise. From baking sheets, cutlery, beautiful bamboo cutting boards, small appliances and even a current cookbook and food book selection, you can usually find what you need. If you get lost in the dark rows of wondrous kitchen items, ask a helpful salesperson.

CHANTAL COOKWARE, *5425 N. Sam Houston Pkwy. West, 713-467-9949.* Chantal's enamel pots are made in Germany, the glass lids come from Japan and the various pieces are designed and assembled here in Houston. Chantal is open to the public only once a year, usually in the fall, when the warehouse has a sale of overstocked, blemished, discontinued and one-of-a-kind items. The rest of the year visit the website (www.chantal.com) to shop the product line.

L'AGLIO, *22100 Westheimer Pkwy., Katy, 281-579-7963.* Italian for "garlic," this Katy kitchen gadget shop features small appliances (e.g. griddles, bread machines, slow cookers, blenders), pot racks, table-top items and gourmet foods, as well as custom gift baskets. In business since 1996, the shop holds evening and weekend cooking classes for adults (usually $35 to $40 per person) and schedules cooking classes for kids and teens during the summer.

SUR LA TABLE, *1996 W. Gray, 713-533-0400, and other locations.* Upscale, roomy stores make shopping for the kitchen entertaining for amateur and professional chefs. The sales staff are usually

PETE'S FINE MEATS

5509 RICHMOND
east of Chimney Rock
713-782-3470
MAP D7

This small shop is a local favorite. And although Pete is gone, his son Mike now runs the store and is extremely knowledgeable. You'll find buffalo, bear, whole suckling pig and snake in addition to aged prime beef cuts, house-made sausage and jerky, and fresh eggs. The staff will season your meat with house-brand spices and sauce at no extra cost. If you call in ahead of time, they will even cook it for you. Pete's Fine Meats is also well known for deer processing, out of which can come its famous deer tamales. (If you buy a hog at the rodeo, you can have it processed here, too.) Fresh turkeys are available for the holidays, but order in advance. In addition to the butcher counter, the lunch counter does brisk business in burgers and steak tacos. Despite being a store stocked with slabs of raw meat, Pete's maintains a quirky, homey atmosphere.

well-versed on their inventory and many are experienced cooks. Expect a foodie paradise of products like unique metal cookie cutters, silicone muffin pans in eye-popping colors, *springerie* (German cookie) molds, plus a kids' section with cooking sets and cute gifts. Along with a whirlwind of whisks, mixers and spatulas, you'll find cutlery and professional cookware, plus mandoline slicers and unusual Japanese steamers. High-end espresso machines and coffee makers from France and Italy will catch your wandering eye.

TONY'S BAR SUPPLY, *5201 S. Wayside, 713-641-2277.* Tony's Bar Supply feels like it should be to-the-trade only, but anyone can shop here. Founded in 1963 and now located just outside the South Loop, this restaurant supplier carries everything for a bar except (as its website notes) the alcohol. You'll find bar appliances (such as sinks and refrigerators), chemicals for cleaning draft-beer lines and concession machines. What the home cook and host will be more interested in are the glassware, bartender kits, cocktail napkins in bulk, garnishes and mixes.

WILLIAMS SONOMA, *4060 Westheimer, 713-212-0346, and other locations.* Here's the crème de la crème of fine cookware stores that originated in the once sleepy wine country town of Sonoma by founder Chuck Williams. Design-worthy store layouts suck in even the most seasoned cook with their sumptuous tablescapes and coordinating color palettes. Shiny hammered European brass cookware sets compete with Calphalon, Le Creuset and Mauviel in every size imaginable. Crystal stemware and trendy wine decanters beckon along with functional glassware, which are popular for the savvy bride and her wedding registry.

LOCAL FLAVORS

> **12141 WESTHEIMER**
> west of Kirkwood
> **281-558-8225**
> www.phoeniciafoods.com
> **MAP** B7

PHOENICIA SPECIALTY FOODS

Upon entering the warehouse that is Phoenicia, the scent of spices is overwhelming. While probably not designed for the purpose of making customers giddy with excitement, it very well does. Phoenicia Specialty Foods is an offshoot of Phoenicia Deli, directly across Westheimer, and carries products from countries around the world while specializing in Mediterranean and Middle Eastern cuisine. It's fun to get lost in the aisles browsing the exotic items such as hookahs and Arabic fruit leather, but it's also not a bad place to do your weekly grocery shopping. The olive bar is one of the best deals in town, and halal beef and whole lamb are available in the meat section. At the lunch and prepared-foods counters, you can purchase a Greek salad or *babaganoush*, among other things, by the pound. The beautiful bakery displays baklava alongside chocolate croissants and Turkish delight. Digestive biscuits are shelved beside Kinder Eggs and jars of mango chutney. There's an entire aisle devoted to canned beans. Overall the experience is akin to spinning around in a teacup to "It's a Small World," but pleasure replaces the dizziness.

The offerings at Phoenicia are a feast for the eyes as well as the stomach.

PICNIC

> **1928 BISSONNET** at Hazard
> **713-524-0201**
> www.picnicboxlunches.com
> **MAP** E7

Picnic, created by the owners of the nearby Raven Grill, feels homey, like a hybrid of the traditional neighborhood bakery, sandwich shop and coffee shop. The seating inside is one giant — and we mean giant — picnic table, but no matter, the whole point is to enjoy this stuff outdoors. The specialty is the box picnic lunch, which includes a sandwich, fruit salad, chips, cookie and pickle. The counter holds a map of good picnic spots that includes parks both nearby (e.g. the Cullen Sculpture Garden at the MFA and

Miller Outdoor Theatre in Hermann Park) and farther afield (the Water Wall near The Galleria). Cookies, cakes, brownies and scones are baked daily in house as are the homemade breads, including the daily special bread. Try to make it on Monday for cinnamon raisin or on Tuesday for cranberry pecan.

PIE IN THE SKY

3600 N. LOOP 336 WEST near Old Montgomery Rd., Conroe
936-760-3301
www.pieintheskyco.com
MAP North of D1

It's lofty for a restaurant to assign its food a heavenly quality, but then again what pie-lover has not thought along those lines anyway? This modernized Conroe diner uses bright green paint and galvanized metal to create a cheerful environment in which to enjoy the food — reliable menu items such as the Angus burger and turkey melt. But pies like apple lattice and Mississippi Mud demand you save room for dessert. Self-taught baker and owner/chef Marline Stubler's personal favorite is the Bumbleberry, an original recipe that involves an assortment of berries. Her pies are also available at Rice Epicurean markets and Barnaby's restaurants around Houston. Some pie flavors such as the fragile banana cream and chocolate meringue need to be ordered a day ahead.

Owner Marlene Stubler started her pie business making minis for the family convenience stores.

RAINDROP CHOCOLATE

When Don Burke opened RainDrop Chocolate, he wanted to bring a different kind of chocolate shop to Houston with none of the factory-processed confections. Instead he aimed for a return to the rich flavors

810 WAUGH between Allen Parkway and W. Dallas
713-524-2864
www.raindropchocolate.com
MAP E6

of traditional chocolate as found in Mexico and South America. Using all-natural ingredients and unexpected combinations, the truffles here are so delicious they really are like drops from heaven. Alongside traditional milk, white and dark chocolate sit delightful flavors including lavender, English mint, chipotle-tequila and Champagne rose. Not

LOCAL FLAVORS

convinced? RainDrop also has arguably the best gelato in town, light, creamy and bursting with flavor, just like you'd find in Italy.

RAO'S BAKERY

6915 CYPRESSWOOD
at Southampton Dr., Spring
281-251-7267
www.raosbakery.com
MAP C1

Open since 1941 in Beaumont, Rao's has finally brought its legendary cakes, gelato and pastries to the Houston area via Spring. Widely known for their king cakes around Mardi Gras time, they have a selection of more than two dozen gourmet cakes available whole or by the slice. The six-layered Dobasche — a triple serving of fudge, vanilla and walnuts — is impossible to resist. If that sounds like it might spoil your diet, there are sugar-free chocolate and white cakes that taste almost as good as the real thing. Rao's also has a nice menu of breakfast, lunch and dinner items. The panini sandwiches are worth a try, if you can tear your eyes away from the cakes, cookies, brownies, tarts, cream puffs and other pastries. If not, well, sometimes you just have to eat dessert first.

RICE EPICUREAN MARKET

5016 SAN FELIPE near Post Oak Blvd., and other locations
713-621-0422
www.riceepicurean.com
MAP D6

Rice Epicurean was Houston's first upscale food store. Now Whole Foods and Central Market have entered the scene and Rice Epicurean has taken a bit of a backseat, though many of its older, well-to-do customers have remained loyal. It is also the oldest family-owned supermarket chain in Houston, which has not changed hands since its founding. The store features all the usual suspects: gorgeous produce, gourmet deli section and prepared foods, fine wines and a bakery. We also appreciate that Rice Epicurean often supports small start-up Texas food companies.

RUGGLES CAFE BAKERY

2365-A RICE BLVD.
near Morningside
713-520-6662
www.rugglesgrill.com
MAP E7

This popular branch of the Ruggles mini-chain serves up more casual, inexpensive fare. All desserts, which range from English trifle to the Charlotte's Web (chocolate cake melded with espresso pudding and Heath bar bits), could feed a small family for $5.95. The patio overlooking the Rice Village neighborhood is a nice place to enjoy a full meal, complemented by the delicious sweet potato fries and the BYO-wine policy.

Personal Favorites
MAKING & GIVING CHOCOLATES

Heidemarie Vukovic, award-winning chocolatier, pastry chef and owner of Chocolate Harmony, shares her favorite sources for chocolate-making supplies.

CENTRAL MARKET (*3815 Westheimer, 713-386-1700*) has the city's largest selection of packaged chocolate, including varieties from Valrhona, El Rey and Belcolade. It's great to see this higher quality of chocolate now so readily available.

I also recommend **HOUSTON PECAN COMPANY** (*7313 Ashcroft, Suite 212, 713-772-6216*). Owners Leon and Shirley Cooper have run this business in the same location for 35 years. The dried fruits and nuts are fresh, and the owners are always helpful. I like to use various nuts and dried fruit in my chocolate, and the freshness is very important.

PATH OF TEA (*2340 W. Alabama, 713-252-4473*) is owned by Thia McKann. This tea shop offers a large selection of teas that are fair trade and organic. I have been interested in infusing various teas into my chocolate fillings. One that is really enjoyed is my Chai Tea, which won the Best Chocolate Truffle award at the Austin Chocolate Festival in 2007. Other selections that work with chocolate are yerba maté, Earl Grey and Thin Mint Houjicha (Japanese mint tea).

Another small place off the beaten path I like to visit for pastry tips and bags for piping the chocolates is **AMAZING CAKE SUPPLIES** (*6057 Bissonnet, 713-665-8899*). You can also get canisters for your airbrush machine if you don't use a generator. They offer various food coloring, garnishing tools, gold and silver dust to decorate your chocolates and much more.

And, finally to present your chocolates in a pretty gift box, I think **PALMER PACKAGING** (*1613 Richmond, 713-524-5413*) is the best. Bob and Barbara Nicodemus have been selling packaging in Houston for many years. There's a huge selection of boxes, bags and ribbons to put it all together. If you're looking for a particular style or theme, Bob will research it for you. They both are very helpful, as is as their staff.

Heidemarie Vukovic recently started teaching chocolate classes with Leisure Learning. Her chocolates can be found at Path of Tea, A Moveable Feast (seasonally), Pleasant Hill Winery and Cricket's Creamery & Cafe. Visit www.ChocolateHarmony.com.

LOCAL FLAVORS

RUSSIAN GENERAL STORE

9629 HILLCROFT
south of S. Braeswood
713-721-7595
MAP C8

When President Ford signed the Jackson-Vanik amendment to a foreign trade bill in 1975, it opened a door within the Iron Curtain that allowed some 500,000 people to emigrate from the Soviet Union to the United States over the following years. Some 40,000 Russian-speaking immigrants settled in Texas cities. The Russian General Store came into existence to serve that community in Houston. Located in a part of Southwest Houston where many Soviet immigrants first settled, the store offers nostalgic items such as real Soviet-style Fanta and Soviet-era style table salt. It also stocks a huge variety of sausages, including numerous kinds of salami; smoked meats and fish; Russian-style dairy products; frozen Siberian dumplings; canned condiments and fruits from Russia, Bulgaria, Bosnia, Poland and other Eastern countries of culinary promise; candies and pastries; Russian beers and Georgian wines. Souvenirs ranging from Turkmen sheepskin hats to fine Russian porcelains, a Russian-language bookstore and a video lending library are also on hand. In general, for any given item, from potatoes to caviar, the prices are the lowest in Houston. The friendly bilingual staff are always ready to explain and guide non-Russophones in their purchases.

RUSTIKA CAFE & BAKERY

3237 SOUTHWEST FWY.
at Buffalo Speedway
713-665-6226
www.rustikacafe.com
MAP D7

Among the simplest of Houston's culinary pleasures is the breakfast taco. At Rustika, the brainchild of Mexico City-born Francis Reznick, the breakfast taco is more akin to a burrito. Improved by the addition of some of the green homemade salsa, this warm roll-up of all things comfortably delicious and the huge variety of migas plates draw crowds on weekend mornings. Empanadas like the chicken *mole* are also good with the salsa, while the pumpkin is more or less the redesigned pie of your traditional Thanksgiving. The clean, homey interior makes for a cheerful environment to toss back a few baseball-sized macaroons as well.

SANDY'S PRODUCE MARKET

Sandy's is part health-food store, part grocery store, part restaurant, part neighborhood community meeting place. If you care about what you put into (or onto) your body, surely you will want to explore Sandy's, which was founded by Sandy and Faith Arch in 2000. Aside from the fresh produce (mostly from smaller, organic producers), there are areas dedicated

12171 KATY FWY.
near Kirkwood
281-870-9999
www.sandysmarket.com
MAP B6

to herbs, spices, natural sweeteners and dietary supplements. Organic meat is available fresh and frozen. A big draw here is the enormous buffet lunch, which is very popular in the neighborhood and with nearby office workers. Diners sit at mismatched antique wood tables. A tea server will bring hot or iced beverages. Live music offerings range from a pianist to an oompah band. With its used books, earnest community events (a recent evening combined a writing seminar and dinner) and literature for massage therapists and crystal healers, this sure doesn't feel like SUV-driving over-achieving West Houston. We love it for that!

SORBETTO'S

The walls decorated with arches and frescoes of Italian scenes set the casual European vibe, and the gelato does not disappoint. Thirty flavors of gelato and sorbetto mean tough decisions: coffee or limoncello? mint or coconut? Fortunately,

14008 MEMORIAL
at Kirkwood
281-531-0637
www.sorbettos.com
MAP B6

there are no wrong answers. Every flavor from creamy to tart to sweet is really that good. And just when you thought all your decisions were made, the smoothies are also made with 100 percent fruit. The coffee and beverages, with options ranging from espresso and iced coffee to chai tea and Italian sodas, are also spot-on delicious. Fortunately you don't have to choose between these all at one time — Sorbetto's is the kind of place you'll keep coming back to.

2117 CHENEVERT at Gray
713-655-7847
www.stir-it-up-coffee.com
MAP E6

STIR-IT-UP COFFEE HOUSE

While some coffee shops tend towards libraries in their unbreachable silence, Stir-It-Up maintains a fun atmosphere with its reggae-themed vibe and friendly counter staff. The sleek interior is colored red green and brown, both modern and relaxing. There is a serious focus on simple food at this coffeehouse. To accompany the fair-trade coffee, a small breakfast selection including toast and bagels is available, and for lunch there is an inexpensive sandwich menu that touts the intriguing Jamaican-style patties. Wednesday is tamale day, and on Friday and Saturday the shop sells breakfast tacos. Unlike many coffeeshops, this one is open only until 6 p.m. on most days. Also, don't over look the mini-shop within the coffeehouse, Ra*Jah, which sells handmade soaps, vintage clothing, painted ties and ethnic jewelry. It's owned by friends Maria Belmarez and Faith Cisneros.

STONE MILL BAKERS

2518 KIRBY at Westheimer
713-524-6600
www.stonemillbakers.com
MAP E6

Stone Mill is proud of the fact that it grinds its own wheat and the breads are made without added fats, oils and preservatives. All that healthful stuff aside though, the fluffy freshness can't be beat. Whole-wheat sourdough, Montana wheat and jalapeño cornbread are the most-purchased loaves. Avoid the cookies, which are fantastically large but lacking in flavor, and order one of the sandwiches instead, specifically the curried chicken salad on cinnamon raisin bread, a mouth-pleasing harmony of sweet and savory. The deli closes at 5:30 p.m., and aside from the standards, certain breads are available only on certain days of the week. Avoid disappointment by checking online or calling ahead to see what's available.

SUGARBABY'S

3310 S. SHEPHERD at Branard
713-527-8427
www.ilovesugarbabys.com
MAP E6

Cupcake experts — or your 5-year-old — will tell you that the crucial feature of any cupcake is the icing-to-cake ratio. The ideal number varies for everyone, but Sugarbaby's caters to the icing lovers. And the icing is good, especially the masterful cinnamon cream cheese frosting on top of the applesauce cupcake. True balance is achieved within the store itself, however, where elegant black and white tiling works with the wildly pink decor to create a welcoming environment for a larger demographic than the name of the store implies. Parking in the back is tight, but there is ample seating inside.

Sugarbaby's is a couture cupcake boutique that makes us nostalgic for carefree days before carb consciousness.

SUPER H MART

1302 BLALOCK
between I-10 and Westview
713-468-0606
MAP C5

Long anticipated, this South Korean-owned supermarket chain finally opened in Houston in May 2008, settling not in Chinatown where you might expect, but in Spring Branch, an area that is becoming known for its Korean restaurants, churches, bookstores and bakeries. This location, a former Randall's grocery store, has had a complete makeover, and it's all for the good. There's an astonishing seafood counter (including many kinds of live fish, even abalone), excellent meat counter where you can order marinated *bulgogi* and super-thin-sliced beef for *shabushabu*, a wall of kimchee of every kind, well-priced produce, fresh noodles and tofu, and much more — not to mention the extensive food court. Here's where you'll find a dumpling counter, sushi bar and cafe for hot stone bowl *bibimbap*, Korean short ribs and spicy soft tofu stews. In other cities, H Mart has been likened to a Whole Foods for Asian foodstuffs — and we agree with the comparison. It's clean, well priced, customer friendly and fun to shop. Note: The chain began as a Korean grocery store, but the concept has expanded to cover all Asian groceries. This is a must-visit.

SUPER JORDAN IMPORTED FOOD & BAKERY

5922 HILLCROFT
just north of Hwy. 59
713-953-1000
MAP C7

Houston's Persian community shops at this small tidy market (next door to Bijan, the Persian restaurant) for dry food staples, jams, syrups, tea, canned beans, herb blends, sweets and much more. Fresh roasted nuts are set out for serving yourself, and you may sample before buying. Tea sets and hookahs will tempt, too. Of particular note: It always has fresh and sometimes warm *barbari* (long flat bread) and a glass case of beautiful-looking pastries, as well as a few cured charcuterie items. Farsi-language videos and CDs are available, along with publications. Prices are in English, but not much else is.

SUPER VANAK INTERNATIONAL FOOD

5692 HILLCROFT
near Westpark Tollway
713-952-7676
MAP C7

This unassuming grocery looks more like a convenience store than anything else, but once inside, past the trickling water fountain and tired potted plants, it provides an enjoyable foray into Persian food basics. A little section is dedicated to baked desserts, another to plums and pomegranates, and

LOCAL FLAVORS

Recommended

STARBUCKS: NOTES FROM THE COFFEE GROUNDS

By M. Yvonne Taylor

Starbucks may not have the same cachet among hipsters as the indie favorites, but it is the mother ship, the comfort food of the caffeine-seeker. Her success has profoundly influenced many other purveyors and consumers of hot liquid adrenaline. If you always want the same drink made the same way, you go to Starbucks. But sometimes, Starbucks actually succeeds in creating a unique culture in individual stores that keeps regulars loyal to a particular locale. Here are 10 locations that break from conformity and reflect a varied slice of Houston:

STARBUCKS AT WILLOWBROOK

7606 FM 1960 West, 281-897-9912
This location is open 24 hours a day, seven days a week. It's large, with plenty of seating and electrical outlets, which is really important for the many latte- and frappuccino-drinkers sporting laptops. People here are very busy, working diligently on novels, term papers, business deals and the occasional first date.

HIGHLAND VILLAGE STARBUCKS

4081 Westheimer, 713-961-1847
This store is not for the fashion-challenged, as Pilates-toned mavens, high-society fashionistas and Jimmy Choo-shod execs, along with those who want to be them, abound. I don't even think you can order a whole milk latte here without someone sneering at you from behind a pair of Donna Karan sunglasses.

THE TWO STARBUCKS IN THE RIVER OAKS SHOPPING CENTER

2029 W. Gray, 713-522-3029
2050 W. Gray, 713-942-7030
Comedian Lewis Black not-so-lovingly immortalized these two locations by quipping, "There is a Starbucks right across the street from a Starbucks! And ladies and gentleman, that is the end of the universe." But, according to a die-hard regular of the south side location, the two shops couldn't be more distinct: "Lawyers and bankers heading downtown stop in, along with trust-fund beneficiaries and a group from the Montrose. Many regulars know each other and the staff by name. Just across the street, the drive-in Starbucks seems to have a younger, more in-a-hurry crowd."

MONTROSE STARBUCKS

3407 Montrose, 713-521-7278
Montrose is still home to a large gay and lesbian population, but you wouldn't know it these days. Yuppies, urban-pioneering families and three-story townhomes have all but taken over. However, the Starbucks on Montrose at Hawthorne positively pops with Pride. Beautiful men and the guys who love them lounge over lattes, some having just met face to face after having had a few cyber conversations. More than most locations, this one feels like a real neighborhood hangout. According to patron Leo, it's the baristas. "Angela sets the tone for the whole joint.

She always remembers your name as well as your favorite drink. She is one those people who has a ray of sunshine coming out of her a**."

STARBUCKS AT WESTHEIMER AND POST OAK
2521 Post Oak Blvd., 713-621-7685
Just as The Galleria is the best people-watching place in Houston, this location, across the street from the modern-day megalith, features coffee drinkers who reflect the cosmopolitan diversity of the city. Sitting "in the round" of the large cafe offers onlookers views of other patrons as well as the tempestuous traffic, nonstop shopping and constantly swirling scene of the "uptown" Houston. This store is so roomy and well laid-out that it's easy to pass three, four, five hours or more without realizing it. The wood and metal design echoes the beautiful functional flourishes that mark Galleria-area intersections.

SPRING STARBUCKS & KINGWOOD STARBUCKS
18565 Kuykendahl, 281-655-1595, 2515 Green Oak, 281-359-8975
Ever seen *Witches of Eastwick*? Update it a little, throw in some *Desperate Housewives*, and hand them black coffee instead of a black caldron, and you could set their stage at either of these locations. The Houston Metroplex Witches Meet-Up takes place once a month at the Spring Starbucks, and Wiccans are purported to meet at the Kingwood location. Think it odd that a group of pagans would choose a master-planned community to meet in? Well, what could be more apropos than a coven of witches meeting each phase of the moon in The Livable Forest?

STARBUCKS ON I-45
6001 North Fwy. near Tidwell, 713-697-8945
When most people think Starbucks, they still think upper-middle class suburban moms driving, well, Suburbans, or Inner-Loop caffeine-intoxicated artistic types. But visit this relatively new Starbucks and you'll visit a Starbucks full of people who represent the predominantly black and Hispanic neighborhood in which it's located. Baristas call their patrons "sugar" instead of just offering them the sweet stuff for their drinks. The manager walks around to make sure everyone is "taken care of."

NONEXISTENT STARBUCKS ON 43RD AT ELLA BLVD.
The northwest corner of Ella and 43rd has been begging for a coffee spot for years. This eclectic neighborhood just outside the Loop is filled with just the right demographics for a happenin' coffee joint — the youngsters, the momsters, the former Inner Loopsters and more who have to drive to 610 or 290 for a cup of the good stuff. Come on, Starbucks! If you build it, they will come. EDITOR'S NOTE: *As we go to press, a Starbucks location is under construction on this corner.*

Having returned from a stint in Portland, Oregon, Houston writer M. Yvonne Taylor is now safely ensconced in suburban Atascocita, where she teaches English. She drinks Starbucks every day.

LOCAL FLAVORS

LOCAL FLAVORS

another to canned goods and pickles. Not really capable of meeting weekly grocery needs, Super Vanak is still a good resource for finding imported goods not available except in small specialty shops like this one.

TÉ HOUSE OF TEA

1927 FAIRVIEW at Woodhead
713-522-8868
www.tehouseoftea.com
MAP E6

A European sensibility (via Irish native Alyson Bell) and Asian approach (via Hong Kong native Connie Lacobie) blend to make this small house smooth and pristine. Blond woods, jazz tunes, rotating art exhibits, light meals and quality teas harmonize for a sophisticated feel. Indulge in delicate Dolce Vita tea of lavender and rose or the exotic African Night (Congo mango, coconut). Feeling proper? Try the Victorian menu of dainty sandwiches, tea cookies or scones with jam and clotted cream.

THIERRY ANDRE TELLIER CAFE & PASTRY SHOP

2515 RIVER OAKS BLVD. at Westheimer, and other locations
713-524-3863
MAP D6

After 31 years in its original River Oaks location, this French/Swiss/German pastry shop spread its wings a couple years ago to open the Uptown Park location, followed by a Tanglewood location scheduled to open in late 2008. Pastries are made in the River Oaks store and delivered to the other stores several times daily. The breakfast and lunch menus are similar. The specialty at this cozy Alpine cottage is quiche Lorraine, but the beautiful French pastries deserve savoring. Holiday treats — king's cake, elaborate gingerbread houses, Valentine assortments, chocolate Easter bunnies, marzipan figures, bûche de Noël — are especially popular and sell out early.

THREE BROTHERS BAKERY

4036 S. BRAESWOOD at Stella Link
713-666-2551
www.3brothersbakery.com
MAP D8

Founded by Max, Sigmund and Sol Jucker in 1949, this uncomplicated neighborhood institution produces sourdough French bread, corn rye and German farmer's bread, as well as celebrated Danishes filled with intense fruit centers, pecans or cream cheese. Ten different bagel varieties are all water-based. The real forte of Three Brothers, though, is the challah — three varieties — the black and white cookies, and the rugelach. The bakery also sells sugar-free and *pareve* treats for those with dietary restrictions.

WALDO'S COFFEE HOUSE

1030 HEIGHTS BLVD. at 10th
713-869-0700
MAP E6

A little Heights bungalow has a new life as a coffeehouse and live-music venue. The menu is, as we go to press with this book, just coffee and tea drinks and sweets: Cake is $3.75 a slice, bar cookies are $2.50 each, muffins $2, biscotti $1.75 and granola bars 92 cents. Live music on Saturday nights, with BYOB. Free WiFi. Our companion asked, But how do they make any money? We have no idea.

WHO MADE THE CAKE?

1811 S. SHEPHERD at San Felipe
713-528-4719
www.whomadethecake.com
MAP E6

All brides — and presumably their grooms as well — labor anxiously over their wedding days for one reason: At the end of the day, they get to eat cake. From that supposition, it follows that the source for the cake is very important. Who Made the Cake? is at the high end of custom cakemaking, a design studio that can craft towering confections for celebrations of all kinds. "Confectionary Artist" Nadine Moon is at the helm, creating sugar flowers and bows and hand-painted designs. The store can serve any size event but requires notice a month in advance.

WHOLE FOODS MARKET

2955 KIRBY at W. Alabama, and other locations
713-520-1937
www.wholefoodsmarket.com
MAP E6

Despite being an invention of wayward free-love Austinites, all types of organic and natural foods appreciators both hippie and yuppie flock to this bright, principled business. You won't find your typical brands of soda or lunchmeat here. Instead, products aimed at satisfying the store's "whole body" commitment — including the chain's 365 brands — line the shelves. If health food isn't your thing, never fear. Dietary supplements may get their own dedicated section in the store but so do warm pizzas, a cheese and charcuterie counter, an olive bar, a good wine selection and an excellent butcher. The food samples are a good enough reason to visit the store, although we hate to admit our greedy impulse to abuse them.

Whole Foods devotes more space to produce than most supermarkets because of their commitment to organics.

spirited houston

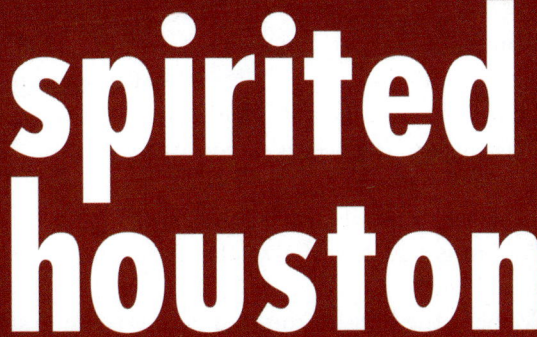

From a picnic table at the neighborhood icehouse to an overstuffed sofa in the hotel lobby bar, from intimate spaces devoted exclusively to adoration of the grape to a quiet martini enjoyed in a clubby chamber of leather and wood, from the cheeky-chic atmosphere of a lizard lounge to a raucous Irish pub on March 17, the Houston wine and spirits scene is a tableau of intoxicating variety. Let's take a look.

There are places that serve only wine, or only beer, and places that are equal opportunity saloons with rows of hard-liquored soldiers standing at attention, ready to be jiggered. You can find a cozy nook for two tucked inside a dim den, or seek out where the in-crowd imbibes and find there's not even room for your elbow at the bar.

In recent years, we've seen a breeding frenzy of wine bars — a trend that's taken *flight* into the rarefied air of sniffing bouquets from three glasses at a time for just a few dollars per trio.

We've seen musty, old-fashiony brown-bag stores explode into gigantic, glittering retail palaces that sell not only mega-lists of liquor and wine but have delis for pâté and cheese, stock booze-related paraphernalia and have >>

separate, climate-controlled rooms for coddling hand-wrapped cigars.

We take our sports seriously in Houston and patronize bars as stuck on plasma TVs and broadcasting the big games as they are to making sure the beer is discounted when the Astros are in town.

We have a slew of Irish pubs — so many in fact, an out-of-towner might suspect the whole of Houston hails from the Emerald Isle.

We have the long-in-the-tooth, gray-bearded stalwarts that have served a pint, a highball, a shot and a blast to our father and to our father's father.

We have those spots that love the college crowd and prove it by mixing techno noise for dancing between sips of Almond Joy martinis.

Some of our casual taverns welcome dogs, while some snazzier saloons are fussy about what you wear. Warning: Such places will bounce you out if your garb of choice is a T-shirt and jeans.

Some places feature live cowboy bands, some have DJs, some have cool jazz and some have jukeboxes with playlists that range from controlled and thematic to schizophrenic mayhem.

Heck, we even have a winery down in Santa Fe, just 10 miles from the Gulf of Mexico.

All in all, it's a spirited Houston experience.

So, a toast and a tap of the glass to the Houston wine and spirits scene, where seekers of morning libation, noontime tippling, sunset solace and 2 a.m. last call have a nonstop assortment of intemperate zones to choose from. Ne'er need there be a dry lip left in the house.

13 CELSIUS

3000 CAROLINE
at Anita
713-529-8466
www.13celsius.com
MAP E6

Enter this vintage 1927 building — a site that once dry-cleaned the business suits that walk around downtown — and you'll find stylish leather sofas, a 40-foot white marble bar and an inviting candlelit courtyard. Wash and press now a thing of the past, this comfortable retreat takes its name from the correct temperature to store wine and its inspiration from European *enotecas* (wine bars). Cozy up into one of those let's-not-hurry sofas; from there you can view the perfectly cooled, ever-expanding wine cellar through a large picture window. (Bottles may be purchased for $5 off retail.) The inspiration of owners Ian Rosenberg and Mike Sammons, this downtown tasting room also serves port, sherry, beer and even a great espresso. Limited appetizers, but the wine sips well with a selection of charcuterie meats and cheeses. Opens at 4.

A+

A+ provides a chic-yet-comfortable atmosphere in the heart of downtown.

1117 PRAIRIE at
Fannin, in the Alden Hotel
832-200-8800
www.aldenhotels.com
MAP F6

Sleek and hip, in an intimate nook opposite the boutique hotel's acclaimed *17 restaurant, the bar setting is backed by jazz, soul and R&B, offering a change of pace for hassled business travelers as well as a slew of savvy locals. Expertly crafted cocktails, delivered by a waitstaff that seems as happy to be here as happy-hour patrons, are served up in glassware as groovy as the surroundings. From 4 to 7 p.m. the drinks are priced to put anyone in a good mood (try the lavender martini), and the selection of sophisticated snacks are also priced amiably (shrimp tacos, $2 a pop). Valet parking available, but you can also park on the street. Do whatever it takes to get into this vibrant milieu.

ABSINTHE BRASSERIE

609 RICHMOND
at Greeley
713-528-7575
www.absinthelounge.com
MAP E7

Like a Rive Gauche hideaway, there's a Parisian bar feel to this secret spot on the map of Houston's own "Left Bank," the deliciously unconventional Montrose. If you didn't know it was here, you might drive by and marvel at the splendid gothic double doors, but *sans* a sign, you would pass on to some neon-lighted bar up the street. Once in, however, most visitors become regulars, drawn by the ambience, the fairly priced wine and bar drinks, and the homemade pizza. Music is soft and jazzy through the twilight hours when patronage is spare, but after 8 the place kicks into gear and sometimes gets loud and jam-packed. Martinis are poured into easy-to-handle stout, stemless glasses, served by one of the friendliest bartenders in town.

Let Absinthe owner/startender Ralph Rager make his signature Hallucinating Melon for you.

ACQUA LOUNGE

For the musically inclined of the greater Houston area who venture forth seeking cocktails and a bite before attending a concert at the nearby Cynthia Woods Mitchell Pavilion, this contemporary hotel lounge offers 40 wines by the glass, a fully stocked bar and food served from 11 a.m. to midnight. For travelers staying at the hotel who came to The Woodlands for things other than listening to music outdoors, cocktail hours stretch out stylishly at the renovated lobby bar. Visiting on a Thursday night? Expect to find live entertainment.

1601 LAKE ROBBINS DR., in The Woodlands Waterway Marriott Hotel, The Woodlands
281-367-9797
www.thewoodlandsmarriott.com
MAP North of D1

AVANT GARDEN

A new baby on the bar playground, Avant Garden tries to be everything to everyone. There is so much going on inside and outside this renovated old house, it makes your head spin. How do they love us? Let us count the ways: weekday happy hour with $2 draft beer and $4 mixed drinks; on selected Tuesdays belly dancing; on Wednesdays open mike talent night; occasional art sessions with live models for sketching; a DJ; jazz and classical music; weekly wine tastings; Brazilian sirloin night on Sundays with tango dancing — whoosh! Four separate areas for socializing: upstairs, downstairs, front porch and back patio (where Christmas lights twinkle). The food is cute: little cleverly stuffed empanadas, quiches and some wildly original cheesecakes (e.g. blue cheese, walnuts and orange marmalade) built to be wine-friendly. Opens daily at 4 p.m.

411 WESTHEIMER near Taft
832-519-1429
www.avantgardenhouston.com
MAP E6

BAKER STREET PUB & GRILL

> **5510 MORNINGSIDE #100** at Times
> **713-942-9900**
> www.sherlockspubco.com
> **MAP** E7

The fact is, Rice Village fairly teems with pub choices. Like Starbucks, sometimes dueling pubs sit right across the street from each other (go ahead, raise a tankard to the fellow in the window opposite). Seems to work fine though, with enough thirsty customers to go around. At this particular spot, the goings-on are lively, the crowds are predominantly Rice University students or doctor types who meander over from the nearby Medical Center, and the draw seems to be the relatively low-priced happy hour drinks (maybe the best in town). Running from 2 to 9 p.m. Monday through Saturday and all day Sunday, $1.75 will buy selected drafts and well drinks, $2 house wines and $6 selected domestic pitchers. An interior of low lights and woody aspects, the English pub model is alive and well here. The food menu includes cod strips beer-battered in Bud, nachos and spinach and artichoke dip. People really squeeze in on weekends.

BAR ANNIE

> **1728 POST OAK BLVD.** near San Felipe
> **713-840-1111**
> www.cafe-annie.com
> **MAP** D6

The slimmer sister of the acclaimed Cafe Annie, this bar beats most everybody else in town for the most urbane food offered on the lounge circuit. The bar menu reads like a gourmet's wish list. This is bistro dining at its best, with a chipotle-sauced octopus ceviche, tuna tartare with truffles and serranos, shrimp cocktail with lobster roe tartar sauce, queso that's made with artisanal cheese and charred chiles, filet mignon and even a cheeseburger ($16, additions like bleu cheese $2 extra). Small tables line the dividing wall between bar and main dining area. There are barstools covered in zebra skin if you want to drink balloon glasses of red wine or sip a hand-shaken martini while chatting with the barkeep. Popular with Houston's rich and powerful.

BELVEDERE

> **1131-01 UPTOWN PARK** near Loop 610 and Post Oak Blvd.
> **713-552-9271**
> www.belvedereinfo.com
> **MAP** D6

Some say "sleek chic" and others say "skip it," but there's rarely an indifferent response from those allowed to enter this too-cool-for-school bar on the edge of the Galleria area. The vibe is exclusive, with some folks cover-charged to enter (inside poop says if the doorman doesn't like the cut of your jib, you are docked), while others sail through on schooners of savvy. Cameras located all over the inner sanctum replay shots of guests on screens in the bathrooms. DJs roll out funk, soul and jazz, but the urge to shake your booty must be tempered to a jerk or two because there's no dance floor. Impressive interior, including an entire wall with LED light fixtures. With food catered by Gary Mercer's City Kitchen, Belvedere is a "city" saloon — hayseeds need not apply.

BISTRO BAR

701 TEXAS at Louisiana, in the Lancaster Hotel
713-228-9500
www.thelancaster.com
MAP F6

Cleverly located in the Theater District, the cozy Lancaster Hotel has the distinction of being convenient to all downtown amusement venues. Just a hop, skip and a jump from Jones Hall, the Alley, Wortham Center and the Verizon, can there be a better choice for grabbing a quick jigger of Scotch before a show? The bar is tiny by comparison to other watering holes, but a hole it is not. Instead you will discover a most sophisticated stopover when pre- or post-theater. Sited cozily within the Lancaster's intimate 62-chair restaurant, the Bistro Bar won acclaim from *Food & Wine* magazine as one of the 10 best booze dispensers in the U.S. A soft-spoken spot for discussing the plays of Albee or why Wagner must bluster so, the bar is a perfect coda to a performing-arts evening. Live piano on Fridays and Saturdays. Valet parking.

BLACK LABRADOR PUB

4100 MONTROSE north of Richmond
713-529-1199
www.blacklabradorpub.com
MAP E7

Rising at the north corner of perhaps the most visually appealing "strip center" in the city, a big sip of Merrie Olde England awaits inside the ivy-covered brick edifice that regulars refer to simply as the Black Lab. Low ceilings in the interior suggest that it's cold out there on the moors, so drinking your Boddingtons by the fireplace is a jolly good thing to do. Darts, of course. And outside you'll find a giant chess-playing surface that begs for real people to stand in for pawns, bishops, knights, queens and kings. There's a single-malt menu, as well as beer from around the world. Authentic British pub fare when you're craving bangers, bubble and squeak or a whipped-cream-topped spotted dick. Limited parking in front, but the garage behind honors tickets validated by the hospitable pub. Open 7 days a week for lunch and dinner, Sunday brunch.

BLACK SWAN PUB

4 RIVERWAY at Woodway, in the Omni Houston Hotel
713-871-8181
www.omnihotels.com
MAP D6

Underneath one corner of the expansive Omni Houston Hotel, you'll find a terrific "basement" bar that's more than 20 years old, has been recently renovated and is named for a couple of resident mascots. In the mood to strut yourself? On Friday and Saturday nights from 9 p.m. till 2 in the wee hours, DJ-spun tunes invite all rhythmic feet to take to the dance floor. It's known as *the* place to go after weddings to keep the dancing/party going. Those who like breathing room, take note: It gets crowded on Saturdays. Fully stocked to quench all thirst preferences, and some signature martinis worth their weight in originality are served across the granite and copper bar. Sit close to the bartender on leather-bottomed, tall wooden bar chairs or snag one of the curtained seating nooks or a spot by the fireplace. Light snacks, no cover, parking validated and Thursday is jazz night. Shorts and swimsuits prohibited. Closed Sunday and Monday.

RECIPE HUGORITA

Created by sommelier Sean Beck
Hugo's, 1600 Westheimer, 713-524-7744

The signature drink at Hugo's is frequently named "Best Margarita in Houston." Each individual margarita is shaken table- or barside and poured into Mexican blown-glass margarita glasses in front of the guests. Sommelier Sean Beck recommends using a blanco or silver tequila in margaritas. "This style is clean and fresh and is never aged in oak. This is important, as oaky flavors tend not to mix well with lime and citric flavors." ¡Salud!

1½ oz. Sauza Silver Tequila
1 oz. simple syrup

¾ oz. Hiram Walker Triple Sec
1½ oz. fresh lime juice

METHOD: Place all ingredients in a shaker with ice and shake to mix well. Pour into margarita glass and garnish with slice of fresh lime. (Serving note: Best served straight up or on the rocks.)

BLANCO'S BAR & GRILL

3406 W. ALABAMA
at Buffalo Speedway
713-439-0072
www.houstonredneck.com
MAP D7

Happy hour starts at 11 a.m., which should be a warning: This joint is Texas-friendly. Honky-tonkin', boot-scootin', gimme a cold Pearl beer Texas-friendly. Good ol' boys swear by the hamburgers and don't mind the potholed parking lot. The dance floor's got ample space for waltzing your cutie around to the sounds of fine, live Texas bands that saunter in Wednesdays to Fridays. On Saturday nights they close for private parties and on Sundays they pray and sleep. Smoking's okay, but outdoors where it's possible to still hear the yodeling.

THE BOOM BOOM ROOM

2518 YALE at 25th
713-868-3740
MAP E5

Retro, funky and as mellow yellow as saffron, hip is not out of joint here. Look for the apple-green one-story building and follow your nose as it leads you into where the paninis are grilling and the Champagne fizzles with mixtures sublime (try the kir royale and don't miss the $1.50 mimosas served from 10 a.m. to 5 p.m. Saturdays and Sundays). There's nothing elegant about this wine and comfort-food destination except maybe the candlelight, which underscores its coolness rather than suggesting it's trying for upscale. Very casual, with jazz, blues and R&B played live Thursdays and Fridays, and on Saturday starting at 10 p.m., if you're lucky, the piano man will appear on the small stage. Happy hour discounts daily 5 to 7 p.m. Parking can be troubling when the place is packed.

BREWERY TAP

717 FRANKLIN
at Milam
713-237-1537
MAP F6

A hundred years ago the now-defunct Magnolia Brewery mixed its barley and hops in the exact location that currently houses this scruffy but amiable corner bar near Market Square. Long-time regulars bring their dogs, satchels full of stories to share and occasionally pull from their pockets that special dart for competing in the Wednesday night tournament. You'll find an eclectic array of personalities from the downtown street parade bellying up for the popular German Spaten Lager or sticking close to home with a Shiner Bock. It has a full bar, draft beer in 35 varieties and a wide choice of tunes on the jukebox. No food, but always a soccer game on the tube.

The Ultimate Food Lover's Guide to Dining in Houston **89**

BRIAN O'NEILL'S IRISH PUB & RESTAURANT

> **5555 MORNINGSIDE**
> near Times
> **713-522-2603**
> www.brianoneills.com
> **MAP** E7

This is the genuine article, or at least the bar is. It was designed and constructed in Ireland, shipped over to the States, then installed at its Rice Village location. (Claim is that Irish fairies brought the works over. But unable to verify the fact, we leave it to parenthetical hypothetical.) Full-bar service, with a bunch of alluring special deals like 50-cent mimosas on Sunday, $2 Long Island iced teas on Tuesday, $3 tidbits for mouth-popping at happy hour, plus $2 house wine during that venerated time slot. Occasional live music, no cover. Great outdoor seating. Rabid sports fans gather here to watch games. Note: O'Neill's has a sister act going on in The Woodlands called The Goose's Acre Bistro & Irish Pub (*21 Waterway Ave., 281-466-1502*). Seems the fairies installed the bar there also. Located on the waterway, it's a swell spot for inside/outside imbibing.

THE BULL & BEAR TAVERN AND EATERY

> **11980 WESTHEIMER** at Kirkwood
> **281-496-6655**
> www.thebullandbear-tavernandeatery.com
> **MAP** B7

Heads up, soccer and rugby fanciers: The big-screen TV broadcasts both sports whenever they are played in some corner of the world. And devotees of Guinness, write this down in red: Guinness is always $3.50 a pint, that's Monday through Sunday — a fine choice for washing down a dozen hot wings on Monday nights when they go for just $4. There's a long menu to plow through, with U.K.-type food aplenty. Try the Cornish pasties (a mixture of ground beef, potatoes, peas and carrots cuddled inside a warm pastry shell) or chicken curry. For Texas taste buds, hope they're making jalapeño meatloaf on the day you visit. Behind the bar, a march of beer taps are smartly turned out and count upwards of 30. Pizza's half off on Thursdays, karaoke starts at 9 p.m. on Fridays, dart tournaments and Texas hold 'em in this feel-at-home West Houston staple.

BYZANTIO CAFE & BAR

> **403 W. GRAY** at Taft
> **713-520-6896**
> www.byzantiohouston.com
> **MAP** E6

Renovation of a brick house in one of Houston's oldest neighborhoods brought the Mediterranean to bar-hoppers who enjoy a taste of the exotic with their cocktails. Gorgeous patio and several

SPIRITED HOUSTON

comfortable rooms to wander through while searching for the place the belly dancer performs from 10 to 11 p.m. on Thursday nights. (Caveat: On belly-dancing nights the bar is busy!) Touted as having the longest happy hour in the city, it's 4 to 10 p.m. Monday through Thursday, noon to 8 p.m. Friday through Sunday, with well drinks going for $2.25. Full food service lunch and evenings — try the pita with *tirokafteri*, a fiery blend of feta, olive oil and serrano peppers. Among the specialty drink concoctions, the Ouzotini stands out for kicking up the ouzo with a splash of peach schnapps. *Opa!*

THE CAPITAL GRILLE BAR

5365 WESTHEIMER
between Sage and Yorktown
713-623-4600
www.thecapitalgrille.com
MAP D6

If you're someone who believes the smell of money is therapeutic, someone who grows misty-eyed when ogling Big Spenders (all dressed in coats and ties) mingling at the bar, someone who is willing to pay $9 for a well drink, this upscale lounge is for you. The booze comes pricey but consider this: It's such a nice setting for taking a wallet whipping. Located across the foyer from the dining room where the $40 steaks are served, the bar relaxes those in stress over the stall of their $50 million merger deal. With its comfy chairs and demur lighting and willingness to serve not only great drinks but a little lobster on the side, the lounge has been known to cool the spirits of hot shots and warm the bosoms of ladies looking to unwind after a spa day. With all the romance of a platter of raw oysters, the bar opens at 5 p.m. and closes down at 10 nightly. There are more than 400 wines to choose from — the list won the 2007 *Wine Spectator* Award of Excellence. Prepare to be surprised: complimentary valet parking.

CECIL'S TAVERN

600 W. GRAY
at Stanford
713-527-9101
MAP E6

Forget "Tavern" — locals just call it Cecil's. This was one of Houston best dive bars until a fire several years ago caused the beloved beer-soaked carpet and cushy couches to be replaced with more "proper" pub attire. Wooden floors and hunter green walls are in their place, and thankfully so are the flock of loyal regulars, lining the bar, filling the many private conversation nooks and packing the patio, one of the best in town. Here, you'll find students, musicians, artists and bike messengers mingling with more corporate types. The jukebox mix is phenomenal, and the bartenders welcoming. If you like some sport with your drinks, there are pool tables and darts.

Recommended
CHOICE BARS FOR GROWN-UPS

To begin or end an evening with a well-made drink in a civilized setting, we recommend:

A+, *1117 Prairie, in the Alden Hotel, 832-200-8800.* Sleeker, hipper and more comfortable than most business travelers expect, A+ draws a savvy local crowd, too.

BAR ANNIE, *1728 Post Oak Blvd., 713-840-1111.* With octopus ceviche on the bar menu, this is not a joint for Junior. Food- and wine-savvy sophisticates mosey in expecting a refined product and service, and get it.

BISTRO BAR, *701 Texas, in the Lancaster Hotel, 713-228-9500.* This tiny bar is a convenient and civil place to rendezvous before the symphony or theater, both of which are just across the street.

THE COTTON EXCHANGE BAR & LOUNGE, *202 Travis, 713-213-1141.* Lawyers, bond daddies, women in suits. This is where the professional office types go to unwind. It's cool and classy — no giggling over martinis made with ice cream here.

DOWNING STREET PUB, *2549 Kirby, 713-523-2291.* This handsome cigar bar, which still has its slightly-smoky haze because tobacco counts for 20 percent of its sales (making it law-abiding), supports a diverse and well-heeled clientele.

THE HOUSTONIAN — THE BAR, *111 N. Post Oak Lane, 713-680-2626.* Kids would call this place a snore, which is just fine with those of us who like our drinks well-made and courteous and attentive service. Elegant appointments, so pick a date and try it out.

THE REMINGTON BAR, *1919 Briar Oaks, in the St. Regis Hotel (pictured below), 713-840-7600.* In a rich setting and manned by an expert bartender, The Remington offers a broad selection of expense-account liquors.

THE STATE BAR & LOUNGE, *909 Texas, 713-229-8888.* A classic lounge atmosphere on the second floor of the Rice Lofts in the heart of downtown. A balcony overlooks the Main Street bustle.

SPIRITED HOUSTON

CÉZANNE

4100 MONTROSE north of Richmond
713-522-9621
www.blacklabradorpub.com
MAP E7

While many denizens of the bar world work themselves into a sweat on the dance floor, Cézanne sits this one out — sits back and grooves in 40 chairs to be exact. An intimate, romantic jazz club that invites those with musical erudition to settle in close to the cool sounds blown by local jazz artists and musicians from San Francisco, New York and other places where jazz thrives, the music starts at 9 p.m. and goes till 1 a.m. See the website for a list of acts scheduled to perform. There's usually a cover and a one-drink minimum from the full-bar set-up. Located above the Black Labrador Pub, the kitchen will send up appetizers and desserts.

CHRISTIAN'S TAILGATE BAR & GRILL (aka CHRISTIAN'S TOTEM)

7340 WASHINGTON at I-10
713-864-9744
MAP E6

Owner Steve Christian says he had to change the name of the icehouse (Christian's Totem, owned by his family for three generations) to Christian's Tailgate Bar & Grill because "fellahs kept coming in here asking for to-go beer." To add to the confusion, he hasn't taken down the "Totem" sign and doesn't plan to. So, please know when you're looking for a cold one to drink with possibly the best burger in the great Southwest, that tin building with the wooden deck riveted to its side is a bar and grill, not a convenience store. Open from 11 a.m. to 9 p.m. neon lights abound in the interior, which some folks find more comforting than a wood-burning fireplace. Visits from the bearded wonders ZZ Top are not unusual, and at Christian's second location (*2000 Bagby, 713-527-0261*) he keeps Macallan Scotch for some doctors who don't mind that it goes for $20 a pop. Lots of beer as well as a full-service bar at both locations.

CHRISTOPHER'S WINE WAREHOUSE

1958 W. GRAY near S. Shepherd
713-524-9144
www.christopherswine.com
MAP E6

In this haven for prosperous wine lovers who crave Burgundies with a passion that matches owner Christopher Massie's, the stars are handcrafted, estate-bottled French wines — emphasis on the Burgundy region. Christopher's also features rare and limited bottles from the Rhône Valley, Italy, Spain and the California coast. Interestingly, being the rep for the California wines stocked on

Christopher's Wine Warehouse is an attractive loft-style warehouse stocked with rare and limited-production wines you won't find elsewhere.

the premises (many Pinot Noir producers on the list), Massie guarantees that the crates that arrive at his store have traveled directly from the wineries — no stopovers in the hot Arizona sun. Weekly email notifications will keep you informed of inventory updates. (Sign up on the website.) Christopher's does not sell wine over the internet, but accepts orders via email, fax and by telephone.

25712 HWY. 290, SUITE C at Spring-Cypress, Cypress
281-758-1682
www.corkcafe.com
MAP West of A2

CORK CAFE

Pristine in concept, this northwest Houston wine bar is a well-cut gem. Some careful thinking by owner Kaleb Kothe and a lot of excellent taste went into creating an atmosphere congenial to patrons seeking the Omar Khayyám ideal of "a jug of wine and thou." The wine selection approaches 100 international varieties available by the glass, or purchase a bottle to take home. Designed sleek and modern in a shotgun style, it has tables lining one wall and leather-seated bar chairs standing barside opposite the dividing cork-tiled floor. It takes a ladder to reach the many high bins holding the cafe's cache of wines. With an affable service staff ready to serve plates of cheese or some signature desserts, you can take your sips and bites inside or out on the patio. Themed wine tastings on Wednesdays and Saturdays.

THE CORKSCREW

With its deep green exterior accented by canary yellow signage, you can't miss it — oh, and by the way, this is a wine bar that shouldn't be missed. Close to downtown on the hot-hot-hot Washington Avenue corridor, it's

1919 WASHINGTON near Sawyer
713-864-9463
www.houstoncorkscrew.com
MAP E6

owned by brothers Doyle and Andrew Adams, who are on site every night overseeing a staff that they're crazy about and want us to be, too. One staff member is the official in-house truffle maker. (Try the cayenne-laced chocolates.) There's romantic lighting in the primary bar and in two adjacent rooms that can be booked for functions. Consider organizing a group to partake of The Corkscrew's private wine tutorial in the Big Red Room. More than 300 wines rotate through the stock at any given time, and the owners will open any bottle as long as you promise to drink at least a couple of glasses. Tends to get quite loud. Hungry? Order pizza from Candelari's to be delivered to your table. It's the thing to do. Opens at 4 p.m. every day. Check the website for upcoming music performances.

Don't let the casual vibe fool you — The Corkscrew is serious about wine.

202 TRAVIS at Franklin
713-213-1141
www.cottonexchangelounge.com
MAP F6

THE COTTON EXCHANGE BAR & LOUNGE

The reemergence of this good-looking space under new proprietorship was a welcome event. Located on the second floor of the old Cotton Exchange Building, echoes from the past have been kept intact. Built in 1884, the structure's interior merits an appreciative nod for the quality exacted by the original builders. What you will find in the 21st century are ceilings, columns, flooring and murals just as they were in the 19th century. Elegant furnishings have been added by the new owners — search out the big leather sofas with big ol' cocktail table nook. The clientele is weighted with professional-type peeps — doctors, lawyers, one or two Indian chiefs — enjoying the full-service bar. Monday through Thursday the bar opens at 4 p.m. On Friday and Saturday expect to find DJs playing an eclectic range of music. For its architectural charm alone, the lounge is the quintessential downtown after-work destination.

COVA

5600 KIRBY at Nottingham
713-838-0700
www.covawines.com
MAP E7

5555 WASHINGTON at TC Jester
713-868-3366
MAP E6

Monsterville Horton IV (yes, his real name) is a wine expert extraordinaire, and the fact is proven on the first visit to either of his restaurant/wine bar/retail shop locations. Wine veneration oozes like a room-temperature brie. The Washington location is more relaxed and demure (check out the Sunday night "Jazz on the House" happening) than the Kirby original, but both share the same quality and service. Functioning as wine shop during the day, at 5 p.m. the kitchen opens with hot and cold tapas (e.g. smoked salmon with shallot crème fraîche), artisan cheeses and charcuterie platters, and there are 40 wines offered by the glass and great wine flights to try. Join the Wine Club and get your own engraved mahogany locker, plus 10 to 20 percent off retail wine purchases. Monday through Wednesday happy hour is 4 to 7 p.m., with $5 menu selections. Menus vary by location.

DECO

510 GRAY at Brazos
713-659-4900
www.decohouston.com
MAP E6

Chic and modern defines this hip dance club. Regulars sends kudos to the smiling bartenders, who serve up the club's "come-on" — 25 wines offered at $5 a glass, and the wine list changes every couple of weeks. On Thursdays, there are $3 drinks and live music after 10 p.m. Downside here is the lack of multiple bathroom stalls. Sometimes the line to relief stretches out onto the dance floor, which can confuse the mood. The indoor lounge is romantically illuminated, and banquettes add an extra comfort angle. Tapas for when you crave a munchie, and an outdoor patio for drinking in the night. Valet and street parking.

DOWNING STREET PUB

2549 KIRBY at Westheimer
713-523-2291
www.downingstreetpub.com
MAP E6

Ten years ago this place was all about booze and smoke. In its current mode (the distinction: "pub" has been added), a food menu rises from the cigar ashes, with offerings like a smoked-salmon sandwich and imported cheese trays. The crowd is younger these days, too. But, the well-heeled don't go to Downing Street to eat. They come for the plush leather couches, the huge mahogany cocktail tables and the 400-square-foot humidor that provides the proper temperature for pampering a long list of cigars for sale. (The website scrolls out the selections available. The local smoking ordinance does not apply here because 20 percent of sales is tobacco.) Offered a 90-plus single malt Scotch array, you could try the 50-year-old Macallan ($300 a shot). Or call for a snifter of the Remy Martin Louis XIII, or order a "Simon Brooking," a concoction made of 12-year-old Dalmore Scotch, an orange slice and ginger ale. Happy hour begins at 10 a.m., a wildly civilized decision. An extensive and impressive wine list is paired with sturdy stemware that would fit in the masterly clutch of Prime Minister Churchill, were he still around. Good choice for office party groups who want to spread out on the clustered couches and schmooze the night away.

D'VINE WINE OF TEXAS

609 BRADFORD, SUITE 105 between 6th and 7th Sts., Kemah
281-334-8300
www.dvinewineusa.com
MAP East of I9

Located close to the Kemah boardwalk, (an amusement area replete with restaurants, boutique shops, roller coaster and a host of seagulls), this wine shop offers wines by the bottle or glass. A pretty interior welcomes visitors who might want to partake of the tasting bar — try three wines for $5. Or you can "make your own" wine with consultation from the D'Vine experts on grape varieties, process, fermentation, labeling, etc. After eight weeks, stop back by to pick up the handmade, customized vintages that can be for personal use or given as gifts (but not sold). Hours are noon to 7 p.m. Tuesday through Saturday, noon to 6 p.m. on Sundays. After hours, you can take over the entire Tuscan-styled establishment for private parties. Dress casual, as this spot is laid-back relaxed.

THE FIRKIN & PHOENIX

After a string of restaurants came and went from this space on lower Westheimer, the Firkin & Phoenix has finally carved out a niche as a cozy neighborhood hangout. Part of a chain of British-style pubs that originated in Canada and is now expanding into the U.S., the Firkin offers great beer selection, a fairly broad menu (we recommend the secret salmon) and savvy waitresses sporting "Working at the Firkin" shirts who always remember your "usual." There's plenty of plush velvet seating and flat-screen TVs in every direction. However,

1915 WESTHEIMER, between S. Shepherd and Hazard
713-526-3100
www.firkinandphoenix.com
MAP E6

this is not necessarily the best venue for watching sports, depending on the night, since karaoke is king on Thursdays, and there are occasional live music acts, poker nights and theme-based parties.

Recommended
TASTING AWAY IN MARGARITAVILLE

The margarita: mysterious, mythical and marvelous. It has the power to take away your legs or fortify you with the courage to do the unthinkable. Served straight-up chilled and chic or as frozen frat-party slush, it's Houston's official cocktail. Here are five outstanding sips.

CAFE ADOBE, *2111 Westheimer, 713-528-1468, and other locations.* The Adobe's Meltdown Margarita is served on the rocks crowned with Grand Marnier. It's big, strong and a little rough around the edges — just what you need on a Friday afternoon. The frozen fruit choices (raspberry, mango) are sweet, attracting a younger clientele who perch on these legendary patios.

CAFE ANNIE, *1728 Post Oak Blvd., 713-840-1111.* The temple of Southwestern cuisine sports an equally elegant signature cocktail. The "RDG" margarita is hand shaken tableside and poured into a generous crystal goblet. Gently intoxicating and beautifully balanced with pricey smooth tequila, Cointreau and fresh, pulpy lime juice. Ahhhh, a sip of Hollywood.

HUGO'S, *1600 Westheimer, 713-524-7744.* This smooth operator is hand shaken and poured up gorgeous in a heavy Mexican blue-rimmed goblet. Silver tequila, lots of fresh lime juice and bright triple sec make the Hugorita a classic choice. Choose from six different margaritas — all superb — or straight tequila flights. (Want to make your own Hugorita? See recipe on page 87.)

NINFA'S, *2704 Navigation, 713-228-1175, and other locations.* Any Houstonian worth her salt knows the familiar flavor of a Ninfarita. Mama Ninfa's original frozen pale green potion is snowy, sweet-tart and lip-puckering limey. Pity those who have consumed too many, or worse, not any! Slurp slowly to prevent dreaded "brain freeze."

SPANISH VILLAGE, *4720 Almeda, 713-523-2861.* Visit the Village for a sneakily wicked concoction prepared with fruity lime juice, triple sec and lots of good silver tequila. Never made with mixes, these refreshing cocktails go down easy. Beware of strangers after consuming the "high octane" (lightly frozen but stronger) version.

THE FLAT

> **1701 COMMONWEALTH** at Haddon
> **713-521-3528**
> **MAP** E6

Smallish and hip, this Montrose lounging spot can't be called trendy — neighborhoody is more like it. Great music, whether from owner Ziggy Morrow's iPod or the DJ spins. Local art from Koelsch Gallery graces the walls. Lots of youngish patrons with the bloom still in their cheeks standing at the bar order signature drinks. Frozen mojitos elicit approving sounds during weeknight happy hour (5 to 9 p.m.). Expect to hear DJ-spun music (funk, electronic, urban soul, R&B, jazz), and there's a teensy dance floor for those who like to sway. Bar food plates nachos, eggrolls, wings, etc. with some clever flavor enhancements. Martinis fly from shakers at a steady pace, and beer is not the flavor of choice here. Street parking. Wanna feel like a welcome regular? Get to The Flat.

FOUR SEASONS HOTEL LOBBY BAR

> **1300 LAMAR** at Austin
> **713-650-1300**
> www.fourseasons.com
> **MAP** F6

Snug as a bug in a great lounge. Expect plush, overstuffed couches — with pillows no less — in this off-the-main-lobby comfortable setting. Accented in colors of cerise and citron, with a shiny corner baby grand and art on the walls, it feels like you're sitting in the living room of your wealthy sister. No snob is she, but a most congenial sister with impeccable taste who invited 50 of her closest friends in for drinks. It can get crowded, especially if the divine Gilberto is tickling the ivories. (The pianist has a loyal following of fans.) A bar reminiscent of the days when bars were elegantly appointed, this is a spot to try for well-crafted cocktails after work. Serving bar menu food all the way to closing: Monday to Thursday 5 p.m. to midnight, Friday and Saturday 5 p.m. to 1 a.m. Flattering low lights are a girl's best friend.

FOX SPORTS GRILL

> **5175 WESTHEIMER**, in The Galleria
> **713-439-1369**
> www.foxsportsgrill.com
> **MAP** D6

While Mom's away (shopping), Dad can play. Just drop him off at this venue for food, drink, play (honking big pool tables, etc.) and plasma screen sports-watching, and know he'll still be there when you return with something cute from Armani. This California import has successful franchises all over, and though a sports bar, it is blessedly free of team logos and neon beer signs. There is a huge contemporary American menu: The Fox sampler has cheese fries, smoked wings and chicken tenders going for $12.95, and on Saturday and Sunday, it opens at 2 p.m. with bottomless mimosas to wash down a variety of omelets and breakfast burritos. Happy hour Monday through Friday, 3 to 7 p.m. and again 10 to 11 p.m. will get you $5 margaritas, $4.75 imported beer and $4 well drinks. Enormous desserts.

FRONT PORCH PUB

217 GRAY near Bagby
713-571-9571
www.frontporchpub.com
MAP E6

A comfortable after-work pit stop, many young professionals on the trek out from downtown might call this place home. There's no pretension at this abandoned-garage-turned-pub, but there is certainly a crowd to fight on weekend evenings. The old garage door is opened up to the Houston air on fine-weather days, although the namesake front porch is massive enough so that outdoor seating isn't usually hard to find. The porch swing, however, may very often be occupied by whispering lovers so you'll have to wait your turn. There are more than 100 varieties of beer, from Bud Light to Belgian, and a full bar complemented by simple bar snacks. Steak Night is every Tuesday and Thursday. A spinoff, the Porch Swing Pub (*69 Heights Blvd., 713-880-8700*), recently opened where Cosmos Cafe once was. Like its Midtown sibling, Porch Swing Pub is popular and casual.

THE GINGER MAN

5607 MORNINGSIDE near University Blvd.
713-526-2770
www.gingermanpub.com
MAP E7

If you love beer, this is the jackpot. The Houston edition of The Ginger Man, which takes its name from the J.P. Donleavy novel, is the oldest of the four Texas Ginger Mans (or should that be Ginger Men?) and one of Houston's favorite bars for beer and conversation. A fixture in Rice Village since 1985, it boasts an entire wall of draft beer, and the beer menu constantly evolves as new or seasonal brews become available. (Visit the website to review the amazing beer line-up; we tried counting and stopped at 175.) There's almost no food served here — just pretzels, artichoke dip, salami and cheese platter, and such — but you can walk 100 yards in any direction and find a good restaurant. Parking and seating are both at a premium, so you might like to visit at a non-peak time. In fine weather, sit outside on the front or rear deck. A discount is offered to service-industry employees on Monday nights.

Personal Favorites
BEST GAY BARS

By Johnny Hooks

In the beginning there was Montrose. From the 1970s through the 1990s, the majority of gay bars found homes in the counterculture neighborhood that once was the epicenter of all things queer. Cut to 2008. The gay experience has spread far and wide, from Spring to the west side, to the Heights and points south. Houston is a diverse and multicultural city and its gay bars reflect that: Country bars, video lounges, classic discos and neighborhood haunts all inviting and unpretentious, like the our city itself. Nevertheless, the best gay bars are still, mostly, in Montrose.

GUAVA LAMP, *570 Waugh, 713-524-3359, www.guavalamphouston.com.* The ultimate video lounge, Guava Lamp is located in a pleasant shopping center. It's a bit like the interior of Jeannie's bottle on *I Dream of Jeannie,* decorated with gorgeous jewel-toned fabrics on the many huge banquettes that circle the room. The bar area is in the center of the space, lit with tiny chandeliers. Guava Lamp hosts many national acts, such as drag superstars like Lady Bunny and Jackie Beat, as well as local celebutantes such as Toddicus and national gay touring acts like the delicious-to-the-ears-and-eyes, Eric Himen. Regular events include karaoke Wednesday and Sunday and happy hour buffet every Friday. The clientele is a mix of A-list gays, lesbians and straights. The handsome and friendly bar staff offers a plethora of cocktails. No cover, except for events. Open to 2 a.m; valet available.

IN-N-OUT, *1537 N. Shepherd, 713-589-9780.* This "metro-social" lounge is one of Houston's newest gay bars, located (thankfully) in The Heights. With so many GLBT members of the community moving to "Montrose North," it's no wonder someone finally woke up and opened a bar there. While non-descript on the outside, inside welcomes you with plush seating areas on the lower floor that also includes a pool table. A rear patio was recently added, and weekends find a variety of grilling and picnic-style events. Huge flat screens fill the walls, so no matter which way you turn, there's always something to look at. Speaking of, the friendly, handsome bartenders — usually dressed in shorts or jeans and not much else — are easy on the eyes and heavy on the pour. Open til 2 a.m. No cover, no valet.

JR'S BAR AND GRILL and **SANTA FE BAR AND PATIO**, *804 and 808 Pacific (respectively), 713-521-2519. www.jrbarandgrill.com.* The number one "stand and model" bar in Houston, JR's at one time actually had a working grill. This bar is home to Houston's award-winning drag queen extraordinaire, Kofi. On Monday, Kofi hosts the best Male Dance (read *strip*) contest in town; other weekly events include "2-4-Tuesdays" with $2 well, wine and frozen drinks and karaoke contests held on Thursday and Sunday nights, hosted by Marsha Carlton, Kofi and Lana Blake. Expect lots of shirtless go-go boys in underwear, video games and, natch, a pool table. JR's is a tradition, as is the promise of "never a cover." Drink specials abound, with every night offering specials on longnecks, Shiners, frozen drinks and more. Split into two separate sides, JR's is on the left and inside you'll find a cool, classic gay bar. The right-hand side is the Santa Fe Grill and Patio, which at one time was a separate bar. No valet.

THE RIPCORD, *715 Fairview, 713-521-2792, www.theripcord.com.* The daddy of all leather bars, the Ripcord is a dimly lit, multi-level bar with video games and pool tables throughout to keep you acting as if you're not staring at some of Houston's hottest men. On Friday and Saturday evenings, nearly everyone from the nearby Pacific Street scene makes a "loop" through The Ripcord. The infamous patio can get pretty wild, so enter at your own risk. The cocktails are cheap, and the music is slamming with different themes each night, focusing mostly on older "classic" gay bar fare. Of note, this bar only accepts cash, no credit or debit cards allowed; an ATM is located at the entrance. This is also Houston's only bar with its own leather store in-house, called Black Hawk Leather. Pick up the perfect pair of handcuffs or a studly leather cop's hat. No cover, although special events may cost. No valet. Open very late.

SOUTH BEACH THE NIGHTCLUB, *810 Pacific, 713-529-7623, www.SouthBeachTheNightclub.com.* Houston's premier gay disco, located in the heart of Montrose, South Beach is as close to Studio 54 as Houston gets. South Beach is generally full of 20- to 40-year-old dancing, shirtless men. Even society boldface types have been known to grace the dance floor. Surrounded by a raised bar area, a waterfall and go-go boys strutting their stuff, the dance floor packs them in with spectacular laser lighting, disco balls, a killer sound system and a fabulous feature that has Houston written all over it: Liquid Ice Jets deliver the relief you need to keep grooving, with the power to drop the temperature of the club 20 degrees in a matter of seconds. This award-winning bar has multiple special events, including visits from the best DJs in the world, drag superstars and dance events like Madonnarama. Cover charge varies. Open 9 p.m. to 5 a.m. Wednesday through Sunday. Valet and off-street parking available.

Johnny Hooks has been a writer for 20 years. His work appears in PaperCity Magazine, OutSmart Magazine, The Houston Voice, Fad Magazine *and* The Texas Triangle. *He resides in the Woodland Heights with his family of cats.*

GOODE'S ARMADILLO PALACE

> **5015 KIRBY** at Bartlett
> **713-526-9700**
> www.thearmadillopalace.com
> **MAP** E7

You can't miss this spot, for two reasons: (1) there's a 14-foot shiny metal armadillo out front, and (2) owner Jim Goode's museum/saloon/cookout/live music show/beer garden is so tasty and so much fun it would be a crying shame to drive on by without going inside. So now you've crossed the threshold, what catches your eye? Maybe the leather Western saddles that take the place of regular bar stools. Maybe the snakeskins that border the wallpaper. Maybe all the paraphernalia hanging around that pays tribute to the great Texas traditions. Maybe the fact that Jim's cubed venison chili has never met a bean and never will. Maybe you like the shuffleboard, pool, domino games and cold beer iced down on the patio. Vittles here include Frito pie and armadillo wings, and there are specialty drinks made from good whiskey if beer's not your thing. There's always somebody live fiddling up a storm (see the website for music schedule). Not the best parking, y'all, but y'all might as well make do because, as Jim says, "Come on in here — we've got smooth whiskey, live Texas music and Goode eats!"

GRAPPINO DI NINO

On your way to a theater event downtown? Take a jog off Memorial or Allen Parkway to find Vincent Mandola's paean to his Italian roots, and quite a song it is. Feels like you're stepping onto the terrace of a villa in the Tuscan countryside. Tables are scattered across the terrace for patrons to

> **2817 W. DALLAS** between Montrose and Waugh
> **713-528-7002**
> www.ninos-vincents.com
> **MAP** E6

sit and sip a few glasses of wine before venturing on or, if not in a rush, stay to try something from the *spuntini* menu — light appetizers that include zucchini chips ($7), prosciutto and figs in season ($8), carpaccio with hearts of palm or several varieties of four-inch pizzettes. Stop by after the show for *dolci di giorno* — Mandola's homemade desserts. Live easy-listening music Thursday through Saturday for dancing al fresco, or partake of full menu dining inside where the rustic decor again transports patrons to Italia. Some service issues have marred tranquility in the past, but we trust this lovely place now has its act in order. They start serving the beer, wine, grappa and drinks at 4 p.m. Monday through Saturday. Huge parking lot.

GRIFF'S SHENANIGANS CAFE & BAR

We cling to traditions long after they have waned in relevance out of

> **3416 ROSELAND**
> near Harold, one block east of Montrose
>
> **713-528-9912**
> www.griffshouston.com
>
> **MAP** E7

nostalgia, habit and stubborn resistance to change. Perhaps for all these reasons people still flock to Griff's — decrepit in appearance but highly favored by Montrose neighborhood regulars. Griff's is the oldest surviving sports bar in Houston, founded in 1965. At first glance the place looks grungy, with plastic cups strewn across the floor and back porch. But Griff's is practically an institution for sports fans who come to watch and holler at the television collectively. On certain game days the bar hosts a party bus that will shuttle inebriated fans around town. As a testament to its Irish flair, Griff's also boasts "Texas' largest St. Patrick's Day festival," a multi-day event with live music, cook-offs and, of course, drinking. On normal weekends, however, customers will find the usual suspects just hanging out enjoying the 25 varieties of beer. Join in if you, too, want to become a member of Griff's Army. Parked close by, if not out on lease with party patrons, is the Griff's party bus.

HAAK VINEYARDS AND WINERY

> **6310 AVENUE T**,
> 1.8 miles south of Hwy. 6, Santa Fe
>
> **409-925-1401**
> www.haakwine.com
>
> **MAP** Southeast of I9

And now for something completely different. Imagine making a date with your sweetheart for a picnic in the country, driving about 25 miles out of town and when asked: "Where are we going?" you get to answer: "To a vineyard." Located just 10 miles from the Gulf of Mexico, this three-acre vineyard comes with a 11,000 square-foot, gray stone winery where scores of events take place — some on a grand scale, like their Greek Festival, their sumptuous feast nights and their summer concert series, and some on a more casual note, like the pruning day that's paired with an oyster fry or tapas served with toe-tapping music. A dream brought to fruition by owners Raymond and Gladys Haak, the vineyard started in 1969 when Raymond began experimenting with grape varietals that might grow well in our humid coastal Texas climate. The future brought not only healthy plants but also a multitude of awards for the wine produced. Summer and winter hours for tours and tastings differ, so check times on the website. Tuesday through Friday, lunch is served at the winery 11 a.m. to 1:30 p.m. Call for special group events, private parties or to stage a wedding amongst the vines.

THE HARP

> **1625 RICHMOND**
> near Dunlavy
> **713-528-7827**
> **MAP** E7

If you liked the pub scenes in the John Wayne film *The Quiet Man*, you will love The Harp. Step inside a somewhat renovated house on the edge of the Museum District and don't expect fancy — there is nothing slick about this hangout. Dim — and as comfy as your 10-year-old bathrobe — The Harp welcomes dogs to wander in if they bring along a customer. No food, but on hand are a bevy of menus from nearby restaurants for ordering in a sustenance delivery. There's a wee bar from which you might request a Guinness, or call for the namesake brew, Harp Lager, on tap. Tables scattered willy-nilly outside. Trivia night is Tuesday at 8. Be careful where you park; many cars have been towed from the parking lots of inhospitable businesses that rub up against the tavern. There's a weekly dart tournament and occasional live music.

Recommended
PUB FOOD

All of the hotel bars and spotlighted restaurant bars listed in this chapter have good food, often the kitchen's most ambitious menu offerings in smaller servings. These four spots serve the best pub food in town. It may be humble, even greasy, but sometimes it's exactly what you want.

BLACK LABRADOR PUB, *4100 Montrose, 713-529-1199.* The Black Lab serves a broad menu, but you should stick with its English pub specialties, such as fish pie, steak and kidney pie, beef Wellington, ploughman's lunch, and bubble and squeak.

KENNEALLY'S IRISH PUB, *2111 S. Shepherd, 713-630-0486.* An Irish pub famous for its pizza? Strange but true. It's only fitting that the Shamrock Special is topped with corned beef. Good burgers, too.

McGONIGEL'S MUCKY DUCK, *2425 Norfolk, 713-528-5999.* This is a full restaurant, but we like the pub food best: Stilton cheeseburger, shepherd's pie, Scotch egg, bangers and mash, and Welsh rarebit.

RED LION PUB, *2316 S. Shepherd, 713-782-3030.* Come here for the biggest serving of fish and chips in the universe (with requisite mushy peas on the side). Or try the Cornish pasty, sausage rolls or mini hamburgers.

THE HIDEAWAY

> **3122 DUNVALE** near Richmond
> **713-977-3515**
> www.hideawayondunvale.com
> **MAP** C7

There is always a mixed bag of personalities at this unpretentious watering shack that's located far enough west of The Galleria to invite a letting down of hair, a kicking off of shoes. From good ol' boys to real estate ladies, from trollers to entwined twosomes, from the single-suited gent to groups from the telephone company, everybody packs in, orders up and begins lively conversation. Dubbed as a live-music venue, restaurant and sports bar, The Hideaway attempts to cover all bases, and usually does. Tuesdays it's $12 steak night (16-ounce ribeye, baked potato, salad), plus the "Big Ass Blues Jam" featuring groups that fit the description. Weekends bring out even more melodies. (Check website for scheduled bands.) Like some chow? The kitchen opens for lunch and stays frying till 1 a.m. every night. For $5.50 you can have a half-pound of fried mushrooms with horseradish dip or a patty melt ($5.75), or try a shrimp po'boy ($6.75). Sunday and Monday, happy hour from open to close. Generous parking.

HILTON AMERICAS LOBBY BAR

> **1600 LAMAR** at Crawford, in the Hilton Americas
> **713-739-8000**
> www.hilton.com
> **MAP** F6

Inside the belly of this behemoth hotel (24 stories, 1200-plus rooms) find a pair of oases awaiting caravans of guests ready for some luxurious imbibing. In the ground floor Lobby Bar, drinks are dispersed from a bar flanked by an enormous egg-shaped blue and gold relief featuring a portion of the planet (the Americas). Vignettes of tables and red leather chairs make a comfortable setting for throwing back a couple of pomegranate martinis or Texas tea, which blends vodka, tequila, rum, Cointreau and some other ingredient we're too tipsy to recall. Appetizers offered during the daily bar hours of 11 a.m. to 2 a.m. include quesadillas, buffalo chicken wings and a $3 shrimp cocktail. But it's that 24-floor ride up the elevator that will take you to the suck-in-your-breath drama of the Skyline Bar & Grill. Floor-to-ceiling windows give a view of Houston that lets the sparkling city spill out before you. Voted "Best Bar with a View" by *Texas Monthly*, the Skyline opens at 5 p.m. and goes to 2 a.m. Have event tickets? Get off the barstool and walk just one block to the Toyota Center, two blocks to see an Astros game at Minute Maid Park.

SPIRITED HOUSTON

HOUSTON WINE MERCHANT

2646 S. SHEPHERD
near Westheimer
713-524-3397
www.houstonwines.com
MAP E6

Owner Scott Spencer is a winer. In his case, that's not a disparaging remark because the man knows his wines. And we, his customers, must be thankful that whenever we're in the need of a bit of oenological instruction, a taste or two of what's new from the world's vineyards and some careful and congenial suggestions for taste-bud stimulation, Spencer is the wine merchant to see. Believing it only wise that we taste before we buy, he offers free wine tastings every Friday 5 to 7 p.m. and every Saturday 2 to 4 p.m. Tastings are usually themed and run from staff favorites to "over the top reds," from Champagne to the mouth-watering wines of Louis Latour. Fine liquor is also available, but wine is center stage here. Join the Wine Club and receive two bottles of choice wine each month, delivered to your home or office, for $39.99 plus tax, delivery included. There were 12 bottles of the 2006 Petrus on hand when last we looked, $1,999 each. Oh, to win the lottery and indulge!

Stop in for Houston Wine Merchant's weekly wine tastings.

THE HOUSTONIAN — THE BAR

111 N. POST OAK LANE
between Memorial and Woodway, in The Houstonian
713-680-2626
www.houstonian.com
MAP D6

Over the years The Houstonian's 18-acre resort/spa/club complex has put its roots down firmly amongst the trees. Positioned in one of only two forests in the inner city, the winding drive leads you to the hotel's entrance. Give your car to the valet, enter, take a right and another right. You are now inside The Bar (yes, just Bar — it recalls Holly Golightly and her cat named Cat, don't you think?). Please be seated and someone will be right over to take your order. Look around. Expect to see women in designer shoes and men with bulging portfolios. The Bar seats up to 125, but it does not draw a big after-work crowd. Instead, it is a relaxing comfort zone with fine drinks, appetizers from Olivette (the restaurant next door) that include tempura shrimp with sweet chili sauce and fried calamari. In the summer months, the outdoor Gazebo Bar opens for cocktailing around the pool. Ah, wilderness.

INN AT THE BALLPARK — ATRIUM BAR & LOUNGE

> **1520 TEXAS** at Crawford
> **713-228-1520**
> www.innattheballpark.com
> **MAP** F6

This Landry's-owned hotel sits right across the street from Minute Maid Park, and the Atrium Bar is a swell place to meet for a drink before or after the ballgame. At the main entrance of the lobby lounge a life-sized bronze of famed Houston pitcher Nolan Ryan in mid-windup greets patrons, and the baseball theme continues in everything from the railings (bronze bats and baseballs) to the carpets. Overhead a paned glass ceiling reveals the skylit night (or day) to you. Several looming trees placed around the expansive bar are artificial — fake trees seem unnecessary when there is all that luscious light. Plush leather furnishings pull up to carved wood cocktail tables lending an atmosphere akin to a legal library or gentleman's club. Interspersed throughout are tall street lamps, with faux gaslights that accentuate the outdoor 19th-century London effect. Some opt to sit at the Ballpark Bar to get a plasma TV fix, but all enjoy a venue for civilized drinking before crossing the street for beer and Astros. If too crowded, try the bar at Vic & Anthony's next door.

KAY'S LOUNGE

> **2324½ BISSONNET** between Kirby and Greenbriar
> **713-528-9858**
> **MAP** E7

What's so special about Kay's? Nothing, really. Which is exactly what this venerable dive's many fans seem to like. It's the antithesis of trendy, so there isn't a line at the door or at the bar. Its seedy unpretentiousness is a relief when all you want is a pitcher of beer — Lone Star is served by the pitcher and bucket — sports on the TV, maybe some pool. Dating from 1939, Kay's has (no surprise) a wonderfully diverse jukebox. Most of the year, Kay's is usually crawling with students from Rice and UofH, but during the Houston Livestock Show and Rodeo, it fills up fast with a different crowd. Live Texas country music on Wednesdays and Thursdays.

KELVIN ARMS

> **2424 DUNSTAN** at Kelvin
> **713-528-5002**
> www.kelvinarms.com
> **MAP** E7

Touted as Houston's only Scottish pub, the most "Hoot mon" identifier (Scottish slang for "Yo, dude") about the place is its regal roll call of fine Scotch whiskey. Recommended are the "Tasting Tours," where lairds and laddies, ladies and lassies can opt to swig Scotch on the Knight's Tour (2 from column 1, 2 from column 2, $12), the Lord's Tour (2 from 1, 1 from 2, 1 from 3, $15) or the Royal Tour (2 from 2, 1 from 3, 1 from 4, $35). Scotches in abundance include Macallan 25-year-old, $35 a swig; Glenmorangie 18-year-old, $18; and eight-year old Sheep Dip at a reasonable $6.75. If beer is your poison, 20 varieties are on tap, with Fullers ESB, Belhaven Twisted Thistle IPA and Boddingtons among the listed brews. Second most Scottish hook is the shrine to Sean Connery, with photos and junk celebrating Scotland's favorite son. On August 25, they even throw 007 a birthday party. Happy hour 3 to 7 p.m. draws in crowds who seem to like the Vault Room — a real vault, vintage 1940s, inside the converted bank building. There are darts and game boards and an outdoor patio, but no music from Scotland on the juke.

2111 S. SHEPHERD near Fairview
713-630-0486
www.irishpubkenneallys.com
MAP E6

KENNEALLY'S IRISH PUB

There's not an Irish eye in the house that forgets to smile when throwing back a draft or two at this jolly neighborhood bar. Folks of other persuasions are wont to grin widely, too, when visiting proprietor John Flowers' well-established pub (circa 1983 and counting). A real patron pleaser, the spot has also gotten kudos from the pros who write about food and booze. Try the "Shamrock Special" thin-crust pizza that's topped with corned beef. Tradition is alive and well during the St. Patrick's Day madness, when the green thing thrives during the pub's annual festival. The Irish-American publisher of the fine food guide you are now consulting recommends the homemade potato chips ($2.35) and gets almost giddy when she discusses the home-style cheeseburger. Mini corn dogs are also on the menu, and draft beer flows like the loving tears of Mother Macree. Open 3 p.m. to 2 a.m. Tuesday through Sunday and from 4 p.m. to 2 a.m. Monday.

LA CARAFE

The ghost was spotted back in the late 1960s by a group of fringed-and-beaded hippies who had descended into the murky bowels of this irresistibly adorable dive on Market Square for some late-night wine. Since then

813 CONGRESS at Milam
713-229-9399
MAP F6

no other sightings have been reported, but there are stories about bar glasses flying through the air and smashing against walls, and there are those cold spots that make the hairs stand up on the back of the neck.

The building that houses La Carafe is more than 160 years old and listed on the National Register of Historic Places. The bar that's located down those gloomy stairs has been functioning since the 1950s, making it one of the old "haunts" on Houston's saloon scene. When the sun goes down, candles (with a wax build-up of more than 25 years) are lit on tables to ease patrons' nervousness about what might be lurking in the shadows. And someone will drop coins in the jukebox, so that Etta James or Louis Armstrong or George Harrison can ease tension by

---

RECIPE **THE PEACHY KEEN**

Created by owner/chef John Sheely
Mockingbird Bistro Wine Bar, 1985 Welch, 713-533-0200

Mockingbird owner/chef John Sheely created this drink in honor of Robert Earl Keen, one of his favorite singers. Country singer/songwriter Keen is a native Houstonian who has gone on to national fame with his popular albums, including *Gringo Honeymoon* and *West Textures*. Keen lives outside Fredericksburg, in the heart of the Texas Hill Country, famous for its rolling ranches as well as its many peach orchards. "I went to Fredericksburg hoping I would run into Keen," says Sheely. "But the best I could do was get inspiration for a drink in his honor."

1½ oz. vodka
1 oz. Mathilde Pêche Liqueur
wedge of fresh Texas Hill Country peach for garnish

METHOD: Combine vodka and liqueur in cocktail shaker with ice. Shake until well chilled. Serve in a martini glass with Texas Hill Country peach wedge.

warbling (whistling?) in the dark. With some respectable wines to choose from and beer served in frosty mugs, customers soon drown their fears, especially when the bartender is a friendly sort who will pooh-pooh all that ghost nonsense. It's a cash bar only, so come packing bills. The spot is great for easy conversation over a drink or two. Just don't wander off from the light and the living.

LA COLOMBE D'OR — THE BAR

3410 MONTROSE
near Hawthorne
713-524-7999
www.lacolombedor.com
MAP E6

Once upon a time we dreamed we died and went to La Colombe d'Or. It's a happy thing to report that heaven serves gourmet French food. But inside the 1920s vintage mansion the food is located around the corner from this tiny golden nugget of a bar, and it's the bar we're here to talk about. To give a clear picture of why this place is so special, it's helpful to know that the mansion was built to be the home of oilman Walter Fondren (a man who gave his name to streets and things around Houston). Now functioning as one of the world's tiniest luxury hotels (with just six suites), the bar most likely was Fondren's private home office or a small parlor. The place is snug, but utterly fine looking and it reeks of romance. (Jacket and tie romance, this is special-occasion stuff.) Want to charm a potential Prince Charming? Want a place for wooing a wench? Escort your sweetheart into the bar for martinis at twilight, for Champagne at midnight. And if you desire to stay over until morning, pre-arrange for a string quartet to be waiting upstairs in one of the suites. Ask them to play blindfolded and order up a pitcher of brandy Alexanders.

LIVE SPORTS CAFE

Consider the list of amusements: darts, pool, foosball, poker, karaoke, hip-hop dances, 25-plus TVs for game watching, and maybe best of all, fruit-flavored hookahs. Who could ask for more? For

407 MAIN at Preston
713-228-5483
www.livesportscafe.com
MAP F6

those of you who did ask, you may consider attending on Wednesdays to get the $1 bargain on domestic beer and well drinks, or take advantage of the Tuesday night steak deal that's so nicely priced you might as well order two. The lounge is located on the ground floor (enter on Preston), the second floor is given to games, and the rooftop patio gives you a bird's eye view of Main Street. Happy hour goes 2 to 7 p.m., and draft beer is discounted before and after Rockets games if you produce a ticket and/or stub. Play Texas hold 'em at 7 and 10 p.m. on Tuesdays and Fridays, then bring your best voice in on Fridays from 9 p.m. to 2 a.m. to belt out tunes karaoke-style. Finger food (bacon-cheese fries, jalapeño poppers, potato skins, onion rings), plus pizza, buffalo wings and burgers.

> **2327 GRANT** north of Fairview, east of Montrose
> **713-528-8342**
> **MAP** E6

LOLA'S
L-O-L-A, Lola's. Like your favorite junkyard dog, this place is scruffy, dark and has no ID, but it's loveable nonetheless. There's no sign and it's kinda hard to find (look for a house with gray aluminum siding), but word of mouth keeps it alive. This is where the coolest of the cool Montrose rockers and artists wet their whistles. The place is a visual orgy, between the tattooed patrons and the walls covered with likenesses of rock legends, bumper stickers and impromptu graffiti. Drinks are as intoxicating as the killer juke, loaded with the best of indie and punk rock, which perfectly suits the place — no Josh Grobin here! Look up "dive" in the dictionary, and you'll find Lola's. A true taste of inside-the-Loop Montrose.

THE LOUNGE AT BENJY'S
If you do it right, they will come. Above all the deliciousness of the downstairs namesake restaurant, The Lounge at Benjy's is a Rice Village destination of decade-old dependability. With its combination of cool cocktails, light bites and stylish interiors, this is a favorite destination for serious food aficionados as well as the hip set seeking a place to see and be seen. For tasty unwinding after work, the bartender touts the Rain-tinis (a mix of Rain vodka, Patron Citronage and pureed strawberries) and the Jack Daniels Blueberry Lynchburg Lemonade (yes, Virginia, it is made with blueberries). There are 20 wines served by the glass, and appetizers to tickle forth a call for more wine (do the pork dumplings when offered). Free parking in the lot, and free to have a good time upstairs.

> **2424 DUNSTAN** at Kelvin
> **713-522-7602**
> www.benjys.com
> **MAP** E7

THE MAGNOLIA BAR
Hot-listed as a Condé Nast "best new hotel" in 2004, the Magnolia Hotel is a 22-story renovated landmark building that has got it going on. The "it" is visible everywhere — in service, amenities, decor. But even if you're not a registered guest, you are welcome to saunter up

> **1100 TEXAS** at San Jacinto, in the Magnolia Hotel
> **713-221-0011**
> **MAP** F6

SPIRITED HOUSTON

to the second-floor bar for cocktails and tapas between 5 and 11 p.m. (The bar closes earlier than most, but six hours is long enough to get a respectable buzz on.) Expect a huge space fitted out in contemporary furnishings (ottomans in cherry pink, lime, butter and black) that bespeak a futuristic designer had his/her way here. With live jazz, billiards and a plasma TV, there are enough distractions to prove the hotel's promotional tag line: "a place of playful elegance." The hotel is located in downtown's central business district. Should you need to sleep over, they serve cookies and milk at bedtime.

MARFRELESS

2006 PEDEN at McDuffie, behind the River Oaks Theatre
713-528-0083
MAP E6

What's behind the blue door? Well, first you must find the blue door. Not an easy task unless you've been round this corner before, as legions of homegrown Houstonians have. There is no sign outside, so newcomers take heed: Romance is behind the blue door — romance, cold martinis served in metal glasses, gin out the wazoo and a real chance you might fall down in the almost-no-light lighting within. Marfreless serves its drinks *con amor*. For years it was touted as a notorious make-out bar, and that still holds true, but the action is now mainly upstairs where the lion's den gets even darker and the couches are as numerous as beds in a hospital ward. Trust us, there's trysting going on, especially at "nightcap time." But before the "wheeee" hours, they offer happy hour between 6 and 8 p.m. Candles flicker everywhere, and the music is classical. Stay till 2 if you dare — just remember to watch your step.

McELROY'S IRISH PUB

A Dublin native, the affable publican Max McElroy lent his name to this attractive spot that is as energetically fused as an Irish jig. Notice is given to Max's decor, especially the red leather banquettes, which have a story behind them. (Ever know an Irishman who did not have a story to tell?) Max purchased 62 pieces of furniture from the Rice Hotel's legendary Old Capitol Club, and it was the horsehair-stuffed couches from that venerable power bar that found a new home at McElroy's. Accented with green walls and the expected shiny dark wood, the bar hosts dart tourneys. Sporting events play on the TV. Umbrella tables are scattered around the outdoor beer garden, where local bands play occasionally and where the annual St.

3607 S. SANDMAN just south of Richmond near S. Shepherd
713-524-2444
www.mcelroyspub.com
MAP E7

Recommended
HOIST A PINT

Brewheads have many options in Houston. Here are 11 bars that boast wide-ranging beer selections and, most important, serve it fresh.

BEAVER'S, *2310 Decatur, 713-864-2328.* This new barbecue roadhouse (opened in late 2007) has an extensive beer list, including ales, wheat beer, porters, stouts and ESBs.

BOONDOGGLES PUB, *4106 NASA Rd. 1, Seabrook, 281-326-2739.* More than 40 beer taps and a true pub atmosphere make this a welcome fixture in the Clear Lake area.

FLYING SAUCER, *705 Main, 713-228-9472.* Boisterous young crowds frequent this high-ceilinged outpost of the small North Texas chain to enjoy its roughly 80 draft beers.

FRONT PORCH PUB, *217 Gray, 713-571-9571.* This casual beer-centric spot at the edge of Midtown has around 40 drafts, a big patio and an efficient staff that keeps crowds well plied.

THE GINGER MAN, *5607 Morningside, 713-526-2770.* Since 1985, the G-Man has been the best of the local beer bars (and one of the best in the country) with a terrific selection (175 beers and counting) and laidback beer-garden feel, plus a cosmopolitan crowd.

HANS' VILLAGE BIER AND VINO HAUS, *2523 Quenby, 713-520-7474.* Quaint Hans' has a relatively small but well-chosen list of beers that will keep most imbibers happy. Includes a beer garden with a bocce court.

KELVIN ARMS, *2424 Dunstan, 713-528-5002.* Sporting a Scottish flavor and an impressive array of single malt whiskies to match, the Kelvin Arms features more than 25 beers on tap.

McGONIGEL'S MUCKY DUCK, *2425 Norfolk, 713-528-5999.* This intimate live-music venue has about 30 draft beers served in 20-ounce imperial pints, including many British and hop-heavy offerings.

RED LION, *2316 S. Shepherd, 713-529-0321.* This cozy English pub serves about 20 draft beers, all in imperial pint glasses, and has a decent pub kitchen and whiskey selection, to boot.

RICHMOND ARMS, *5920 Richmond, 713-784-7722.* Though this clubby pub affects a British accent, the 80-plus draft beer and numerous bottled choices come from all of the best beer regions. Poured in imperial pint glasses.

THE STAG'S HEAD PUB, *2128 Portsmouth, 713-533-1199.* The 35 or so draft beers and plenty of wood-lined bar space make this a fine choice for socializing or just imbibing.

Paddy's Day celebration will forever be scored to the sound of bagpipes. Open Monday through Saturday 3 p.m. to 2 a.m. and on Sunday from 4 p.m. to 2 a.m., this spot loves big groups to crowd in cozily together. No food, but who needs grub when a pint or a whiskey stops the grumbling?

McGONIGEL'S MUCKY DUCK

2425 NORFOLK
near Kirby
713-528-5999
www.mcgonigels.com
MAP E7

Here you get your rarebit in more ways than one. Order a lovely Welsh rarebit (ale-infused cheese toast) while enjoying live music in a nightclubby setting that *Billboard* magazine tagged as one of the top 20 acoustic venues in the country — rare bit indeed, eh? The Irish-English-themed layout is funky, with tables snuggled up very close together, little table lamps, faux wallpaper bookcases, a fine looking bar and a performance stage flanked by a red curtain. There's an outdoor patio for smokers and others who like the night air more than the airs coming from "open mike" sessions on Mondays (expect everything from singers to comedians, from poets to tale-tellers). On Wednesday eve starting at 8, a longtime tradition places Irish/Celtic music at the head of the class. (See website for calendar of music events.) Beer and wine only, but the bar boasts one of the longest lists of Champagne you'll find in town. There's an extensive wine list, and the beer is imported draft and many bottled choices. Happy hour 5 to 7 p.m. offers bar tidbits for free, but you should try something from the menu because the food is very good. They've recently added a private room available for parties.

MOSAIC

530 TEXAS at Bagby, in Bayou Place
713-236-1100
MAP F6

Young (and restless) professionals will begin dropping in at 10 p.m. (when the bar opens Thursday through Saturday), with absolutely no thought of sleep or that they have to be at their desks bright and early next morning. They will be dressed in "business casual" (a euphemism for no flip-flops, no flimsies, no floozies, no running shorts, no lederhosen), since being well-dressed for successful drinking is of prime importance here. These bar owls have come to Bayou Place to sip cordials in the late-night air — there is a killer patio that overlooks the Theater District. There is no food, so they would have dined earlier. DJs pamper them with music that fits their age and lifestyle, and until 2 a.m. they make conversation that would not challenge a college don. Next door, the RocBar is the naughty sister to Mosaic's controlled persona.

MUGSY'S

3200 KIRBY at W. Main
713-526-5595
MAP E7

Our first impression is this is a set out of a mob movie. All it needs is a guy is sitting at a table with a fork of twirled spaghetti nearing his mouth. Suddenly another guy comes busting in with a machine gun and mows him down mid-bite. That's the look of Mugsy's. It's a good thing it doesn't serve food — no one would be able to eat without nervously watching the front door. What it does serve are top-notch cocktails from a well-stocked bar. This place has a customer base that's flat in love with their neighborhood "speakeasy." A recommended diversion is The Bloody Mary Deal — the owner offers a money-back guarantee if his Marys do not send you into euphoria. Naturally, the drink has the color of spilled blood, and a spicy, tasty quaff it is. Open Monday through Friday 4 p.m. to 2 a.m., Saturday from 8 p.m. to 2 a.m., and Sunday 6 p.m. to 2 a.m.

NOTSUOH

314 MAIN between Preston and Congress
713-409-4750
www.myspace.com/notsuohmusic
MAP F6

Notsuoh is not really like anything else in Houston. At its most basic, Jim Pirtle's strange little place is a downtown lounge/bar. You might even think it's fairly typical at first glance. But once inside it becomes clear that there is way more going on than you thought. It's small, cozy even, with one side filled by a stage. It's there that you might catch an up-and-coming indie band, a poetry slam, a lecture, even a theatrical piece of some sort. On the walls is artwork from local artists, and the crowd is usually mostly 20-something artist types. The bar itself is located farther in the back, but Notsuoh is as much a coffeehouse as a bar. Furniture is shabby-chic, with the emphasis on shabby. The place is full of eclectic stuff, from mannequin parts to bicycles to bird cages. And the name? It's "Houston" spelled backwards, which probably explains Notsuoh better than anything we could write.

OPORTO CAFE

3833 RICHMOND at Cummins
713-621-1114
www.oporto.us
MAP D7

The original name of the Portuguese town that was the birthplace of port wine, Oporto succeeds in its ambition to transport us to the sunny seaside to partake of regional libations, food and the ambience associated with the small, relaxed cafes found in the wine-producing countries of Europe. A lunch spot by day and a tapas bar by night, Oporto distinguishes itself from other similar spots around town with its cuisine and a heady list of wines concentrated on labels from Portugal, Spain and Italy. Try the potato and chorizo soup (cup, $3.95) and wash it down with lime-hued Vinho Verde. Or order a rose petal-scented Spanish Esperanza to sip with piquillo pepper rellenos (stuffed with shrimp and crawfish, sauced and cheesed). On Thursdays live flamenco guitar music heightens the impression we have been transported to Iberian bliss, so try one of their Madeiras to hold the mood. Specialty drinks, Portuguese desserts and a sharp service crew.

RED LION PUB

This spot is owner Craig Mallinson's "local." Born in England, where he was educated in the art of keeping a public house, Mallinson says a local is what we Texans would call a neighborhood bar. Styled to meet all necessary requirements of a U.K. local, the sanguine Lion has its brass, its wood paneling, its red leather booths, its fireplace in the back room and its 20 drafts of British beer on the wall. It also has comestibles associated with the isles across the pond, such as roast beef and Yorkshire pudding (Sundays), the fried English breakfast (Saturday and Sunday) and sausage rolls served with HP sauce (everyday). There's no freezer in the

2316 S. SHEPHERD
at Fairview
713-782-3030
www.redlionhouston.com
MAP E6

Personal Favorites
GREAT SPORTS BARS

Selected by Brian Ching

FOX SPORTS GRILL, *5175 Westheimer, 713-439-1369.* Good food. I like the variety of TVs.

FRONT PORCH PUB, *217 Gray, 713-571-9571.* Great outdoor area. Tremendous atmosphere.

KOBAIN, *3720 Raymond, 713-862-9911.* Perfect for meeting friends. Roomy and relaxing.

PUB FICTION, *2303 Smith, 713-400-8400.* Great location. Walking distance to all Midtown clubs. Great atmosphere.

TAVERN, *1340 W. Gray, 713-522-5152.* Ping Pong. Enough said.

Brian Ching plays forward for the Houston Dynamo. Ching led the team to its first of two MLS championships in 2006 and was also on the 2006 USA World Cup team.

kitchen (a source of pride for the amiable publican), guaranteeing all dishes are prepared fresh. Appetizers abound, and some are solidly American, like the quartet of mini burgers that can be shared with your bar mates. Speaking of mates, ladies take note: Men like this pub. Soccer games are aired on the bar TV, and happy hour goes to 7 p.m. Monday through Saturday and all day and night long on Sunday. Have a tankard of Old Speckled Hen and sing "Rule Britannia"!

THE REMINGTON BAR

1919 BRIAR OAKS at San Felipe, in the St. Regis Hotel
713-403-2759
www.theremingtonrestaurant.com
MAP D6

Forever and anon a playground for grown-ups, this is absolutely not the place for 20-somethings seeking tequila shots, foosball and being packed in like chewing gum sticks. No. Instead, sitting barside or comfortably ensconced around the corner in the very chic lounge, you will find gents graying at the temples who are in the black on the ledger book, ladies in (designer) red, 40-ish corporate whizzes, people from out of town who can afford the price of a St. Regis bed, and ladies of a certain age who would never submit to choking down a Jell-O shot, even if sent over by an off-course toy-boy. The mixologist does put together a wicked traditional martini here, and he is savvy to what a Gibson is. If you must have a sweet martini, the Remington's signature Wedding Cake uses vanilla vodka. An elegant destination, it offers live music for dancing at the end of the week. Light fare is offered in the bar, such as chicken tostadas, lobster crab bisque and satay of lemongrass beef tender with red curry coconut peanut dip. Quick, bring us a generous glass of Louis Roederer Brut Premier ($40 a gulp). Check the website for upcoming bands and performers. The Remington Bar is soigné — making it either an oddity or a blessing in the saloon world.

RICHARD'S LIQUORS & FINE WINES

2124 S. SHEPHERD near Fairview, and other locations
713-529-4849
www.richardsliquors.com
MAP E6

Perhaps the Cheers of retail liquor stores, everybody knows the name of this Houston purveyor of spirits. Family owned for more than half a century, Richard's has brown-bagged booze for your father and your father's father since 1950. As the business grew, its stock and trade became more diversified with fine wines, fine cigars from the Dominican Republic and upscale gift items being added to the shelves and bins and humidors. The staff, knowledgeable and eager to offer recommendations, shares a commendable professionalism at all six locations. Offering in-store specials every day, the wine is always premium quality whether modestly priced or rare vintage. Specialty items for connoisseurs of wine and spirits: Pierre Ferrand Ancestrale $479.99, Johnnie Walker Blue (authenticated with a serial number) $199.99, Remy Martin Louis XIII $1,549. Bar-related gift items include decanters, flasks and Champagne buckets, and Richard's puts together great gift baskets. For a special occasion, consider the pairing of Les Cailloux Châteauneuf-du-Pape and Thomas Sancerre packed together in a good-looking wooden box, $85. Or the quartet of California Pinot Noirs, $180. Customers in neighborhoods surrounding each of the six locations can call for home delivery.

5920 RICHMOND near Fountain View, and other locations
713-784-7722
www.richmondarmsonline.com
MAP D7

RICHMOND ARMS

Like an old English cottage set upon the Cornish coastline, the Richmond Arms has deeply planted roots that suggest, even if the whole of Richmond becomes a parking lot, this venerable and well-loved pub will forever survive. Picnic tables outside, and in keeping with its authentic public house theme, there are dark corners, booths and 84 beer varieties inside. Special deals and activities of a variegated allure lure customers to come back often. Monday, take $1 off the price of a martini. Tuesday is Quiz Night, with prizes awarded to teams displaying the highest erudition. Also on Tuesdays, chicken curry is served and you can have a second helping of the stuff for free. When the Toad Club meets, a line-up of antique and exotic cars will be parked outside — you are welcome to make up-close scrutiny of the autos and to chat with the owners. There's a $20 cover and 12 TVs turned on when there's a broadcast of an international rugby match. Food service includes the Prime Minister burger, which is smothered in mushroom gravy, or try the banger sandwich, or Sunday the chicken pot pie. And, this is one of the last places in town to find liver and onions a staple on the menu.

RIO RANCH BAR

Located in a separate room off the main restaurant (itself a dining creation of the Schiller Del Grande restaurant team), the wood-floored, western artifact-strewn Rio Ranch Bar is so Texas-inspired you'll want to run home and change out of

9999 WESTHEIMER between Gessner and Beltway 8 in the Hilton Westchase Hotel
713-974-1000
www.rioranch.com
MAP C7

Belly up to the bar and enjoy a "grande" cocktail at Rio Ranch, a Hill Country-style watering hole.

your Nikes into cowboy boots. There is no saloon nude hung over the bar; instead the mural is of a subject dear to every bona fide child of the great Lone Star state — a cowboy herding cattle. Cedar bar chairs belly up to the snaking bar top, and there are chairs and tables placed around white columns so you can sit and chow down on selections from the bar menu. A durn fine choice for Westsiders looking for a comfortable happy-hour destination, the clock on special deals runs from 4 to 7 p.m. New to the establishment is the Setanta Sports Channel, which broadcasts soccer, rugby and other sporting events on high-definition TVs. (To see what's coming up, the website has a calendar of events.) No trouble finding the restrooms — look for the half-moon carved in the door.

ROLL-N SALOON

4200 SAN FELIPE
just east of Mid Lane
713-622-7487
MAP D6

Located inside the West Loop across from the train tracks, Roll-N Saloon is a freak show of sorts. Imagine a train car falling off those train tracks, tumbling over and its interior decorated like a frat house. That would pretty much describe this wrong-side-of-the-tracks dive. Regulars are a mix of yuppie bankers, accountants, collegiates and single dads, and the bartenders are gruff good ol' boys. Don't come here expecting much in the way of silicon enhancements or "atmosphere." A friend of ours who now lives in Norway explained it best: Roll-N is an acquired taste, and you're either hooked or you're repulsed. Photos and chalk doodles cover the walls, the games are always on, and there is Golden Tee and pool for the sportsmen. Our favorite thing about the Roll-N? The music. The Roll-N has the best jukebox in Houston, hands down. Random detail: Contributors to this guidebook once watched police give a DUI to a drunk bicyclist who was leaving the Roll-N.

RUDYARD'S BRITISH PUB

A funky spot in funky Montrose, this place teeters on being tagged a lowdown dive bar, but its popularity defies

210 WAUGH at Welch
713-521-0521
www.rudyards.s425.sureserver.com
MAP E6

Personal Favorites
TOP BYOBs

By Charles M. Bear Dalton

While I know of more than 40 Houston bring-your-own-bottle (BYOB) restaurants, I tend to visit a few favorites over and over. The following have very good food and good (if casual) service. But most do not have good wine glasses, and they sometimes run out of glassware. I generally suggest you BYOG (bring your own glasses) as well as BYOB. I do. And don't forget that most BYOB places charge a corkage fee — about five to 10 dollars a bottle.

CORELLI'S, 5640 Westheimer, 713-629-4424, and 3229 Hwy. 6 South, Sugar Land, 281-491-8900. This is my neighborhood BYOB hangout. They have a beer and wine permit and a small wine list but allow BYOB. It's the only BYOB where I routinely see families with young kids.

COLLINA'S ITALIAN CAFE, 3835 Richmond, 713-621-8844, and other locations. There are four Collina's locations, but I think this one is best. While it can be noisy and sometimes runs out of clean glasses, the food and service are always good. Now that the school across Richmond has been torn down, I expect Collina's will get a beer and wine permit but will still encourage BYOB.

LA VISTA, 1936 Fountain View, 713-787-9899, and 12665 Memorial, 713-973-7374. La Vista now has a beer and wine permit and a small wine list, but most of their business is still BYOB. This indoor/outdoor spot has great Italian food worthy of fancier digs and the best service of any of the BYOBs. No reservations, and there is always a wait. Be sure to BYOG.

LUCIO'S BYOB & GRILL, 905 Taft, 713-523-9958. Lucio's is a good American neighborhood restaurant that happens to be in a dry area and so doesn't have a wine list. The food is terrific and the entrees and specials stand out. Among this group, Lucio's alone both takes reservations and has better-than-average wine glasses.

VIETNAM RESTAURANT, 605 W. 19th, 832-618-1668. This Heights hangout serves very good Vietnamese food in a dry part of town. I like the Vietnamese eggrolls that you wrap in lettuce, the green beans, the asparagus, the Vietnam beef and, especially, the soft-shell crab. BYOG.

YUM YUM CHA, 2435 Times, 713-527-8455. It is a treat to eat dim sum with great wine, such as a fine drier-style Riesling, unwooded Pinot Gris, red Burgundy or spicy cool-climate California Syrah. BYOB at dinner only, and never on Sundays.

Charles M. Bear Dalton is the fine wine buyer for Spec's and teaches about wine at Rice University's Glasscock School of Continuing Studies, the U of H's Conrad Hilton School of Hotel and Restaurant Management, and the Wine School at L'Alliance Française.

clumping it with undesirables. Think Virginia Woolf gone beer-hound rocker, coming in every Monday at 6 to eat the free hot wings downstairs. Or, Mick Jagger unknown and un-Stoned, playing electric bass with an indie touring band upstairs. Having an Upstairs and a Downstairs, it is not reminiscent of the elegant British television series, but rather a mishmash of trash and treasures beloved by dart leaguers who compete every Monday and Wednesday, adored by regulars who call it "Rudz," patronized by those happy to pay the reasonable cover charge to cram in for the comedy and the music. The food's above par, with a decent cheeseburger, plus tater tots, corn dogs, pizza and, for some reason, a nice lady-like salad. Special events are so common here they should be called usual events. Parking is nightmarish, but you can get Tall Boys and Kazi's for a dollar on Sunday. Monday through Sunday the well drinks go for $3.25 all day.

2522 FAIRWAY PARK DR. between Hempstead Hwy., Antoine and Hwy. 290

713-713-686-9494

www.saintarnold.com

MAP D5

SAINT ARNOLD BREWING COMPANY

Taking its name from the patron saint of brewers, Saint Arnold is the oldest microbrewery in Texas. Given the restrictive state alcohol laws, that's only since 1994. Guided by beer-lover and former investment banker Brock Wagner, Saint Arnold today brews five beers year-round, plus five seasonally, as well as an ever-changing series of extreme single-batch beers called Divine. All the beers are made in the traditional German and craft method with only malt, hops, yeast and water, no adjuncts. The hoppy, medium-bodied Amber Ale is one of the three original beers and the brewery's workhouse. Other notables include the Cascade hop-heavy Elissa IPA; Fancy Lawnmower, a light Kölsch-style ale; and the crisp Summer Pils, a Bavarian style pilsner. The Saturday tours have grown very popular in recent years, often attracting up to 500 people, and the brewery is a must-visit for beer-lovers. Saint Arnold

Saint Arnold has captured Houston's imagination with its community involvement, funky style and great beer.

purchased a larger facility in mid-2008, a warehouse north of I-10 and just east of downtown. The new building will allow brewing capacity to be increased five-fold. The new location will also include air-conditioning for the brewhouse and nicer and more numerous restrooms, allowing more frequent tours. Wagner expects to be in the new location by mid-2009.

SALUD! WINERY

3939 MONTROSE, SUITE C at Branard
713-522-8282
www.saludwinery.com
MAP E7

Brothers Brad and Charles Odom created a small-batch winery and tasting room smack in the middle of the city that has turned out to be a real wine-crowd pleaser. Thirty wines are available for tasting with an array of appetizers from the kitchen, but the coup de vin here is the onsite wine-making. Within this multi-storied dream of an Italian palazzo there dwell shiny steel vats filled with wine the customers have made themselves. All you have to do to make wine, too, is to call up the Odoms, reserve a space for yourself or take along 10 of your best friends, and then begin your guided wine-making tour. Using imported grapes from around the world, each step of the process is explained during hands-on instruction. Nine weeks later, the wine is ready for bottling and personalized labeling and you get to take home two cases. (Several experienced customers recommend opting to make the red Italian Amarone.) Open Tuesday and Wednesday 11 a.m. to 9 p.m., Thursday through Saturday 11 a.m. to 11 p.m., and Sunday 1 to 9 p.m.

SAMBUCA

A modern-day supper club and all that jazz: As a live-music venue, the high note here plays in perfect pitch. With jazz as the set piece, and a smattering of R&B, soul and Latin, expect to find

909 TEXAS at Travis
713-224-5299
www.sambucarestaurant.com
MAP F6

performances by top bands seven nights a week. The dancing's not for jerks or slams, but draws nicely dressed people to the floor who remember what they were taught in Miss Cynthia's Dance Class in the eighth grade. Sit at the bar as long as you like, enjoying some expertly mixed drinks and nibbling from the appetizer menu. It might irk you to know there's a two-hour limit on squatting in the faux-leopard booths to have dinner — and double irk to find there's a hefty minimum price per person for that dinner. But count to 10 and breathe in the sexy ambience. Located on the first floor of the historic Rice Hotel, downtown worker bees buzz in for a happy hour that goes to 7. No dress code on weeknights, but lose the shorts on weekends or even the valet will frown and say "No, no."

SCOTT GERTNER'S SKY BAR & GRILLE

3400 MONTROSE
at Hawthorne
713-520-9688
www.scottgertner.com
MAP E6

Ladies are greatly favored at this penthouse nightclub that is touted for the spectacular city views outside and the jazzy, danceable music inside. Men must prove they are 23 to enter, but females are only required to be 21. After 8 p.m. men pay a $10 cover, but on Wednesdays and Thursdays the ladies sweep in free of charge. And Thursday is a hot time to step up to this aerie in the sky because salsa is the rhythm of the night, dance lessons are free and $5 will get you a 36-ounce mojito. There's a long list of Do Not's for the gents: Do not even think of getting in if flip-flops are on your feet, your jeans are baggy (ironed jeans with a crease are okey-dokey), you're wearing a hat, your shirt is sleeveless (men's shirts must be sleeved and buttoned up) or you came from the gym in warm-ups. Ladies have no dress code, but to be safe, wear something. Owner Scott Gertner is a fine musician and his band is as cool as his club. (Other performers also appear, so check the calendar on the website.) Two sweeping terraces hug the club — one for food and the other for drinking in the twinkling Houston skyline.

SHAY McELROY'S IRISH PUB

909 TEXAS at Main
713-223-2444
www.mcelroyspub.com
MAP F6

A second enterprise from Max McElroy, this drinking den is located on the ground floor of the Rice Lofts in downtown. Look for the dancing green leprechaun on the sign outside, then step into a bar imported intact from Ireland and accessorized by wood paneling, Irish etched glass and legions of beer and liquor. The space is smallish, but all the better for rubbing elbows with others who have come seeking what you are seeking — a pint or a cocktail, a feeling of party and maybe a pun or two exchanged for good measure. It offers window-table views and outdoor seating for sightseeing — the MetroRail stops at the corner, so you can sip happily while watching the world detrain. Children are not allowed and you will be sternly spoken to should you attempt to bring one in. Full bar, no food.

THE SOCIAL LOUNGE & PATIO BAR

3730 WASHINGTON
at Yale
713-426-5585
www.thesocialinfo.com
MAP E6

With the idea in mind to revitalize the nearby dry Heights area as a nightlife destination, the owners of this ambitious new lounge have a "party, party, party" philosophy that they are hell-bent to

Recommended
WINE EDUCATION

Want to learn more about wine? Houston's better wine retailers regularly host in-store tastings — check websites for details. Or sign up for a class at one of the following.

CENTRAL MARKET, *3815 Westheimer, 713-386-1700.* The upscale grocer has two or three wine-centric classes per month run by its own wine and beer manager or visiting instructors.

THE CORKSCREW, *1919 Washington, 713-864-9463.* To arrange for private wine tutorials in the Big Red Room, call Doyle or Andrew Adams — the congenial brothers will arrange for their sommelier to speak to your group.

D'VINE WINE OF TEXAS, *609 Bradford, Kemah, 281-334-8300.* The D'vine experts at this cozy shop will teach you how to make your own wine that will be custom bottled for delivery eight weeks after the fermentation process is completed.

L'ALLIANCE FRANÇAIS DE HOUSTON, *427 Lovett, 713-526-1121.* Predictably, the wine school here focuses on French wines. Classes are taught by Bear Dalton, fine-wine buyer for Spec's and a longtime *My Table* magazine contributor.

RICE UNIVERSITY, SUSANNE M. GLASSCOCK SCHOOL OF CONTINUING STUDIES, *713-348-4803.* Bear Dalton is also instructor of several continuing-education wine courses. Check the course catalog at www.gscs.rice.edu.

SALUD! WINERY, *3939 Montrose, 713-522-8282.* Another pair of brothers dedicated to your wine instruction (and enjoyment), Brad and Charles Odom have installed a slick small-batch winery on the premises. For an unusual party, gather some friends and learn how wine is made.

SONOMA RETAIL WINE BAR & BOUTIQUE, *2720 Richmond, 713-526-9463.* Offers wine classes every two weeks and holds wine dinners that are hosted by knowledgeable winemakers and wine reps.

UNIVERSITY OF HOUSTON CONTINUING EDUCATION, *713-743-1060.* The International Sommelier Guild, in cooperation with UH Continuing Education, offers a Wine Fundamentals Certificate (designed for the novice) and Sommelier Diploma Program courses. See www.uh.edu/academics/dce/prog/sommelier.html. Note: The Conrad Hilton College also offers courses in wine and spirits, which are part of the Wine & Spirits Management Institute. However, you must be a UH student to enroll.

VINEYARD ON THE SQUARE, *16135 City Walk, Sugar Land, 281-277-1851.* Wine classes for both beginners and seasoned oenologists. Advance payment requested to reserve a seat — call for a calendar.

follow. With a gaggle of DJs primed to spin tunes every night the place is open, the music ranges from pop to R&B to hip-hop to soul to rock. Many nights are themed, so that when the second day of the week comes around we'll remember it is "Red Cup Tuesday," which means drinks will be poured into oversized red plastic cups giving a bigger jigger's-worth for the bucks. (Check the website for other themes.) The Art Guys' huge Absolut bottle, swathed in 1,000 coats of paint, is permanently installed next to the patio bar where food is dispensed from an Airstream trailer (menu designed by chef Lance Fegen, who's at Glass Wall). The interior main bar is a restored antique barback out of a joint on the South Side of Chicago. There's no cover charge to avail oneself of all this fun, and free parking across the street comes courtesy of a business that has no nocturnal use for its lot.

2720 RICHMOND
near Kirby
713-526-9463
www.sonomahouston.com
MAP E7

SONOMA RETAIL WINE BAR & BOUTIQUE

Good choice for a birthday girl or boy because that first lovely flute of Champagne is a freebie. And if you want more perks from this unfussy, upscale wine bar, plan a surprise for a loved one (or somebody you're hoping to persuade to be a loved one), and Sonoma will arrange for the fresh flowers, have the Champagne iced in the bucket and on the table, cook up a special meal, and even hire the limo to whisk you from a perfect evening to the residence of your choice. There are more than 150 wines to order by the glass, and should you like what you taste, receive a 20 percent discount when you purchase a case. They also serve 15 varieties of beer. The food's unusually good: Try the honey-drizzled Brie or the hand-tossed thin-crust pizza with three cheeses (manchego, mozzarella, goat) or the prosciutto, Swiss and basil pesto crostini. Live jazz plays cool on Thursdays from 7 to 11 p.m., and on Saturday a DJ is in control of the acid-jazz scene starting at 10 p.m., ending at 2 a.m. Wine classes, wine dinners and a pretty room for parties add to the bouquet of pleasure.

SPEC'S WINES, SPIRITS & FINER FOODS

You would have to be from another planet to not know Spec's. For those ETs among us, some facts: The warehouse store at the Smith Street location is the mother ship for this close encounter with the divinely perfect bottle-and-bonuses-plus retailer. There are close to

2410 SMITH near McGowen, and other locations
713-526-8787
www.specsonline.com
MAP F6

two acres of store to wander through, stocked with some 40,000 labels of wine, spirits, liqueurs, beer and gourmet food. Walk right into the humidor to peruse 900 cigar varieties, and follow your happy nose over to the 5,000-square-foot deli to get a closer whiff of the delicacies on display. Overwhelmed? Over-excited? Well, it's not over yet. Spec's roasts its own coffee beans, cooks up lunch specials weekly, publishes its own newsletter and spirits magazine, holds wine classes, presents the savviest staff in town for wine selection consultation, has an exhaustive but exquisitely detailed website covering everything you need to know about the operation, including an online tutorial about wine and food pairing, and it throws a Cheese Festival annually in September. There are 30-plus stores in the greater Houston area, but the Mother Ship needs to be visited for the sheer pleasure of seeing the "spec"-tacle up close and personal. All stores open Monday through Saturday 10 to 9. All cash purchases receive a five percent discount.

2128 PORTSMOUTH at S. Sandman near Richmond
713-533-1199
www.stagsheadpub.com
MAP E7

THE STAG'S HEAD PUB

There's a manly feel to this English-styled pub — the reinvented Ale House — as if the tweed-coated laird will step inside any minute bringing along his burly gameskeeper who is trailed by a very male, drooling bull mastiff. A wrap-around bar is centered in the room, and there are wooden bench chairs and tables set in corners for pleasant chats with buddies or solitary drinking. Over-30-somethings seem to define the demographic. Hungry? Try the potato soup or the Hawaiian pizza topped with jalapeños as well as pineapple, ham and cheese. Five-buck pitchers are offered Monday and Tuesday after 4 p.m., Wednesday draft specials, and on Thursday it's "well-tini" — select martinis $4. From 1 to 3 p.m. on Sundays the pub serves the Great British Sunday Lunch as well as a traditional English breakfast. The expected international sports are shown on the TV, darts are thrown and there is an inviting patio. Tap beers number 35 or so, and there's a wine list.

THE TASTING ROOM

There are now three Tasting Rooms placed strategically around Houston. (Check out the Midtown location on Gray and the River Oaks location at W. Alabama near Kirby.) A former Continental Airlines pilot, co-owner Jerry Lasco also studied at the NYC

1101-18 UPTOWN PARK near Loop 610 and Post Oak Blvd., and other locations
713-993-9800
www.tastingroomwines.com
MAP D6

Peter Kump Cooking School, which bestowed not only expertise in the culinary arts, but obviously he's the man to see to make wine flights. Each of the three locations has a different Flight Night — three wine samples for a small sum. (The website keeps you updated on the pricing, scheduling and various theme nights.) Cushioned chairs on the patio, gourmet pizza and cheese platters, and beer if you really must. The Uptown location's hours are Monday through Friday noon to midnight, Saturday noon to 1 a.m.

Taste, linger and socialize at The Tasting Room, a wine cafe that is serious about wine education but casual in feel.

TAVERNA WINERY & RESTAURANT

12820 HWY. 105 WEST, five miles west of I-45, Conroe

936-588-6464
www.tavernawinery.com

MAP North of D1

Like adventures in wine and food beyond the borders of the city? Never thought we'd say this, but head for Conroe. A town not known for donning a culinary crown, there is a jewel out there in the north country. Seek and ye shall find a sprawling complex consisting of one gourmet restaurant, one wine tasting room, one retail shop stocked with goodies and wine accessories, one nice patio within scent of the herb garden and one expansive lawn for concerts when the weather's good. The tasting room opens daily at 4 p.m. and stays open until 9 on weekdays and Sunday, until 10 on Saturday. Try the five wee but tasty wine sips for $5, purchase bottles in a price range of $18 to $40 (with some premium vintages also available) from a stock of more than 100 labels, and partake of small bites from the tapas menu — calamari, marinated olives, pâté. Check the website for Taverna's special-events schedule and summer concerts.

T.K. BITTERMAN'S

Trendy never shows up here. And you won't find T.K. Bitterman's winning bravos on anyone's "Best" list. It's hard to pin down exactly what kind of drinking hole this is. One thing is certain, it's not themed — that

2010 W. ALABAMA
east of S. Shepherd

713-529-8979

MAP E7

is, if you don't count the shrine to the Chicago Cubs. That there is the mounted head of a billy goat on the wall conjures a vague memory of some cobwebby baseball story, but you can sit with your back to the thing if it makes you queasy. The bar's been around for quite awhile, and many of the frequenters seem to be members of the journalistic arts (writers for the 6 o'clock news, documentary filmmakers, obit assemblers, unpublished crime novel hacks, publicists). Other fields are represented too, but all seem to have one commonality — they take their drinking seriously. The mixed drink is alive and well at T.K. Bitterman's, with the martini weighing in at about seven ounces. Not a lounge lizard destination, more a net for catching bar flies who like to sit at the bar on a bar stool and talk, or not talk, to the bartender. Open 4 p.m. to 2 a.m. Monday through Friday, 6 p.m. to 2 a.m. Saturday and Sunday. Dogs are welcome.

THE TREE HOUSE

1611 LAMAR at Crawford
713-337-7321
MAP F6

With a verdant setting among the oak trees of Discovery Green — the new park in front of the George R. Brown Convention Center — this sprawling rooftop spot is magical and unlike anything else in the city. It sits atop The Grove, a restaurant from the Schiller Del Grande group that opened in early 2008. In keeping with the trend at several new area bars, mixology engenders the same seriousness as the chef's efforts. So come casual and try one of the many innovative drinks, such as a lychee martini, Champagne mango cosmo or pomegranate margarita. (The tequila bar pours some 35-plus choices, including rare hard-to-find tequilas.) Chef Ryan Pera's bar menu is fun and includes pulled pork sliders, babyback ribs and pizzettes, though the break-out app winners seem to be deviled eggs and duck meatballs. Getting back to the setting: It's possible you've never seen the downtown skyline from this perspective before. For an hour or two, it will make you glad to live in Houston.

UNDER THE VOLCANO

2349 BISSONNET at Morningside
713-526-5282
MAP E7

Going to make this short. There's a bouncer who will check your I.D. There are voodoo masks on the wall. There is a jukebox that might remind you of HAL in *2001: A Space Odyssey* — a machine gone loopy in a good way. There is a frozen screwdriver that fans of the drink do not find comparable to an orange slushie. There are pisco sours and Singapore slings and Cuba libres to be had, but you must queue up at the bar (or more accurately, fight the crowd at the bar) to nab them. There is a

Recommended
DRINKING UP CLEAR LAKE

So you and your friends are heading to Clear Lake for a weekend by the water? Here are some of our favorite watering holes for sharing drinks and laughs before turning in back at the condo.

CARLOS BEER GARDEN, *18018 Hwy. 3, Webster, 281-554-6062.* We love this place — a good ole Texas icehouse with every kind of person imaginable and some of the best burgers around, plus a barber shop attached that is accessible from the bar. Grab a table or sidle up to the bar with the regulars, and be sure to bring a roll of quarters for the pool tables and jukebox (we love the variety of rock and country). Leave your watch at home and just have fun with beers by the bottle, glass (*ahem*, plastic cup) and pitcher. Carlos is very local and very casual — kids welcome — and a darn good time. We miss the Wall of Shame, but karaoke Tuesdays is shameful enough. Open 10 a.m. to midnight Sunday to Friday, 10 a.m. to 1 a.m. Saturday. Oh, and if you need a keg, they also do rentals.

LANCE'S TURTLE CLUB, *2613 ½ NASA Rd. 1, Seabrook, 281-326-7613.* This classic Clear Lake spot actually floats on the lake so you can feel it sway with the waves — good to know, in case you think you already had too much to drink. Hold onto your drinks when boats pass by. This barge bar is fun and very local. If you wanna become a turtle, you gotta ask Lance. Once he says yes, you can give the secret pass phrase — "You bet your sweet a** I am!" when asked if you're a turtle. Full bar with bottle beer only, shot specials and the signature frozen rum-based drink, the Bushwacker. Decent burgers and sandwiches, nice jukebox of classics, and live bands Wednesday to Sunday. Don't miss the best part of the bar: Look for the stairwell to the left of the main bar, which leads to the upper deck with covered seating and an awesome view of Clear Lake. Open daily 11 a.m. to 2 a.m.

MONKEY BAR, *605 6th St., Kemah, 281-334-7800.* George of the Jungle would feel right at home in this friendly and playful monkey-themed local bar. Bring in a monkey (item, not a live one!) and get a free drink. Located near the Kemah Boardwalk and local gift shops, you can head to the area and make a (lazy) day of it. There are both an inside and an outside bar, so don't let weather bother you. Great beer selections (35 bottled and 17 on tap, including Lone Star at a bargain price), specialty shots, pool tables and a digital jukebox with a good mix. There is also live music on Saturday and Sunday. The staff is friendly, and bikers are welcome.

NOAH'S ARK BAR & GRILL, *4438 Boulevard St., Bacliff, 281-339-2895.* Pass up the Kemah happy hour, 2 to 7 p.m., when you get $1 off both mixed drinks and drafts. If you're a college student who has the proper identification, you will find more like you here. (If, on the other hand, you feel alien to the scene and are cocksure that this isn't the hangout for you, skip happily across the street to Kay's Lounge — an iconic, beloved dive that's been around since the 1930s. Monday at Kay's is free-hotdog day.) By the way, locals call it simply "the Volcano."

VINE WINE ROOM

12420 MEMORIAL
between Gessner and Beltway 8

713-463-8463
www.vinewineroom.com

MAP C6

One of the good-guy proprietors, Joe Rippey makes friends of his customers with his personal easygoing amiability and his public-pleasing fine taste in wine. This is, literally, the coolest wine bar in Houston — the temperature inside is set to baby the stock — so our host has several shawls on hand should a bare-shouldered lady's teeth start clacking. There are about 200 wines from small and unique estates around the world to buy by the bottle. Per glass the wine choices run from $5 to $36, and the imported beer goes for $5. Inside the setting is Old World charm, with antiques and artwork to accentuate the style. Outside you can participate in the "Pairings on the Patio" event every Tuesday, with wine, food and live jazz,

Bored-walk and have a homegrown experience at this awesome biker bar where everyone is welcome. If you want laid back with a view (and the occasional rumble of Harleys), this is a great choice. Two front decks and another massive one upstairs have spectacular views of Galveston Bay, located just across the street. Fave drinks include the doctor-it-yourself bloody Marys and tangy margaritas. Fresh Gulf seafood, burgers, Mexican dishes and even steaks and salads taste better with a bucket o' cold beers. Weekends feature a breakfast buffet from 8 a.m. to 1 p.m. and live music at night. Poker nights Monday through Thursday.

OUTRIGGERS, *101 Bath, Seabrook, 281-474-3474.* Arrive by boat or car at this seafood grill and oyster bar that has an upstairs bar popular with the locals. Multi-level decks provide awesome views of the water, passing boats and the sunset — outdoor tables go quickly on sunny days, so get there early. Our friends love the bloody Marys with housemade pepper vodka. Get a few plates of fried whatever — it's all good — and some raw oysters and just kick back and relax. On Mardi Gras weekend, they do a Yachty Gras boat parade with local decorated boats tossing beads to patrons. Boat docks available with no advance notice.

6 to 9 p.m., $25 per person. On Saturday wine tastings begin at 3 p.m., and live jazz soothes the soul from 6 to 10 p.m. Limited appetizer menu, but you can order in food from area restaurants.

VINEYARD ON THE SQUARE

16135 CITY WALK
between Hwy. 59 and Town Center Blvd., Sugar Land
281-277-1851
www.discovervineyard.com
MAP A9

An ultra-modern interior, with cool paintings, hardwood floors, couches in soft beige and peach and accented by black leather benches, this wine bar/retail store draws us southwest out of Houston for a classy lounge on the Sugar Land side. Divided into two sections inside — one for tasting 48 wines by the glass, one for buying from a selection of 250 bottles. Outside there is an expansive patio dotted with banana-colored umbrellas to keep the sun off your appetizer plate (try the poached shrimp with lemon vinaigrette) and wine. Monthly wine classes are geared toward both the beginner and the seasoned connoisseur. Local artists have showings in this pretty place, and live music events are always scheduled at week's end. The retail shop is open Monday through Saturday 11 a.m. to 9 p.m.; wine bar opens at 11 Monday through Saturday, closing at 10 on weekdays, at midnight Friday and Saturday.

VINO 100

11693 WESTHEIMER
#140 at Crescent Park Dr.
281-759-4100
www.vino100houston.com
MAP B7

This far-Westside boutique tasting room/wine shop has limited seating, but folks seem to enjoy mingling while sipping wine as though at a private cocktail party. The knowledgeable staff provides astute but easily understood wine chatter, so that you are never in the dark about what you are drinking. Matter-of-fact they have a "wine barometer" that gives comprehensive details about their shelves' 100 wines — bouquet, flavor, body, price, etc. — with ratings compiled by Vino 100's tasting panel. Priced at $25 or less, the wines run the spectrum, including red, white, sparkling and dessert wines. Wines by the glass change weekly, and there are usually at least 15 from which to choose. At happy hour (1 to 5 p.m.) take $2 off that glass. Many special events (check the website) pair food and wine, $10 to $20 per person.

WARREN'S INN

Like a grizzly-bearded, aged-cheese geezer, Warren's has the endearing (and enduring) charm of the grandpa you want to hug and kiss in spite of the beard. He's funny and eccentric and set in his ways. Surrounded

307 TRAVIS at Congress
713-247-9207
MAP F6

by a parade of odd characters that like to sit around guzzling the overly generous pours, a great many of the people you meet at Warren's are veterans at the bar game. Of course new faces will pop in — young professionals who heard about the killer martinis here, the lost *trendetti* who need directions to Mosaic — but don't be surprised to spot the judge who heard your divorce case this morning, or that *Chronicle* columnist whose snapshot is forever frozen in your morning paper. It can get claustrophobic, but forget about it and have a chicken sandwich. Punch up Sinatra on the jukebox and raise a toast to a joint that's so unfashionable, it's fashionable. Warren's sits smack on Market Square, where things old and legendary should.

WEST ALABAMA ICE HOUSE

1919 W. ALABAMA at Hazard
713-528-6874
MAP E7

For the uninitiated, icehouses are like open-air bars. Unique to the Lone Star State, they pock the Texas back roads like warts on a toad. They have long been a refuge for morning drinkers (who often marathon into the night) and often appear to have given birth to a litter of pickup trucks that — parked as they always are, nose in — seem to be nursing at a steady flow of bottled beer. That said, the West Alabama Ice House began as a back-road joint in 1927 when it sold great chunks of ice (and occasional intoxicants) to the denizens of small-town Houston. In its current incarnation, located just a couple blocks from the Menil Collection, it squats still in its original form with pickups nosed in and unshaven Methuselahs milling around. Everybody comes here — bikers, students, professionals, soccer moms — and dogs and kids come along. Unless you're already here, it is difficult to understand what the draw is. There is no AC, the only place to sit is at a picnic table outside or on one of the few stools inside, no food to speak of (except hot dogs on Friday, and burgers and tacos on Saturday) and beer, beer, beer.

People of every description gather at the West Alabama Ice House to chill out with a cold beer, music (live or jukebox) and conversation.

SPIRITED HOUSTON

(Someone once wrote a haiku dedicated to the icehouse — the poem repeated the word "beer" 17 times.) You can play horseshoes under shade trees while sucking down a dozen or so longnecks. Many generations of Houstonians have stopped by to grab a cold one here — many of them at 9 a.m. when the icehouse opens.

THE WINE BUCKET BOUTIQUE & BAR

2311 W. ALABAMA
at Revere
713-942-WINE
www.thewinebucket.com
MAP E7

Giving credit where it is most gratefully due, Junico Velarde and his wife Tracy started the wine bar/wine store trend in Houston. Formerly the GM of the Grotto on Woodway (now gone), Junico had the warm woods and wicker demure setting ready to go in 2001, and those who first discovered the spot quickly got the word out that something deliciously original had entered the local bar scene. Cool and intimate, this lovely, low-lighted interior is the setting for choosing from 50 wines offered by the glass or bottle. Happy hour here is called "the grape hour," and it happens from 4 to 6 p.m. Monday through Thursday when reds are $6, whites $5. There are weekly themed tastings, and special events such as the Champagne and popcorn affair ($25 per) and an all-day Valentine's celebration. The adjacent shop is a Disneyland for wine aficionados — silver ice buckets, stem charms, Riedel glassware, wine openers, books, wine racks and such. Uncomplicated wine bites add flavor to the sipping. Background jazz and outdoor seating.

ZIMM'S MARTINI & WINE BAR

4321 MONTROSE
near Richmond
713-521-2002
MAP E7

Far from the madding meat markets, strangers do not hit on strangers at Zimm's. Rather they pat the bartender on the back for making a perfect (yet pricey) martini. It can get crowded late at night, but voices mostly chat in low register and we haven't heard of any bodice-ripped young things dancing on tables. Mostly it's a place for reserving one of the leather-couched and wingback-chaired conversation circles. Or strolling into the dark, semi-private back room for a romantic, yet wholly proper, interlude with your date. It's a class act that draws in folks who have plenty of money for a bar-night splurge. The wine list urgently needs updating, but they do warm the brandy snifter. Weekend DJ, no food, valet parking, street parking or parking behind the bar. Monday through Thursday 4 p.m. to 1 a.m., Friday and Saturday 4 p.m. to 2 a.m.

my table
HOUSTON'S DINING MAGAZINE

  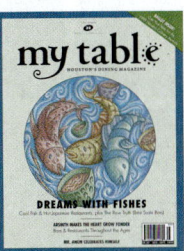 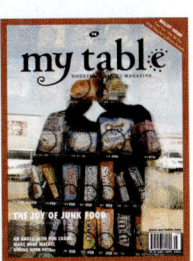

READ WELL

·

EAT WELL

  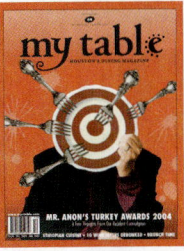 

·

LIVE WELL

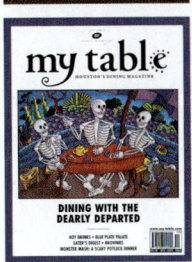   

Subscribe today!
www.my-table.com

restaurants & cafes

If you've used this book in chronological order, then you've already shopped for food and had a few snacks (section one, *Local Flavors*) and stopped off for drinks (*Spirited Houston*). Only now, in the third and final section, *Restaurants & Cafes*, do we approach meal time. Houston's restaurant scene is ready for its close-up.

So just how lively is the local restaurant scene?

The office where this book was edited is in an older neighborhood inside Loop 610. Five minutes from here is first-rate French, Vietnamese, pan-Latin American, Thai, Belgian, Spanish, Cuban, Chinese, Jewish deli, Moroccan, Japanese, Mexican, Italian, Greek, English pub food, "rustic European" and American of every variety, including barbecue, Gulf Coast seafood, burgers, health food, soul food and big-ticket steaks.

Such variety has become commonplace in Houston. There's a sushi restaurant in practically every neighborhood, a recipe for an ethnic-spiced chicken dish in every pot, a Monopoly board of clustered restaurants seen from every freeway.

All of this great food wouldn't mean much if people didn't support their local restaurants, and we do. Houstonians like to point to research >>

collected by the editors of the *Zagat Surveys** as evidence of our love for dining out: Year after year, we have been first among the nation's cities for eating out most often. And not to toot our own horn, but how many cities support a paid-circulation restaurant magazine such as *My Table: Houston's Dining Magazine*, now in its 15th year of publication?

We have included a few national chain restaurants in this chapter, but mostly we did not. You will certainly find those places by yourself. Instead, we want to guide you to Houston's best independent restaurants and locally grown chains, funky holes in the wall and ever variable ethnic treasures. We take particular delight in directing you to a hallmark of Houston dining — the casual fine-dining spots, where you will eat exquisite food and dressing up is not required.

As you will notice, this guidebook does not score restaurants. We think the simplified shorthand of scoring actually shortchanges restaurant-goers. Restaurants do not operate in an clinical vacuum. How can you pin a numeric or letter grade on an enterprise that changes a little with every breakfast, lunch and dinner? What we've tried to do is give you a summary of our experiences. Our listings are not long — you can read most in about 20 seconds — and if a place is included in the book you may assume there are reasons we find it worthy, even if a few blemishes give character to the overall quality.

So please be seated, tuck a napkin under your collar, pick up a fork, and get ready to dig in.

---

* *According to the 2008 Zagat Survey, Houstonians dine out more often than do residents of any other major American city.*

*17

The Alden Hotel is home to one of the most beautiful modern dining rooms in Houston, with red brocade walls, white wingback dining chairs and glimmering chandeliers, the perfect backdrop for an elegant meal. The departure of executive chef Ryan Pera — he went to The Grove — leaves the traditional American cuisine in the hands of talented newcomer Wes Morton, former executive sous chef at Navio in the Ritz-Carlton Half Moon Bay. Morton has tweaked the menu and focuses on bringing in fresh ingredients from local markets, but favorites like the black truffle macaroni and cheese, seared foie gras with roast pineapple and coriander, and braised wagyu short rib remain. Dinner entrees start at $24, yet the three-course lunch and brunch menus are a great value at $17.

1117 PRAIRIE at San Jacinto, in the Alden Hotel
832-200-8888
www.17food.com
MAP F6

*What's black and white and red all over? The interior of *17.*

59 DINER

3801 FARNHAM between S. Shepherd and Greenbriar, and other locations
713-523-2333
www.59diner.com
MAP E7

A blast from the past that doesn't take itself too seriously, this spot boasts good roadside food and a culinary trip down memory lane. It's also filled with icons from the Eisenhower years and the early days of rock 'n' roll. Plastic booths (including a couple of big Hollywood-style booths), an old-fashioned soda fountain and daily blue-plate specials make it a smart choice for kids, too. You'll find good hamburgers and fries, as well as breakfast. For a Mexican-style breakfast, try the migas — three eggs scrambled with creamy cheese, chopped onions, bell pepper and jalapeños and tortilla strips, served with warm tortillas. At lunch, order a chocolate shake ("rich enough to be your landlord"), cheddar fries and the chicken-fried steak. Any surprise that the motto here is "Eat Heavy"? Open 24 hours.

100% TAQUITO

Set incongruously in a long, homogenized strip center across the freeway from Lakewood Church, this quirky spot is a fun, colorful, fast-casual concept serving Mexican street food. It's like walking up to a taco truck at

3245 SOUTHWEST FWY. west of Buffalo Speedway
713-665-2900
www.100taquito.com
MAP D7

a construction site or the Airline Farmers' Market, except it's in air-conditioned comfort and there are no flies. All menu items are served à la carte, and the size of the tacos is smaller than you'd expect for the price. Still, 100% Taquito fans — and we count ourselves among them — rave about the *sopes*, tortas, *tacos al pastor* and the *tacos de tinga* (tacos with spiced brisket), plus *aguas frescas*. If you see a green VW in the middle of the restaurant, you know you're in the right spot.

A MOVEABLE FEAST

It's a good name, for this health-food restaurant and store really has moved around a bit since its debut in 1971. The current (and, seemingly, permanent) location near Memorial High School is a great spot for people-

Recommended
GREAT ARCHITECTURE

Here are five local restaurants and a bar that are worth visiting for the buildings that house them.

ARTISTA, *800 Bagby, 713-278-4782.* On the second floor of the airy Hobby Center for the Performing Arts, designed by Robert A. M. Stern and opened in 2002, this Cordúa-operated restaurant showcases the modern grandeur of the Houston skyline with extensive use of glass and vaulted ceilings. Stunning food and view.

CAVA BISTRO, *301 Main, 713-223-4068.* This narrow three-story 1889 building with a prominent corner turret, vaulted ceiling and dramatic arched windows on the second and third floors was designed by Houston's most exuberant Victorian-era architect, George Dickey. Serving upscale bistro food, it is a captivating spot near a downtown light-rail stop.

KRAFTSMEN BAKING, *4100 Montrose, 713-524-3737,* and **BLACK LABRADOR**, *713-529-1199.* This small shopping center, designed by Ray Bailey Architects in the late 1980s, is a wonderfully pleasant urban space near the Museum District and University of St. Thomas. It's a rare example of intelligent reuse.

LA CARAFE, *813 Congress, 713-229-9399.* One of the three oldest buildings downtown, the narrow, two-story structure was built as the Kennedy Bakery Building in 1861. It retains much of its original detail, which creates a funky/charming atmosphere at this longtime bar.

LA COLOMBE D'OR, *3410 Montrose, 713-524-7999.* This bold early 1920s structure was once the home of Walter Fondren, a founder of Humble Oil, and works well as an intimate restaurant and hotel. It's a reminder of the time when Montrose Boulevard was millionaires' row.

> **9341 KATY FWY.**
> at Echo Lane
> **713-365-0368**
> www.amoveablefeast.com
> **MAP** C6

watching while dining inside or outside on light sandwiches and fruit smoothies. No longer strictly vegetarian, but still healthful and fresh tasting, fare varies from Tex-Mex to hummus to Southern-inspired cornbread and beans. The spinach, mushroom and tofu quesadillas are tasty, and the vegetarian burgers are famous among the no-meat crowds (burgers with beef and grilled chicken are also available). Wine by the glass is a mere $.99 and beers are $1.50. The large health food store in which the restaurant is located offers vitamins and supplements, tea, coffee, books and aromatherapy. Both cafe and store are closed on Sunday.

ADDISABA

What's an adventurous eater to do now that Thai and Indian cuisine have become mainstream? For a unique culinary experience, make the trek to southwest Houston for Ethiopian food from Addisaba. The setting is bleak, near Sharpstown Center, but the people are friendly and sometimes there is live East African music. In lieu of utensils, the dishes (which might be compared to stir-fries or hearty stews) are eaten with hands or with the spongy, slightly sour bread called *injera*. Part of the menu is vegetarian (try the *yemissir wot*, a spicy red lentil stew), but lamb and beef dishes are a specialty. *Kitfo* is basically Ethiopian steak tartare: top quality raw meat, finely minced, flavored with spiced butter. Addisaba offers it either raw or cooked. Be brave and go for the raw. If you're unsure about what to try, there are several combination plates for sampling different dishes. Also be sure and try the Ethiopian honey wine — it makes a nice digestif. Dishes are cooked to order, so don't come in a hurry.

> **7668 DE MOSS**, east of Fondren between Clarewood and Bellaire Blvd.
> **713-995-0333**
> **MAP** C7

ALADDIN

At the happening intersection of Westheimer and Montrose, this place looks kind of dorky from the street, but it's warm and inviting inside. Cafeteria-style service gives way to huge portions and lots of Lebanese food. We love the fresh fruit juice and the fresh-baked pita bread. Shawarma, kabobs, gyros, all manner of dips and salads (tabouli, lentil, cucumber, etc.) and dolmades are well

> **912 WESTHEIMER** at Montrose
> **713-942-2321**
> www.aladdinhouston.com
> **MAP** E6

prepared and priced very reasonably. The lunch buffet is a big hit, but we also like the idea of reserving the cozy little room off to the side for a dinner with friends. The owner (related, no surprise, to the Fadi restaurant folks) is very friendly and will construct pretty much any combination of foods you like. There's off-street parking in the back.

3055 SAGE at Hidalgo
713-622-2778
www.alexanderthegreatgreek.com
MAP D7

ALEXANDER THE GREAT GREEK

This comfortable spot started under the watchful eye of proprietor John Gioldasis and has since passed into the capable hands of Voula Kouluriotu. Meals begin with feta cheese and olives in a puddle of good olive oil and end with sludgy Greek coffee. Service is especially fine: As in Europe, our waiter knew precisely what we should order. We listened, and he was right. Also as in Europe, the pace might be slower, but there will plenty to enjoy in exchange for patience. Try the mixed appetizer plate to share and mixed seafood lightly sautéed in garlic, wine and butter. This is not the most beautiful restaurant in Houston — it's awfully blue for our taste — but the Greek food has been (if you'll pardon the Emerilism) kicked up a notch. The chef stirs, bakes and grills new interest into the same old Greek dishes, managing to make them taste almost like a voyage of discovery. Entertainment at night includes George Kitidis on the mandolin-like Greek bouzouki and the popular belly dancers.

AMAZON GRILL

Restaurateur extraordinaire Michael Cordúa (of Américas, Churrascos and Artista fame) has taken his pan-Latin cuisine and gone fast-casual with Amazon Grill. The self-service cafe boasts good chicken and fish dishes as well as deliciously flaky empanadas, puffy tacos, ceviche, enchiladas and the popular ta-kit-o kit. All guests can nosh on the plantain chips and chimichurri sauce, a Cordúa restaurant staple, and entrees come with a house salad. For dessert, choose the locally famous *tres leches* cake or, our

5114 KIRBY between Westpark and Bissonnet
713-522-5888
www.cordua.com
MAP E7

9600 WESTHEIMER at Gessner
713-933-0980
MAP C7

favorite, the s'mores that you prepare yourself with a tiny hibachi. Lush plants and exotic touches don't completely mask the hollow feel of the room, magnified by the inevitable noise of a family-friendly atmosphere. (This is a very popular family-dining choice and often crowded.) To escape the din, find a seat on the patio or come at happy hour, when margaritas, mojitos and other Latin-themed drinks are a mere $2.

AMÉRICAS

1800 POST OAK BLVD. between San Felipe and Westheimer
713-961-1492
www.cordua.com
MAP D6

21 WATERWAY just off Six Pines Dr., The Woodlands
281-367-1492
MAP North of D1

The original Post Oak Boulevard location may be the most exotic-looking restaurant in the universe, with a stunning (if hallucinogenic) pre-Columbian impressionistic design by architect Jordan Mozer. Alas, as we go to press, that entire shopping center is coming down. However, Mozer has been hired to design the replacement Américas just a hundred yards away. As for the food, chef/owner/impresario Michael Cordúa has coupled the Old and New Worlds in a kitchen that uses indigenous New World foods, prepared and presented in both traditional and experimental ways. The menu was originally built on Cordúa's signature churrasco — a flavorful grilled beef tenderloin with chimichurri sauce — plus other meats, such as the roasted pork filet mignon with corn tamalito, grilled shrimp and crabmeat and the chicken breast crusted with plantain and chontaleno cheese over black bean sauce. With the May 2008 opening of The Woodlands version of Américas, everything has been cranked up even higher. That location, with a design by Studio Gaia, is sleek and modern, but still tells the story of the Américas with visuals that suggest the European lust for gold or the virgin rain forest. Even the sail-draped waterside terrace suggests a Spanish galleon. For the new restaurant, Cordúa has hired his son David Cordúa, chef Jonathan Jones and dessert chef Plinio Sandalio. The three young men have gone where no Houston restaurant has previously gone — e.g. ahi tuna brûlée (a kind of ceviche), softshell crawfish taquito, slow-cooked Berkshire pork "ribpops" and crisp roasted wild salmon with grilled romaine. The atmosphere at both locations is lively, so quiet conversation is difficult. A true crossroads.

AMERIGO'S GRILLE

Casey and Nancy Kosh's classic Italian-accented steakhouse put The Woodlands on the culinary map. The Northern Italian cuisine served up by executive chef Arturo Osorio since 1994 commands a fervent

25250 GROGANS PARK off Sawdust, The Woodlands
281-362-0808
www.amerigos.com
MAP North of D1

Amerigo's put The Woodlands on the local culinary map.

following, including some regulars who drive from Memorial for the near-perfect entrees like angel hair-crusted red snapper, linguini with lobster and shrimp, New York strip steak, veal scaloppini, even occasional wild game. The elegant dining room is a much-needed break from the chain restaurants prevalent in the area.

Wine Spectator named Amerigo's "One of the Best Wine Lists in the World" in 2007, although the by-the-glass selection is not as wide as some in Houston. Thursday through Sunday, head upstairs to the second-floor piano bar for cocktails and live music.

AMICI

16089 CITY WALK at Plaza Dr., Sugar Land
281-242-2800
www.amicitownsquare.com
MAP A9

The latest branch of the Vallone empire is from Tony Vallone's son Jeff Vallone and long-time Tony's restaurant chef Bruce McMillian. The duo have created (on Sugar Land's Town Square) an upscale yet informal restaurant that echoes back to the 1990s heydays of the original Grotto. McMillian cooks expressive Neapolitan-inspired fare that is true to its roots while indulging in some modern Gulf Coast expectations. Dishes range from handmade ricotta dumplings with prosciutto and broccoli rabe, grilled calamari that is stuffed with spinach and bread crumbs, a chilled seafood medley tossed with lemon and olive oil, to lasagna and chicken parmesan. Among the robust entrees is a long-time Vallone favorite, the tender pan-fried pork loin finished with roasted capers, olive oil and lemon. The dining room is large, noisy and fun, and there's a patio as well. As at all Vallone restaurants, good people watching.

ANDREA RISTORANTE ITALIANO

Chef Andrea Pintus, a native of Sardinia, has been cooking in Houston for the past 20 years, most notably 13 years at Patrenella's. His business partner, Luigi Campioni, recently arrived from Europe with a background in restaurant management. Together they've created a new (early 2008) little Italian outpost on far-west Westheimer. Choose from among sautéed clams, *insalata di tonno e*

12513-A WESTHEIMER at Dairy Ashford
281-496-9443
www.andrearistorante.com
MAP A7

Personal Favorites
WHERE I GO FOR JEWISH FOOD
By Ted Powers

Houston's cultural melting pot has everything. It's no surprise then that in this city once best known for its barbecue, Tex-Mex and fried shrimp, Jewish cuisine thrives. Here are eight places I like. Some are kosher, some not, as indicated.

CAFE AT THE J, *5601 S. Braeswood, 713-729-3200.* Located in the Jewish Community Center, Cafe at the J serves gefilte fish, matzoh ball soup, Israeli salads, falafel, *borekas* (stuffed pastries), corned beef and pastrami sandwiches. Try what I call the kosher Reuben — grilled pastrami and sauerkraut on rye. Great coffee bar. *Kosher*

KENNY AND ZIGGY'S, *2327 Post Oak Blvd., 713-871-8883.* The best New York Jewish-style deli restaurant in town, with a full line of smoked fish, triple-smoked pastrami, age-cured corned beef and featuring Hungarian goulash, stuffed cabbage, Romanian tenderloin steak, matzoh ball soup and knishes. *Not kosher*

MADRAS PAVILION, *3910 Kirby, 713-521-2617.* Vegetarian Indian restaurant with cuisine from as many as six different regions of India. *Dosas* — light and low-calorie crêpes made from rice and lentils — are a must. *Kosher*

NEW YORK BAGEL & COFFEE SHOP, *9720 Hillcroft, 713-723-5879.* Like a typical New York luncheonette, this is the place to meet lots of people from the community and eat chicken soup with huge matzoh balls, chopped liver, a large variety of smoked fish, blintzes, eggs and onions, potato latkes and fresh bagels. *Not kosher*

SABA'S, *9704 Fondren, 713-270-7222.* Salads, sandwiches, entrees such as lasagna, eggplant parmesan and baked ziti, Greek and Israeli salads, falafel and *borekas*. Also regular, deep dish and stuffed-crust vegetarian pizza. *Kosher*

SUPER PITA, *9806 Hillcroft, 713-723-6400.* A neighborhood pita bakery, owned and operated by a third-generation baker serving regular and whole wheat pita, some topped with *zahtar* (sesame, sumac, thyme), stuffed pitas filled with potatoes, mushrooms and spinach, challah and cakes. *Kosher*

SUZIE'S GRILL, *5925 S. Braeswood, 713-729-5741.* Suzie's serves falafel platters with Israeli salad, *borekas*, chicken and beef kabobs, shawarma, soups, Persian stews such as *khoresh*, salads and dips. Dill rice and dried cherry rice are not to be missed. *Kosher*

THREE BROTHERS BAKERY, *4036 S. Braeswood, 713-666-2551.* A Houston institution and tradition. If all you purchase are bagels, challah and some danish, you would not believe what you are missing. Every day it produces pumpernickel, baguettes, po'boy rolls, wedding cakes and lots more. *Kosher*

Ted Powers is food editor for the Jewish Herald-Voice *(celebrating its 100th anniversary). Go to www.jhvonline.com for his weekly column, restaurant articles and recipes.*

fagioli (tuna and white bean salad), gnocchi in gorgonzola sauce blushed with a hint of tomato, some 19 distinct pastas, risotto or grilled meat or fish. Daily specials — we liked hand-made manicotti stuffed with sautéed spinach and cheese, covered in homemade tomato sauce — keep things interesting. Andrea serves wine and beer, and the menu offers many suggestions for pairing wine with the kitchen's output. Closed Monday.

ANTICA OSTERIA

2311 BISSONNET near Greenbriar
713-521-1155
www.anticarestaurant.com
MAP E7

Antica Osteria is an utterly comfortable Italian restaurant for Baby Boomers. The food is not bold or fabulous or even particularly memorable, but the whole package is easy to like and very appealing. The former bookstore has been revamped as a candlelit — it's open for dinner only — and cozy venue with dining areas that ramble throughout the old house. Is it a good place for a romantic dinner for two? Yes! It's from Velio DePlano (previously with Trattoria Da Velio) and Ray Memari, and gives consistently solicitous service, partly evidenced in that they will readily serve half-portions of the pasta entrees for an appetizer, or *primo*. The menu is much more Italian than Italian-American — a couple of the highlights are the braised lamb shank and sautéed chicken breast with prosciutto in wine sauce. There are always a few nightly specials that are likely to entice, plus classics like spaghetti alla carbonara, veal Milanese and eggplant parmesan. The wine list is not extensive, but there are many well-priced bottles. Don't leave without the fresh-made cannoli for dessert.

AQUARIUM RESTAURANT

410 BAGBY at Memorial
713-223-3474
www.aquariumrestaurants.com
MAP F6

Any veteran Houston diner can rattle off a dozen seafood establishments that have better food than the Downtown Aquarium. At none of those places, however, will they try to guess your weight for an extra couple of bucks — and award you a plastic fish if they fail. Granted, many patrons would gladly pay *not* to have their avoirdupois evaluated (or mentioned at all), no matter how enticing the prize. But these are probably not Downtown Aquarium kind of people. Such people are equally unmoved, no doubt, by hearing that they are mere minutes — seconds, if they step sprightly — from leaving their table and climbing aboard a miniature train headed on a Shark Voyage, pausing within a tunnel where the creatures swirl in a see-through tank above them. And no amount of oohing and aahing about the beckoning Ferris wheel will melt the cold hearts of the anti-Aquarium elitist. On the other hand, your grandkids and Aunt Mimi from Des Moines will probably love this place. More than $38 million was spent by Tilman Fertitta's Landry's Restaurants, Inc. to redevelop two city-owned downtown structures into a six-acre theme park that includes a public aquarium, seafood restaurant, ballroom, casual cafe, lounge, midway, Ferris wheel, train and carousel. The Aquarium Restaurant offers a variety of seafood dishes, including coconut shrimp, grilled mahi-mahi, crab salad and fried calamari, as well as steak, pasta, salads and enormous desserts at prices that admittedly outpace the quality of food. There is, after all, no question that Aquarium is as much about total sensory gratification as it is about putting seafood into your mouth. But this impressive Disney-esque restaurant — stunning architecture, a well-stocked 150,000-gallon aquarium right in the dining room — is definitely a scene.

Kids love Aquarium's massive fish tanks as a colorful backdrop for dining.

ARCODORO RISTORANTE ITALIANO

5000 WESTHEIMER
at Post Oak Blvd.
713-621-6888
www.arcodoro.com
MAP D6

This sophisticated restaurant is striking and stylish, matching its well-attired crowd who seem to have aspirations for the Costa Smeralda. Owned by Efisio and Lori Farris (who also have Arcodoro & Pomodoro restaurant in Dallas), Arcodoro emphasizes grilled meat and seafood, simply prepared. The cuisine is mostly from the long-neglected Italian outpost of Sardinia, which will be novel to most diners. (For a primer, see Efisio's 2007 cookbook, *Sweet Myrtle and Bitter Honey: The Mediterranean Flavors of Sardinia*.) Excellent dishes such as *sa fregula* (a type of couscous with clams in saffron) and *gnochetti Sardi al cinghiale* (Sardinian-style dumplings with a *ragù* of wild boar) aren't readily found anywhere in this country. Classic Italian dishes fill out the rest of the menu, which features freshly made pastas, beautiful fish flown in from the Mediterranean and a wood-burning oven for turning out unique pizzas, chicken and an excellent steak. Located just underneath Morton's of Chicago, this is a pretty setting — all earthy tones of gold, brown and russet — although it can be very noisy. On a fine day, choose to sit outside under one of the umbrellas. Arcodoro is a must for anyone who enjoys Italian food and it's one of the top Italian restaurants in the area.

ARMANDOS

> **2630 WESTHEIMER** at Kirby
> **713-520-1738**
> www.armandoshouston.com
> **MAP** E6
>
> **2234 E. NASA RD. 1**
> east of El Camino Real
> **281-291-8828**
> **MAP** Southeast of I9

Given the flashy crowd that eats here, the Mexican food is surprisingly plain. Start with a margarita: powerful, clean and not too sweet. Then move on to the mostly straightforward, confidently commonplace presentation of the usual suspects — enchiladas, fajitas, tacos, nachos, flautas and quesadillas. The original Armandos was a notable fixture on Houston's culinary landscape back in the 1980s with the eponymous owner Armando Palacios serving up "River Oaks Tex-Mex," as it was described affectionately by some and dismissively by others. His establishment, first located on S. Shepherd then later on Westheimer, seemed to occupy a sweet spot between upscale and down-home, where bracing margaritas and a vaguely exclusive atmosphere allowed *gabacho* patrons to convince themselves the bland enchiladas were *mucho excellent-o*. Since its 2007 reopening in these plush Westheimer digs (the previous location of River Oaks Grill) after a seven-year hiatus, Armandos has begun to cultivate a younger and trendier crowd. (Example: A new late-night menu is meant to bring in the club-goers after midnight.) There's even a sign on the side of the building now. The current edition of Armandos has dark pumpkin walls and big mirrors, formal linen-set tables and gracious wait people. Our advice: Keep your focus narrowed (on tacos al carbon, *nopales* salad, guacamole and margaritas are all recommended), let the service coddle you and revel in the snug, lush Mexico City-style setting. The Clear Lake edition opened in 2008.

ARTISTA

Set in the Hobby Center, Artista distills everything Michael Cordúa (Américas, Churrascos) has learned about restaurants, then makes a blind leap of faith in downtown Houston. The

> **800 BAGBY** between Rusk and Walker, in the Hobby Center
> **713-278-4782**
> www.cordua.com
> **MAP** F6

menu is limited and less Latin than his other restaurants; it's more about, simply, how Houston likes to eat now. One of the interesting aspects of the menu is that diners choose their protein, then mix-match it up with vegetable, starch and a sauce. (Of course, if you prefer, you can let the chef choose for you.) Located on the second floor lobby of the Hobby Center for the Performing Arts, Artista is a visual stunner. Its most outstanding feature is a lofty wall of glass that frames the Houston skyline to the northeast — and from that height, conveniently focuses one's downtown view on sky and graceful architecture rather than road-blocks and traffic snarls. Seating is comfortable and the giant windows show off a truly spectacular view of downtown, only topped by the panorama offered by the patio. Service at lunch can sometimes be iffy, but before a theater performance the staff is skilled at timing your dinner so you don't miss the curtain.

1180-1 UPTOWN PARK BLVD. north of Post Oak Blvd.

713-621-1180

www.arturosuptown.com

MAP D6

ARTURO'S UPTOWN ITALIANO

An elegant yet comfortable addition to Uptown, Arturo's on a pretty day really does seem like a slice of Tuscany, with the stately porch perfect for a languorous afternoon and gold-hued walls inside. The service is superb and while the menu does not break new ground, it features classic Italian cuisine nicely prepared. The ravioli stuffed with chicken and mushrooms and topped with white wine sauce and jumbo lump crabmeat is not to be missed; other standouts include the veal scaloppini, tuna tartare, yellow bell pepper soup, bowtie margherita pasta and apple tart. A good wine list is made better by knowledge-able waiters who offer spot-on suggestions. Don't be surprised if chef/owner Arturo Boada or co-owner Bill Sadler stop by your table.

Take a seat on Arturo's patio and dine al fresco.

ASHLAND HOUSE

> **7611 WESTVIEW**
> east of Wirt
> **713-682-7611**
> www.ashlandhouse.us
> **MAP** D5

Once actually on Ashland Street in The Heights, this ladies' lunch spot moved to the Spring Branch area in 1996 to a little ranch-style bungalow remarkable for the two trees growing up through the middle of it. The food is rather dreary luncheon fare, salads and sandwiches, but it seems to charm a certain older clientele. The apricot iced tea is a refreshing touch.

AU PETIT PARIS

> **2048 COLQUITT** at S. Shepherd
> **713-524-7070**
> www.aupetitparisrestaurant.com
> **MAP** E7

Since opening in November 2007, this tiny dinner-only bistro set in a bungalow has had Montrose/River Oaks foodies abuzz. Its homemade ambiance might remind you of the now defunct Chez Georges on lower Westheimer: burnished dark woodwork and hardwood floors in an intimate dining room, lace curtains on the windows, the walls butter-yellow above and claret-red below plastered with blurry Impressionistic cityscapes, shiny copper pots and colorful posters advertising absinthe and other things oh-so-French. But the out-of-the-gate menu is ambitious and expensive (entrees start at $23 and go up into the $30s). We very much enjoyed the food here, including traditional onion soup, a salad topped with poached egg and bacon, duck confit and "salad" of crabmeat with white beans. You might also try frogs' legs, oxtails with wild mushrooms and sautéed scallops. The restaurant is the co-creation of chef/owners Eric Legros and Dominique Bocquier. The menu is pure French, but things are not always quite what you expect, due, probably, to a language gap.

AURA

> **3340 FM 1092**
> between Cartwright and Hwy. 6, Missouri City
> **281-403-2872**
> www.aura-restaurant.com
> **MAP** B9

Frédéric Perrier, who used to have Cafe Perrier on Mid Lane and was the opening chef at Ruggles Grille 5115, and his wife Michelle aim their current effort at the local neighborhood, Township Square Mall of Missouri City. The idea, Perrier explained, is to offer a cherry-picked selection of dishes from all of his past restaurants. These include bouillabaisse, *filet au poivre* and other bistro standards, as well as American dishes with a French twist: buffalo sliders with foie gras and a to-die-for "surf and turf" composed of grilled scallops that are split and topped with

RECIPE **CREOLE BARBECUE SHRIMP**

Pesce, 3029 Kirby, 713-522-4858

This is Pesce chef Mark Holley's take on an old Creole favorite that marries his experience cooking at Commander's Palace (New Orleans) and Brennan's (Houston) with other cooking styles that have influenced him through the years. It's a delicious appetizer that also makes a great entree.

For each serving:
2 slices garlic bread (optional)
1 Tbsp. vegetable oil
5 shrimp (36-42 count), head-on, peeled to tail and deveined
1 Tbsp. finely chopped garlic
1 tsp. Creole seasoning
⅓ cup Creole Barbecue Sauce (below)
½ lemon
1 Tbsp. white wine
1 sprig fresh rosemary
1 Tbsp. heavy cream
1 Tbsp. cold unsalted butter

METHOD: Toast bread in a 350-degree oven. In sauté pain, heat oil over medium heat until very hot, but not smoking. Add shrimp and sauté for 30 seconds. Add garlic and Creole seasoning and sauté another 15 seconds or until shrimp are three-fourths cooked. Do not burn garlic! Deglaze with white wine. Add Creole Barbecue Sauce, squeeze in juice from lemon and drop lemon half in pan. Add rosemary and heavy cream; reduce sauce by half or until slightly thickened. Remove toasted bread from oven and place on a warm plate. Spoon shrimp in center leaving sauce in the pan. Return sauce to stove over low heat and whisk in cold butter until melted and sauce is creamy. Pour sauce over shrimp. Garnish with lemon and rosemary. Serves 1.

Creole Barbecue Sauce
2 Tbsp. vegetable oil
½ cup yellow onion, small dice
¼ cup garlic, minced
1 cup shrimp shells
3 lemons, peeled and quartered
3 Tbsp. fresh ground black pepper
2 Tbsp. Creole seasoning
1 cup Worcestershire sauce
3 cups shrimp stock
½ cup heavy cream

METHOD: Heat oil in medium saucepan over medium heat. Add onion and cook, stirring occasionally for 2 to 3 minutes. Add garlic and sauté. Add shrimp shells and cook for 4 to 5 minutes. Add lemons, pepper, Creole seasoning, Worcestershire, shrimp stock, cream and bring to a simmer. Lower heat and cook on low simmer until sauce has reduced by one-third, or about 2 cups. Strain sauce through fine mesh. Makes approximately 2 cups.

braised short ribs. Save room for dessert: The crème brûlée, profiteroles and baked-to-order apple tart are not to be missed. The wine list is great and affordable, too, with bottles starting at $19, and the cafe setting is pleasant. Our only issue was with the service, which seemed hit or miss.

AVALON DRUG CO. & DINER

2417 WESTHEIMER just east of Kirby
713-527-8900
www.avalondiner.com
MAP E6

12810 SOUTHWEST FWY. in The Fountains, Stafford
281-240-0213
MAP B9

The Westheimer location is a circa-1950 drugstore lunch counter Houston classic. (This is not its original location, however; it's moved a bit since 1938.) Poached eggs and grits, fluffy pancakes, pecan waffles and a tart greeting from the ageless waitresses who man the counter have made this River Oaks institution a long-time favorite among the city's movers and shakers, many of whom grew up at the Avalon Drug and today use it as a second office. It's an old-fashioned small-town spot — the real McCoy — so be prepared to get up and pour your own coffee during the noon-hour soaps. Speaking of noon: Many swear the hamburgers here are the best in town. We wouldn't go that far, but they are darn good, and the made-to-order milkshakes are fabulous. (The fries here are awful, however.) For what it's worth, Avalon was named one of the nation's top 10 diners by the Roadfood.com folks. The Stafford location is a spin-off, a diner without the history.

AZUMA/AZUMI

Stunning interior design (paper lanterns, heavy wooden beams, bamboo chairs) vies with a creative menu that goes from teapot seafood soup (served in a child-sized teapot with a tiny cup) to the robata-

5600 KIRBY at Nottingham, and other locations
713-432-9649
www.azumajapanese.com
MAP E7

cooked skewers to hot-rock cooking at the table. These offerings aside, the focus of the menu is still firmly on the sushi, prepared well and culled from high-quality ingredients. It's owned by brothers Yun and Hubert Cheng, who also have the new Soma on Washington Avenue. One of *My Table*'s reviewers thought Azuma had the best sushi he's had in Houston — "I even liked their giant clam, generally not one of my favorite dishes." We've heard complaints from others about Azuma's service, but never experienced anything less than eager-to-please professionalism. The fact that the restaurants are often completely packed — it's a popular date place — may sometimes overwhelm the staff.

BABA YEGA

2607 GRANT at Missouri, east of Montrose
713-522-0042
www.babayega.com
MAP E6

Perched on a quiet street off of Montrose, this cozy house-turned-restaurant is a wonderful, quirky hideaway for enjoying a menu that has a healthful bent. The sandwiches and salads are all good: The veggie burger, for example, comes piled with all the avocado, sprouts and cheese you could possibly want. The back patio, adjacent to fragrant gardens and a decorative pond, is a terrific spot for lingering over brunch on a sunny day. Inside, it's a rabbit warren of little rooms stuffed with vintage stuff. The clientele is eclectic — well, so is the staff, for that matter — ranging from business suits to performance artists. So sit back and watch the parade of folks that is Houston. The expansion into the adjoining property takes away some of the inn-like charm, but we doubt it will impair your enjoyment at this Montrose classic. The brunch buffet often includes poached salmon, omelets, waffles, chicken and veggies, all very light on sauce and oil. A vegetarian-friendly restaurant, obviously.

BACKSTREET CAFE

Tracy Vaught's long-popular restaurant — it celebrates 25 years in 2008 — seems to have become a bistro organically, if not completely by accident. Chef Hugo Ortega's menu is filled with items like jalapeño fettuccine, shrimp cheesecake, shellfish risotto, red corn chicken enchiladas and pecan-crusted chicken, plus crabcakes and meatloaf. It's hardly French, to be sure. But by serving creative and well-made takes on upmarket local comfort food, coupled with Sean Beck's expansive and intelligent wine list, all in a setting that includes one of the city's nicest al fresco settings, Backstreet Cafe *is* a classic Houston bistro, one of our favorites. Ease into Saturday or Sunday brunch with a bloody Mary on the plant-edged brick patio with the splashing fountain, located just across from Tila's, on the cusp of River Oaks. We'll have the bacon-wrapped shrimp over mashed potatoes and spinach, please.

1103 S. SHEPHERD between W. Dallas and W. Gray
713-521-2239
www.backstreetcafe.net
MAP E6

Recommended
BRUNCH

Sunday brunch is the meal when we tuck into delicate comestibles most of us would never eat any other day of the week: huge stacks of pancakes squishy with maple syrup. Hollandaise sauce by the boatload. Pork and eggs in myriad combinations. Brunch even has its own drink menu — mimosas, milk punch, bloody Marys. Yes, bring on Sunday brunch!

ARCODORO RISTORANTE ITALIANO, *5000 Westheimer, 713-621-6888.* A fashionable Euro/Persian princess/Latin crowd gathers for brunch at Arcodoro, including many overworked folks from the Med Center enjoying a meal out. This is more about unhurried family get-togethers than roll-out-of-bed-in-running-suits fueling. The Sardinian menu includes salads, egg dishes (try *uova al pomodoro*, two eggs cooked in a wood-burning oven, covered with a fresh tomato sauce and pecorino), pastas, meat and seafood.

BACKSTREET CAFE, *1103 S. Shepherd, 713-521-2239.* Backstreet has long been famous for its brunch, served 11 a.m. to 3 p.m., due in equal parts to the pleasant patio and chef Hugo Ortega's (the same who co-owns Hugo's) well-grounded American menu (e.g. ribeye and eggs, crabcakes and eggs, brioche French toast). Brunch is relaxed and fun, drawing a diverse crowd, including families, couples of all ages, gay and straight diners, small parties and large. The Bob Chadwick Trio begins playing at noon.

BRENNNAN'S OF HOUSTON, *3300 Smith, 713-522-9711.* Is there a Houston brunch-lover alive who is unaware of the Texas-Creole fare served at this *Vieux Carré*-style restaurant? Or of the charming patio? Classic eye-openers like Sazerac and milk punch? Hollandaise-glazed eggs Sardou, smothered beef *grillades* and grits, and bananas Foster? This is the mother of all jazz brunches, and you must indulge yourself at least once.

HUGO'S, *1602 Westheimer, 713-524-7744.* Tracy Vaught and Hugo Ortega offer Sunday brunch 11 a.m. to 3 p.m., and it's a great way to sample the menu. Brunch offerings include *cochinita pibil* (pork cooked in banana leaves), ceviche, *chilaquiles* topped with a fried egg, tamales, *costillas de res en salsa verde* (beef short ribs in green sauce) and an egg station.

KIM SON, *12750 Southwest Fwy. at The Fountains Center, Stafford, 281-242-3500, and 10603 Bellaire Blvd., 281-598-1777.* Some would argue that Kim Son serves the best dim sum in Houston, and this is a marvelous way to kick off a Saturday or Sunday. All the steamed dumplings, buns and lotus-leaf bundles are here, as well as wide and flat *fun* noodles, *congee* (rice porridge) and the pan-fried and deep-fried dumplings. An exotic end-of-week treat.

LE MISTRAL, *1420 Eldridge, 832-379-8322.* French food doesn't have to be expensive, and this reasonably priced spot that has recently been rebuilt is French to the *coeur*. Try the *oeufs Florentine* (poached eggs with sautéed spinach, garlic and béchamel sauce), quiche Lorraine, tarragon-scented chicken pot pie or a *croque monsieur/madame*. Desserts and brunch drinks round out the menu, which is served on Sundays 11 a.m. to 3 p.m.

QUATTRO, *1300 Lamar, in the Four Seasons Hotel*, 713-276-4700. The formula here is simple: Combine one part 55-foot appetizer buffet (e.g. oysters and crab claws, fresh shrimp, blinis and caviar, breakfast pastries), one part choose-an-entree (try the eggs Benedict or cinnamon-scented sweet brunch risotto) and one part chocolate dessert bar. Mix with a pitcher of bellinis or bloody Marys. Consume. Grin ear-to-ear. Offered Sundays 10:30 a.m. to 2:30 pm.

RAINBOW LODGE, *2011 Ella Blvd., 713-861-8666*. Pretty in its new location, this bayou-side hideaway offers one of the city's most glorious settings for brunch. Just walking into the cozy lodge foyer will make you shiver with anticipation. A recent visit yielded housemade breakfast sausages, an open-faced omelet strewn with grilled vegetables, thick juicy pork chops and, yes, even pancakes. A stiff bloody Mary will smooth out Sunday morning kinks.

RAVEN GRILL, *1916 Bissonnet, 713-521-2027*. The quiche changes every week, but you might also like the brunch migas served with black beans and green chili cheese grits, Southwest enchiladas topped with a fried egg or eggs Benedict topped with ancho Hollandaise. Be sure to order one of the excellent bloody Marys. Casual ambiance suits the West University neighborhood, and there's a slouchy patio blooming with fresh herbs and flowers. The restaurant's pet chicken might be there too. Brunch served 10:30 a.m. to 3 p.m.

RIO RANCH, *9999 Westheimer, in the Westchase Hilton*, 713-952-5000. Comfortable and handsome ranch-house setting and an appealing buffet (with omelet and waffle stations) make this a top-notch brunching spot on the west side of town. We've long been a fan of the limestone-and-cedar interior, but it's the food — fresh fruit, smoky breakfast meats, cheesy potatoes, hot cinnamon buns and ethereal pancakes — that made us semi-regulars.

SHADE, *250 W. 19th, 713-863-7500*. Claire Smith (*My Table* magazine's 2004 Restaurateur of the Year) offers the much-lauded Shade waffle with eggs, apple-smoked bacon and berries. The menu is always evolving, but we recently liked a composed salad of chicken, Stilton and green apple; a fried green tomato and bacon sandwich; a Mediterranean sampler plate; and a grilled sirloin steak sandwich on sourdough with watercress and grilled red onions.

TILA'S RESTAURANTE & BAR, *1111 S. Shepherd, 713-522-7654*. Early risers will appreciate that Tila's begins serving Sunday brunch at 10 a.m. (through 3 p.m.). There are American brunch items such as French toast and eggs Benedict, as well as many savory Mexican dishes, including huevos rancheros, *chilaquiles*, roll-your-own breakfast tacos and great Mexican cocoa.

BAMBOO HOUSE

540 WAUGH between Allen Parkway and W. Dallas
713-522-3442
www.bamboo-house.org
MAP E6

Stephanie Chow's pan-Asian fusion menu may give you pause here: How can one kitchen produce such disparate foods and do them all so well? What we've found is that everything here is just a little bit better than at almost any other Asian restaurant we can name. The dumpling wrappers are thinner and tenderer, the vegetables fresher, the meat better quality, the presentations more carefully planned. Standouts include the teriyaki ribeye, crab dumplings, Singapore noodles and Thai curry chicken. There's also tempura, even sushi. If there's a criticism to be made, it's that the kitchen runs slightly to the sweet side.

BARBECUE INN

116 W. CROSSTIMBERS west of N. Main
713-695-8112
MAP E5

Despite its name, this is the spot to come for great chicken-fried steak with cream gravy, fried chicken or fried seafood, particularly the fried shrimp. Frying is good! The barbecue is nothing to sniff at, either; the brisket especially is wonderfully tender. Good family dining, with excellent pies, all served in a comfortable dining room that looks like it hasn't been updated since the place opened in the 1960s. Judging by the lines that go out the door, it doesn't seem like anyone minds.

BARNABY'S CAFE

604 FAIRVIEW between Taft and Montrose, and other locations
713-522-0106
www.barnabyscafe.com
MAP E6

This funky quartet of modern diners has a large and loyal following for its California-tinged comfort food. Healthful options abound, from enormous salads to vegetarian-friendly entrees, including the best spinach lasagna in town. For meat lovers there are also baby back ribs, the popular Doctor Gale's meatloaf, grilled turkey burgers and chicken burritos made with whole-wheat tortillas. Each location is open for brunch on certain days, but only Baby Barnaby's, next door to the original Fairview location, offers it up every day. The menu is once again simple and full of the classics: Eggs, buttermilk or fruit pancakes, French toast, waffles and a breakfast burrito comprise most of the main offerings. The bacon is thick, crisp and excellent, and the fair trade and organic coffee is charmingly served in small individual pots. Simple food, fair prices, open setting, fun crowd — all that a neighborhood spot should be. One caveat: Depending on the location, parking is limited, so be prepared to walk a bit.

BB'S

2710 MONTROSE
just north of Westheimer
713-524-4499
www.thebetterbite.com
MAP E6

BB's is a Cajun outpost from a young guy named Brooks Bassler. The menu is mostly straightforward stuff — New Orleans-style po'boys, red beans and rice, boudin balls, grits and grillades, fried catfish and étouffée — and unexpectedly good. Po'boys are made using a wonderful loaf, and we enjoy both the roast beef and fried shrimp versions. Muddy thick gumbo also pleases. This ultra-casual spot is open to 4 a.m. Thursdays through Saturdays, and there's a small breakfast menu. The owner hopes to grow his little low-key Cajun concept and has plans to eventually open several locations around town.

BEAVER'S ICE HOUSE

2310 DECATUR south of Washington
713-864-2328
www.beavershouston.com
MAP E6

First of all, Beaver's Ice House is *not* an "ice house" by any traditional measure of the term. What ice house, we ask, lists a $118 Hanzell Chardonnay on its wine list? What ice house has a wine list? So let's appreciate that the name is ironic and have some fun here. This Washington Avenue-area restaurant fired up the grill in late 2007 and has been sending out great chunks of smoky brisket, North Carolina-style pulled pork, fabulous Jolie Vue Farms' sausage and pork ribs since. This we like. The restaurant (whose name, no surprise, has launched a thousand jokes) is from Monica Pope of T'afia, but it's run by chef/GM Dax McAnear and sous-chef Gabe Godell. As you might expect, the menu is a smart, fun read. We like the spicy-sweet Asian-style "Jon-Jon noodles," "Old School" potato salad and the meats, particularly that sausage. The setting is casual, like a noisy roadhouse, and there's a wonderfully deep and well-chosen beer list that is worth a visit in and of itself.

BECKS PRIME

2902 KIRBY between W. Alabama and Westheimer, and other locations
713-524-7085
www.becksprime.com
MAP E6

This homegrown chain of upscale burger-and-dog shacks is best loved for its thick mesquite-grilled hamburgers, grilled ahi tuna sandwiches and homemade strawberry milkshakes. But there's more than that, too, including stuffed baked potatoes, chili and various salads. "Hot Plates" include outrageous concoctions such as The Kitchen Sink (grilled chuck patties, sautéed onions, bacon, Swiss cheese, guacamole, lettuce and tomatoes). Recently the management has been taking the menu even more upscale, adding grilled T-bone steaks served with baked potatoes and Caesar salad. In fact, we've noticed it's now "Becks Prime Restaurants," no longer "Becks Prime Drive-Thru." At four of the eight locations you can drive through, however. But it's better to laze on the deck at one of the picnic tables. Most of the locations are well sited, snuggled under fine old trees — the Augusta location is said to be shaded by the largest and oldest live oak in Houston — or, in the case of the Memorial Park location, overlooking a golf course. Park your car and stay awhile.

BENJY'S

2424 DUNSTAN
at Kelvin
713-522-7602
www.benjys.com
MAP E7

The setting of this Rice Village restaurant is lean, with kind of a Los Angeles art gallery look that is both hip and retro. Teeny tulip-shaped lights are suspended from single black wires from the black grid ceiling, and framed photographs line the wall. In the back, the kitchen is semi-open. The spare design makes a great backdrop for the food and clientele, who are mostly young, with great hair, dressed in black. The menu features a flavorful Modern American cuisine that plays the familiar against the exotic: pizza with sushi-grade tuna, brie and portobello crêpes, tea-smoked duck breast, crisp Asian-influenced salads. On weekends, brunch's crunchy French toast is topped with cool fruit and berries. Presentation is very architectural and carefully arranged, often vertically. The upstairs Lounge at Benjy's offers a see-and-be-seen scene for Houston, with pretty young things perched on couches and outdoors on the patio. Happy hour is popular, with appetizers and premium drinks all going for $6.

BERRYHILL BAJA GRILL

This tiny, white-collar taqueria (the original location) hits just the right note between kitsch and offhand sophistication. The decor consists of photos of Mexican beaches, a wonderfully hideous Elvis painting

2639 REVERE just off Westheimer, and other locations
713-526-8080
www.berryhilltamales.com
MAP E6

and a roll of paper towels on each table. As good as the namesake tamales are, the linchpin of the entire operation — and what everyone comes here for — is the fish tacos. Sweet, farm-raised catfish fillets are lightly

Recommended
CHEAP & GREASY BURGERS

As perilous as it sounds, cheap and greasy is just the way we like our burgers when the mood strikes. Here are a handful of dives without frills or pretentious price tags that do the old-fashioned burger right.

BELLAIRE BROILER BURGER, *5216 Bellaire Blvd., 713-668-8171.* This mom-and-pop burger joint is the classic greasy spoon for flame-broiled burgers with a true smoky flavor. Bellaire regulars don't seem to mind that the interior remains trapped in the 1960s and the cramped room can fill with grill smoke. The Deluxe Burger is crowned with chili, cheese and onions. Note: It's worth the trip alone for the rich, real milkshakes.

BUBBA'S TEXAS BURGER SHACK, *5230 Westpark, 713-661-1622.* At venerable Bubba's, it feels like you are on some old Texas farm market road in the middle of nowhere. Ironically, you are in a shack under the freeway not too far from The Galleria. The moist burgers are not huge, but they ooze with grease and the meat is high quality. Expect such surprises as buffalo burgers, jalapeño potato salad, fancy chips and designer sodas, plus a cast of characters for people-watching.

CHRISTIAN'S TAILGATE GRILL & BAR, *7340 Washington, 713-864-9744, and 2000 Bagby, 713-527-0261.* The never-frozen, freshly ground meaty burgers and the tanned, caramelized-sweet O-rings at these two icehouses are among the city's finest. Diehards swear the original on Washington (once called Christian's Totem) tops the newer Midtown location. Regardless, they are both male magnets for ice-cold beer in frosty mugs and two-fisted burgers with a side of sports TV.

LANKFORD GROCERY & MARKET, *88 Dennis, 713-522-9555.* This rumpled, circa-1940s retro market where Montrose meets Midtown is the Holy Grail for some burger lovers. Lankford handles the all-American burger with unwavering detail, starting with choice ground beef and a deft griddling technique for a moist and meaty charred masterpiece. Expect a right-on ratio of fixings slapped between sweet toasted buns. No credit cards. Yep, it's that old-fashioned.

PETE'S FINE MEATS, *5509 Richmond, 713-782-3470.* What could be finer than a freshly ground beef burger from a meat market? This family-owned sleeper serves an amazingly beefy charred burger (a steal at $3.29) stacked with fresh crisp fixings on a toasted sesame bun slathered with mayo and mustard. The bacon double cheeseburger is the bomb, especially washed down with an old-style root beer. Take some high-quality meats (e.g. ribs, steaks, sausage) home from the case to grill.

SOMEBURGER, *745 E. 11th, 713-862-0019.* Fast, hot retro-burgers are yours for under three bucks at one of the few true hamburger "stands" left in Houston. Heights regulars walk up to the window to order, then grab a picnic table under the tree out back or take it packing. We love the buttery griddled buns and homestyle sliced fixings, but carnivores should look elsewhere for big beef.

battered and fried, tucked into two corn tortillas, heaped with cilantro and the thinnest red cabbage threads and drizzled with a sweet-hot sauce. Additionally, don't miss the shrimp and avocado salad punched up with horseradish-spiked remoulade. On weekends Berryhill has been taken over by the young crowds of Houston's rapacious brunch scene for breakfast tacos and margaritas, especially at the Montrose location, the only Berryhill to serve the yummy frozen bellini.

BE-WICHED BISTRO

1844 WESTHEIMER
just east of Hazard
713-520-5300
www.bewichedbistro.com
MAP E6

Just opened in December 2007, this tiny spot is adjacent to The Cookie Jar and directly across the street from Lanier Middle School's athletic field. With its small size, copper-topped bar and urban vibe, Be-Wiched is the closest thing Houston has, looks-wise, to a modern Parisian bistro. Walking in, you half expect to see a chalkboard advertising the *prix fixe* options. Fortunately, it doesn't need one: The reasonably priced menu includes European-inspired salads, pizzas, panini and quiche, and we are especially partial to the pumpkin lobster bisque with fresh crab crostini. Have it with a half sandwich or small salad — a match-up that makes this an amazing dining bargain. Its sibling, the popular bakery The Cookie Jar, is next door, so if you've no time for dessert, grab a cupcake for the road on your way out.

BICE

5175 WESTHEIMER
at Sage, in The Galleria
713-627-2423
www.bicehouston.com
MAP D6

If Antica Osteria is the comfortable neighborhood Italian restaurant, here's a model from the other side. Located in The Galleria, it's strictly a destination restaurant, and there's nothing comfy or cozy about it. This is the Giorgio Armani of local restaurants — crisp, expansive, confident, understated. The food — Northern Italian pastas, risotto, grilled hunks of meat — is ambitious, occasionally even splendid. Sophisticated service. Portions are small, prices are high. It's part of an international chain.

BISTRO CALAIS

Comfortably located in a 125-year-old Texas cottage overlooking manicured gardens and a glass conservatory on a quiet street just off Westheimer, Bistro Calais churns out enjoyable, straightforward French bistro-inspired fare at good prices. The menu has morphed from its traditional narrow French focus into one with a wider range of influences

2811 BAMMEL LANE off Westheimer near Kirby
713-529-1314
www.bistrocalais.com
MAP E6

today. It offers oven-roasted quail with mustard pan sauce, braised rabbit salad, mussels and steak frites, yes, but also seafood gumbo, smoked salmon, fish and chips, seafood pasta marinara and several dishes with avocado, mango or pineapple. The capable cooking is complemented by a wine list that is all French and Californian. Live music on Wednesdays (see the website for music schedule). Great Sunday brunch, too.

BISTRO DON CAMILLO

Georges and Monique Guy opened this spot in January 2008, then almost immediately sold it to son Jean-Philippe Guy, who also owns Bistro Provence out on Memorial. The menu will remind you of Bistro Provence, with the addition of a few Italian items, such as gnocchi, ravioli and cannelloni Niçoise. ("I love pasta," explains Jean-Philippe.) The hybrid makes sense, as so much of the cooking along the French-Italian Riviera coast shares ingredients and technique. A meal here begins with a hunk of the ladder-shaped bread and herbed olive oil. There are brochettes, duck leg confit, rabbit stew and steak frites. Pâtés are among the starters, and the duck mousse, duck and pork rillettes, tapenade, etc., can also be vacuum-packed to take home. We're especially fond of the pizza from the wood-burning oven.

6510 DEL MONTE just off S. Voss
713-782-3011
www.bistrodoncamillo.com
MAP C6

BISTRO LANCASTER

Now under the culinary direction of chef Jamie Zelko — voted the "Up-and-Coming Chef of the Year" for the 2007 Houston Culinary Awards — this charming Theater District restaurant is finally regaining some of its past glory. So perfectly convenient to the Alley Theatre, Jones Hall and the Wortham, it's worth a visit to try the seared blue crabcakes, osso buco, wild mushroom risotto or the tangy citrus Caesar with ahi tuna, or finish up the evening here with a nightcap. For breakfast or

701 TEXAS at Louisiana, in the Lancaster Hotel
713-228-9500
www.thelancaster.com
MAP E6

The Lancaster's intimate English-style bistro is handy for pre- or post-theater dining.

brunch, choose the eggs Lancaster, two poached eggs on English muffins with ham, avocado and hollandaise. Service kinks are still being ironed out, but when everything is working Bistro Lancaster is sexy and fun.

BISTRO LE CEP

11112 WESTHEIMER
near Wilcrest
713-783-3985
www.bistrolecep.com
MAP B7

This French-accented offshoot of Joe Mannke's much-admired Rotisserie for Beef & Bird (now closed) is a homespun number, quite different from its grand progenitor. The prices are moderate, and the interior is understated with rustic pine furnishings and cozy, if often loud. Here you can enjoy such time-tested and rich dishes as *pâté de canard, poisson meunière, coq au vin,* pot-roasted rabbit, steak au poivre, pan-roasted calf liver with apples, onions and bacon, plus *tarte tatin* and strawberries Romanoff. The wine list is moderately priced, with most bottles priced below $50, as well as a remarkable 30-plus selections by the glass that are served in generous 8-ounce pours. Bistro Le Cep also serves Sunday brunch. The menu lists traditional breakfast foods, such as eggs Benedict, French toast, etc., but we were more interested in selections like liver and onions, grilled pork chop with creamed garlic potatoes and red cabbage and the oddly appealing chopped sirloin steak topped with gorgonzola.

BISTRO PROVENCE

Old-fashioned homey meals start with *fougasse* (a crusty twist of warm Provençal bread) and olive oil, then proceed to such resolutely old-time bistro dishes as *confit de lapin* (rabbit confit with prunes), pig's feet in

13616 MEMORIAL
between Wilcrest and Kirkwood
713-827-8008
www.bistroprovence.us
MAP B6

white wine, mustard, garlic and parsley sauce, chops and steaks, grilled sausages and *boeuf cocotte* (beef stew with black olives). In a culinary world where "fusion" is the point of so many menus, it's refreshing to find a kitchen unaffected by foreign influences. There's no "slight Asian accent." Maybe a nod to the prevailing Latin influence? No. A few Southwestern touches in a sauce? Nope. Ah, the glories of traditionalism! There are more than a few places in Houston that call themselves bistros. Most are too fancy and too expensive for the description. This is a bistro. In any other Houston restaurant, customers would whine about the chairs and tables being too close together. Here, it feels exactly right. And even though people hover around the front door waiting for a table — the crowd often spills outside, where folks sometimes lean on the parked cars — the manager seems able to move everybody along with a minimum of discontent. You may like the house's homemade pâté, a lusty salade Niçoise or the traditional *soupe au pistou* from Provence. This location was a pizzeria in another life, so the Guy family made good use of the wood-burning oven. They offer four pizzas, including a favorite seafood version. The simple, understated dining room, with an open kitchen, wood-beamed ceiling and a few French advertisements on the walls, is casual and inviting, although with the tables packed tightly it can get loud. There's a cheery blue and yellow color scheme (the colors of Provence) with a pervasive feeling of fraternity: You are among people who share your very good taste in classic food.

> **5510 MORNINGSIDE**
> near University Blvd., and other locations
> **713-526-5551**
> **MAP** E7

BLACK WALNUT CAFE

Though the ordering set-up and menu layout are both a bit goofy, the three Black Walnut Cafes provide well-made food. That's the bottom line. And, as it happens, some of the more irritating features of the menu (e.g. silly punctuation, schizo fonts and prices taken out to four decimal points) are being phased out as we edit this book in mid-2008. Apparently the attention such features got from users was not the kind that the management had hoped for. So what should you eat here? There's breakfast (omelets, quiche, kolaches, steak and eggs, breakfast quesadilla and breakfast burrito), as well as lunch and dinner. For the latter, choose from entree salads (e.g. hot bacon and spinach, fried chicken tender salad, blackened salmon Caesar), sandwiches, pot roast, fried chicken, noodle dishes, flat-bread pizzas and more. The menu goes on and on and may be one of the most diverse in town. If you can't find something you want to eat here, you're not hungry.

BLUE FISH HOUSE

This small sushi bar and pan-Asian restaurant, which recently had some renovations, is next door to the Hobbit Cafe. They're both in a little offbeat retail development behind a messy hedge. The sushi at Blue Fish is excellent and fresh, and we've never had a problem with service (despite the suggestion that we might, given the signs that state misunderstood orders cannot be returned). The menu is larded with

> **2241 RICHMOND**
> between Greenbriar and Kirby
> **713-529-3100**
> www.bluefishhouse.com
> **MAP** E7

RECIPE **TEXAS VENISON CHICKEN-FRIED STEAK**

Ouisie's Table, 3939 San Felipe, 713-528-2264

"In one of our weekly food meetings, we got into a discussion about chicken-fried steak and its origin," says Elouise "Ouisie" Adams Jones of this signature dish. "We agreed the Germans who immigrated to Texas in the mid- to late-1800s had a great influence on how steaks, particularly tough ones, were prepared. After all, the dish was guaranteed to be tender after being pounded and quickly fried (like wiener schnitzel). I'm sure the cooks and trail bosses running cattle on long, hot and dusty, or cold and wet, trails in the wilderness of Texas were pleased when one of the group bagged a deer and found it to be the best chicken-fried steak around."

12 venison backstrap pieces (three per person),
    sliced ¼-inch to ⅓-inch thick
salt and pepper
1 cup all-purpose flour
3 eggs, lightly beaten
1 cup milk
1 cup heavy cream
2 cups panko (Japanese breadcrumbs),*
    seasoned to taste with salt and pepper
1 Tbsp. finely chopped fresh parsley
1 tsp. finely chopped fresh thyme
equal parts grapeseed or canola oil, and butter

Panko is available at most grocery stores.

METHOD: Lightly salt and pepper meat and pound out meat with heel of hand or wooden mallet. Combine flour with ½ tsp. each salt and pepper in large bowl. In separate bowl, combine eggs, milk and cream. In third bowl, combine and mix panko, parsley and thyme. Dip slices of venison in flour, coating both sides; shake off excess and dip into egg mixture. Dip into seasoned panko, coating sides and pressing into meat. In large iron skillet, heat equal amounts of grapeseed or olive oil and butter (just enough to cover bottom) until very hot, about 350 degrees. Fry pieces three at a time (do not crowd) until golden brown, turning once. Be careful not to overcook or venison will get tough. Ouisie's Table serves this with gravy on the side, a mess of greens, wild rice risotto with butternut squash and mushrooms and corn pudding. Cream biscuits round out the meal, with a slice of lemon pie waiting in the wings. Serves 4.

witticisms (e.g. Thai Me Up, Thai Me Down is a salad and Dumb and Dumpling is an order of vegetable dumplings), which are probably funnier after a sake bomb or two. We like the fusion cooking that lets us pick a protein, then pick a sauce, such as Thai red curry or spicy basil sauce.

BOMBAY BRASSERIE

2414 UNIVERSITY BLVD. #214 at Morningside (upstairs)
713-355-2000
www.thebombaybrasserie.com
MAP E7

3005 W. LOOP SOUTH
north of Richmond
713-622-2005
MAP D7

In a pleasant white-tablecloth atmosphere, Bombay Brasserie serves up memorable Northern Indian cuisine. The lunch buffet, offered daily, puts other buffets to shame with an expansive rotating menu of 19 dishes that always includes well-prepared classics like tandoori chicken, saag paneer and chicken tikka masala. They have also introduced *tava* (also spelled *tawah*) cooking to Houston, a technique for seasoning and grilling vegetables and chicken, said to be used in five-star hotels in India. The naan is fluffy and soft, the spices are plentiful but not too heavy, and the service, though stiff, is attentive and prompt. This spot is a can't-miss for Indian food-lovers and novices alike.

BRASSIERE MAX & JULIE

4315 MONTROSE
south of Richmond
713-524-0070
www.caferabelais.com
MAP E7

Laurence and Chris Paul, owners of Cafe Rabelais, created this white linen- and lace curtain-bedecked restaurant serving hearty French favorites on a pleasant stretch of lower Montrose, and it's just what the neighborhoo needed. It's the old Aries location, jazzed up with a new Art Deco entrance but keeping that same great treetop balcony upstairs. The cooking is hearty and not terribly dissimilar from its sibling, but it adds some traditional brasserie favorites such as chilled shellfish platters and *choucroute*, that Alsatian sauerkraut favorite. Chef Jeff Boudreaux's menu seemed heavy when the restaurant first opened in August 2007, but in winter it was exactly right. Other menu possibilities: sautéed sweetbreads, bone-in ribeye, foie gras, steak tartare and frites, and *cassoulet Toulousain*. And delivering the check in a beer glass is a nice tip of the hat to brasseries' beginnings as breweries. By the way, owner Chris Paul, who is a well-informed oenophile, offers an extensive French wine list, including many by-the-glass selections and Champagne splits.

BREAKFAST KLUB

> **3711 TRAVIS** at Alabama
> **713-528-8561**
> www.thebreakfastklub.com
> **MAP** E6

Despite its name, the Breakfast Klub is open not just for breakfast, but also lunch. The kitchen, however, tends to mix the two meals in an unfamiliar but cool way: A popular order is for fried chicken wings and waffles, as is catfish and grits. The setting is informal — form a line to order, and your food will be brought to the table — and it's always entertaining to talk with the strangers who converge here. Sometimes the line is out the door, though it seems to move quickly. But we do suggest you go earlier rather than later, especially on

Recommended
MEXICAN BREAKFASTS

In this city you can have a Mexican breakfast any time, any day. But there's something special about digging into a Saturday-morning plate of migas or *chilaquiles* that simply starts the weekend off on the right note. Here are five spots we're devoted to.

GOODE CO. TAQUERIA, *4902 Kirby, 713-520-9153.* Jim Goode's version of a Houston taqueria creates hefty masterpieces with eggs, potatoes, beans and tortillas, turning these into Tex-Mex combinations such as eggs scrambled with a choice of bacon, chorizo or *nopalitos,* plus laudable versions of migas, huevos rancheros, *huevos a la mexicana* and even a Mexican omelet.

GORDITAS AGUASCALIENTES, *6102 Bissonnet, 713-541-4560, and other locations.* The breakfast menu here is similar to most local taquerias, but the food seems more carefully prepared. Glorious refried beans and *chilaquiles* are topped with crumbles of white cheese, and the potatoes are cubed and perfectly fried. Try the fresh-squeezed juices, *aguas frescas, licuados, atole* and hot chocolate.

JARRO CAFE, *1521 Gessner, 713-827-0373.* Beatles posters (instead of kitschy knick-knacks) are on the wall, and the breakfasts and unique salsas also break with Tex-Mex tradition. Try the *chilaquiles* topped with a thin beef steak and a couple of fried eggs or a breakfast taco stuffed with pieces of omelet.

MARIA SELMA, *1617 Richmond, 713-528-4920.* The artful Mexican breakfasts are accompanied with fresh thick corn or flour tortillas. *Aguas frescas* in a half-dozen different flavors are offered, all made at the restaurant.

TEOTIHUACAN, *1511 Airline, 713-426-4420, and other locations.* The familiar Tex-Mex breakfasts are always enjoyable and a terrific value. Great salsas, delicious hot tortillas and recommended vegetable omelet.

Saturday. Owners and staff are friendly, and the restaurant has a warm vibe — it's like being in the kitchen of a favorite aunt. Other menu stalwarts include the Green Eggs & Ham (the eggs are green with spinach, peppers and chives), biscuits and gravy, salads and sandwiches. There are also daily specials, such as red beans and rice with hot water cornbread on Mondays. See the website for the regular line-up. Closes at 2 p.m. Closed Sunday.

3300 SMITH at Stuart
713-522-9711
www.brennanshouston.com
MAP E6

BRENNAN'S OF HOUSTON

The Texas-accented neo-Creole menu here just keeps getting better and more appealing, with game, seafood and poultry all putting in an appearance. The menu's longtime classics, brought over from New Orleans, are still here, including turtle soup, oysters Rockefeller, gumbo ya-ya and chili-fried oysters. Plus chef Randy Evans has introduced dozens of new variations on traditional ingredients, such as shrimp with "biscuits and gravy" and flatiron steak. The *vieux carré* patio, with massive live oaks, splashing fountain and graceful plantings, may be the most charming spot for lunch or brunch in the entire South. The kitchen is utterly reliable, and a glassed-in kitchen table puts one lucky sextet of diners square in the middle of the culinary action each evening. From the moment you step out of your car at the valet stand until you tuck a praline in your pocket when exiting two hours later, you will find the service here as cordial and polished as it comes. There's a devotion to good manners drenched in old-style Southern graciousness that is forged with a brisk Houston downtown edge. It's exactly right. Want a lasting memento of your meal here? Buy a copy of chef Randy Evans' cookbook, *The Kitchen Table*.

BRENNER'S

A few years ago Tilman Fertitta and his Landry's Restaurants Inc. reopened Brenner's, the long-time Westside steakhouse that had closed in 2002 after more than 65 years in business. More than $1 million was spent refurbishing the building, which had begun to look pretty awful. The redo brought this beloved steakhouse back to life, and for that we're thankful. Besides its prime beef, Brenner's was known for

10911 KATY FWY.
between Brittmoore and Wilcrest
713-465-2901
www.brennerssteakhouse.com
MAP B6

1 BIRDSALL just off Memorial
713-868-4444
www.brennersonthebayou.com
MAP E6

German-style potatoes and wonderful blue cheese dressing, both of which are still on the menu. Landry's also expanded the garden and added a gazebo for special events and weddings. "Having eaten at the old Brenner's and observed its sad decline," wrote our *My Table* reviewer, "I thoroughly enjoyed my recent visits to this transformed, upbeat, yet untrendy dining room." In 2007, Landry's rescued another landmark location: the old Rainbow Lodge, which was pushed out of its longtime home on Birdsall at Buffalo Bayou by the landlord. Landry's took over the soon-vacant location and opened Brenner's on the Bayou, hardly missing a beat.

Classic steakhouse dishes are the bill of fare at Brenner's.

BRIO TUSCAN GRILL

1201 LAKE WOODLANDS DR., in The Woodlands Mall, The Woodlands
281-465-8993
www.brioitalian.com
MAP North of D1

This Columbus, Ohio-based chain operates three of its Brio concepts in Texas, and just this one in the greater Houston area. Americanized Tuscan fare — e.g. grilled steaks and lamb chops, house-made pasta dishes, flatbreads — round out a menu that also includes slightly more specialized items, such as "chicken under the brick," mushroom ravioli with brown butter and lobster risotto. Weekend brunch —pancakes, crêpes and frittatas — is a welcome addition to the area. Hearty diners might like the "Bistecca & Sweet Potato Hash." Very pretty dining room, but Brio is even more attractive for the outdoor dining area. The restaurant is child friendly, and on some early evenings the munchkins tend to get a bit rambunctious.

BROWN BAG DELI

This Houston-grown chain of sandwich shops is from the same people who have Barnaby's, so they understand casual dining and busy working folks' need to get in and out quickly. The way it works is meant to expedite the sandwich-ordering process: Pick up a

2036 WESTHEIMER, just east of S. Shepherd, and other locations
713-807-9191
www.thebrownbagdeli.net
MAP E6

brown bag that is printed with all the various choices of breads, meats, cheeses and condiments. Check off the way you want your sandwich built, add your name and pay. The people behind the counter now have your instructions and build your sandwich to suit. Simple, eh? Makes it easy, too, on the executive assistant who has to pick up lunch for the office and then distribute the sandwiches. Choices are basic and predictable — roast turkey, roast beef, honey-baked ham, egg salad, pimiento cheese, etc. — and the sandwiches are perfectly fresh and straightforward. There is also a limited menu of sides (e.g. Zapps chips, cole slaw, potato salad), plus desserts. Open 11 a.m. to 6 p.m Monday through Saturday.

THE BROWNSTONE

2736 VIRGINIA off Westheimer near Kirby
713-520-5666
www.brownstone-houston.com
MAP E6

The most overstuffed dining room in this part of town boasts a rococo collection of antiques and chandeliers, altogether a setting that will go right to your head. The menu could not be more classic — châteaubriand, beef carpaccio, herb-crusted salmon, rack of lamb — but the kitchen doesn't always pull it all off. The service and atmosphere (harp music, anyone?) are perfect for a long, languorous dinner, if your food expectations are not terribly high. For a small group (12 would be a crowd), reserve the tiny wine room: low-ceilinged, lit by candles and lined with wine racks, it feels like another world, another century. In fact, this restaurant seems like a special-events spot with little interest in attracting a discerning dining-out crowd. It's more about being in a pretty place for a bridal shower or Easter Sunday brunch with the in-laws. And by the way, all the antiques are for sale.

THE BUFFALO GRILLE

3116 BISSONNET east of Buffalo Speedway
713-661-3663
www.thebuffalogrille.com
MAP D7

1301 S. VOSS between Woodway and San Felipe
713-784-3663
MAP C6

If you wake up craving an honest bacon-and-eggs breakfast, then Mac and Betty McAleer's diner/grill is the place to go. The pecan-smoked bacon is thick, crisp and just sweet enough to keep the smoky flavor from being bitter. And the eggs — well, you name it, they make it. Perhaps the most distinctive item on the breakfast menu is the cream cheese-and-green-onion omelet, but there is a whole list of Mexican egg dishes, too. The restaurant (the Bissonnet location is the original, open since 1984) is justly famous for its enormous pancakes. You have to wait on line to place your order, so arrive early, especially if you have children in tow. At lunch or dinner, the menu is a traditional Texas diner hybrid, with Tex-Mex dishes (e.g. *chile rellenos*, King Ranch spinach enchiladas) as well as burgers, fried catfish, chicken and dumplings and chicken-fried steak.

THE BURNING PEAR

16090 CITY WALK, in the Sugar Land Marriott, Sugar Land
281-275-5925
www.theburningpear.com
MAP A9

The Sugar Land Marriott Town Square and chef/restaurant consultant Grady Spears partnered a few years ago on this 184-seat hotel restaurant. The menu features regional cuisine from Southeast Texas, the Texas plains and Hill Country, the Gulf Coast and the Texas *frontera* with a modern twist. To wit: prickly pear-glazed boar ribs, fried green tomatoes, pan-seared redfish with shrimp Creole sauce and an award-winning smoked porterhouse pork chop. Other than a set of horns mounted prominently above the look-into kitchen, the interior decoration is relatively subdued and tasteful — no neon Lone Star flags, no cowhide tapestries, no Bob Wills blasting away on the PA system. Instead, it's white-linen tablecloths (redundantly covered with white butcher paper), banquettes, dark mahogany chairs with brocade backs and chic dim lighting. For groups there is a central wine room for private functions, plus a bar offering Spears' signature cocktails. The Sunday buffet brunch is popular, as is the new outdoor patio overlooking Town Square. By the way, that intriguing, slightly francophonic name, Burning Pear, refers to the practice of searing the spines off prickly pear cactus so that cattle can eat it.

CADILLAC BAR

1802 SHEPHERD
south of I-10
713-862-2020
www.cadillacbar.com
MAP E6

Some things, happily, never change. Despite new spiffed-up digs, at Cadillac Bar that list includes awesome margaritas and the noise of very happy dudes and dudettes reverberating off the walls. The Tex-Mex food is above average, with good mesquite-roasted pork carnitas, *pollo flameado*, bacon-wrapped stuffed shrimp and ceviche alongside the traditional offerings. The legendary "shooter girls" tequila shots make the Cadillac a hoot every time and a fun spot to take good-sport friends who can handle the sensory overload. Thankfully there are no more Magic Marker-isms on the wall — the Cadillac is more upscale these days. This Cadillac Bar, inspired by the Nuevo Laredo original, has spawned locations in Kemah and Dallas.

CAFE 101

9889 BELLAIRE BLVD.
just east of Beltway 8
713-272-8828
MAP B7

Prominently located off Bellaire in the new and ever expanding Chinatown, Cafe 101 welcomes customers with its bright neon lavender sign. A sharp divergence from the typical Chinatown restaurant, Cafe 101's innovative décor, mini-skirted waitresses and food presentation makes it a pioneer in bringing Taipei's trendy club atmosphere to Houston. The forte of 101 is its vast array of colorful and tasty drinks, ranging from sweet and dark teas to blended fruit smoothies and various bubble tea combinations. The light dishes have Korean, Japanese and Chinese/Taiwanese influences, and each dish comes with a medley of small sides dishes of the day. Seafood hotpots are popular, and Taiwanese-style shaved ice with a combination of fruit, jelly and bean mix-ins is a must-try dessert. With K-pop music blasting and colorful drinks and sushi dishes whizzing past the turquoise-lighted tables, Cafe 101 is a Chinatown experience worth a visit, especially if you're under 30.

CAFE ANNIE

1728 POST OAK BLVD. at San Felipe
713-840-1111
www.cafe-annie.com
MAP D6

We're not the first to observe that Cafe Annie *could* rest on its laurels from time to time, but almost never does. Food and service are always presented at full tilt. One of Houston's most highly rated restaurants is an elegant, high-ceilinged bistro with many unusual touches. The mahogany paneling, for example, was all cut from the same tree so that the grain forms a repeating pattern around the room, though your attention might be more drawn to the exuberant floral arrangements and dramatic artwork. James Beard Award–winning chef/co-owner Robert Del Grande's Southwestern menu is full of surprises, such as black-bean terrine (see recipe on page 236), pan-roasted branzino, "chicken fried" Gulf shrimp, sweet plantain tamales, Texas red fish in a banana leaf and slow-roasted suckling pig. The award-winning wine list has many fans, too. If money is no object, go here. Forget to make a reservation? For dinner Bar Annie, a cross between a club and a cafe set inside the restaurant, serves similar top-notch Southwestern fare in a more relaxed setting that's also easier on the pocketbook. As we go to press in mid-2008, a new Cafe Annie is being built just across the parking lot from this location. It's all part of an enormous development of the Post Oak at San Felipe intersection. (As noted previously, Américas is also getting a new building.)

CAFE BENEDICTE

15455 MEMORIAL
between Eldridge and Hwy. 6
281-558-6607
MAP B6

Sporting a type of menu that might come from cosmopolitan Marseille — or from an immigrant restaurateur who hails from there — Cafe Benedicte features broadly Mediterranean items bolstered by some American beef-hearty dishes to appeal to the burghers and globe-trotting energy industry workers of west Memorial. It appears right on the mark, as the dining room is usually packed during the lunch hours. In an airy and comfortable setting looking out onto a green belt, there are pastas, paella, couscous, entree-sized salads, grilled items such as tuna and swordfish, and more identifiably Greek, Spanish and North African dishes. Meals are prefaced with excellent breads, and a fine wine list makes the visit more enjoyable. Note: It's owned by the same couple who runs nearby Lynn's Steakhouse.

CAFE EXPRESS

1422 W. GRAY
west of Waugh, and other locations
713-522-3100
www.cafe-express.com
MAP E6

These high-tech yuppie delis with full bars and extensive patios are from the Schiller Del Grande Restaurant Group, the people who run Cafe Annie, The Grove and Taco Milagro. Adorable little pizzas, wholesome salads and photogenic sandwiches are specialties. Chicken salad with pistachios is a passion for many fans, and the desserts are divine. We are especially fond of the lavish condiment bar, called the "oasis table," where diners help themselves to salad toppings, dressings, grated cheese, olives, cornichons, sun-dried tomatoes, breadsticks and more. Just be careful not to over-order, as it's easy to get carried away. The chain, briefly owned by Wendy's before being bought back by the original owners, has already expanded to Dallas. Cafe Express was one of Houston's earliest "fast-casual" restaurants — order at the counter, take a beeper, pick up your food when ready — and it is still the gold standard.

CAFE EXTRAORDINAIRE

5120 WOODWAY
at Sage, in the Houston Decorative Center
713-622-4600
www.afehouston.com
MAP D6

Good food is synonymous with good design, believes Charles Cohen of Cohen Brothers Realty and owner of Houston's Decorative Center. A couple years ago he partnered with Mary Jo Caya, co-owner of caterer A Fare Extraordinaire, to open Cafe Extraordinaire in the atrium space of

Recommended
AL FRESCO DINING

Our fickle Houston weather may not be perfect all the time, but when it's good, it's great. So get outside! Here's our pick of prime alfresco dining. Be it a terrace overlooking the city, a handkerchief-sized garden or an enchanting flower-filled patio with a romantic fountain and grapevine trellises, you will have it made in the shade.

ARTISTA, *800 Bagby, 713-278-4782.* Owner Michael Cordúa is known for restaurants with dramatic, over-the-top ambience, and this downtowner on the second floor of the Hobby Center is no exception. The stylish terrace offers stunning views, making it a romantic stop pre- or post-theater for creative South American cuisine. Indoors, the black onyx bar is also a favorite for cocktail hour.

DAILY REVIEW CAFE, *3412 W. Lamar, 713-520-9217.* This pint-sized cafe has a bounteous, well-tended garden behind the tall fences. If you crave green grass, homegrown vegetable and herb gardens and a country-style wood-decked porch for lollygagging, this is your al fresco spot. Come for a leisurely brunch and chow on dishes you prefer not tackling at home, such as buttermilk biscuits and gravy, warm gingerbread with whipped cream, grilled salmon and eggs with hollandaise.

GRAPPINO DI NINO, *2817 W. Dallas, 713-528-7002.* Escape to Italy, for at least a few hours. Just order an Italian wine and the Italian cheese sampler with walnuts, honey and tall crunchy breadsticks. Then take in the beauty of blooming wisteria on the patio trellis and listen to the gurgling fountain, live music and the murmur of office dwellers who choose this relaxing spot to come out of their shells. There are heaters for cool evenings and endless other excuses to return again and again.

HUGO'S, *1600 Westheimer, 713-524-7744.* This patio tucked away on the west side of Hugo's is quite the find. The metal chairs aren't exactly luxurious, but the space is thoughtfully designed, with a gorgeous wall fountain paved in pretty Mexican tile, beautiful handcarved Mexican wooden doors securing both entrances and tall creamy adobe walls muffling the noise of bustling lower Westheimer. Order the sensational salmon tacos and a Hugorita. You'll notice it feels like Friday here.

MONARCH RESTAURANT, *5701 Main, 713-526-1991.* Hollywood glamour meets Museum District classic at this hot new (circa 2007) hotel restaurant. The terrace is everything it should be — and where *you* should be — on that clear fall day or balmy summer evening. The sophisticated space is roomy yet intimate, with shaded umbrellas and a bird's-eye view of Hermann Park and the surrounding museums.

OUISIE'S TABLE, *3939 San Felipe, 713-528-2264.* Lots of Houston cafes serve Southern food, but Elouise Adams Jones has created a comfort food shrine with clever twists on classics. Her meticulously landscaped Bear's Garden is delightfully private from San Felipe and boasts artsy water fountains, shaded cozy tables and neat rows of bamboo plants mixed with other native flora and fresh herbs. Kick back and stay a while; dessert is dynamite.

Houston Design Center that was once JAGS. It's sleek, open and stylish, and the similarly sophisticated menu changes with the seasons and might include a chilied shrimp wrap with avocado and jicama, smoked salmon pizza with goat cheese, pickled onions and arugula, and salmon over fresh spinach with habañero and red onion jam, as well as a selection of daily specials. Open for lunch only Monday through Friday. Note: The shops at the Houston Decorative Center are open to the trade only, but Cafe Extraordinaire is open to the public.

CAFE LE JADEITE

1952 W. GRAY at Driscoll
713-528-4288
www.cafelejadeite.biz
MAP E6

Qin Dynasty on Buffalo Speedway spawned a second concept a couple of years ago, likewise from owner Randy Chow, and this is a stunner. The maximalist dining room is broken up into cozy niches, with a soaring ceiling, dramatic glass accents and Chinese sculpture. The kitchen promotes a contemporary blend of Eastern and European cooking with winning dishes such as osso buco, chargrilled Colorado lamb chops, salt and pepper calamari, rainbow shrimp and Mongolian beef. A mixing of flavors also makes for some truly spectacular desserts like mango crème brûlée and honey crispy banana A very reasonable three-course prix-fixe lunch menu falls more traditionally into the Asian genre. For tipplers, the expansive menu of martinis and single malt scotches leave little to be desired. Some evenings, there's a pianist.

CAFE LILI

This friendly, family-run Lebanese cafe is known for its shawarma and falafel sandwiches, as well as excellent mezzas (try the hummus loaded on a piece of warm pita bread), including tabouli, babaganoush and *fatoosh* (chopped cucumber and tomato salad). Friendly and efficient counter service and fresh, well-prepared food are hallmarks. It's often crowded during lunchtime with Galleria-area office workers; in the evening it becomes a local hangout for the city's Lebanese community. Order from the menu, or check the chalkboard for the daily special. An interesting wine list features a small number of Lebanese bottles. We also like the bottomless cups of Turkish coffee.

5757 WESTHEIMER west of Chimney Rock
713-952-6969
www.cafelili.com
MAP D7

CAFE MONTROSE

This laid-back, family-run eatery on lower Westheimer serves laudable

> **1609 WESTHEIMER**
> just west of Mandell
> **713-523-1201**
> www.cafemontrose.com
> **MAP** E6

versions of classic Belgian dishes such as *moules frites, boeuf carbonade* (beef stew made with beer) and *waterzooi* (a sort of creamy chicken stew). The requisite *pommes frites* (delicious when swiped through the side of mayonnaise) and the various sauced versions of the steamed mussels are each probably the best in the city. Delicious! The buckets of mussels alone make Cafe Montrose worth a trip, despite the shaky (and sometimes downright rude) service. The desserts with Belgian chocolates are not bad, either. This is a comfortable place that is not fine dining, but it's a good complement to its more ambitious neighbors, including Hugo's, Da Marco and Mark's. There is a small selection of wines, with a few excellent Belgian ales.

CAFE PIQUET

> **5757 BISSONNET**
> near Chimney Rock
> **713-664-1031**
> **MAP** C7

Our favorite Cuban-American named this as her favorite Cuban restaurant in Houston, and it's not hard to see why. Despite the strip mall location, inside the restaurant is clean and modern with walls covered in Cuban memorabilia to add character. The menu sticks to the basics — well-made Cuban favorites like *yuca frita* (lightly fried yuca), *papa rellenas* (balls of mashed potatoes stuffed with ground meat, then fried), *croquetas* (ham croquettes), *empanadas*, *picadillo* (seasoned ground beef), *masitas fritas* (fried pork chunks), *ropa vieja* and *pargo entero frito* (whole fried snapper). Obviously the deep-fat fryer sees a lot of action, as is true at all Cuban cafes. Service has some hiccups but the prices are reasonable, and the delicious, authentic Cuban food keeps people coming back.

CAFE PITA+

> **10890 WESTHEIMER** at Lakeside Country Club Dr.
> **713-953-7237**
> **MAP** B7

Cafe Pita+ is a real charmer of a Bosnian restaurant. Small, cozy and comfortable, hidden away in a strip mall just outside the Beltway, it seems pretty near the Platonic ideal of the little ethnic restaurant that foodies are always on the hunt for. The service goes along with the whole feel of the place — eager to please and informative. Start with a mezze plate, which comes loaded with traditional cured meats and sausage (one selection, *pastrma*, is like the darkest, best-tasting pastrami you'll ever find), a particularly tangy Bosnian feta, olives and hot peppers. Accompanying the platter is *kajmak* (a rich mixture of feta, cream cheese and sour cream), *ajvar* (a relish, or salsa if you will, of roasted red peppers, eggplant and a few chilies) and warm pieces of freshly baked *lepinja*, the traditional Bosnian bread. If you can only try one entree, make it the *cevap* — juicy spiced sausages tucked into a large round of split, buttered and toasted *lepinja*. You might also consider a plate of sardines, thin-crust pizza or lamb shank. The setting may be modest, but prices are low and portions are generous, making Cafe Pita+ a great place to try something new.

CAFE RABELAIS

2442 TIMES between Morningside and Kirby
713-520-8841
www.caferabelais.com
MAP E7

This is an intimate place in Rice Village where the Gallic charms are readily apparent. Quaint and often boisterous (despite its small size), the current location serves robust Provençal-inspired fare and is a perfect fit among the other small ethnic restaurants in this part of town. From the chalkboard menu, foie gras, escargot, duck pâté or *boudin noir* can start a meal, while veal kidneys in mustard sauce, duck breast with a prune and port sauce or a ribeye with fresh shallots provide the heft. There are always several salads, including a salade Niçoise and another with chèvre, grilled eggplants, tomatoes and basil. The Franco-centric wine list is surprisingly lengthy and award-winning, and there are many choices to complement the food. Besides impressing with its wine list, this little French bistro wins the hearts of Houstonians with its cozy setting and simple, authentic cuisine. Note: It can be very busy and they don't take reservations, so go early or late.

CAFE RED ONION

Owner Rafael Galindo now has a string of popular Latin American restaurants, most emphasizing seafood. The names vary — e.g. Cafe Red Onion, Red Onion Seafood & Mas, Red Onion Taco Cantina — but if it contains the words "Red Onion," it belongs with the group.

3910 KIRBY between Richmond and Hwy. 59, and other locations
713-807-1122
www.caferedonion.com
MAP E7

The food can loosely be characterized as Latin fusion. Galindo himself is from Honduras, but Mexico is obviously a part of the mix here, as are Peru and the Caribbean. All of the restaurants provide a festive atmosphere and good values. Among the attractions: pineapple salsa with the tortilla chips to begin, "Latino sushi" creations and 100-plus kinds of tequila.

CANDELARI'S PIZZERIA

6002 WASHINGTON
east of Westcott, and other locations
832-200-1474
www.candelaris.com
MAP E6

We're a long time out of college, but eating at Candelari's makes us feel like a university student all over again. These are neighborhood joints with the typical drawbacks — sometimes noisy, sometimes crowded, spotty service — but great food. Started by two Bellaire High grads, Candelari's was first known for its Italian sausage (still packaged and sold separately), with a deep dish or thin crust pie more of a staging ground for the signature meat. Our favorite pizza, "King Mike's," is topped with Italian sausage, sundried tomato chicken sausage, pesto, roasted garlic, bacon, portobello and feta. All but the Bellaire location have a daily lunch buffet. Delivery available.

CANTINA LAREDO

11129 WESTHEIMER
at Wilcrest
713-952-3287
www.cantinalaredo.com
MAP B7

Part of Dallas-based Consolidated Restaurant Operations, Inc. — it also owns Spaghetti Warehouse, El Chico Cafe, Good Eats and others — Cantina Laredo is an upscale Tex-Mex that's done a good job of not feeling corporate. The menu includes several kinds of enchiladas (our pick: Veracruz, with chicken, spinach and Monterey Jack), "top-shelf guacamole" that is made tableside, tacos al pastor and chicken chimichurri salad. Mole dishes, daily fish specials and signature sauces such as chipotle-wine with portobello mushrooms and sautéed artichoke hearts and roasted red pepper set this apart from your standard Tex-Mex — it's more like Mex-Mex. A live band plays on weekend nights, so if it's quiet conversation you want, stick to lunch or weekdays. For a tête-à-tête over margaritas and chips, snag one of the cozy two-person booths.

Holy guacamole! Dive into Cantina Laredo's tableside Mexican classic.

CAPITAL GRILLE

5365 WESTHEIMER
between Sage and Yorktown
713-623-4600
www.thecapitalgrille.com
MAP D6

What can we tell you about The Capital Grille, one of the big-boy players in Houston's steakhouse wars? Pour yourself a martini, close your eyes and visualize a grand, beautifully appointed bastion of Republican dining featuring expensive steaks, expensive side dishes and expensive wine. In fact, it's reported that The Capital Grille has the highest check average of any restaurant chain in the country. It's the kind of restaurant that is often described as "a man's restaurant": clubby dark wood, cushy Oriental carpeting, gorgeous oversized light fixtures, hunting trophies on the wall. Everything is crisp white napery, heavy flatware and good wine glasses. The wine list runs to a couple hundred selections, while the menu is only about one-tenth as long. If you order a martini to start, your waiter or waitress will deliver a miniature shaker to your table and ceremoniously pour your drink into an oversized glass garnished with olives and onions. You order dinner à la carte, and a single appetizer will cost you what a whole meal costs at many other Houston restaurants. But you will eat a meal built around excellent meat cut into obscenely thick hunks and an award-winning wine list. You will also be cosseted by polished service, so pampered into submission that, by the time you're ready for a cigar, you won't think twice about dropping $40 for a good smoke. Note: The bar is a popular meeting place and within easy walking distance of Galleria-area hotels.

CAPTAIN BENNY'S HALF SHELL OYSTER BAR

8506 S. MAIN
between Kirby and Murworth, and other locations
713-666-5469
MAP E7

There are three of these beached boat-shaped restaurants now, but the location near Reliant Park still sets the standard for fresh oysters, fried shrimp and chowders. Just the right amount of Gulf Coast tackiness makes this a Houston original. Mix your own blend of cocktail sauce with the provided catsup, horseradish, lemons and Tabasco. Captain Benny's is tacky and not so very clean, but friendly service and fine cheap seafood provide a welcome taste of old Houston.

CARMELO'S

The Sicilian-influenced Continental dishes can be quite good at this white-tablecloth stalwart that has been a fixture on the western stretch of Memorial for a quarter-century. Much of the menu and presentation

> **14795 MEMORIAL** west of Dairy Ashford
> **281-531-0696**
> www.carmelosrestaurant.com
> **MAP** B6

follow a timeworn model, but the ingredients are fresh and true, and the kitchen can shine with its more soulful Southern Italian creations. A lunch special of an eggplant stuffed with quickly sautéed seafood then baked seemed straight from a fine ristorante in the *Mezzogiorno*, and can even excite a diner from northern Italy not prone to praise things Sicilian. Pastas, veal and steaks will satisfy most diners. Fresh fish, including salmon with Champagne sauce and grilled swordfish, make this as much a seafood as Italian-restaurant destination. Good tiramisu and a worthy wine list. The setting is comfortable and unpretentious and the service eager to please. A roving accordion player is hokey, but nice.

Recommended
SOULFUL HOUSTON

Houston supports quite a few casual neighborhood restaurants that serve home-style or country-style African-American comfort food. Don't expect much in the way of décor, but do count on a hearty, straightforward meal for a fair price.

BIG MAMA'S HOMECOOKIN', *7129 W. Broadway, Pearland, 281-412-4445.* The meat-and-three is $10, and the sides are particularly good: yams, Creole okra, cabbage cooked with ham hock, dirty rice. There's a steam table with various entrees, but you can also get cooked-to-order fried shrimp.

BREAKFAST KLUB, *3711 Travis, 713-528-8561.* Serving up breakfast (mostly) and lunch with Southern and Creole roots, the Breakfast Klub is located near the nexus of the Third Ward, Montrose and the Museum District. On weekend mornings there are lines out the door. Try the fried chicken wings and waffles, catfish and grits or "Green Eggs and Ham."

THIS IS IT!, *207 Gray, 713-659-1608.* This is It! is the best and probably oldest soul food restaurant in town. Serving lunch and dinner, it has been around in several locations in the Fourth Ward since 1959. The menu is slow to change, and regulars like it that way. Meat, three sides and cornbread go for about $10. The meatloaf is world famous.

YO' MAMA'S SOUL FOOD, *5332 Antoine, 713-680-8002.* Yo' Mama's serves good soul food on the near north side. The cooking is slightly less heavy than most other soul food purveyors, though certainly not light. The steam table changes daily and might include smothered pork chops, fried steak or gumbo.

CARRABBA'S ITALIAN GRILL

3115 KIRBY between Richmond and W. Alabama, and other locations
713-522-3131
www.carrabbas.com
MAP E7

Carrabba's original Kirby location is still owned and operated by cookbook author and PBS cooking show host Johnny Carrabba and remains hugely popular after 20-plus years. This home-grown chain — with locations now all over the country, thanks to OSI, the parent company of Outback Steakhouse — helped define the exuberant Sicilian-rooted Gulf Coast cooking that is today one of the best-loved staples of the Houston dining scene. The kitchen perpetuates its *nuova* rustic reputation with well-tended grills and some of the best filled pastas in town. Don't overlook the surprisingly good pizzas on chewy, slightly charred crusts, either, or the seafood salad that is a smartly dressed toss of bitter greens, grilled shrimp and scallops. Perhaps these yuppie havens are no longer the hottest of the hot. No matter: There's still *always* a crowd. Best seat in the house for eating pizza is at the open kitchen bar next to the oven — lots of action and great aromas from the cranking kitchen.

CARTER & COOLEY

375 W. 19TH between Heights Blvd. and N. Shepherd
713-864-3354
www.carterandcooley.com
MAP F6

A lovely old building (circa 1921) in the Heights with a high ceiling of pressed tin and marble-topped tables is the setting for this breezy sandwich shop known for its sandwiches (Reuben, BLT and muffaletta are specialties), Texas-style chili, soda fountain and health-food items. The staff is exceedingly accommodating, so if you don't see what you want, just ask. However, don't ask for a hamburger — they don't serve 'em.

CATALAN FOOD AND WINE

5555 WASHINGTON just west of TC Jester
713-426-4260
www.catalanfoodandwine.com
MAP E6

Local gourmets were practically in a tizzy by the time Catalan swung open its doors in 2006. The Spanish/American comfort food concept brought together Charles Clark and Grant Cooper (of Ibiza), chef Chris Shepherd (Brennan's), wine guy Matthew Pridgen (Mark's American Cuisine) and GM Antonio Gianola (Da Marco). Now that's a pedigree. The result is noisy, lively and fun, and the food is great. The wine list, coming in at 23 pages, is diverse and features guides on topics like bio-dynamics, grower Champagnes, dry rosé and cider. The menu offers sharable small plates, including spicy garlic shrimp, crabmeat croquettes, calamari with jalapeño lime dressing and asparagus wrapped in prosciutto and *bufala mozzarella*. For those not in the mood to share, regular entrees such as red wine-braised short ribs, seared pork chop, seafood stew and a Colorado lamb quartet are also well-cooked, although considering the price some find the dishes to be on the small side. Note to adventurous eaters: The chef is always ready to serve a cut of meat you may not have previously sampled, including chunks of cane syrup-braised pork belly on sugar cane skewers, crisp-fried strips of pigs' ears (and you thought they were just for dogs!), marrow bones and black blood sausages.

One of Catalan's signature dishes is syrup-braised pork belly.

301 MAIN at Congress
713-223-4068
www.bellarestaurants.com
MAP F6

CAVA BISTRO

Cava Bistro occupies an odd little site in the historic Sweeney & Coombs Building that the previous tenant — Osteria d'Aldo — had fashioned into a mock grotto, complete with cavernous rock spines arching along the ceiling. Cava Bistro kept the cave-like motif, which is nicely done in a rugged, faux-wine cellar sort of way that stops just short of kitsch. (Though you probably can't resist cracking a small joke about Bruce Wayne and the Bat Cave.) About a dozen four-tops are shoe-horned into the intimate dining room. Another eight or so tables are available on a covered patio. The compact kitchen, which is still big enough to boast a wood-burning oven, is open, and a small bar takes up most of one wall. If you're at all claustrophobic, Cava Bistro may be a tad too *intime,* but many will enjoy the convivial spirit of the surroundings. The pleasantly eclectic fare is not easily categorized, though a Moroccan influence makes a distinct impression — a chili paste dipping sauce for the bread basket, couscous, the zesty harissa aioli dressing for the calamari and a stunningly piquant marinade called *charmoula* that combines cilantro, cumin, paprika and a dozen other ingredients. The *charmoula* is used on the most memorable dish at Cava — a succulent oven-roasted whole red snapper. You will also enjoy potato gnocchi, given an edge with feta cheese; port-glazed beef tournedos served atop a heap of creamy polenta and crowned with stringy *pommes frites*; oxtail pie; leek tart; and chicken strudel. Cava does a lively lunch trade, as it's near the Harris County Courts complex. Evenings are quieter.

CHARIVARI

2521 BAGBY at McGowen
713-521-7231
www.charivarirest.com
MAP E6

A slice of the very Old World in the midst of youth-centric Midtown, Charivari (supposedly old French for "beautiful good mix") and Transylvania-born chef/owner Johann Schuster quietly serve up refined European cuisine. The menu changes seasonally — the restaurant celebrates white asparagus, for example, every spring. Evergreen appetizers include a "Dracula" garlic soup, escargot, beluga blinis and "Budapest-style" foie gras; entrees encompass such fascinating choices as Transylvania pork filets, Wienerschnitzel, spätzle with wild mushroom sauce, seafood *choucroute* and a ribeye "Café de Paris" that is dry-aged for 20 days. Presentation is very nice (albeit old-fashioned, with silver domed dishes placed before diners in unison) and service is impeccable, attracting a power lunch crowd by day and a more mature set at night. The dining room can feel a bit stiff, especially when the crowd is sparse.

CHEZ NOUS

217 S. AVENUE G two blocks south of Main St., Humble
281-446-6717
www.cheznousfrenchrestaurant.com
MAP G2

Gerard and Sandra Brach opened this little French country inn in a former Pentecostal church in the mid-1980s. Since then they've brought in some co-owners (currently, executive chef Stacy Crowe and maître d'/sommelier Scott Simonson), but everything else has remained pretty much the same over the past 20 years. Situated in a modest residential neighborhood in Humble, a few blocks off Main Street, this is the kind of place you'd brag to your friends about discovering on a trip through Napa Valley, say, or Vermont. It's a French restaurant of decades past, so full of charm you almost expect the bartender to wear a straw boater. Most of the menu's offerings are sturdy, classic dishes with good sauces, and there's a generous wine list. Recommended: house-made charcuterie, steak *marchand de vin*, shrimp Provençal and snails sizzling in thick garlic butter. Here's everything you love about French restaurants, but without the hauteur. Recognized for excellence by *Zagat, Gourmet* and the *Mobil Travel Guide*, it's worth the 30-minute drive from Houston.

CHINA VIEW

Finding the View first time can be something of adventure. Persevere. Located on the eastbound frontage road of I-10, this spacious, gracious Westside establishment serves some of the best Far East food in the city.

11113½ KATY FWY.
between Kirkwood and Wilcrest
713-464-2728
www.chinaview.us
MAP B6

Robin Luo spent a number of years traveling throughout his native China as a tour guide before taking an M.A. in culinary arts from University of Houston's Hilton School. He and wife Judy finally opened their own restaurant in 1998. Building on their experience and frequent return visits to Robin's homeland, China View's extensive menu is in a constant state of change. That can make for adventurous dining. Seafood dishes, such as the honey walnut salmon, are a specialty, but standards like pine nut chicken with snow peas are treated with respect. There's a dim sum buffet on weekends, and the chef offers a lavish tea-tasting party with five-course dinner, perfect for a group night out.

CHURRASCOS

2055 WESTHEIMER
at S. Shepherd
713-527-8300
www.cordua.com
MAP E6

9705 WESTHEIMER
at Gessner
713-952-1988
MAP C7

These popular eateries, now 18 years old, are the foundation of Michael Cordúa's restaurant empire, and it was the namesake churrasco that started it all. (See page 257 for Cordúa's recipe for Churrasco with Chimichurri Sauce.) It's a flavorful quick-grilled cut from the tenderloin that takes its name from Argentina and is perfect for a city that loves beef. Even if the churrascos weren't so good, people would come to Cordúa's South American steakhouses for the irresistible plantain chips and chimichurri sauce that is served at the start of every meal. (Miraculously, more of that garlicky chimichurri finds its way onto the churrascos as a rich baste.) What else? Rich and soft *maduros*, a quintet of ceviches, variously filled empanaditas, bacon-wrapped shrimp and arguably the best version of *tres leches* ever. The excellent beef, sexy tropical Latin flavors, festive atmosphere, earnest service, good drinks and value-priced

Tres leches is the signature dessert at Churrascos, and the city's gold standard.

Chilean wines make this pair of restaurants well-suited for our city. We only wish there were more locations.

CHUY'S COMIDA DELUXE

2706 WESTHEIMER
just west of Kirby
713-524-1700
www.chuys.com
MAP E6

18035 NORTH FWY.
at Research Forest, Shenandoah
936-321-4440
MAP North of D1

The Houston area has two popular outposts of the Austin original, both offering campy and noisy singles fun along with fairly typical Tex-Mex food. Enchiladas are a specialty, as are crispy flautas and "Big As Yo' Face" burritos. The addictive ranch-based creamy jalapeño dip (or "Creamy J") used to be only available to regulars in the know, but now it comes standard with the chips alongside a chunky pico de gallo. The restaurant walls and even ceilings are covered with themed knickknacks ranging from a school of colorful wooden fish to hubcaps to a shrine to Elvis Presley. Service is quick and portions are generous, so don't over-order. Be sure and grab a margarita — the strawberry margarita is particularly good, if you like that sort of thing. Chileheads: Keep an eye peeled for the annual summertime chile promotion.

CIRO'S ITALIAN GRILL

9755 KATY FWY.
between Bunker Hill and Gessner
713-467-9336
www.ciros.com
MAP C6

This used to be a little hideaway in Spring Branch. But expansion of Interstate 10 forced it to move farther west and across the freeway, and a glossy expansion came with that. The northern Italian menu includes a number of heart-healthy selections as well as good seafood. The variety of breads for the table earns raves, and the lasagna, pork chop and seafood pasta are particularly good, with large portions. It's always noisy and crowded, but you can now buy Ciro's various sauces to prepare similar meals at home. The jarred goods are available at the restaurant and many area grocery stores.

CLEBURNE CAFETERIA

A popular, non-chain cafeteria known for fresh, made-from-scratch squash casserole, broiled chicken, carrot salad and turkey with dressing. Cleburne's is popular among an older set, of course, but also much liked by West U-area families. It's also a good lunch spot, with its proximity

> **3606 BISSONNET**
> at Edloe
> **713-667-2386**
> **MAP** D7

to Greenway Plaza, but go early because the line often is out the door. It burned down several years ago, much to the despair of its loyal clientele. But the Mickelis family rebuilt it better than ever, and so Cleburne (named for the downtown street where it first originated) endures. Word to the wise: Bring your checkbook, it's cash or check only.

Personal Favorites
WHERE I GO FOR DIM SUM
By Dorothy Huang

Houstonians who know about dim sum love it. I make it my business to introduce newcomers to this fun way of eating, small plate by small plate. Here are five restaurants that are consistently good.

FUNG'S KITCHEN, *7320 Southwest Fwy., 713-779-2288.* Besides traditional dim sum, Fung's Kitchen offers many innovative vegetarian dishes, such as steamed snow pea tips, dumplings, bean curd roll with cilantro, pan-fried veggie buns and black fungus (black cloud ear mushrooms) with black vinaigrette.

KIM SON RESTAURANT, *12750 Southwest Fwy., 281-242-3500, and 10603 Bellaire Blvd., 281-598-1777.* It offers two locations for dim sum. Diners with no experience in dim sum dining can use the picture menu to guide their selections.

NEW GOLDEN PALACE RESTAURANT, *8520 Bellaire Blvd., 713-776-8808.* This is the oldest dim sum restaurant in Houston and still maintains its popularity. Some contend it's Houston most authentic dim sum experience.

OCEAN PALACE, *11215 Bellaire Blvd., 281-988-1688.* Ocean Palace is conveniently located in Hong Kong City Mall and serves great dim sum seven days a week. The mall is a cultural experience not to be missed!

YUM YUM CHA, *2435 Times, 713-527-8455.* It's a small 30-seat restaurant run by a father-daughter team. The unique picture menu is very helpful for first-timers. The cafe serves nothing but dim sum, six days a week.

Dorothy Huang is a Chinese cooking teacher and author of Chinese Cuisine Made Simple. *She frequently offers Chinatown walking tours (which include a dim sum lunch). You can attend one of her cooking classes at Central Market, L'Aglio, Sur La Table and Williams-Sonoma. For information, email chinesecuisinedh@aol.com.*

COLLINA'S ITALIAN CAFE

> **2400 TIMES** at Morningside, and other locations
> **713-526-4499**
> **MAP** E7

This *pizzeria e ristorante* is a longstanding neighborhood choice for casual Italian cuisine and meeting friends. But what it's best known for is a long-standing BYOB policy. Yes, you can bring your own wine (see Bear Dalton's sidebar, *Top BYOBs*, page 121) to drink with their pasta, calzones or pizza. All pies have yeasty dough, puffy edges and crisp bottoms, and whole-wheat crust is also available. Our favorite: the Mona Lisa with roma tomatoes, mushrooms, spinach and feta. Retro selections include a Hawaiian pizza with Canadian bacon. This is a good choice for families with kids.

CORELLI'S

> **5640 WESTHEIMER** at Chimney Rock
> **713-629-4424**
> www.corellis.com
> **MAP** D6
>
> **3229 HWY. 6 SOUTH** at Williams Trace, Sugar Land
> **281-491-8900**
> **MAP** A9

Rather like Collina's but a little more ambitious in the kitchen, this neighborhood Italian eatery features pastas (e.g. lasagna, manicotti, spaghetti with *sugo rosa*, fettuccine primavera), several salads, pizza — and a liberal BYOB policy. An off-the-menu-secret: In lieu of alfredo, ask for the cream sauce with black pepper. It's especially good on seafood dishes. For a twist, try the dessert pizza. With a clean but casual vibe and attentive service, Corelli's is an excellent value and great for families. Another plus: delivery service to surrounding businesses and homes.

COURSES

> **1900 YORKTOWN** south of San Felipe, in The Art Institute
> **713-353-3644**
> www.artinstitute.edu/houston
> **MAP** D6

This is the "practice" restaurant in The Art Institute where student chefs cook and the public is welcome. Located on the sixth floor, Courses serves an à la carte lunch Monday through Wednesday, and Wednesday through Friday dinner is served as a five-course tasting menu with a wine pairing. (Call to confirm, since the restaurant-service schedule is changeable.) There is also a deli option with sandwiches, soups and salads available to go on weekdays. The cuisine changes weekly with the course load and includes genres such as Italian Bistro, Bay Area Seafood, Old World French and Flavors of Summertime. Sometimes the students practice the style or recipes of celebrity chefs.

Service can be bumpy, so this is not the place for a hot date or important business meeting. But it is fun and the price is right.

CRAPITTO'S

2400 MID LANE just north of Westheimer
713-961-1161
www.crapittos.com
MAP D6

This Italian-American restaurant stands apart from its glitzy Galleria neighbors, housed in a remodeled 75-year-old farmhouse that's full of charm and liked by an older crowd. We love the beautiful deck and dining under the fine old live oaks. Regulars rave about the crabcakes, lasagna, pan-sautéed snapper, salmon florentina and cheesecake. Prices are on the expensive side, but service is quite personable — it's not unusual to see owner Frank Crapitto greeting diners.

CRICKET'S CREAMERY & CAFFE

315 W. 19TH between Heights Blvd. and N. Shepherd
713-869-9450
MAP E5

Packed with gewgaws and tchotchkes, this little cafe/ice cream bar is easy to mistake for just another antique shop. Veteran shoppers know it as the perfect midpoint for a refreshment during an afternoon of combing through the West 19th shops. It has ice cream and gelato, as well as frappes, smoothies and hot teas and coffees. Hungrier? It also features a breakfast menu that includes Belgian waffles, granola and pastries, and at lunch owner John Krug prepares daily-fresh soups and, sometimes, vegetable lasagna and meatless loaf. Don't be like us and wander in looking for a hamburger: It's a vegetarian cafe. A tasty meat substitute is the black bean burger on sourdough with tomato pesto mayo.

CULLEN'S UPSCALE AMERICAN GRILL

11500 SPACE CENTER BLVD. south of Genoa Red Bluff
281-481-3463
www.cullensgrille.com
MAP I9

Everything's bigger in Texas, and Cullen's Upscale American Grille is the biggest new kid (it opened in early 2008) on the block, racking up 37,000 square feet. Inside, though, the rooms are designed to a human scale and can feel almost intimate. Finishes are natural materials: granite, marble, limestone and wood accented with earth tones. The main dining room seats 250 and, depending where you're seated, your view could be into the state-of-the art kitchen through a curved wall of glass. Cullen's menu, designed by executive chef Paul Lewis, is American with ambitions. The Frito pie-style starter, for example, boasts Berkshire pork in the chili, toasted tortilla chips, Texas goat cheese, two kinds of cheddar and crème fraîche. You'll also find prime rib, steaks and chops, seafood, chicken, duck, homemade pizzas and sandwiches. The wine list is very 21st century with a computerized wine tablet that allows patrons to search wines by type, vintage, region and price. Cullen's, named after owner Kevin Munz's son, is also surprisingly kid friendly for a grown-ups' restaurant — video games on flat screen televisions in the sports bar/waiting area, a children's menu, children's dessert menu and a nice selection of non-alcoholic specialty drinks. Cullen's Live, the two-story main bar, features various genres of live music.

5510 MORNINGSIDE between University Blvd. and Times
713-526-3400
www.damico-cafe.com
MAP E7

D'AMICO'S ITALIAN MARKET CAFE

"D'Amico" is an old name in Houston eateries, going back to the 1970s. Nash D'Amico closed all his restaurants in Houston and Galveston to concentrate on this concept, a combination Italian grocery store, deli and cafe all in one. It's not fancy — it's comfortable, a real family spot, maybe even a little funky. You eat at tables near cases of wine and bottles of olive oil; a few feet away, folks are buying hunks of cheese to take home; over there, cooks are preparing a dish. It's crowded but full of energy. Fresh pasta is made daily, and Village regulars order favorites like chicken piccata and veal marsala to eat in or carry out, as well as purchase pantry staples. The baked pasta dishes are particularly good, and the outdoor patio is a favorite spot for families where children can play without disturbing other customers.

DA MARCO

In a small house on Westheimer, Marco Wiles' Da Marco serves truly excellent food that represents the best of many of the northern Italian regions with far more than a dash of creativity and talent. It is appealing and

1520 WESTHEIMER just east of Mandell
713-807-8857
www.damarcohouston.com
MAP E6

sometimes eclectic, but always flavorful and sometimes sublime. Here you are expected to dine in the Italian fashion with antipasti, a first course, a meat or fish entree and separate sides. There are many tempting seasonal options for each course, like a salad with frisee, taleggio and pears; sweet corn ravioli with lobster; freshly made pappardelle with rabbit; sea bass with grapefruit and vinegar; calf's liver with polenta; and, *cavolo nero*, black cabbage. In the fall, during white truffle season, come here to have a blizzard of naughty truffles shaved over your pasta. Tables are rather close together but the room never feels too crowded (though it is occasionally a bit loud). Servers are extremely knowledgeable about the wine list as well as what constitutes traditional Italian cuisine and Wiles' interpretation. It's all done expertly. This is not only the best Italian restaurant in Houston, but also, possibly, the best restaurant in the city. Along with the cooking, the top-notch wine list is strictly Italian. Bring lots of *lire*.

3412 W. LAMAR at Dunlavy
713-520-9217
www.dailyreviewcafe.com
MAP E6

DAILY REVIEW CAFE

For well over a decade now, this tucked-away spot just south of Allen Parkway has been dishing up Southern-inflected modern comfort food that suits keen local sensibilities desiring healthy or hearty. There are not too many restaurants where you can indulge in a nearly artisanal chicken pot pie and a good bottle of wine, and enjoy them on an expansive patio when the weather cooperates. Other Houston-attuned dishes include a lobster taco with yellow tomato salsa, black bean chili with cheddar and pico de gallo, achiote grilled shrimp with grilled sweet potatoes, and an ancho- and cumin-rubbed aged New York strip steak, all served in a comfy atmosphere that avoids pretension. Note: We've always found parking on the street to be a challenge here.

DAMIAN'S CUCINA ITALIANA

This Midtown classic set in a stolid stand-alone building has been a well-worn stop for downtown businesspeople since it opened in the 1980s. Owned by the affable Frankie Mandola and Bubba Butera — it was founded by their relative Damian Mandola — Damian's does not excite quite as it once did, but it remains a fine-dining Houston favorite. The cooking might be described as upscale Gulf Coast Southern Italian-American — think of it as the godfather to Carrabba's — and flavors and portions are both generous. In a dining room made cozy by low-ceilings and lights, you can enjoy specialties like plump chops with prosciutto, fontina and mushrooms in a Marsala sauce; braised pork shank over cannellini beans; and, *linguine fra diavolo* with a medley of seafood including lobster and lump crabmeat in a piquant marinara sauce. The charming Italian ambiance, robust food and snappy waiters wending their way through the dining

3011 SMITH between Elgin and Tuam
713-522-0439
www.damians.com
MAP E6

room make an absolutely comfortable environment. Good choice for business or romance.

DANTON'S GULF COAST SEAFOOD KITCHEN

> **4611 MONTROSE** just south of Hwy. 59
> **713-807-8883**
> www.dantonsseafood.com
> **MAP** E7

Chef/owner Danton Nix and partner Kyle Teas opened a seafood spot in the location that has seen many tenants in the past few years, including Redwood Grill and O'Rourke's Steakhouse. Nix is an alumnus of Goode Co. Seafood and Joyce's, and the experience is evident on the menu — a perfect Houston confluence of Texas Gulf seafood with generous Cajun and Mexican influences — and its stellar execution. Grilled items are wood-fired over oak and hickory, and the gumbo is cooked for up to 18 hours to get its signature flavor. The sophisticated setting and service sets Danton's in the top tier of Cajun joints in Houston. The old bar area, to the left of the front door, is now an oyster bar. Go slurp a dozen or two when the bay water is cold and the oysters are sweet.

DARBAND SHISHKABOB

Named after an Iranian special-occasion restaurant in a park-like setting, much enjoyed by Tehranis, Houston's version of Darband is a culinary delight in a decidedly downscale setting. It's located among the many Mideastern, Indian and Pakistani

> **5670 HILLCROFT** between Harwin and Westpark
> **713-975-8350**
> **MAP** C7

shops and cafes that line this multi-cultural wonder that is Hillcroft. As we said, it's a very modest little spot, but many insist that it has the best kabobs in the city. We especially love the lamb kabobs and *koobideh* (seasoned ground-meat kabobs). Often whole Mideastern families are here dining together, enjoying kebobs, rice and grilled tomatoes, followed by sweet tea. Delicious fresh flat bread is a welcome lagniappe. A newer, flashier spot, Darband Bar & Grill, recently opened at 2707 Fountain View, 713-975-8352.

DEL FRISCO'S DOUBLE EAGLE STEAK HOUSE

> **5061 WESTHEIMER** at McCue, in The Galleria
> **713-355-2600**
> www.delfriscos.com
> **MAP** D6

After its grand opening — complete with a red carpet, paparazzi and sky-slicing spotlights — Del Frisco's grabbed the title of fanciest new restaurant of 2007. It boasts luxurious interiors, including a

Snack on this.

my table

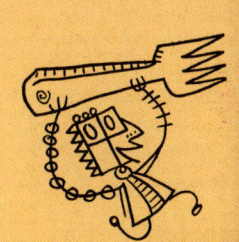

DO YOU GET HUNGRY BETWEEN ISSUES OF MY TABLE?

SIGN UP FOR SIDEDISH, OUR HIGH-CALORIE E-NEWSLETTER DELIVERED EVERY OTHER WEEK OR SO BY EMAIL.

VISIT WWW.MY-TABLE.COM TO SIGN UP FOR A FREE SUBSCRIPTION TO SIDEDISH.

Recommended
DINING SOLO

These casual spots provide a comfortable atmosphere for solo diners.

A MOVEABLE FEAST, *9341 Katy Fwy., 713-365-0368.* When your amigos head to a greasy Mexican joint for lunch, you can remain virtuous. This natural foods cafe provides one of the best vegetarian and vegan selections in the city. Order dishes that never make you feel deprived, like fresh fish, soy cheese enchiladas or the famous veggie burgers from the front counter. If boredom strikes, head to the adjoining health food store for products galore. You deserve it.

CAFE EXPRESS, *6570 Woodway, 713-935-9222, and other locations.* Nowhere else will you find a portion of pasta so preposterously large and delicious that it is a challenge to lift your head out of the bowl long enough to strike up a conversation with a companion. Solution? Dine alone at this dependable Houston-grown chain devoid of bothersome waiters, yet populated with tiny tables both inside and out that are ideal for the lone diner.

FADI'S MEDITERRANEAN GRILL, *8383 Westheimer, 713-532-0666, and 4738 Beechnut, 713-666-4644.* If you're alone and craving truly delightful tabouli, hummus and warm pita bread, head for this colorful cafeteria-style Middle Eastern cafe. Midday clientele consist of herds of lone businessmen grabbing a quick bite between appointments; after a meal, indulge in some sweet baklava.

GOODE CO. TEXAS BARBEQUE, *5109 Kirby, 713-522-2530, and 8911 Katy Fwy., 713-464-1901.* When craving succulent Texas mesquite barbecue without a buddy, head over to Houston's favorite smokehouse. The line moves like lightning, which is great news for the singleton. Pay up front, then take your tray to a lone booth or picnic table in the back and dig into that delectable fresh-chopped brisket sandwich. Alone for the whole day? Pile on the onions.

MISSION BURRITOS, *2245 W. Alabama, 713-529-0535, and other locations.* When it first opened, Mission was a breakthrough in burritos: They'll make it any way *you* want. What could be more perfect for the lonely burrito addict? Grab a tray and tell the staff what goes into your personal burrito as you move down the line. Once you have a beautiful, unique burrito, sit down at one of the outside tables and people watch.

PICNIC, *1928 Bissonnet, 713-524-0201.* Enjoying a delicious blueberry muffin, apple tart or chorizo scone in silence is a perfect way to begin the day. The early eater can catch a yummy brunch (minus the crowd) from around 10 to 11:30 a.m.; the late luncher is likely to be left alone to enjoy a delectable chicken salad sandwich between 1:30 p.m. and the closing time at 5. The cute cafe is also a favorite spot for avid readers, despite the somewhat hard picnic benches.

hand-painted Italian glass ceiling and light fixtures, 40-foot windows with a striking view of the skylines of the Galleria and downtown Houston, and a second-story mezzanine, accessible by elevator, with its own bar. Speaking of which — the bar action is sizzling. Known for its prime steak and *fab-u-lous* crab cakes, Del Frisco's is set in the renovated retail complex that formerly housed Lord and Taylor. The two-story space can get quite noisy, and the layout is certainly more about see-and-be-seen than an intimate dinner. Nevertheless, the view is stunning and executive chef Steve Haug's food can be sublime. The kitchen and service staff were a little rocky in the beginning but wrinkles seem to have been ironed out.

9777 KATY FWY.
at Memorial City Way
713-464-6900
MAP C6

DENIS' SEAFOOD HOUSE

This noisy, New Orleans-flavored spot serves fresh seafood any which way. The open kitchen turns out etouffée, gumbo, boiled crawfish in season and great jumbo lump crab. We liked the fresh fish-ordering concept: The blackboard lists the catches of the day, and your choice is then served grilled, sautéed or blackened (though the last option tends to be over-seasoned and overcooked to our taste). For a bit more coin you can also add one of seven seafood sauce toppings like the Florentine, a delicious shrimp, scallop and crawfish-laden spinach cream sauce. The lovely atmosphere (there are beautiful mosaic walls with tile work by noted Houston artist Dixie Friend Gay) is not always matched by the level of service.

DHARMA CAFE

There are only a handful of tables at John Gurney and Susan Ralph's cozy little spot, where one fan describes the ambiance as "sacred and sincere." Think Big Sur, and you might have a feeling for the funky setting with its

1718 HOUSTON AVE.
near Crockett
713-222-6996
www.dharmacafehouston.com
MAP E6

shelf of poetry by Allen Ginsberg and books on Buddhism. The Sunday brunch menu — sort of West Coast with a French flair — includes amazing homemade scones, pancakes and waffles, pasta dishes, and eggs cooked to order, served in a buffet for an extraordinary value at $15. The mimosas are excellent, and your first glass (you'll want more) comes free with the buffet. The menu is vegan- and vegetarian-friendly, with tempting salads, pizza and sandwiches along with entrees of cedar-planked salmon and blueberry chicken breast. The small space can be surprisingly romantic at night.

DIVINO

> **1830 W. ALABAMA**
> between Woodhead and Hazard
>
> **713-807-1123**
> www.divinohouston.com
>
> **MAP** E6

This is a comfortable neighborhood eatery and wine bar in the *osteria* and *enoteca* traditions that features a small menu of items mostly from Emilia-Romagna, where executive chef and co-owner Patrick McCray trained. Though not terribly ambitious, the kitchen's straightforward renditions of dishes from this region, which is the favorite among many Italian gastronomes, will please most. There's not much about the exterior that will draw you in — it could be a doctor's office. But neighborhood regulars like it, and there is a decent wine list. Several Sundays a year Divino opens up its cellar for retail wine sales at deep discounts.

DOLCE VITA PIZZERIA ENOTECA

> **500 WESTHEIMER**
> between Taft and Montrose
>
> **713-520-8222**
> www.dolcevitahouston.com
>
> **MAP** E6

We've never been to this casual pizzeria/wine bar from Marco Wiles (of the peerless Da Marco, see above) when it wasn't packed. Don't be misled by "pizzeria" — this ain't no Pizza Hut. The thin and slightly scorched wood-fired pies are the draw to be sure, but there is also a bold menu that includes a unique array of appetizers including shaved Brussels sprouts with pecorino cheese, preserved fried whitefish, fried croquettes of pumpkin and goat cheese, the deep-fried rice and cheese *supplì* and several tasty Italian cheeses. The pastas are a pan-Italian collection of simple, amazingly flavorful dishes: shell-like orecchiette with escarole and sweet sausage; spaghetti with grated cheese and black pepper; *bucatini* with octopus, chilies and tomatoes; and the hearty gnocchi with ragù. The nightly entrees might be braised pork served with polenta, braised lamb, grilled sausage with peppers, or sea bass. And it's all smartly complemented by the all-Italian wine list. Terracotta-hued walls and exposed brick and tile lend a casual charm to this old, only-slightly-renovated two-story house.

DONERAKI

> **2836 FULTON** between Quitman and Hays, and other locations
>
> **713-224-2509**
> www.doneraki.com
>
> **MAP** F5

The original Fulton Street Doneraki is still the place to go for an authentic barrio-style Mexican-food experience. The suburban locations, though less distinctive (and less grimy) than

RECIPE **OYSTERS DAMIAN**

Tony Mandola's Gulf Coast Kitchen, 1962 West Gray, 713-528-3474

"Back in the early 1980s, my brother Damian had tasted a fried oyster with salsa on top at some restaurant," recalls chef/owner Tony Mandola. "I thought about it and felt that cold pico de gallo on a hot cornmeal-battered fried oyster would be a great complement/contrast. It worked! I gave it my brother's name for giving me the idea."

Breading mixture
2 lbs. yellow cornmeal
2 Tbsp. salt
1 tsp. cayenne pepper
1 tsp. black pepper
1½ tsp. garlic powder

Pico de gallo
12 oz. diced roma tomatoes
3 oz. diced yellow onion
1 diced fresh jalapeño
juice of 1 whole lime
1 tsp. salt

2 dozen freshly shucked oysters on the half shell
¼ cup all-purpose flour
1 gallon vegetable oil
rock salt (optional, see note below)
1 lime, cut into 6 wedges

METHOD: Combine breading mixture ingredients and set aside. Combine pico de gallo ingredients and refrigerate until ready to use. Remove oysters from shells, saving shells, and drain away excess juice. Place drained oysters in a bowl and add the flour, gently coating the oysters. Heat vegetable oil to 350 degrees. Gently bread the oysters with the breading mixture and place in oil for 2 minutes. Remove and drain excess oil by placing on paper towels. Place a layer of rock salt on 6 plates and set 4 oyster shells on each plate. Put one fried oyster on each shell and top with pico de gallo (be sure to drain any excess juice from pico de gallo so oysters won't get soggy). Garnish each plate with lime wedge. Serves 6.

Note: A layer of rock salt keeps the oysters from sliding around on the plate. You can substitute lettuce leaf or anything else to prevent this.

their forebear, bring in droves of fajita-munching customers to noisy, festively overwrought cantina settings. The service is hit-or-miss, but the free queso with the chips is a nice touch. Enchiladas and the grilled options are always tasty, plus the margaritas are decent and at $12 for a pitcher it's hard to say no. A live mariachi band on the weekends is fun for those who want the full-sensory trip to Mexico but it does make conversation almost impossible.

DRY CREEK CAFE

544 YALE at 6th
713-426-2313
www.drycreekcafe.com
MAP E5

Housed in a refurbished 1930s gas station, the cafe is in a dry part of the Heights, but you are welcome to bring your own beer or wine — and plenty of folks do. Like Onion Creek, its sister cafe a few blocks east, the Dry Creek patio is full of laid-back charm, great for sitting outside dragging on a bottle of sharp beer. The burgers are tasty, and the salads and sandwiches are also good bets, especially the grilled ahi tuna. Breakfast is serviceable, with all the classics plus less common dishes like chicken and waffles, a crab omelet and a lox plate. Nice staff, though sometimes overworked. This is a really wonderful example of building re-use.

EL MESON

This odd little hybrid near Rice University is part Cuban, part Tex-Mex and part Spanish. The decor is modest and the service is sometimes slow, but the home-cooking nevertheless has plenty of neighborhood fans, including Rice students and faculty.

2425 UNIVERSITY BLVD. near Morningside
713-522-9306
www.elmeson.com
MAP E7

Try the rustic paella, shrimp *al ajillo* or Cuban chicken with black beans, plantains and garlic. The kitchen also does a smashing whole roast baby pig. El Meson translates as The Tavern, not an inappropriate name for a place with an award-winning list of Spanish and South American wines as well as a potent margarita and pitchers of sangria. Don't expect too many frills, but the personable owner, Peter Garcia, does warm up the ambience. On Wednesdays, enjoy the flamenco guitarist.

Peter Garcia wears many hats at El Meson — chef, wine director and host.

EL PUEBLITO PLACE

If you ask fans of this comfy Richmond Avenue cafe what they like about the place, odds are they'll rave about the patio before

> **1423 RICHMOND** just east of Mandell
> **713-520-6635**
> www.elpueblitopatio.com
> **MAP** E7

getting around to the food. And usually they like the food well enough, too. Owners Eduardo and Monica Lopez specialize in Mexican and Guatemalan cuisine. The fish tacos are a lunchtime favorite, as is the platter of grilled chicken and black beans served over fried plantains. The kitchen also turns out some tasty and bargain-priced seafood such as Crazy Snapper. Your vegan friends will be pleased to find super-sized veggie wraps on the menu. Enjoy a margarita on the patio before, after or with dinner. If you have a group, reserve one of the semi-private covered tables that are curtained off cabana style.

EL PUPUSODROMO

Though they still seem to operate below the foodie radar, in some parts of Houston *pupuserias* are as common as taquerias. This trio of modest cafes offer a taste of one of Houston's lesser-known Latin American cuisines. The Salvadoran food touches on the familiar: *Tamals* are similar to their Mexican cousins (though lighter), and sprightly pickled-cabbage *curtido* tops the namesake *pupusas*, which are something like gorditas in Mexican cooking. These *pupusas* are stuffed with cheese, *chicharron* (cracklings), meat and/or beans. To eat, spoon on some of the *curtido* or the table salsa, then fold in half like a taco. This is not fiery fare, although the salsa does spark things up a bit. Try also the *plátanos fritos con crema y frijoles* — fried sweet plantains, *crema* and refried beans. The earthiness of the beans plays off the sweetness of the plantains, and the rich cool crema brings the whole thing together. Another odd but winning combination is *yucca con chicharrones*, which is yucca (either boiled or fried), dressed and then sprinkled with crunchy bits of *chicharron*. We prefer the fried, which is like eating French fries topped with pork. There are some negatives regarding quality — we repeat, these are modest little storefronts — but the food is not scary in the least.

> **5802 RENWICK** between Hwy. 59 and Gulfton, and other locations
> **713-661-4334**
> **MAP** D7

> **910 SHEPHERD** at Washington, and other locations
> **713-802-9145**
> www.elreytaqueria.com
> **MAP** E6

EL REY TAQUERIA

Got five bucks? If so, you may feast here. Although bare to the bones when it comes to decor, the food is priced to bring you a princely plate for pennies. We love the drive-thru convenience at the

Shepherd location, even when they get the order wrong. Kudos to the Cuban tacos, tucked with fajitas, black beans, sweet *maduros* (ripe plantain) and a shmear of *crema*. We also like the rotisserie-roasted chicken, tortilla soup, *tortas* and the house mayonnaise that's laced with habañeros. Breakfast tacos start at $1.25. This is not a spot we'd choose to spend a lot of time in, but it's a good choice for take-out.

EL TIEMPO

3130 RICHMOND
between Buffalo Speedway and Kirby, and other locations
713-807-1600
www.eltiempocantina.com
MAP D/

Where else in the country would people flock to restaurants to pay so much for a Tex-Mex fix, albeit upscale Tex-Mex? Here you will find often-excellent and relatively expensive takes on the humble fajita, Gulf fish and crab dishes done in Tex-Mex fashion, as well as potent margaritas (don't forget the shot of Patron on the side) served in noisy settings. The Richmond location is somewhat family oriented, while the Washington location is frequented by a more "date night" crowd, making it the ideal location to visit if you plan to burn off calories dancing the night away later on in Midtown. We like sitting on the cool and shady patio at the Richmond location, sipping sangria (with *real* fruit in it), sharing Queso Joey (queso with spicy ground beef) and the beef and shrimp fajitas with friends early in the evening. Happy hour does exist, but for short hours and at the bar only (not at your table), which can be confusing. El Tiempo's Montrose location is called 1308 Cantina (it's at 1308 Montrose). It's a great place to kick off a bachelor party or girls' night out. Our very favorite menu item: the carnitas-stuffed taco "musico." Ask for it extra spicy.

EMPIRE TURKISH GRILL

Don't expect tent-draped, cushion-scattered, hookah hubble-bubble Turkish exotica here. Rather, this is a friendly and inviting restaurant that sports white tablecloths and an elegantly western ambience. Respectful nods to authenticity are found in the 100 percent halal meats — a sumptuous variety of chicken, beef and lamb dishes cooked to heavenly perfection and flavored even loftier. The traditional *sis kebab* (or shish kabob) with chargrilled chunks of marinated lamb and the *döner kebab* sliced from the vertical spit are both palate-pleasers. And you can't go wrong with any dish featuring eggplant. *Patlican salatasi* (eggplant salad with garlic, peppers and lemon juice) and *babagannus* are

12448 MEMORIAL
between Gessner and Beltway 8
713-827-7475
MAP C6

wonderful, but our heart belongs to the *imam bayildi* ("the Imam fainted"): Cold roasted baby eggplant with onions, tomato, parsley, garlic and olive oil, it's splendid heaped on the warm flat bread that accompanies every meal. Most notable, there is an array of salads and vegetable appetizers that will work your taste buds into a frenzy — among them, *tarama* (red caviar spread), *labni* (yogurt cheese dip) and the familiar Mideastern hummus and tabouli. Owner Kamil Ramazanoglu recommends creating your own cold appetizer plate — five choices, $9. This is a Turkish delight reincarnated from the old Lantern Inn. Complete your tour of the Empire with sweet desserts and Turkish coffee.

ERIC'S RESTAURANT

4800 CALHOUN in the University of Houston's Hilton Hotel (Entrance 1)
713-743-2513
MAP F7

Go in knowing there will be hits and misses. Both waiters and kitchen staff are students in the Hilton College of Hotel and Restaurant Management, and though their hearts are in the right place, their heads aren't completely filled as yet with seasoned restaurant savvy. Stress happens here. Still, it's kind of special to have a wannabe gourmet restaurant — named for hotelier Eric Hilton — smack dab in the center of U of H, making it a useful venue for dining if you're taking in a play or concert elsewhere on campus. In this food-making and food-service laboratory you will find breakfast, lunch and dinner served seven days a week and an 18 percent gratuity for parties of eight or more. Give them a chance, for from today's in-training food-service aspirants will come tomorrow's celebrity chefs and restaurateurs. Note: There's a handy parking garage under the hotel.

ESCALANTE'S

Escalante's must be doing something right. This Tex-Mex purveyor began life as a single location on Woodway at Voss in 1993 and now boasts three other upscale addresses — Town & Country, Meyerland Plaza and Highland Village — and more on the drawing board. Just be prepared, prime locations can mean somewhat premium prices. The crowds here seem to take it in stride. They rave

4053 WESTHEIMER at Drexel, and other locations
713-623-4200
www.escalantes.net
MAP D6

At Escalante's, one of every four tables orders chef Rodrigo Juarez's guacamole, which is made tableside.

Recommended
OPEN VERY LATE

It's after 11 p.m. You've just walked out of the Edwards' screening of Russell Crowe's latest movie, and you're hungry. If you're like us, you can never think of a single late-night place and end up at some drive-thru or fluorescent-lit chain restaurant. Here's our list of safe bets for very late dining.

59 DINER, *3801 Farnham, 713-523-2333, and other locations.* These bebop diners are always good for a burger, fries and a Coke float, plus breakfast is served anytime. Open 24 hours.

HOLLYWOOD VIETNAMESE & CHINESE, *2409 Montrose, 713-523-8807.* Popular with the Montrose club crowd, the menu here offers a little bit of everything, especially Asian seafood choices. Open to 2 a.m. Sunday through Thursday and to 4 a.m. on Friday and Saturday nights.

HOUSE OF PIES, *3112 Kirby, 713-528-3816, and 6142 Westheimer, 713-782-1290.* With more than 40 sweets on the menu, the legendary House of Pies bakes a dessert for every craving in addition to its menu of short-order offerings, such as breakfast and burgers. As well known for its colorful waitstaff as for its food, House of Pies is visited by the most varied assortment of locals and it can get rowdy as the hours wear on. Open 24 hours.

KATZ'S DELI, *616 Westheimer, 713-521-3838.* This late-night Austin import blends traditional deli-style fare with more innovative takes on New York items, such as the Cheesecake Shake, a beverage that begins with an entire slice of cheesecake. If you're not in an adventurous mood, the Reuben sandwich is superb. Since the doors don't even have locks, customers can get anything they want — even fried pickles — at all hours. Remember its mantra, "Katz's Never Kloses."

MAI'S RESTAURANT, *3403 Milam, 713-520-7684.* In 1975, not long before Houston transformed itself into the ethnic melting pot it is today, owner Mai Thi Nguyen's parents opened Houston's first Vietnamese restaurant. Authentic Vietnamese food is on hand at Mai's until 4 a.m. on the weekends, 3 a.m. on weekdays.

SPANISH FLOWERS, *4701 N. Main, 713-869-1706.* Some people go to Spanish Flowers for the breakfast, served 24 hours, and some only eat the dinners. Both are worthy at this hacienda in The Heights. The menu is solid and includes chiles rellenos, fajitas and various tortas, as well as classic Mexican egg dishes. The restaurant closes between 10 p.m. Tuesday and 9 a.m. Wednesday for cleaning.

TAN TAN, *6816 Ranchester, 713-771-1268.* This "New Chinatown" spot has been dishing up Americanized Chinese and Vietnamese food for years, and it is perhaps at its best in the wee hours. (It's open 'til midnight during the week, 3 a.m. on the weekends.) The menu is hu-u-u-ge, with nearly 400 choices. It's especially popular with club kids.

about the decor, service and menu. Regulars recommend the white cheese chili con queso, *enchiladas verdes* and guacamole. Hungry first-timers might want to go for the Escalante Especial, which includes empanadas, enchiladas and bacon-wrapped shrimp. Enjoy a top-shelf margarita while watching the waiter prepare your guacamole tableside.

FADI'S MEDITERRANEAN GRILL

8383 WESTHEIMER at Dunvale
713-532-0666
www.fadicuisine.com
MAP C7

4738 BEECHNUT at Loop 610
713-666-4644
MAP D7

Fadi's offers Middle Eastern cuisine that is fresh and wholesome, and it is one of the most popular of its cafeteria-style genre. You push a tray along the counter where the tempting vegetables and salads, then hot foods, are handsomely displayed. Order one of the pre-set combination plates, or pick and choose as you like. There are kabobs, shawarma, roasted chicken, sometimes lamb shank. The process is very flexible. Portions are large, but ultimately healthful so the guilt of wolfing down an entire one-meat-and-three-sides plate is minimal. The staff here is very polite and happy to make a recommendation if it's your first visit. Delicious hot pita bread and freshly squeezed juices are available, as well as a selection of authentic desserts, including baklava. Whatever you don't finish, take it to-go; you'll be craving it again later.

FARRAGO

Subtitled "world cuisine," this aptly named hodgepodge borrows from many culinary traditions. Alas, it is not particularly innovative anymore — at least not like it was back in 2000 when it first opened. Back then, this was a cutting-edge place, one of the early pioneers in Midtown. The crazy mixed-up menu still has some winners, such as the pecan-crusted, cream cheese-stuffed French toast, *posole*, grilled salmon and the curried mussels. There's also an all-American half-pound burger and pizza. Given all the bars nearby, it's no surprise that Sunday brunch draws a crowd looking to get well lubricated on the bottomless mimosas and pink lemonade martinis. Patrons are younger and seemingly less demanding today than during the restaurant's early years. Even so, with the bright colors, concrete floors, pleasant outdoor dining and opportune people-watching scene, the place still buzzes.

318 GRAY at Bagby
713-523-6404
www.farragohouston.com
MAP E6

FEAST

219 WESTHEIMER
between Bagby and Taft
713-529-7788
www.feasthouston.com
MAP E6

A gustatory adventure for well-traveled palates, this labor of culinary love is the newest brain food from Meagan and James Silk and Richard Knight. The two guys are Brits who have toiled with great success in the foodie world abroad. They describe their food as rustic European fare, but it tasted rustic English (with great heaps of imagination) to us. The menu changes daily — depends on what kind of odd cuts of meat are delivered, quips Silk, a butcher by training — and always takes its vegetable influence from what's fresh seasonally. Some days you'll find a ham and parsley terrine, or the terrine might combine pigeon, pork and prune. Oxtail-stuffed cabbage, roasted pork belly, squid with chorizo and shepherd's pie topped with Gloucester cheese and leeks have been spied on the ever-flipping bill of fare. On a recent visit, the starters included "A Bowl of Necks," including chicken, quail and duck necks. A lovely rear garden (no street view!) feels like a pub in Sussex. Very nice wine list with good choices by the glass, and spotted dick with custard for dessert.

FIELD OF GREENS

2320 W. ALABAMA
between Kirby and Greenbriar
713-533-0029
www.fieldofgreenshouston.com
MAP E7

Beloved by eschewers of all that's meaty, this vegan/veggie/healthy-eating cafe does serve a few dishes featuring tuna and wild salmon, but the food thrust here is vegetarian replacement ingredients used in standard menu items. Order a burger and the patty may be made of falafel or soy chicken or portobello mushroom. Want a barbecue sandwich? Expect the organic barbecue sauce to be dribbled over grilled wheat roast, served with a side of tofu fries. There's a daily vegan soup and a breakfast menu with a line-up of breakfast tacos that includes one with soy sausage. Smoothies and tofu chocolate cake will satisfy the sweet-tooth. No corkage fee is charged at this BYOB establishment. It is a wee short on ambience, those stark green walls being reminiscent of an elementary school cafeteria. Reading matter of the expected alternative-lifestyle genre is available near the entrance.

FLEMING'S PRIME STEAKHOUSE

In a city that seems to acquire a new steakhouse every week, six-year old Fleming's has carved out a special niche. Part of the credit must go to the general manager/partner, Maeve Pesquera, who has built a large base

> **2405 W. ALABAMA** east of Kirby
> **713-520-5959**
> www.flemingssteakhouse.com
> **MAP** E7

of loyal fans from her days at Tony's and many new best friends. It also helps that this is intentionally not another "men's club" steakateria. The handsome interior has a lighter, brighter touch that appeals to both men and women. A long bar prides itself on offering 100 wines by the glass and is a congenial place to begin your visit before adjourning to a banquette where you can, we hope, converse with your companion without shouting. Wet-aged, hand-carved USDA Prime beef is the star attraction here. Sides include such old favorites as iceberg wedge salad, shoestring potatoes and creamed spinach. There is also a newer Fleming's location in The Woodlands at 1201 Lake Woodlands Dr., 281-362-0103.

FOGO DE CHAO

> **8250 WESTHEIMER** between Voss and Fondren
> **713-978-6500**
> www.fogodechao.com
> **MAP** C7

This *churrascaria*, Houston's oldest such Brazilian steakhouse, is an impressive place to take meat-lovers, if not your PETA friends. It's an all-you-can-eat concept, with waiters roaming the dining room with enormous skewers of grilled meat that they want to serve. Turn your table token to green-side-up, and waiter after waiter will stop to dispense a piece of meat onto your plate. This might be any of some 15 various cuts of beef, lamb, pork, chicken, linguiça, pork ribs and fatty-delicious ribeye. You can use your little tongs to take the meat as it's being sliced. If you're showing green, you'll be overwhelmed with meat. Quick, turn the token to the red-side-up to make them stop. Don't overlook the estimable salad/vegetable bar. Meat aside, our favorite treat here is the funny little cheese buns. Wow, we could eat a dozen. It's all presented in a handsome room suitable for impressing visiting corporate bigwigs or treating the family.

FOUNTAIN VIEW CAFE

> **1842 FOUNTAIN VIEW** south of San Felipe
> **713-785-9060**
> **MAP** D6

As neighborhoody as they come, what Avalon is to River Oaks and the Buffalo Grille is to West U., the Fountain View Cafe is to Tanglewood. Businessmen leave their jackets in the car and line up with well-buffed ladies in their workout togs. Soccer team boys cram in for pancakes and bacon, lone white-haired gents eat Reubens while perusing the newspaper and quartets of golfing buddies sit outside telling fish stories. Moms with strollers and strollers out for a walk with Mom stop by for the daily blue plate specials and the thick shakes. Order a single biscuit and the gravy is served in a bowl as big as your head, while the coleslaw is served in a Dixie cup. Open only for breakfast and lunch, many a hungry local has peered past the Closed sign into darkness at 6 p.m. and wept.

> **3736 WESTHEIMER** east of Weslayan/Willowick
> **713-572-8600**
> **MAP** D6

FRANK'S CHOP HOUSE

Two Franks — Frank Crapitto (Crapitto's Cucina Italiana) and Frank Butera (who helped open Carrabba's so many years ago) — partnered to open this spot in summer 2008, in the space where Joyce's Ocean Grill was. They do indeed serve steaks and chops, but the emphasis here is on a lighter, fresher, less testosterone-driven menu and ambiance. Expect many locally sourced vegetables, including Crapitto's own famous homegrown tomatoes.

FRENCHIE'S

So, what's in a name? Brothers Frank and Giuseppe Camera, who own both this Clear Lake-area restaurant and Villa Capri just down the road, have establishments very clearly Italian. Slinging pasta since 1979,

> **1041 NASA RD. 1** just east of I-45
> **281-486-7144**
> **MAP** Southeast of I9

the brothers are from the island of Capri, so it's no surprise that their food is a favorite among visiting Italian astronauts. (The walls are covered with NASA memorabilia and photos of celebrities posed with the Cameras.) During the day Frenchie's is a hectic counter-service spot that hits high on the noise level. It settles down a bit at night when table service puts people in their seats. Expect a lengthy wait for a table, especially on weekend nights. This is a place loaded with character and local color. It's not fine-dining, but decor, service and presentation put the "Ah" in customer satisfaction.

> **3919 SCOTT** at Wheeler, and other locations
> **713-748-2233**
> www.frenchyschicken.com
> **MAP** F7

FRENCHY'S CHICKEN

Fans of this funky fried-chicken chain — the Scott street location near U of H and Texas Southern University is the one to visit — are legion. Gathering its troops since the late 1960s, this walk-up, unprepossessing fast-food shack puts patrons through the drill with long lines, long waits and an aversion to credit cards (take cash to be safe). The cooking style leans heavily to the Creole/Cajun side, serving cayenne-laced fried chicken — many insist it's the best fried chicken in Houston — along with jambalaya and red beans and rice. Dirty rice can also be dished up, with collard greens, corn muffins and a really great bread pudding. Mention Frenchy's Chicken to a veteran customer and expect to see some salivating. There's something to be said about nostalgia for food you grew up with.

RECIPE **TO-DIE-FOR FUDGE PECAN PIE**

Dessert Gallery, 3200 Kirby, 713-522-9999, and two other locations

Sara Brook, Dessert Gallery owner and Houston's dessert diva, says, "This pie is so chocolate-y that it tickles going down — the true test of sufficient chocolate content. This pie is to-die-for (hence the name) whether you eat it room temperature, warm, cold or frozen, with or without ice cream, with or without fudge sauce over the ice cream. The possibilities are endless. Too bad the recipe only makes one pie."

1 10-inch pie shell, unbaked
1 cup (2 sticks) unsalted butter
5 oz. unsweetened chocolate
2 ½ cups sugar
½ cup half & half
4 whole eggs
1 egg yolk
1 ½ tsp. vanilla
¾ cup pecans, toasted

METHOD: Preheat oven to 425 degrees. Bake pie shell for 7 minutes. Remove from oven and cool. Reduce oven temperature to 350 degrees. Melt butter and chocolate in microwave. Add sugar and half & half and stir until sugar dissolves and mixture is smooth. (You can put the mixture back in the microwave to melt the sugar if necessary.) Beat eggs and yolk to blend in a small bowl. Gradually add eggs to slightly cooled chocolate mixture — you don't want to scramble the eggs — stirring until thick and smooth. Stir in vanilla. Pour batter into partially cooked pie shell and sprinkle pecans on top. Bake for 35 minutes or until completely set. Serves 6 to 8.

FUEGOVIVO CHURRASCARIA

11681 WESTHEIMER
between Wilcrest and Kirkwood
281-597-8108
www.fuegovivo.com
MAP B7

This Miami-based chain (they have three other locations in Florida) opened in April 2008 in a former Champps location. "Fuegovivo" means "roaring fire" in Portuguese and is meant to conjure up the gauchos' roaring fire: Service is rodizio style, with roving waiters bearing swords of beef, chicken, pork, linguiça and lamb. In addition to the grilled meats, a 20-foot two-tiered bar is stocked with some 50 side selections, including *feijoada* (black beans), salads, cured meats, carpaccio, boiled shrimp and traditional Brazilian dishes. Fried polenta and our favorite little cheese buns are on the table. It's a fun

---

Recommended
A MESS OF RIBS

Houston's best local rib purveyor, Williams Smokehouse, burned down in December 2007. But there are several other barbecue joints that will satisfy when you are in the mood for messy, smoky pork ribs.

BAKER'S RIBS, *2223 S. Voss, 713-977-8725*. Ribs are in the name of this small Dallas-based chain for a reason, and the hickory-smoked version are meaty, moist and flavorful. They're even more enjoyable with a few squirts of the warm vinegar-based sauce.

BURNS BAR BQ, *8397 De Priest, 281-445-7574*. Humbly situated in the northern part of the almost-rural Acres Homes neighborhood, the thick ribs are long-cooked and delicious. Many fans claim these are now the best ribs in town, and they might be right. Prepare to wait in line.

LULING CITY MARKET BAR-B-Q, *4726 Richmond, 713-871-1903*. Along with the brisket and sausage, the post oak-smoked ribs are done right here. We're also fans of the distinctive, tangy sauce featuring a faint mustard taste and slow-working spiciness.

PIZZITOLA'S BAR B CUE, *1703 Shepherd, 713-227-2283*. Boasting a barbecue pit that has been in operation since the 1930s, the meaty hickory-smoked ribs make it worthwhile to fight the midday lunch crowds that always fill the place.

THELMA'S BAR-B-QUE, *1020 Live Oak, 713-228-2262*. In this ramshackle shack east of downtown, the meaty ribs are cooked with both hickory and pecan. They are moist and messy — sometimes excellent, other times less so when the service gets overwhelmed.

way to eat, but come hungry. The restaurant is open for lunch weekdays, Sunday brunch and nightly dinner.

7320 SOUTHWEST FWY. between Bellaire Blvd. and Fondren
713-779-2288
www.fungskitchen.com
MAP C7

FUNG'S KITCHEN

This non-Americanized Cantonese spot promises there's a trip to Hong Kong inside … if you can find a place to park outside. There is culinary value in the six fish tanks that are swimming with oceanic creatures destined for the table. The seafood comes in live and fresh from around the world — Alaskan king crab, green mussels from New Zealand, etc. are among the creatures who temporarily pass time in the tanks — and seafood is what you come here to eat. From the book-length menu try the sautéed oysters, sliced abalone with black mushrooms, clams with black bean sauce, shredded dry scallop soup, whole fried fish and memorable softshell crabs served in a blizzard of golden minced garlic. Fried foods noted as "crispy" on the menu are beautifully done; fat-phobes will appreciate the very thin, light, battered crust. Friends have decried occasional cold dim sum. Rare lapses aside, Fung's Kitchen is the city's best mainstream Chinese restaurant.

GIGI'S ASIAN BISTRO & DUMPLING BAR

Located next to Del Frisco's, this handsome bistro with a sexy Asian vibe is the recent work (early 2008) of Gigi Huang, whose family long had

5085 WESTHEIMER near McCue, in The Galleria
713-629-8889
MAP D6

Hunan in The Pavilion. You can enter from the street or from inside The Galleria. If with a group, ask for a table in the "alley," where each cubbyhole is curtained off from prying eyes. Executive chef is Junnajet Hurapan, who emigrated here from New York City and his menu is inviting — samplings include crispy whole baby snapper, "Heavenly Beef" (oven-dried sirloin with coriander seed and chili sauce) and sesame-crusted tuna. There's a major yum factor in the house-made table condiments, including plum sauce and chile oil. Hurapan's wife, Jiraporn, is an expert pastry chef, so save room for her jackfruit crème brûlée, molten chocolate cake or the quartet of tiny cupcakes. As we go to press with this book, future plans call for patio dining and the namesake dumpling bar where diners can watch their dumplings being wrapped and stuffed.

GILHOOLEY'S

222 9TH ST. just off E. Bayshore Dr., San Leon

281-339-3813

MAP Southeast of 19

A few things to know before venturing down to this bayside legend: 1) Be sure to Google the best route from your part of Houston. 2) Take along no children younger than 18; they're not allowed. 3) Expect some of the best oysters on the planet. Oysters Gilhooley, the star attraction, come smoky-grilled on the half shell with parmesan and a secret sauce. Adding shrimp is allowed. We also recommend the gumbo and an excellent half-pound burger. Early risers brag about the breakfast selection, but we wouldn't know. You can't be too casually dressed to offend the locals, but a big-city attitude won't fly here. Just sit back, order a couple dozen of those delicious bivalves along with a cold beer or two, and thank your designated driver.

GLASS WALL

933 STUDEWOOD between Omar and E. 10th

713-868-7930

www.glasswalltherestaurant.com

MAP E5

In more ways than one, we're hitting the Heights here. Located in that section of Houston where dowdy meets do-overs, the Heights area has strange and wonderful things to offer — and chef/co-owner Lance Fegen's newish restaurant falls on the side of wonderful. Winner of the 2007 Houston Culinary Award for Restaurateur of the Year, Fegen subtly brings his love for surfing into the decor theme, but this place is all about food from a chef who loves his kitchen best. Co-owner/front-of-the-house guy Shepard Ross really knows wine, and you can trust him to help guide you. But help might not be required because the partners have taken wine selection to new "heights" in their recommended entree and wine pairings noted on the menu. Acoustics need work — it's very, very noisy when the place is running full out. Dinner only.

Shepard Ross and chef Lance Fegen have brought fine dining to a transitional area in The Heights.

GOODE CO. TAQUERIA & HAMBURGERS

4902 KIRBY at Westpark
713-520-9153
www.goodecompany.com
MAP E7

This Goode Co. production gives new meaning to the words "casual dining." That's why a large slice of Houstonians from corporate types to soccer teams patronize it. The order line moves rapidly enough; you pay up, take your ticket and wait to be called. This allows just enough time to stake out a table on the big enclosed patio or at one of the inside tables. The burgers and chili dogs are worthy, but many come for the Mexican dishes, which can be powered up with potent pico de gallo and salsa from the "fixings" bar. Weekend breakfast platters, served beginning at 7:30, would do your grandma proud: scrambled eggs with strips of crunchy corn tortillas and smoky pork-sausage patties, Brazos River pecan waffles with hot maple syrup, venison sausage, grilled quail, eggs with *nopalitos* and spicy green salsa. (Quiche really would taste pretty wimpy next to this.) Kids will love the strawberry *agua fresca* made with half and half or a cinnamon milkshake.

Recommended
BOILED CRAWFISH

When Houstonians talk about "pinching tail and sucking head," they're talking about eating crawfish. So tie on a bib and dig in. Note: The best, most authentic Cajun restaurants only serve fresh boiled crawfish in season, typically January through June. Avoid disappointment and call ahead to check availability.

BAYOU CITY SEAFOOD 'N PASTA, *4730 Richmond, 713-621-6602.* They boil excellent crawfish here, as well as serve Gulf Coast-styled pasta dishes, gumbo and other South Louisiana-style seafood.

FLOYD'S CAJUN SEAFOOD HOUSE, *20760 Gulf Fwy., Webster, 281-332-7474.* Expect that Floyd Landry boils crawfish the way it should be done, especially if you like them spicy.

MAGNOLIA BAR & GRILL, *6000 Richmond, 713-781-6207.* This jazzy upscale Cajun restaurant is one of the nicest places in the area to enjoy boiled crawfish — only in season, of course.

MARDI GRAS GRILL, *1200 Durham, 713-864-5600.* Down-home and friendly, this Cajun eatery is always packed during crawfish season.

RAGIN CAJUN, *4302 Richmond, 713-623-6321, and other locations.* The original location of this loud and popular chain of casual Cajun eateries is the best one in which to indulge in a big basket of boiled crawfish.

GOODE CO. TEXAS BAR-B-Q

5109 KIRBY between Bissonnet and Westpark
713-522-2530
www.goodecompany.com
MAP E7

8911 KATY FWY. between Campbell and Bingle/Voss
713-464-1901
MAP C6

Jim Goode's pair of Texana-crammed outposts offer what many contend is the best barbecue in town, with standing room only at peak hours. They look cool (and are sure-fire winners for visiting out-of-towners) and also dish up irresistible peppery chicken, beef brisket, Czech sausage, duck and pork ribs, all of it slow-smoked over mesquite. Move along the counter cafeteria-style and then head for one of the inside tables or, at the Kirby location, a picnic table on the patio. Don't pass on the jalapeño cheese bread (we prefer it to a regular bun for the chopped beef sandwich) or pecan pie, either. Though Texas barbecue might have its spiritual home in central Texas, the top Houston purveyors such as Goode Co. incorporate a wider range of influences and skills and pay much greater attention to the sides and desserts. That's all exemplified here.

GOODE CO. TEXAS SEAFOOD

2621 WESTPARK just west of Kirby
713-523-7154
www.goodecompany.com
MAP E7

10211 KATY FWY. west of Gessner
713-464-7933
MAP C6

Jim Goode has been a dedicated fisherman all his life, and he has brought his love for Texas Gulf Coast finny favorites along with Cajun and Mexican variations to the table … and the counter, which many regulars prefer. No competitor has ever been able to equal Goode's sundae-glass *campechana* served here, boosted with cubed avocado and chopped onion. Then there's a wide selection of fresh filets that are offered fried or mesquite grilled, plus lip-blistering gumbo, generously stuffed fried seafood po'boys and what some claim is the best catfish filet in town. Orders arrive at the table as soon as they come out of the kitchen, assuring maximum flavor, if uneven food delivery. Some famous Houston types consider the Westpark location — set in an old railroad car — their hidey-hole restaurant, and it would be indiscreet to name them here. The newer Katy Freeway location is a traditional seafood house and more upscale. Both locations, with their respective gallery of photographs, are a true-life tribute to Gulf Coast fishing.

GORDITAS AGUASCALIENTES

Regulars insist these havens for traditional Mexican food are the real deal.

> **6102 BISSONNET**
> between Renwick and Hillcroft, and other locations
> **713-541-4560**
> **MAP** D7

No Tex-Mex going on here. Instead what comes from these Houston kitchens looks and tastes exactly like fare from kitchens in central Mexico. Mornings will find a host of breakfast tacos that can be washed down with hot *atole* — a drink that mixes masa, cinnamon and chocolate. Lunch and dinner standouts include tortas, *sopes*, the namesake gorditas and tacos. Any of these may be ordered with *barbacoa* (meat from the cow's head), *nopales* (prickly pear cactus, said to guard the body against diabetes), pork, chicken, *chicharron* (cracklings), *rajas* (poblano pepper strips) and other popular fillings. Homemade tortillas, huge bowls of soup and a highly praised green sauce round out the attractions. We know people who do nothing but search for the perfect green sauce, so if you're one of them, Gorditas has got it going on. The Bissonnet location has an especially lively jukebox.

GRAND LUX CAFE

It's only fitting that Las Vegas was the birthplace of this over-the-top chain. It's soaring and oversized, richly embellished and, well, simply grand. Think Gustav Klimt, old Vienna, Cheesecake Factory (its owner) taken to warp fantasy level. It has a pseudo-elegance that's right off the Strip, with chandeliers, marble floors and plush banquettes you could get lost in. Still, Galleria shoppers and nearby office workers find it to their liking because it isn't stuffy dining and the prices are more reasonable than the location might suggest. (It also doesn't hurt that there's ample free parking.) A glance at the lunch and dinner menus indicates a restaurant eager to please as many appetites as possible: Jamaican this, Mongolian that, Mexican whatever; even a bento box, plus burgers, pastas, salads and grilled meat and fish. Taking a clue from its very successful progenitor, there are also delicious baked-to-order desserts.

> **5000 WESTHEIMER**
> just west of Post Oak Blvd.
> **713-629-5565**
> www.grandluxcafe.com
> **MAP** D6

> **807 TAFT** south of Allen Parkway
> **713-522-0995**
> www.gravitasrestaurant.com
> **MAP** E6

GRAVITAS

Gravitas has had buzz since it opened in 2005. A project of Scott Tycer (he once had the red-hot Aries) and Australian chef Jason Gould, it turns out bistro food with a designer's touch in a barebones historic building. The dining room is cool and urbane, with rich dark woodwork — who'd guess

Personal Favorites
YES, HONEY, WE *CAN* TAKE THE KIDS
By Sarah Gish

Although there are more than 11,000 restaurants in Houston, not all are kid-friendly. Because I have two kids of my own — and for my publications — I have scouted many restaurants to gauge their kid-friendliness. Here are several suggestions.

Mexican restaurants are almost always a sure bet — they're colorful, food comes quickly and everyone is usually able to find something they like to eat. **MOLINA'S MEXICAN RESTAURANT** (*7901 Westheimer, 713-782-0861, and 4720 Washington, 713-862-0013*) is a great choice, as is **LOPEZ'S RESTAURANT** (*11606 Wilcrest, 281-568-5639*), which has been around for decades. **CHUY'S** (*2706 Westheimer, 713-524-1700, and 18035 North Fwy., Shenandoah, 936-321-4440*), with its hubcap decorations, is also fun.

SKEETER'S is friendly to families as well as groups of stinky little kids, otherwise known as sports teams. The website (www.skeetersgrill.com) lists its nine locations and posts its full menu, which includes a $3.99 kids' menu. Skeeters encourages diners to doodle while they eat, providing crayons and butcher-paper table covers. Exceptional drawings are displayed on the walls.

HICKORY HOLLOW (*101 Heights Blvd., 713-869-6300*) is one of our favorite places to eat while enjoying live music on Fridays or Saturdays. Kids can dance wildly up front with the band while you nosh and drink. It's a casual Texas honky-tonk in the Heights.

Restaurants with mini-playgrounds for kids get high marks from me, and I like **LUPE TORTILLA'S** (*2414 Southwest Fwy., 713-522-4420, and other locations*). Lupe Tortilla's provides a sandbox and play area for tots while parents can kick back and sip a chilled margarita.

At **BENIHANA** (*9707 Westheimer, 713-789-4962, and other locations*) it's okay to play with your food. *Teppan* chefs regale children and adults with knife-juggling theatrics and expert showmanship.

Chinese restaurants can be very family-friendly and places like **FUNG'S KITCHEN** (*7320 Southwest Fwy., 713-779-2288*) offer dim sum daily. Some have buffets, so small fry can organize their own meal. Plus there's the bonus of fortune cookies at the end.

LUBY'S CAFETERIAS (*1414 Waugh, 713-528-0880, and other locations*) has a family-friendly menu that offers low-priced kids' dishes. The little ones seem to love coasting through the line in their rolling high chairs and enjoy the power of selecting their own meal.

Families traveling to the downtown **AQUARIUM** (*410 Bagby, 713-223-3474*) ought to make a day of it. Houston's first public aquarium features 500,000 gallons of visible underwater tanks, including an acrylic tunnel with live sharks swimming overhead. After a long day of underwater adventure, visit the Marina Matinee cafe or the Aquarium restaurant for a meal of — you guessed it — seafood.

Across the street from the Aquarium, the **HARD ROCK CAFE** (*502 Texas, 281-479-7025*) is a glitzy attraction in downtown's Bayou Place. The menu it's mesquite? — dressed up as a gallery hung with works by well-known local artists. Gould, who has won Houston Culinary Awards from *My Table* magazine for both "Up-and-Coming Chef of the Year" (2006) and "Chef of the Year" (2007), applies a refined touch to such crowd-pleasers as pan-fried calf's liver and a steak frites platter. Though the menu will not daunt even the most timid diner, there are more than a few twists such as the venison chili, crispy veal sweetbreads, buttermilk pierogies filled with cream cheese and marinated lamb served on chickpeas. The menu also offers bistro favorites from many sources: salt cod brandade, *croque monsieur*, baked cheese spätzle, lamb shank with polenta, a sausage plate with sauerkraut, even a pan-fried schnitzel. Don't overlook the bread basket from Gravitas' sister establishment, Kraftsmen Baking, which runs the risk of becoming your meal all by itself. Fine wine list, too, and there's an adjacent lounge that is a draw in its own right on weekends. Park in the back.

12330 SOUTHWEST FWY.
between W. Airport and S. Kirkwood, Stafford, and other locations
281-980-7482
www.gringosmexicankitchen.com
MAP B8

GRINGO'S MEXICAN KITCHEN

Owner Russell Ybarra is a restaurateur who has raked in honors for his savvy entrepreneurial know-how. And he knows his food, which he calls "nacho average Tex-Mex."

includes huge portions of American fare, such as burgers, fries, ribs, chopped salads and milkshakes. Kids love the rock 'n roll memorabilia and can entertain themselves studying the displays until their food arrives.

IKEA (*7808 Katy Fwy., 713-688-7867*), the Swedish home-furnishings warehouse, has a family-friendly dining area complete with use-it-yourself microwaves. You can put the kids in Ikea childcare after eating while you shop.

Finally, a great place where you can have your cake and eat it, too, is **DESSERT GALLERY** (*3200 Kirby, 713-522-9999, and other locations*). Choose from soups, wraps, salads, sandwiches and kid-friendly food like mac and cheese and PB&J sandwiches. You can top off the meal with one of its scrumptious desserts while the kids chow on cupcakes or the super-fun "Design Your Own Cookie Platters" or the "S'mores Pupu Platters" (kids love the name and don't worry, there's no fire). Plus, it always has board games on hand, so no one should be, well, bored.

Sarah Gish owns Gish Creative (www.gishcreative.com), a full-service marketing company she founded in 2000. Her publications include The Summer Book: A Guide to Houston Day Camps for Kids and Teens *and an e-newsletter,* Gish Picks: A Guide to Cultural Activities for Families.

Serving an unexpected signature Cozamel chicken salad, he also ratchets up a time-honored staple with another signature dish — seafood enchiladas stuffed with crawfish tails and Gulf shrimp served in a white wine sauce. Expect the usual sides to also have flair, such as the andouille *baracho* beans. Dining in the Old Mexico-themed setting is a treat, especially when it doesn't cost an arm and a leg. Thin chips for dipping into another celebrated green sauce. In the cantina try the Banderita — frozen strawberry and lime margarita laced with melon liqueur. Family-friendly.

4715 WESTHEIMER just inside Loop 610
713-622-3663
www.grottorestaurants.com
MAP D6

9595 SIX PINES south of Research Forest, The Woodlands
281-419-4252
MAP North of D1

GROTTO

This longtime home-grown favorite first arrived on the local scene in the 1980s as a mural-lined hot spot in Highland Village before landing at its present address near The Galleria. It has an impressive antipasti bar and Neapolitan-inspired *pranzo* selections — ravioli, lasagne, penne, etc. — built with from-scratch pastas. The kitchen also turns out some fine veal and seafood dishes. Business lunch specials feature an entree plus salad or soup for about $16. When you have a little time to relax, order a bellini, some pasta and one of Grotto's wickedly caloric desserts. The staff will make you feel rich and pampered. Since becoming part of the Landry's empire, the brand has been rolled out to places like The Woodlands, Dallas, Las Vegas and Palm Beach.

THE GROVE

The Schiller Del Grande group scooped everyone by getting the contract to operate this high-profile spot in front of the George R. Brown Convention Center and opened it in early 2008. They wisely installed chef Ryan Pera (previously at *17 in the Alden Hotel) to oversee the kitchen. The menu by Pera and foodie-god Robert Del Grande is "American rustic," owing to its focus on rotisserie specialties, steaks and seafood. We loved the Long Island duck meatballs to nibble with drinks, as well as the taste of fiery fish sauce in the deviled eggs, the sensational crab cocktail with remoulade, pulled pork on tiny corn cakes, mirin-brushed

1611 LAMAR at Crawford, in Discovery Green
713-337-7321
www.thegrovehouston.com
MAP F6

Enjoy a cocktail, even dinner, at The Grove's stylish bar.

chicken wings and mesquite-smoked quail. Even the addictive olives are cured in-house. There's a mix of high ceilings, glass, red brick and soothing lime accents downstairs, while on the second level it's so "upscale" that the outside deck soars above the trees. Aptly dubbed The Treehouse, upstairs is a place to wait for your reservations to kick in while quaffing drinks, munching appetizers and schmoozing with the in-crowd. Some people are calling this spot Houston's version of Manhattan's Tavern on the Green. But we disagree. This is all Houston hip.

2925 SOUTHWEST FWY.
between Kirby and Buffalo Speedway, and other locations
713-942-0772
www.guadalajarahacienda.com
MAP E7

GUADALAJARA BAR & GRILL

This big, boisterous choice for Mexican food promises "hacienda style" atmosphere, but don't expect that to translate as quaint and quiet. It does a steady business in families and large parties, so "fiesta" might be a better description. There's a sizable bar that offers the requisite margaritas and cervezas along with a happy-hour appetizer menu. "*Favoritos de la casa*" include seafood enchiladas, the bacon-wrapped Pacifico shrimp, grilled South Texas quail and snapper Veracruz. The fajitas have a menu all their own. Weather permitting, retreat to the patio for more peaceful dining.

HARD ROCK CAFE

Houston's take on the international chain has a strong Texas accent. It's loud fun, abuzz with people mingling and gawking at the memorabilia: the guitars of Rusty Hills, BB King and Harry Wilson, one of Buddy Holly's songwriting contracts and such. Of course, you'll find it hard to not notice the shop where the Hard Rock T-shirts, caps and jackets are sold. Finally there is the food, which is good enough. The down-home menu includes burgers (which

502 TEXAS between Smith and Bagby
713-227-1392
www.hardrockcafe.com
MAP F6

we found messy and delicious), babyback ribs, salads, milkshakes and homemade pie. Children and teens love it, as do adults with a nostalgic bent for classic rock'n'roll. As with Hard Rock's other national locations, it is what it is and maybe not the worst place for a cocktail or a beer after you've been to a performance at nearby Jones Hall, the Alley, Hobby Center or Wortham Center. The Verizon Wireless Theater and Angelika Film Center are both next door. Look for the 35-foot Gibson Firebird guitar in the sky.

HARRY'S
Follow your nose to the spic-and-span stand-alone structure on Bagby near the spur to the Southwest Freeway to find this homage to the great American breakfast. Perfectly cooked large eggs, golden hash browns

Recommended
PIZZA PALACES

Forget a square meal — we love these meals in a circle. Here are some of our favorite Houston pizzas.

ARCODORO RISTORANTE ITALIANO, *5000 Westheimer, 713-621-6888.* Try the thin-crust *profumi sardi* (roasted eggplant mousse sprinkled with goat cheese, topped with slivers of pecorino sardo and a drizzle of bitter honey). Better known as a fine-dining restaurant, Arcodoro has a chef from near Naples (pizza's birthplace), a very hot oven and some unique combinations, both savory and slightly sweet.

CANDELARI'S PIZZERIA, *6002 Washington, 832-200-1474, and other locations.* Excess plays well at Candelari's, bolstered by the excellent house-made sausages. We recommend "King Mike's": Italian sausage, sundried tomato chicken sausage, pesto, roasted garlic, bacon, portobello and feta. Delivery available.

DOLCE VITA PIZZERIA ENOTECA, *500 Westheimer, 713-520-8222.* It's tough to choose the best pizza among the exemplary individual-sized thin and crusty pizzas at Marco Wiles' *pizzeria e ristorante*. First time visit? Order the *prosciutto e rucola*, featuring both prosciutto di San Daniele and mozzarella di bufala with arugula. Excellent wine list.

KENNEALLY'S, *2119 S. Shepherd, 713-630-0486.* This Irish pub is famous for its "Shamrock Special" pizza, which is topped with slices of corned beef, mushrooms, onions and bell peppers. Sounds weird, tastes great.

STAR PIZZA, *2111 Norfolk, 713-523-0800, and 3616 Washington, 713-869-1241.* Insiders order the Joe's pizza, with spinach and garlic atop a crust that is thick and buttery tasting. It's the most popular pizza at Houston's favorite pizza joint. Delivery available.

318 TUAM at Bagby
713-528-0198
www.harrysrestaurantcafe.com
MAP E6

and hefty pancakes are some of the prime attractions. Waffles served with chicken strips, French toast, a shrimp omelet, catfish and grits and a grilled center-cut pork chop are also most worthy for breaking fast. For those who must have their Mexican food at all hours of the day, there are migas, huevos rancheros and generous breakfast tacos. Though open for lunch, breakfast is the reason to visit: Their uninspiring lunchtime steam table spread will only excite the Luby's crowd. Breakfast is served everyday at Harry's, on the weekends 7 a.m. to 2 p.m. We like the classic American-diner setting, and love it that Harry's website plays Big Band music — it puts us "In the Mood."

HIMALAYA

6652 SOUTHWEST FWY. near Hillcroft
713-532-2837
MAP C7

The owner's enthusiasm and love for what he's cooking sets the tone at this Pakistani restaurant. Chef/owner Kaiser Lashkari is large, jovial and nearly messianic in his belief in the quality of his food, and it is his habit to come over to the table to help with your order. Probably he will recommend *resha ghosh*. It's beef, steamed until fall-apart tender, shredded, then stir-fried with what tastes like the full arsenal of Pakistani spices. It is breathtakingly, beads-of-sweat-on-your-forehead good. Nearly as good are two chicken dishes: Chicken *hara mosh* is an extraordinarily spicy green curry thick with herbs that Lashkari boasts of having invented, and *handi* chicken is tomato-y and gingery, more warmly spiced than the green, but equally delicious. Just as good is the *chopli kebab*, a spicy meat patty delicious with the warm parathas. The fresh hot flat bread, in fact, is practically reason enough to come here. Beloved among serious foodies and well regarded in the local Pakistani community, Himalaya is located in a simple, modest setting in the same strip center as London Sizzler and India Grocers.

2243 RICHMOND
between Greenbriar and Kirby
713-528-3418
www.hobbitcafe.verycool.at
MAP E7

HOBBIT CAFE

The granola-and-sprouts crowd has long come here for inexpensive health food and delicious fruit smoothies. These days, the menu lists wine, beer and even — gasp! — several non-vegetarian items. There are plenty of options. The yogurt is a made-in-house creation, they do have carrot juice, but also serve mimosas. Your burger may be fashioned of either good beef or soy and black beans. Still, you won't feel out of place if your Birkenstocks brought you in for apple almond pancakes or a Gandalf sandwich made with piles of avocado, mushrooms and melted cheese. Next time we visit, gingerbread pancakes are on the list as a must-try. Beyond the expected Tolkienesque naming of food items, there's a distinct Middle-Earthiness about the shabby tavern-like building, the pot-holed parking lot and even the hooked shower curtain hanging before the ladies room toilet.

> **2409 MONTROSE** at Fairview
> **713-523-8808**
> **MAP** E6

HOLLYWOOD VIETNAMESE & CHINESE

From an elephantine menu that literally takes you all over the place, the diner may choose to gastronomically visit Paris, Saigon or Peking, all while sitting on a popular patio festooned with colorful adornments and semi-screened from the street by plants. At this restaurant located in the heart of Montrose — once it was the hip Cafe Noche — one may also partake of the international vittles indoors, knowing the signs at the crossroads point toward satisfying a slew of appetites with a kitchen that cooks Vietnamese, Chinese and French. All of it's pretty good, if not spectacular, and we recommend you stick with the Vietnamese offerings. (Wrap-your-own Vietnamese fajitas in rice paper is a good choice.) No Oscar for the cuisine, but this spot makes a nice run for it. Of note: Hollywood is open to 2 a.m. Sunday through Thursday and to 4 a.m. on Friday and Saturday nights. It's located in an area with a high density of gay bars, so it's something of a pick-up joint late at night.

HUGO'S

Hugo Ortega's eponymously named citadel of regional Mexican cuisine is properly pronounced "Oo-goes," but rarely is. Housed in a nicely restored 1920s building, it's been a hit since opening day. (Of course, co-owner/wife Tracy Vaught's other popular properties, Backstreet Cafe and Prego, have a reputation for tasty eating, too.) Don't think of this place as Tex-Mex; the menu has gone far south of the border to introduce Houstonians to the distinctive flavors of places like Oaxaca (the birthplace of *mole*) and Puebla (the birthplace of Ortega himself). And who else would dare offer fried grasshoppers on occasion? Sunday

> **1602 WESTHEIMER** at Mandell
> **713-524-7744**
> www.hugosrestaurant.com
> **MAP** E6

brunch — complete with a Mexican band up on the mezzanine — can be a great introduction to Hugo's. Offerings include *cochinita pibil* (pork cooked in banana leaves), ceviche, *chilaquiles* and *costillas de res en salsa verde* (beef short ribs in green sauce). Other attractions include a pretty and private patio, mixologist extraordinaire Sean Beck and scrumptious desserts by Ortega's brother, Ruben Ortega. Definitely recommended.

HUNGRY'S CAFE & BISTRO

2356 RICE BLVD.
near Greenbriar
713-523-8652
www.hungryscafe.com
MAP E7

14075 MEMORIAL
near Dairy Ashford
281-493-1520
MAP A6

Just a block from the Rice University campus and going on 30-plus years, the Rice Boulevard location has become a neighborhood institution. A half block away from the Village shopping turmoil, there's parking up front, but customers often walk in or take out. Hungry's serves up health-conscious, reasonably priced foods seven days a week with brunch on the weekends. It also caters and delivers. The extensive menu aims to be all things to all people, and that includes kid-friendly selections. You may not be overwhelmed by the food, but you won't be disappointed with this unassuming diner. The Memorial location recently completed an overhaul and built a bar-lounge adjacent.

IBIZA

2450 LOUISIANA at McGowen
713-524-0004
www.ibizafoodandwinebar.com
MAP E6

Although he lost by one point to chef Mario Batali on the Food Network's *Iron Chef*, Ibiza chef/co-owner Charles Clark scores a win every time in his Spanish-inspired restaurant. With wife Sherry and business partner Grant Cooper, the trio stays on point delivering all that's tasteful to a consistently packed house. It's all noisy sophistication here, with spirits high and happy because the food and the reasonably priced wine are so good. The mouth waters thinking about grilled shrimp with smoked jalapeño butter resting on crabmeat cornbread, six-hour lamb shank laced with Spanish mint oil and pan-seared foie gras. Other high notes: ravioli stuffed with snails and boursin cheese napped with an anchovy cream, an amusingly retro wedge of iceberg lettuce with green goddess dressing, venison chop with a sour cherry demiglace and apple-smoked bacon risotto. We could rhapsodize on and on, and so we will ... pork rib roast, succulent and juicy, with a luxurious foie gras blackberry butter atop spicy mashed potatoes, sea bass with mango essence and Rioja broth on a bed of a toothy risotto. Then comes the lovely tradition of Sunday evening paella and sangria that draws us from home to end the weekend on a savory-sweet note.

516 WESTHEIMER
between Taft and Montrose
713-524-2170
www.indikausa.com
MAP E6

INDIKA

With so much good press she could cover a wall, chef/owner Anita Jaisinghani has won praises from such heavyweights as *The New York Times*, *Gourmet* and the *Zagat Survey*. (*My Table* magazine, too!) Her cooking style is touted as Indian fusion, but to our minds "fusion" simply means impressively creative. Dining at her pretty lower-Montrose restaurant is guaranteed to make your mouth happy (on fire, maybe, with some dishes, but still happy). For the coconut lover, try *aviyal* — a vegetable coconut stew served with saffron pilaf and mint chutney, and at Sunday brunch enjoy coconut pancakes heaped with blueberries. Eggplant stuffed with *paneer* (fresh cheese) and cashews rivals the pine nut-stuffed tandoori quail for nutty lusciousness. Try also the fiery *Goan* chicken (dark meat), the banana leaf-steamed prawns, grilled pompano with millet lentil pilaf and the gunpowder salmon. Physically, Indika has a simultaneously high-tech and medieval feel. Tiny spotlights hang from parallel wires that span a dining room bathed in soothing apricot, persimmon, orange and caramel tones. A low burnished-steel picket fence separates the floor-level dining room from a raised section, its row of tables partitioned by what look like jousting-tournament flags. Long banners hanging on the foyer wall sway like pendulums in the breeze admitted whenever anybody enters or leaves. And the wall between the dining room and the bar area has grated windows that suggest a dungeon. Want to try this cooking at home? Jaisinghani shares an understanding of herbs, spices and all manner of foods in a monthly cooking class that's open to all and nicely priced.

Be sure to save room for one of Indika's desserts, traditional or unexpectedly modern.

INKA SOUTH AMERICAN CUISINE

12225 WESTHEIMER
between Kirkwood and Dairy Ashford
832-379-1717
MAP B7

Literally a bright spot in west Houston, Inka is painted in vibrant oranges and yellows and showcases South American folk art. Life-size metal palm trees and one-of-a-kind hand-painted tables make Inka a feast for the eyes, and the food is just as bright. The menu is pan-South American with seven ceviches and four choices for mussels or clams. In addition, beef, chicken and pork are featured in tortas, empanadas and entrees. The excellent *empanadas de puerco*, for example, are stuffed with seasoned shredded pork, a bit of melted cheese and wrapped in flaky pastry. An order includes two huge empanadas, your choice of sweet potato fries, yucca fries or *maduros* (sautéed plantains) and tomatillo-red onion relish. There's a covered patio for outdoor dining, full bar and an extensive coffee menu, thanks to Cafe Inka (its sibling next door), which serves South American coffees, sandwiches and pastries. Although new (opening in 2008), Inka is earning praise for creative presentations and Sunday brunch.

IRMA'S

22 N. CHENEVERT
at Commerce, just north of Minute Maid Park
713-222-0767
MAP F6

For first-timers, please know going in that the menu is speed-recited in Spanish — and since it's understood among gentle folk that mentioning the price is tacky, meal prices aren't mentioned. If not holding a printed menu in your hand is of no consequence to you, everything else will be peachy. It might help push you toward a visit to know that the venerable James Beard Foundation named Irma's one of five 2008 "American Classic" restaurants. There's dubious "classic" in the tawdry décor — it's crammed with junk, Christmas lights, weird gewgaws, campaign posters, neon, old parlor lamps and more — but we adore it. But big "classic" kudos go to the Mexican home cooking here. Owner and *capitán general* Irma Galvan (she's in the safari shorts and combat boots) always oversees front and back of the house with a strong and colorful character: She will pour your lemonade (a miraculous concoction) while barking orders to those in service. Bigwig downtowners love her and love this spot. They'll tuck into chicken and spinach enchiladas, stuffed-with-pork enchiladas and, like the rest of us, get wolfishly ravenous over cheese enchiladas. The *carne guisada* is stuff to write home about, and so is just about everything else.

ISLA COQUI

1801 DURHAM
just south of I-10
713-861-1000
www.islacoquipr.com
MAP E6

For a flavorful slice of Puerto Rico this is the place. Start with the *empanada de queso* (a baked, not fried, cheddar cheese turnover), *bacalaitos* (codfish fritters), *mofonguitos de yuca* (fried cassava balls) and *conitos de plátanos rellenos de camarones* (little cups made of plantain filled with shrimp). You'll find an emphasis on the wondrous plantain here. House specialties, for instance, are all about *mofongos* — fried green plantains mashed with pork cracklings and other ingredients. You can even order a plantain and beef pie (*pastelón de maduros*). Recommendations beyond the exotic banana: Try the *masitas de cerdo* (pork chunks) and shrimp in a sauce of white wine, onions, tomatoes and peppers. For a sweet finish, passion fruit mousse, *tres leches* (does it appear on every Latin menu in town?) and the surprisingly delicious *flan de queso*.

ISTANBUL GRILL

5613 MORNINGSIDE
near University Blvd.
713-526-2800
MAP E7

Casual and easygoing with a delightful little patio, Istanbul is a great meeting place before a pub crawl through Rice Village. (To start your crawl, the Ginger Man is just next door.) Just beware of carb-overload: Istanbul's warm savory bread is your appetizer and is prominent in one of the best entrees, the *kiyamali pide*, something like an individual pizza, with deliciously spiced ground lamb and chopped vegetables. Kids will love the *peynirli pide*, which is a Turkish cheese pizza. And they will probably learn more about Turkey sitting in Istanbul Grill than they do in geography class, as artifacts, maps, photos and evil eyes (called *nazar bancuk*, to ward off bad luck and jealousy) cover the walls and table tops. Must-order here: kabobs. There are all kinds, including lamb, chicken, beef and seasoned ground meat. All succulent and juicy, all come with rice, grilled tomatoes and bell peppers. Friendly waitstaff, horrible parking.

JABOUR'S FINE DINING

14019 SOUTHWEST FWY. west of Dairy Ashford, Sugar Land
281-980-2130
MAP B9

Partners Jody and Joyce Jabour, Kerry Ream and chef Jason Jones serve classic American favorites with a French accent in a relaxing space (it used to be Sugar Creek Grill) with buttery yellow walls, plush dark green carpet and lots of natural light. Jabour's menu features seafood, steaks and their signature crabcakes that are offered as both an appetizer and an entree. The wine room can be reserved for

RECIPE **PAN-SEARED DUCK BREAST WITH SAUCE MIROIR**

Rainbow Lodge, 2011 Ella Blvd., 713-861-8666

The inspiration for this dish reaches back to Rainbow Lodge owner Donnette Hansen's roots, which include a love for the great outdoors and comfort food. "Grilled duck breast, creamed mustard greens, polenta (or grits), a fantastic Pinot Noir and a warm fire … you can't get any 'lodgier' than that."

4 skin-on duck breasts (6 to 8 oz. each)
salt & black pepper
2 Tbsp. olive oil
Sauce Miroir (recipe below)

METHOD: Pre-heat oven to 400 degrees. Pat duck breasts dry with paper towels and place skin-side down on cutting board. Remove any silver skin or sinew. Turn breasts over and score skin (being sure not to cut the flesh) in a crosshatch pattern. Cut lengthwise down the skin and about every quarter-inch, cut across the width to form diamond shapes. This will help the duck breast cook evenly.

Place a stainless steel, non-reactive sauté pan (large enough to fit all four duck breasts without them touching) over medium-high heat. Season both sides of breasts liberally with salt and pepper. Add olive oil to pan and then duck breasts skin-side down. Sear until skin releases from the pan easily, about 2 to 3 minutes. Turn breasts over and sear flesh side for about 1 minute. Turn back over to skin side and place the pan in the oven and roast for 7 to 8 minutes (for medium-rare). Remove from oven. Place duck breasts on a warm plate lined with paper towels and let rest for 4 to 5 minutes in a warm place. Once rested, thinly slice the duck breast.

To plate: Place a spoonful of Sauce Miroir on plate and place the sliced duck breast on top. Serves 4.

Sauce Miroir (Mirror Sauce)

1 bottle red wine (Shiraz or Cabernet Sauvignon will do just fine)
1 large shallot, sliced
1 garlic clove
1 fresh bay leaf
1 sprig fresh thyme
1 Tbsp. black peppercorns
1 cup sugar

METHOD: Combine all ingredients except sugar in a pot and reduce by two-thirds. Add sugar and reduce some more until thickened. Remove from heat and strain through a fine mesh strainer. Let cool to room temperature for use. Sauce will keep in refrigerator for one month before the flavors begin to dull.

private parties of up to 24 guests. Jabour's is still new — it opened in late 2007 — but already winning over a regular suburban clientele.

3607 S. SHEPHERD at Richmond, and other locations
713-524-7400
www.jamesconeyisland.com
MAP E7

JAMES CONEY ISLAND
People can be adamant about where to find the best burgers or barbecue in town. To that short list, add hot dogs. James Coney Island has been an often-named favorite since two Greek immigrants, Tom and James Papadakis, opened their first location downtown in 1923. Brother James's name is on the door because he won a coin toss. For years, the upstairs dining room was fondly known as the "Linoleum Club" by the Houston power brokers who could be found there daily. It took 40 years and an ownership shakeup for a second site to be opened. But some things haven't changed. The original mustard, chili sauce and onion version is still on the menu, and generations of families still chow down with gusto. That original downtown location is gone now, but a chain of some 20 JCIs has sprung up around town.

JAPANEIRO'S SUSHI BISTRO & LATIN GRILL
Mirroring our city's unconventional melting-pot food culture, Japaneiro's offers a relaxed family-restaurant atmosphere by day; at night, it morphs into a trendy nightspot with

2168 TEXAS DR., in Sugar Land Town Square, Sugar Land
281-242-1121
www.japaneiro.com
MAP F6

a distinct Latin flare. The connection is sushi. Japaneiro's signature dishes include the Cabo San Lucas (a double-decker yellowtail tuna roll) and a charbroiled churrasco steak. Imagine ordering a meal that could include mojitos and sushi, charbroiled churrasco and sashimi, salmon tostadas and *hamachi maki* and, yes, even yuca fries and steamed dumplings as sides. The Latin side of the menu will put some rhythm in your shoes so you'll be ready when the staff remove the dining tables for Latin music and dancing on weekends. Open daily for lunch and dinner. It's owned by Robert White, who also has Sasu Sushi.

JASPER'S
After conquering the food scenes in Dallas, Austin and Plano, restaurant impresario Kent Rathbun brought his "backyard gourmet" to The Woodlands and plopped his sophisticated setting and American comfort food menu down on Market Street overlooking the square. Promising

> **9595 SIX PINES** at Lake Woodlands Dr., The Woodlands
> **281-298-6600**
> www.jaspers-restaurant.com
> **MAP** North of D1

diners the experience will be "like eating at my house," Rathbun stimulates appetite with fall-off-the-bone, slow-smoked baby back ribs, an aged Gouda mac and cheese dish that throws in cured ham and fantastic house-made potato chips with blue cheese. The smoked bacon cheeseburger comes with onions braised in Shiner Bock and, by request, can be made with Kobe beef. Desserts are phantasmagorical — banana parfait with homemade 'nilla wafers and a cherry limeade pie are featured among the sweet treats. Aromas of good food blowing down from the north tease city folk into making a drive up to The Woodlands.

JAX GRILL

The Shepherd location is a classic roadhouse smack in the middle of town where fun rules and food bows subservient to the spirited atmosphere. There's a Cajun focus on the fare, with gumbo a standout, and bacon-wrapped shrimp with a jalapeño kick and a surprising oyster hidden in the wrap. Sidle up to the counter to put in your order — burgers, a respectable chicken-fried steak, salads, fried shrimp po'boys, mesquite-grilled fajitas. Live Zydeco music on Friday and Saturday nights boosts the mood even higher, with dancing a must-boogie temptation. (The cavernous space inside doesn't seem spacey enough once the crowds hit.) For dessert, the famous Jax Sack (cherished by diners who ate at the long-gone Jack's on Woodway) is a tall bag-shaped confection made of pure chocolate filled with cream, cake and goodies that serves four. Kids are certainly welcome at the Shepherd location to dance to the music and hang out with their parents, but, in general, the Bellaire location is more family oriented.

> **1613 SHEPHERD** between I-10 and Washington
> **713-861-5529**
> **MAP** E6
>
> **6510 S. RICE AVE.** near Bellaire Blvd.
> **713-668-3606**
> **MAP** D7

> **307 N. SAM HOUSTON PARKWAY EAST** east of I-45
> **281-931-7654**
> www.jimmyg.com
> **MAP** E2

JIMMY G'S CAJUN SEAFOOD RESTAURANT

Kind of stuck out in no-man's-land on the highway to Bush Intercontinental Airport, Jimmy G's takes advantage of the executive airport business in terms of pricing and cursory (but adequate) service. On a recent visit, we had the impression that it seats the few regulars in a small section around the open kitchen, where they receive good treatment, and the majority of traveling flotsam gets dumped into the big space that feels like a cafeteria. The gumbo was looser than what we like, but still nicely smoky with plenty of meat. Also pleasing: shrimp and oyster embrochette, crawfish bisque and crabmeat au gratin (in season).

5161 SAN FELIPE between Post Oak Blvd. and Sage
713-960-0333
www.jimmywilsons.com
MAP D6

JIMMY WILSON'S SEAFOOD & CHOP HOUSE

In the soaring and dramatic space that La Strada once occupied, Denis Wilson and Jim Jard set up shop in late 2007. (Around the same time, they sold their Westheimer location.) The new digs are more upscale than the original location, with dramatically lit photographs of the Texas coast, and racks of wine bottles that soar from floor to ceiling. But this is not a fancy-schmancy spot. It wants to be the Tanglewood/Briargrove area's easy-to-fall-into regular seafood house. We recently spent a pleasant spring evening on the patio and found our dinner to be everything we hoped for: intense flavors, fresh seafood, a lush and naughty richness to the sauces. The accent is Cajun-Creole, and most seafood choices can be ordered broiled, deep-fried or blackened. Ellen Gonzalez is in the kitchen, along with Wilson. And, yes, the ever-popular fried green tomatoes made the move.

JOSEPHINE'S

Remember the scene in *Lady and the Tramp*, where the two dogs share spaghetti at an Italian restaurant? That's what Josephine's will remind you of. Since 1988 Josephine Storenski and husband Johnny have been dishing up Americanized Italian food like *nonna* (grandmother) used to make. This old-school mom-and-pop cafe near the convention center is unpretentious and friendly. At lunchtime, a cafeteria-like arrangement offers a heady array, including minestrone, lasagna, manicotti stuffed with Italian cheeses in tomato sauce, pizza and po'boys (try the meatball po'boy). Sometimes the food sits on the steam table a while too long, and a certain amount of microwaving takes place. Still, folks are fond of this spot. Come dinner time you get to have a waiter for table service, and the kitchen revs up with more ambition, sending out spinach sautéed in olive oil,

1209 CAROLINE at Dallas
713-759-9323
www.josephinesitalian.com
MAP F6

Recommended
OYSTER BARS

There is nothing quite as exhilarating as a raw oyster, tasting alive of the sea.
From scruffy to neighborhood cozy or downright swanky joints, Houston oyster bars are swimming in fresh bivalves being shucked on the spot. Oysters taste best, of course, when the weather and sea water are cool.

CAPTAIN BENNY'S HALF SHELL OYSTER BAR, *8506 S. Main, 713-666-5469, and other locations*. The Captain's righteously shabby "boat" is thankfully still marooned on South Main Street. The kitchen shucks oysters as consistently as a robot right out in the open, so there are no mysteries about freshness. Expect only one type of raw oyster here: the fat, cold and juicy Gulf Coast specimen. Don't miss the draft beer in frosted mugs or the fried catfish. All in all, a bang for the buck.

DANTON'S GULF COAST SEAFOOD KITCHEN, *4611 Montrose, 713-807-8889*. This unpretentious Museum District newbie quickly gained a reputation as the place to scarf excellent happy hour-priced oysters. Don't look for a huge oyster bar — most of the shucking takes place in the nearby kitchen. But those huge iced-down platters glistening with sweet, plump oysters fly out in record speed. If you can break away from the raw oysters, try oysters Kyle, pan-sautéed in spicy lemon-garlic butter. Wow.

GOODE CO. TEXAS SEAFOOD, *2621 Westpark, 713-523-7154, and 10211 Katy Fwy., 713-464-7933*. Both Houston locations created by Jim Goode have small oyster bars where fresh Gulf Coast oysters are being shucked and served on the half shell. The original Westpark location exudes Texas charm in its railroad car, while the Memorial area location is fancier and roomier, too.

McCORMICK & SCHMICK'S, *1151 Uptown Park Blvd., 713-840-7900*. This Portland, Ore.-based seafood chain prints its menu twice daily and always includes an ever-changing menu of oysters from both coasts. Have a dozen of one kind, or build your own sampler. Happy hour occasionally features oyster shooters.

THE OCEANAIRE SEAFOOD ROOM, *5061 Westheimer, 832-487-8862*. Sleek, Art Deco ocean liner look-alike in The Galleria has a separate oyster bar that hits the right comfort note between cozy and swank. Witness dozens of oyster varieties being shucked at the bar daily from Wellfleets to Washington Olympia, Malpeques or Kumamotos. Feel free to mix and match a sampling of the day's varieties.

PESCE, *3029 Kirby, 713-522-4858*. At this cosmopolitan seafood spot, perch at the big marble raw bar and ogle your oysters being shucked or gumbo being dispatched from copper kettles. Daily oyster selections are scribbled on the chalkboard with at least three choices from all over the globe. Watch for Blue Point Connecticut, Martha's Vineyard or Tatamagushi from Canada.

fettuccine Norman (egg, spinach, mushrooms and shrimp in savory cream), oven-fried chicken or fish, veal marsala and a stuffed artichoke so good (and so 1970s Houston) it might be the single item that draws you back for more.

JOYCE'S SEAFOOD & STEAKS

6415 SAN FELIPE at Winrock
713-975-9902
MAP C6

If you're unfamiliar with the location, this reliable Tanglewood-area eatery might be missed, as the restaurant is set back from its San Felipe address. Look for cross street Winrock (a bit east of S. Voss), turn south there and look to the right. Now in the capable hands of Luis and Maeve Pesquera (namesake Joyce retired long ago), Joyce's blends culinary traditions of the Gulf Coast, Southern Louisiana and Mexico, such as blackened catfish enchiladas. Raw oysters, grilled fish tacos, gumbo, fried shrimp, crabcakes with a sauce of poblano peppers and New Orleans-style barbecued shrimp made with Shiner Bock beer all seem to be menu naturals. Note: There's a second restaurant that also belongs to the Pesqueras, which opened in early 2008 in the Tomball area: Pesquera's Ocean Grill & Oyster Bar at 34616 Highway 249 in Pinehurst (281-259-5000). It has a similar menu, serving up lobster and shrimp enchiladas, sautéed mussels, fried catfish, hush puppies and, of course, oysters, oysters, oysters.

JULIA'S BISTRO

3722 MAIN at Alabama
713-807-0090
www.juliasbistro.com
MAP E7

Sleek and vibrant decor with super-saturated colors of magenta, ruby and red-orange, complemented by silver and (oh, thank you!) spanking white tablecloths, fresh flowers, candles, sets up this ultra-urbane dining room for high expectations. MetroRail whizzes by outside, concrete floors guarantee it will get noisy, and it ain't cheap, but this is a welcome change from the mundane with its very modern and sophisticated food. The inspiration of restaurateur Carmen Vasquez, the kitchen is adept, and flavors run rampant. We got giddy over the chipotle Caesar topped with manchego cheese, poblano *mole* on the roasted duck, chorizo in the penne pasta, taquitos made with filet mignon, achiote-marinated pork, red snapper dressed with ginger-mango butter, and the fact you can get *nopalitos* as a side dish. The fusion here happily does not con-fuse. Try the pork sandwich with avocados and plenty of spicy mustard sauce or a salad of baby spinach, chèvre, walnuts and caramelized shallots. Service is eager, if sometimes unpolished. Relax and wait for the food.

KAHN'S DELICATESSEN

2429 RICE BLVD.
between Kirby and Morningside

713-529-2891
www.kahnsdeli.com

MAP E7

Some of us recall being still wet behind the ears when we first visited Alfred's in the Village and tasted our very first Reuben sandwich. Some of us also remember getting that empty feeling in the pit of our stomachs when Alfred's closed. The son of the legendary Alfred Kahn now carries on the superb deli tradition, albeit in a tiny Village hole-in-the-wall. Mike Kahn's resolutely ugly storefront smells worlds better than it looks, offering a tiny whiff of home for transplanted New Yorkers. The overstuffed sandwiches are delicious and gy-normous. Concerning the aforementioned Reuben: the corned beef is layered so high, the sauerkraut is stacked so generously, you'll wish you had a mouth like Joe E. Brown or Carol Channing. There's also homemade chicken liver, and Kahn swears on a stack of rye bread that the lox is never frozen.

KAM'S FINE CHINESE CUISINE

4500 MONTROSE
between Richmond and Hwy. 59

713-529-5057

MAP E7

Big name for a Chinese spot like you might find on a London backstreet. Chic but spare in both decor and menu, this Museum District sleeper draws avid returnees who come for either lunch or dinner and will brook no argument over its appeal. Pork dumplings — steamed or pan-fried — come with a variety of sauces, leaving the diner to concoct the perfect dipping accompaniment. Lightly crisp eggrolls, a salad of chicken breast and greens with a chilled vinegar dressing, orange beef (a fave among regulars), sesame chicken, garlicky green beans with black bean sauce and fine hot-and-sour soup are among the possibilities. Quiet, confident servers bring things with a smile, which helps relieve stress over the less-than-ample parking.

KANEYAMA

9527 WESTHEIMER
between Fondren and Gessner

713-784-5168
www.kaneyama-houston.com

MAP C7

The name loosely translates to "treasure mountain," and though there's no lofty peak in sight, treasures await in the sushi collection. As testament to taste and quality, this Westside restaurant bustles with Japanese customers, joined by the rest of Houston looking for an authentic Japanese food experience. No kitschy karaoke bar, but a surprisingly tasteful and spacious dining room, with three tatami rooms that are entered through sliding rice paper doors. Best spot in the house is at the sushi bar to sample the sparkling-fresh fish prepared by artistically motivated chefs. Owner Keeper Lin describes the sushi preparation as "art for consumption," and the fresh king crab sushi and the ultra fresh salmon sushi prove the point. Also, this may be Houston's best choice for *uni* (sea urchin).

KANOMWAN

736½ TELEPHONE near S. Lockwood
713-923-4230
MAP G8

Maybe the second best thing about this scruffy Thai cafe is the scary owner who takes your order without a smile and rings up your bill holding the same surly demeanor. People who have been eating here forever say he'll eventually warm up to you if you come in often enough and might even begin preparing your dish the way you ordered it and not the way he wants you to have it. Funny guy. Long a Houston underground favorite, the first best thing about Kanomwan is the extraordinary Thai food. Never shying away from the big heat, the kitchen has a frisky hand with the chilies (and lemongrass and basil). It's BYOB until 8:30 p.m., so bring your own cooler stuffed with beer or wine to put out the fire. Know in advance you won't be going for the ambience (dreary to the extreme), and you won't be going because it's conveniently located or even easy to find; you will become a regular because you won't be able to get dreams of the food out of your head. Try the *tom ka gai* soup (coconut milk, chicken and lime), the spicy shrimp and the whole fried snapper with chile sauce.

KASRA PERSIAN GRILL

9741 WESTHEIMER at Gessner
713-975-1810
www.kasrapersiangrill.com
MAP C7

Tucked into a corner of a shopping center in Westchase, this culinary paean to traditional Persian cooking can easily be overlooked by new patrons, but those who have stumbled across it have had quite a trip. The dining room is usually full during the lunch rush, and with good reason. The portions here are generous and come from a kitchen where the *barg* is as tasty as its bite. Kabobs (*barg*) of salmon, chicken, shrimp and one that's skewered filet mignon made us drool (behind a napkin) with pleasure. Seasoned with a wicked garlic sauce and grilled, the tenderloin kabob may be served with fava bean rice or luscious dill rice — both recommended. Of all the kabob platters, however, our repeat favorite is the humble *kubideh*, two skewers of seasoned ground beef. Two other menu standouts: *khorashe bademjan* (lamb shanks that require no knife, served with fried eggplant and a sauce of sour grapes, tomatoes and onions) and the exotic *fesenjan* (chicken prepared in a sauce of pomegranate juice, ground walnuts and saffron). The garlicky hummus receives bravos, and if you are of an adventurous palate, wash it all down with *doogh*, a carbonated yogurt drink. Kasra is, hands-down, our favorite Persian restaurant.

2327 POST OAK BLVD.
between Westheimer and San Felipe
713-871-8883
www.kennyandziggys.com
MAP D6

KENNY & ZIGGY'S

Folks schlep in the whole *mishpuchah* (clan) to have Sunday brunch at Kenny & Ziggy's. This New York-styled deli really packs them in on weekends, and no matter how disparate the taste buds in your group, something satisfyingly yummy will be

Recommended
TOP TORTAS

In Mexico, there is a torta shop on every corner, where the local version of a fancy sub sandwich is constructed on a toasted Mexican *bolillo* roll with layers of mashed bean, meat, tomato, avocado, onion and shredded lettuce. Many are kicked up with chipotle chiles, salsa fresca or chile poblano. Here are four Houston versions.

EL REY TACQUERIA, *910 Shepherd, 713-802-9145, and other locations.* Generous portion of lean, moist rotisserie chicken, sliced avocado, shredded lettuce and tomato neatly piled on a grilled *bolillo* that skirts sogginess. Nice restrained dollop of sour cream; ask for onion and jalapeños to ratchet up the flavor.

GORDITAS AGUASCALIENTES, *6102 Bissonnet, 713-541-4560, and other locations.* Gorditas (like a taco, but made with a much thicker tortilla) are the thing here, but the interior-of-Mexico tortas are also worthy. Take a break from meat and try the delicious cheese torta slathered with refried beans, melted Mexican white cheese, lettuce, tomato, avocado, jalapeños and sour cream.

MEXICO'S DELI TORTAS AND TACOS, *2374 S. Dairy Ashford, 281-679-7790.* Choose from 20 different tortas listed on the blackboard at this tiny window stand. The #1 is a winner featuring spicy chorizo, white cheese and mushrooms, on a sesame-dusted grilled roll spread with black bean paste.

TAQUERIA ARANDAS, *1020 N. Shepherd, 713-880-4686, and other locations.* Tortas prepared on a puffy untoasted Mexican *bolillo* from their adjacent bakery are a little smaller than the others. The barbecued baby goat is sometimes a bit dry, so add the excellent spicy green sauce and sour cream. Big selection of fillings to choose from, including beef tongue and cactus.

found among the 200-plus, cutesy-named menu items. (The Three Faces of Cheese is an example.) The namesake owners have bent over backwards to be forward in their attention to food details. Breads and cakes are baked in-house, and meats are cured and pickled on site. Their smoked fish is overnighted-in from New York and the chicken matzo ball soup has cured more sinus infections than the Mayo Clinic. If you dare to order the $38 eight-decker sandwich (The Zellagabetsky) and can finish it all alone, free cheesecake is your reward. They've got real sour pickles, cold beet borscht, Philly cheesesteak sandwiches, Hungarian goulash, cheese blintzes, fried *kreplach* (filled dumplings) sweet potato pancakes, *kishka* (Eastern European sausage), Boston cream pie, apple strudel and a 2-cents plain (seltzer) that goes for a dollar. A smaller satellite deli recently opened downtown at 1200 McKinney (Houston Center), #374, 713-655-7700. It's called Zig's New York Deli, and now the three-piece suits can hurry in from their skyscrapers to grab a quick Reuben and egg cream.

KENZO SUSHI BISTRO

23501 CINCO RANCH BLVD., in La Centerra Mall, Katy
281-371-8200
MAP West of A7

Since opening in December 2007, Kenzo has been one of the Katy area's most-talked-about newcomers. Executive chef Juna Rorimpandey previously worked with the Miyako group, Uptown Sushi, Noé and The Oceanaire Seafood Room. Owner Charlie Cho was mentored by Donald Chang (Nara, Uptown Sushi), perhaps Houston's most influential Japanese-restaurant owner. The result is a fine-dining restaurant fronted by a full sushi bar. There are many non-Asian specials and menu offerings, and the food presentation is beautiful.

KHUN KAY THAI-AMERICAN CAFE

1209 MONTROSE between W. Gray and W. Dallas
713-524-9614
MAP E6

For 26 years, we dined at the Golden Room, the prettiest Thai restaurant in town and located at this address. Our children pretty much grew up here, nibbling chicken satay dipped in sweet-hot peanut sauce, slurping sinus-clearing hot shrimp soup and finishing meals with sliced mango (in season) and sticky rice. Just as this book is going to press, however, co-owners/cousins Suptra Yooto (front of the house) and Kay Soodjai (chef) are taking the Golden Room apart and reconfiguring it to become Khun Kay Thai-American Cafe, a fast-casual spot. We are not the only ones who will miss the Golden Room. Laments have been pouring in from other longtime customers. Our advice: Settle down, people! We have no doubt whatsoever that the ladies' new venture will be as delicious and welcoming as the Golden Room.

KHYBER NORTH INDIAN GRILL

2510 RICHMOND
east of Kirby
713-942-9424
MAP E7

A visitor finds an attractive exposed-brick interior with lots of tree-sized plants and Oriental carpets hung on the walls, New Age jazz on the sound system and a menu upon which the word "tandoori" does not appear. Instead the marinated meats and ground-meat kabobs are chargrilled. Cooking ethnic for the non-literal-minded, the kitchen tucks pistachios in the *naan*, and the *saag paneer* is a solid mouth-pleaser. Even though the kitchen has its good days and its off days, most who try the lamb *korma* come away routinely satisfied, and the rice pudding has never drawn a negative response. Years ago, Khyber was a hot Indian restaurant, and everyone talked about it. Owner Mickey Kapoor's lunch buffet still keeps them coming in, but it seems sometimes like the place is running on auto pilot. Or maybe it's just that there are so many newer, funkier, more authentic places in town that have dulled our admiration for this golden oldie. Count on Khyber's sign to always include a Kapoor witticism or comment.

KILLEN'S STEAKHOUSE

Ron Killen's steakhouse is housed in the same South Main building as his family's previous casual-dining enterprises, but he has clearly dolled up the place. The floor is still humbly covered with white-flecked red vinyl

2804 S. MAIN ST.,
south of FM 518, Pearland
281-485-0844
www.killenssteakhouse.com
MAP South of F9

tile, but the walls are painted a soothing pale green and adorned with lush Western art. The leaded-glass front doors are handsome, the low-slung ceiling is supported by den-worthy knotty-pine columns, and the food-preparation area is politely hidden behind the kind of opaque glass panel you see in dentists' waiting rooms. When the place is busy the noise level can get a little intense, and the personable servers can get a little stretched, but these demerits won't make much of a dent in your dining experience. Overall, the menu is simple and very well executed. Draped over the edge of a stemmed cocktail glass filled with crushed ice, for example, the five large, plump shrimp are served with a splendid homemade tartar sauce or rémoulade. Among the steaks, Killen's USDA

Prime ribeye comes to the table all alone on a plate, seasoned ever so gently and grilled exactly as ordered. Among the sides, there are steak fries, creamed spinach, cream-spiked macaroni and cheese and, a recent newcomer that everyone is talking about, creamed corn. As we go to press, Killen is planning to move the steakhouse to a newer, fancier, larger location just down the road. This location, he says, will become a casual-dining spot once again.

KIM SON

> **2001 JEFFERSON** at Chartres, and other locations
> **713-222-2461**
> www.kimson.com
> **MAP** F6

"Mama La," her husband and seven kids fled Vietnam in 1980, came to Houston and opened a modest spot where she set about cooking selections from the 250 recipes memorized from the culinary repertoire of her mother-in-law. Now, almost three decades later, four restaurants, three banquet halls and numerous food kiosks all over town relate a most fascinating success story. The flagship restaurant on Jefferson is an enormous palace with koi pond and banquet rooms, and even though the 13-page menu can be daunting, once selections are made the food that comes to the table is glorious. From the regular menu, gold stars go to *Mekong* soup (shrimp, tomatoes, bean sprouts, pineapple, okra in a hot sour broth), *bo nuong xa* (charbroiled Vietnamese fajitas marinated in lemongrass), black-peppered softshell crabs, *chem chep xao lan* (mussels simmered with glass noodles, onions and coconut curry sauce), *bun* (noodle salad) and *chao tom* (shrimp paste wrapped around sugar cane). Some people say Kim Son's Stafford location (*12759 Southwest Fwy. in the Fountains Center, 281-242-3500*) serves the best dim sum in Houston. All the steamed dumplings, buns and lotus-leaf bundles are here, as well as *fun* noodles, congee, and the pan-fried and deep-fried dumplings. Many among Houston's large Vietnamese population have enjoyed these various venues (each larger and grander than the last, it seems) for wedding parties. For the rest of us, Kim Son is always a celebration of good eats.

KING BISCUIT PATIO CAFE

> **1606 WHITE OAK**
> west of Houston Ave.
> **713-861-2328**
> **MAP** E6

Reincarnated from a gas station and various other restaurant tries, Roger Aggoun's funky Woodland Heights shack-with-patio has a Dorothy-in-the-poppy-field view of the Emerald City (or, rather, the downtown Houston skyline). Parking was not a priority when the design was originally executed, so look for a place on a side street or pedal over on your bike. If kitsch is your thing, has King Biscuit got an umbrella table for you! Those who have ventured in warn against visiting during mosquito season. But if it's a cool day, be cool and stop in for spicy buffalo wings, a hoagie roll with meatballs, sauce and mozzarella, black bean veggie burger, salmon croquettes with shrimp remoulade, new potato enchiladas and the fried pickles. Sunday brunch has some tasty choices, including *tchoutchouka* — an Algerian dish of sauteed vegetables. Bottled and draft beer and a standard ho-hum wine list. We like the outdoor patio for laid-back, lazy chats with friends in this fast-paced city.

4100 WESTHEIMER
east of Mid Lane
713-960-8472
www.kiranshouston.com
MAP D6

KIRAN'S

Chef Kiran Verma's upscale and very handsome Indian dining space features a number of Indian standards — creamy *saag paneer*, crisp *pappadum* and chewy *naan* breads, assorted *samosas*, hearty tandoori dishes, cool yogurty *raita* to help quench a curry's fire. But some of these classic trappings have been rethought and reinvigorated. The menu sparkles with unexpected novelties and delights like a perky lump crab salad, a full rack of lamb (instead of the usual minced or stewed variations), a velvety seafood curry, a smoky array of scallops, even a witty crème brûlée served in three petite, separately flavored portions (cardamom, saffron and pistachio). There's also a much-better-than-average wine list, which is rather noteworthy in itself, since wine was long considered a difficult match for the wildly divergent flavors of Indian food. So let Verma or the staff guide you in choosing a bottle. It will be a revelation.

Ask chef Kiran Verma to recommend a wine to go with her modern Indian cuisine.

RECIPE: BLACK BEAN TERRINE WITH GOAT CHEESE, FRESH TOMATO SALSA AND AVOCADO

Cafe Annie, 1728 Post Oak Blvd., 713-840-1111

"I developed the black bean terrine maybe as early as 1983," says Cafe Annie chef/owner Robert Del Grande. "It was one of my first dishes in the then-new direction of Southwest Cuisine. I used a very French form (the terrine) and infused it with Southwestern flavors, drawing heavily on the flavors of Mexico, particularly Oaxaca. It is probably why the dish has endured all these years — it is well steeped in tried-and-true culinary traditions: rustic beans, tart and tangy cheese, rich avocado and spicy salsa."

Black Bean Terrine
1 Tbsp. olive oil
1 oz. apple-wood smoked bacon, small dice
½ white onion, small dice
1 oz. garlic, minced
1 qt. black beans, washed and picked over
4 qt. water
12 oz. goat cheese, well drained and fairly dry (prefer Dallas Mozzarella Company's)
1 shallot, rough chopped
1½ oz. ancho chile, stemmed, seeded and torn into small pieces
4 oz. apple-wood smoked bacon, small dice
8 oz. venison sausage, small dice (prefer Broken Arrow Ranch)
salt to taste
Tabasco to taste
4 oz. (1 stick) whole butter
3 2-cup foil loaf pans
Fresh Tomato Salsa (recipe below)
1 ripe avocado, peeled, seeded and cut into small cubes (for garnish)
cilantro sprigs (for garnish)

METHOD: In large pot, heat olive oil and sauté 1 oz. bacon, onion and garlic. Add black beans and water and bring to a boil. Reduce heat and simmer until beans are tender, about 90 minutes to 2 hours. Drain the liquid and reserve. Grind approximately two-thirds of the beans through a meat grinder with the ¼-inch die or plate. (Alternatively, pulse the beans in a food processor to generate a coarse bean puree.) Combine the ground beans with the remaining whole beans.

Divide the goat cheese into three 4-oz portions and roll into logs of approximately a 1-inch diameter and a length just shorter than the length

KIRBY'S PRIME STEAKHOUSE

1111 TIMBERLOCH PLACE
at I-45, The Woodlands
281-362-1121
www.kirbyssteakhouse.com
MAP North of D1

A favorite in Dallas since the 1950s, Kirby's almost made it into Houston, stopping just north of here in that vibrant stretch of suburbia called The Woodlands. Opening its doors for business in 2004, this Dallas import has a bar where live performances in the jazz genre happen Thursday, Friday and Saturday nights. In the dining room a sommelier will aid in selecting

of the terrine pan. Place the goat cheese logs in the freezer until very firm.

Place the shallots and ancho chiles in a small saucepan and cover with water. Gently simmer until chiles are very soft. Drain all but ¼ cup of the liquid and puree until smooth. Reserve.

In a broad deep skillet, lightly brown the 4 oz. bacon and sausage. Combine the ground bean mixture, sausage/bacon mixture and chile puree. Fry or "refry" the beans. Add reserved bean liquid as needed to adjust the consistency. Season to taste with salt and Tabasco. Remove from heat and stir in butter until well combined.

Fill each terrine approximately half way with the bean mixture. Press the cold goat logs into the bean mixture, then cover with remaining beans. Gently pack and cover with plastic wrap. Refrigerate overnight.

To plate: Remove a terrine from the mold and cut into ½-inch thick slices. In a hot non-stick skillet over high heat, quickly sear the slices. Spoon Fresh Tomato Salsa onto center of each dinner plate. Place the seared terrine slice over the salsa. Garnish with cubes of avocado and cilantro sprigs. Makes 3 terrines; one terrine should yield at least 8 portions.

Fresh Tomato Salsa
2 large ripe tomatoes
¼ white onion, minced
1 serrano chile, minced
½ tsp. fresh lime juice
½ tsp. salt

METHOD: Score the skin of the tomatoes. In a pot of boiling water, blanch the tomatoes and remove skin. In food processor, pulse tomatoes to form a coarse salsa. Stir in remaining ingredients, and season to taste. Chill.

from the 4,000 bottles when time comes to order wine. Now, let's talk menu. For us, it's *déjà vu* all over again. Reading it, we felt like the 1950s had circled back. Scanning the carte we found escargot, lobster bisque, cracked peppercorn filet mignon with Cognac sauce, tournedos with béarnaise, surf and turf (a straight interpretation, not deconstructed or ironic), prime rib, creamed spinach, fettuccine alfredo, iceberg wedge with blue cheese, chocolate mousse and Kirby's coffee (aka Irish coffee). Visions of eating at Maxim's in downtown Houston circa 1958 danced through our head. Not that there's anything wrong with that. To modernize things a bit, at Kirby's in The Woodlands you may choose to dine outdoors lakeside. Maxim's never delivered that option.

KOBE

9313-C KATY FWY.
at Bunker Hill
713-827-8329
MAP A6

This neighborhood favorite had been slicing and dicing sushi and sashimi since 1997 in a pretty, if ultimately tired, setting a couple blocks away. The ongoing construction along the Katy Freeway and the renovation of older shopping centers that it has engendered prompted Kobe's 2008 move to this new location. It was always a quiet place — the sake bomb-swilling skinny-hipped *trendetti* never came here, but plenty of Memorial-area families did. We have no reason to think anything will be much different with the new location. Tempura is fine, and the sushi chefs are willing to make practically anything, even if it's not on the menu. Bento box lunches are generous in the extreme. Try the pan-fried pork dumplings (*gyoza*), small and delicately constructed. For true sushi eaters, we recommend the spicy salmon roll and unagi.

KUBO'S SUSHI BAR & GRILL

This place has been earning raves from customers and critics from day one. *Zagat* previously ranked it Houston's best Japanese restaurant, and roving national restaurant reviewer John Mariani once labeled it one of the eight best sushi purveyors in the nation. Choose a seat at

2414 UNIVERSITY BLVD. at Morningside (upstairs)
713-528-7878
www.kubos-sushi.com
MAP E7

the sushi bar or a table in chic but minimalist surroundings one floor above the hubbub of Rice Village. Miso-bouillabaisse soup whets the appetite as you consider the day's fresh-fish selections. Then leave the rest to Kubo's master chefs. Popular entrees include salmon *hooba-yaki* and garlic beef, but it's the sushi and sashimi that bring people back. Also, better-than-average sake selection, with super-premium varieties available.

LA COLOMBE D'OR

3410 MONTROSE
Hawthorne and W. Alabama
713-524-7999
www.lacolombedor.com
MAP E6

When oil hit rock bottom about 25 years ago, the distressed oil executives who frequented this elegant and baronial mansion found financial relief in a menu set by the daily price of a barrel of crude. The restaurant is not doing that these days, thank goodness. (Oil hit $128 the day we type this.) Still, the modern French food attracts the same executives and other well-heeled, well-traveled Houstonians who enjoy both the cuisine and the once-stately (a little shabby these days) surroundings of the former residence — now a tiny hotel — that once belonged to Exxon founder Walter Fondren. Stop in the wee bar before dinner for an aperitif, the cozy library for brandy afterward. If available, take a peek into the adjacent ballroom and see the interior of an original, centuries-old French salon, imported and rebuilt for private events in Houston.

LA GRIGLIA

2002 W. GRAY at McDuffie
713-526-4700
www.lagrigliarestaurant.com
MAP E6

Electric might be the best word to give diners forewarning about this Italian grill and rotisserie. From the noise level and absolute explosion of colors in everything one looks at, to the frenzy of an attentive and efficient kitchen and waitstaff, calm just does not enter the picture. Once a shining light in Tony Vallone's now-gone collection of restaurants (there's a historic collection of signatures

from another generation of Houston society captured in the cement on the floor from opening night in 1991), the place is now a part of the Landry's Restaurant empire. But gold is gold, and this lively destination is 24-karat. The kitchen is steady, the service polished, the food always better than it needs to be. (This is the restaurant that introduced Houston to shrimp and crab cheesecake.) As for the crowd, this is not the place for clandestine meetings.

La Griglia's menu includes seafood, pasta, salad, wood-fired pizza and more.

LA GUADALUPANA BAKERY & CAFE

2109 DUNLAVY
between Vermont and Fairview

713-522-2301

MAP E6

For those of us who relish the fact that not all good things come in pretty packages, this bakery-cum-restaurant will please on many levels. Based on its lack of curb appeal, one might hesitate to eat here. But once through the door, you will be greeted by a cheerful face, usually the owner's. Trancito Diaz, who once was a pastry chef at the Houston Country Club, will probably encourage you to try one of the pastries with your meal, or to go — and so you should. Mexican breakfast is served all day, but we're partial to lunch and dinner, which start with excellent salsa and chips. Try the *enchiladas verdes* (we're nuts for them), the migas or anything with pork, and be sure to finish with some flan. Next time, come back for first-class *mole*. Until the restaurant obtains a wine and beer permit, you may want to bring your own, or purchase drinks from the adjacent convenience store. Longtime fans of the restaurant will notice that the holes in the ceiling have been repaired and the place spruced up a little — and still the food is as good as ever.

LA MEXICANA

1018 FAIRVIEW at Montrose

713-521-0963

www.lamexicanarestaurant.com

MAP E6

Centuries ago in Old Mexico, whenever a son married, it was tradition to just add some rooms onto the family house for him and his new wife to live in and raise their own family. After a few generations, homes were a confusing sprawl. La Mexicana has been adding on for 30 years to accommodate customers (much better than in-laws), but while it now sprawls every which way, the heart of the original still beats true. Breakfast through dinner, it's a place for no-frills Tex-Mex with traditional gaudy tossed around for decor. Try the *taco de guisado de puerco*, a handmade flour tortilla with cubes of pork in red sauce. Spike anything with the vibrant tomatillo sauce. For breakfast, there are robust huevos rancheros (some have called them the best in town) or migas. A great bakery keeps the cross-cultural clientele happy, too. Unpretentious, homey and a true Houston crossroads.

LA STRADA

This is kind of the Rolling Stones of Houston's restaurant scene. A lot of people know about it, a lot of people have memories — good and better forgotten — in relation to it, and the bones have gotten a little creaky

> **322 WESTHEIMER** at Taft
> **713-523-1014**
> www.lastradahouston.com
> **MAP** E6

after all those years of partying. Rebuilt and reopened after a fire destroyed the original restaurant, Aldo Catania's Montrose-area landmark has had some shaky times this past year, especially as the fickle youth market found new quarters for raucous Sunday brunches. (And the San Felipe location has closed.) Fans say less alcohol-fueled madness is all for the good, letting them concentrate more on the loosely Italian menu with a Californian attitude. So who cares if the infamous Sunday revels are no longer as outlandish? Just because you'd prefer not to see Mick Jagger in tight pants anymore doesn't mean you can't enjoy the music.

Recommended
FRIED CHICKEN

Texas isn't just about beef. Over the years we have fielded many questions from *My Table* magazine readers looking for good fried chicken. Here is where we send them.

BARBECUE INN, *116 W. Crosstimbers, 713-695-8112.* The deep-fryer at this old-school northsider works its wonders on more than just the renowned fried shrimp with crisp-on-the-outside and moist-on-the-inside Southern fried chicken. It's cooked to order and worth the wait.

FRENCHY'S CHICKEN, *3919 Scott, 713-748-2233, and other locations.* Using chickens that have never been frozen and frying them in small batches are two reasons why Frenchy's Cajun-style slightly spicy chicken with its crispy skin and always-moist meat became so popular. The original location near the University of Houston is a local landmark.

HENDERSON'S CHICKEN SHACK, *3811 Ennis, 713-533-0033.* Not far from Texas Southern University, this humble spot features larger-than-normal chicken pieces that are dusted in a batter that hints of cornmeal and then are deep-fried to order.

MAX'S WINE DIVE, *4200 Washington, 713-880-8737.* Max's serious Southern fried chicken begins with top-quality fowl bathed in a jalapeño-studded buttermilk marinade. The finished product is complemented with chipotle honey — which can make negotiating a wine glass between bites a bit messy.

SPANISH VILLAGE, *4720 Almeda, 713-523-2861.* Finding Southern fried spring chicken on the menu of this funky Tex-Mex stalwart might be a surprise. We bet you'll find the crisp, perfectly cooked birds as much of a draw as the restaurant's signature margaritas.

LA TAPATIA TAQUERIA

> **1749 RICHMOND**
> at Woodhead, and other locations
> **713-521-3144**
> **MAP** E6

No one will be challenged by the cuisine in these oh-so-authentic taquerias. Actually, few would ever use the word "cuisine," but that's not down-putting this Mexican-style comfort food. Generally, you won't miss by ordering the savory shrimp tacos: eight to 10 small shrimp that are grilled, folded into double corn tortillas lined with a bed of sharp white onions and cilantro. The effect is hearty and a little spartan, but you can spoon on either of the two good table salsas, too, if you wish. Better yet: the *tortas*, built on toasted *bolillos* smeared with refried beans and sour cream, and your choice of fried fajita, pork *al pastor* or chicken breast. Out-of-town guests unfamiliar with Tex-Mex? Bring 'em in. Not only might they appreciate the mild flavors, they'll also feel authenticated by the conglomeration of mustard-colored walls, flashing neon, casino-like bar and last-minute toss-in of a gurgling fountain. Excellent people-watching, too. It seems all of Houston's strangeness passes through these doors.

LA TRATTORIA

> **6504 WESTHEIMER** between Fountain View and S. Voss
> **713-782-1324**
> www.latrattoria-houston.com
> **MAP** D6

Everyone who loves Carlo Molinaro's cozy little restaurant seems to use the word "intimate" at some point in their praises. Almost everyone who says not-nice things about it usually begins by saying they were there with a large group. We see a pattern here. The fact is, this is an intimate, chef-run kind of place that's not flashy, is usually dependable and won't disappoint even those who claim to know Northern Italian cooking. Its surprisingly deep — albeit pricey — wine list backs that up. Molinaro, originally from Verona, serves classic fare that can often be as good and served just like you will find in a proficient *trattoria* or *ristorante* in the Veneto or Emilia-Romagna. We're especially partial to house-made tortellini with a Bolognese *ragù* or in a sauce of wild mushrooms.

LA VISTA

Cozy is a nice descriptive word to use at either of the two locations of this popular BYOB restaurant. That is if it's a quiet night. Cramped is a better word if the spots are busy, which they often are. No reservations are taken, so plan accordingly. Of course busy-ness indicates the kitchen is serving something people want. In this case that something is an imaginative

> **1936 FOUNTAIN VIEW** south of San Felipe
> **713-787-9899**
> **MAP** D6
> www.fatbutter.com
>
> **12665 MEMORIAL** at Broken Bough
> **713-973-7374**
> **MAP** C6

number of dishes more American than Italian. The kitchen has a knowledgeable way with the spice rack — is that cinnamon, coffee and cumin on the roast pork? Who cares, is the response between bites. (On the other hand, *My Table* magazine's critic noted that the kitchen has a tendency to "ignore the innate simplicity of classic Italian cooking by overdoing things and piling on too many flavors.") La Vista is known for its steamed mussels, and the corkage fee is just $7. There's nothing wasted on pretense at La Vista, including the "vista" that can range from a street-side view of clogged traffic to sweating delivery people at nearby places of business. But the atmosphere is nice and the food can be surprisingly good.

THE LAKE HOUSE WATERSIDE CAFE

This brand-new hamburger bar is the second phase of the Schiller Del Grande restaurant plan — the first phase was The Grove, which opened in early 2008 — for the new Discovery Green Park in front of the George R. Brown Convention Center. Designed by noted architect Larry Speck (former dean of architecture at the University of Texas, who also did The Grove), The Lake House has been designed for family fun. There are burgers, Kobe beef hot dogs, sweet potato fries and grilled chicken salad. In addition to its all-American menu, The Lake House sits on the southern edge of Kinder Lake, which features model sailboat racing and will be frozen over November through February, converting it into Houston's first-ever outdoor ice rink. You can literally skate off the deck of The Lake House come winter time (and skates are for rent adjacent to the restaurant).

> **1611 LAMAR** at Crawford, in Discovery Green
> **713-337-7320**
> www.thegrovehouston.com
> **MAP** F6

LANKFORD GROCERY & MARKET

It may be a walk on the wild side for ladies who lunch, but for the rest of us Lankford Grocery is a great place if you like your burgers a little rough around the edges. There's nothing pretentious here — the food

> **88 DENNIS** 4 blocks west of Bagby, 1 block east of Genesee
> **713-522-9555**
> **MAP** E6

is home-style grilled and fried, and the grungy location is well-hidden — except, perhaps, the mystique that surrounds its street-cred pedigree. If you are fussy about hygiene, this is not the place to eat off the floor (or even the oilcloth tablecloth), but for tasty, old-style breakfast or lunch Lankford's is a memorable experience, much enjoyed by several generations of Houstonians who crave the onion rings, messy non-artisan burgers and dependable desserts. It is usually packed at lunch, so you may have to jostle for service. Credit cards are not accepted. Ladies should wear gloves.

RECIPE **CRAWFISH TORTILLA SOUP**

Brennan's of Houston, 3300 Smith, 713-522-9711

This is a "Louisiana version of a Tex-Mex classic," created in the 1980s by Carl Walker, then-executive chef and now-general manager of Brennan's of Houston.

2 Tbsp. vegetable oil
2 cups diced yellow onions
2 cups corn cut from cob
1 cup diced poblano chiles
1 cup diced red bell pepper
2 Tbsp. thinly sliced garlic
1 lb. fresh Louisiana crawfish tail meat
2 Tbsp. Creole seafood seasoning
1 tsp. chili powder
1 tsp. ground cumin
1 Tbsp. Louisiana hot sauce
1 Tbsp. Worcestershire sauce
3 qt. chicken stock or low-sodium chicken broth
¼ cup chopped cilantro
salt & pepper
½ cup vegetable oil
3 fresh corn tortillas, cut into matchsticks

METHOD: Heat 2 Tbsp. vegetable oil in a large saucepan over medium-high heat. Sauté onions, corn, chiles, bell pepper and garlic for 3 to 4 minutes or until tender. Add crawfish, seafood seasoning, chili powder, cumin, hot sauce, Worcestershire sauce and stock. Simmer for 30 minutes. Add cilantro and adjust seasoning.

To plate: Heat vegetable oil in a large sauté pan; add tortillas. Cook over medium heat until matchsticks are crisp. Remove to a towel-lined plate. Ladle soup into warm bowls and garnish with tortilla strips. Serves 8 to 12.

LAST CONCERT CAFE

1403 NANCE west of McKee, in the Warehouse District
713-226-8563
www.lastconcert.com
MAP E6

This "last concert" has been playing for just shy of six decades and the fat lady hasn't even reached make-up. She may have danced on the tables, helped herself to free-flowing sangria and beer and canoodled amongst the diverse crowd that includes yuppies, neo-punks, factory workers and artists from the nearby warehouses, but she ain't singing yet. Since 1949 when founder Mama Lopez named her new restaurant Last Concert to say this was her last business (she died in 1985 at age 95), in-the-know Houstonians have flocked here, knocked on the door speakeasy-style to get in and proceeded to party away. So have their children and even a few of their grandchildren. Does anyone really care the Tex-Mex food is just mediocre? Does New Year's Eve have to be so close to Christmas? Come on, when the party is great, forget the details. Today Last Concert Cafe is a world-famous Houston secret.

LATE NIGHT PIE

302 TUAM just west of Bagby
713-529-5522
MAP E6

After a late movie or to blunt the hangover that will result from a pub crawl through nearby Midtown, Late Nite Pie offers what more refined eateries do not: overly cheesy and caloric pizza that hits the spot, late at night, without the disapproving looks of staff and other customers. Our own favorite is the Stanky Whore (anchovies, roasted garlic and goat cheese), but beer-drinking frat boys also like to order the Italian Stallion (Italian sausage, pepperoni, roma tomatoes and garlic butter dipping sauce). Late Nite Pie serves brewskies, too, but only until 2 a.m. Novelty menu item: the Guinness Float (that's right — beer and vanilla ice cream). Be ready for young and boisterous crowds, as a large University of Houston crowd can usually be found here after tailgating and during Cougar baseball season. As the designated driver, it's your responsibility to take your boozed buddies here for a New York-style pizza — and let them pick up the tab. LNP also delivers.

LATINA CAFE

1972 FAIRVIEW at Hazard
713-521-2611
MAP E6

A native of Cuba said this place was okay for a restaurant if this were Havana. For Houston, he said, it was great enough to remind him how much he loved the food in his native city. He meant that as a compliment. Surrounded by new townhomes selling for half a million and more, this old, slightly rundown cafe seems remarkably out of place, but the changing neighborhood has only resulted in an increasingly upscale clientele. Daily breakfasts — served, of course, with sautéed plantains and rice — delight people who often look more Norwegian than Cuban. Outside of breakfast, come here also for such island classics as *masas de puerco fritas* (chunks of fried pork), *bistec empanisado* (breaded steak), *ropa vieja* (shredded beef in tomato sauce), Cuban-style sandwiches, even paella.

LAURIER CAFE

3139 RICHMOND between Kirby and Buffalo Speedway
713-807-1632
www.lauriercafe.com
MAP D7

Ready for a career change, Gary Fuller deserted telecommunications, went to cooking school and, with his wife Kelly Kimberly, opened this little French spot a few years ago. Our *My Table* reviewer praised the short and tight French-American menu (steaks, chops, seafood and risotto), noting that it reflected "a minimalist formula." So toss out any preconception you might have of what a French bistro should look like so as not to be frightened off when you first step into the sterile (is this the employees' dining area?) dining room. Laurier Cafe adapts French bistro classics with a modern, local sensibility, creating a menu and atmosphere that most guests come away loving. Some of the seasonal dishes might include pepper-encrusted scallops, grilled asparagus and a poached egg with Parmigiano Reggiano, pan-roasted Peking duck breast on top of creamy polenta and a veal bone-in strip steak served with a dried-cherry sauce. Nice patio on the east side and a snazzy new entrance out front soften the edges. We dare anyone to call the place stuffy.

LE MISTRAL

1400 ELDRIDGE north of Briar Forest
832-379-8322
www.lemistralhouston.com
MAP A6

Of all the French bistros in Houston, this place has perhaps the bluest pedigree via brothers David (chef) and Sylvain Denis (wine guy/front of the house), who grew up in a restaurant family in France. Named after the famous seasonal wind that blows through southern France, Le Mistral is one of three French restaurants on the West side (where French oil executives tend to buy homes) and serves rustic Provence-inspired cuisine. Diners who like the old classics will find happiness with most of the dishes. The biggest complaint among its biggest fans is that the menu doesn't change often enough to go back more than just occasionally. In the summer of 2008, Le Mistral moved about 100 yards north, just to the next parking lot, to a larger, swankier location. The dining room itself is still smallish (but modern and soaring), and there's a large bar with its own bar menu. Other attractions include a private dining room (with built-in AV equipment), 10-seat chef's table off the kitchen, a large outdoor dining area and a retail store (to be called Foody's) that will sell wine, the house salad dressing, terrine of foie gras, charcuterie, etc. The store will also have a cooking school. Finally, there's a bakery in the works; it will be open by the end of 2008, says Sylvain Denis.

LEMONGRASS CAFE

5109 BELLAIRE BLVD. at S. Rice Ave.
713-664-6698
www.lemongrass-cafe.com
MAP D7

The health-food-wary might feel cautious at something called Lemongrass Cafe, but fear not. This sleek, neighborhood cafe puts the shine on Asian fusion cuisine without a slice of tofu in sight. Not that a healthful conscience isn't in the works, it's just well disguised in savory dishes like Korean osso buco and lemongrass pizza. Sophisticated, nuanced and delicious, both the menu and setting are harmonious, detailed efforts. It's like an evening of mental massage while still getting to devour darn good food.

LES GIVRAL'S KAHVE

When someone suggests meeting at "the Vietnamese sandwich shop in Midtown," most locals will know exactly the place. That's because, among the numerous *banh mi* and *pho* joints in Midtown, Les Givral's on Milam is a stand-out. (We're just not all sure how everyone else pronounces it.) Most first-time visitors are drawn in by reports of the habit-forming barbecue pork *banh mi*. Repeat offenders may graduate to the tofu sandwich. As unlikely as it sounds, it is a deliciously subtle concoction, which, with a shake of sriracha and hoisin sauce, looks as lovely as it tastes. There's also a decent selection of *pho* and spring rolls to choose from at the counter, which is manned by faces as fresh as the ingredients. The staff all appear to be 20-somethings, but the clientele cross all the boundaries of age, ethnicity and socio-economics. In fact, Les Givrals probably best represents what is great about eating out in

2704 MILAM between McGowen and Elgin
713-529-1736
www.lesgivrals.com
MAP F6

801 CONGRESS between Travis and Milam
713-547-0444
MAP F6

Recommended
THE HOUSTON "OSCARS"

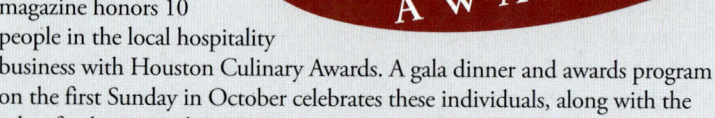

Every year, *My Table* magazine honors 10 people in the local hospitality business with Houston Culinary Awards. A gala dinner and awards program on the first Sunday in October celebrates these individuals, along with the other finalists in each category.

The award winners are always selected by *My Table* readers in a city-wide vote, beginning with an open call for nominations in the magazine's June-July issue. The raw list of nominees — typically numbering in the hundreds — is presented to our nominations committee for winnowing down to five candidates in each of the 10 categories. The final, edited slate is then presented to the *My Table* readership in the August-September issue. Traditionally, postage-paid ballots were bound into that issue, but as of 2008, we have introduced six weeks of online voting to replace the mail-in ballots. The results are kept secret until the big night, when winners are presented with one-of-a-kind glass awards, handmade by artist Gene Paul Michal.

In addition to the reader-selected Houston Culinary Award winners, the magazine staff also selects a well-known food personality — e.g. culinarian, food writer, restaurateur, entrepreneur — to honor with the annual Legends of Houston Restaurants Award.

The Houston Culinary Awards dinner is open to the public, and tickets go on sale August 1. The event always sells out, so we suggest you avoid disappointment and get your tickets early. Contact us at culinaryawards@my-table.com.

HOUSTON CULINARY AWARD WINNERS

RESTAURATEUR OF THE YEAR
1997 Robert Del Grande
1998 Alex Brennan-Martin
1999 Mark Cox
2000 Damian Mandola
2001 Michael Cordúa
2002 Frankie B. Mandola & Bubba Butera
2003 Tracy Vaught
2004 Claire Smith
2005 Charles Clark & Grant Cooper
2006 John Sheely
2007 Lance Fegen

CHEF OF THE YEAR
1997 Mark Cox
1998 Robert Del Grande
1999 Carl Walker
2000 Tony Ruppe
2001 Tim Keating
2002 Hugo Ortega
2003 Mark Holley
2004 Lance Fegen
2005 Robert Gadsby
2006 John Sheely
2007 Jason Gould

UP-AND-COMING CHEF OF THE YEAR
(age 35 or younger)
1997 Claire Smith
1998 Aaron Guest
1999 Hugo Ortega
2000 Alberto Baffoni
2001 Lance Fegen
2002 Scott Tycer
2003 Toby Joseph
2004 Randy Evans
2005 Bryan Caswell
2006 Jason Gould
2007 Jamie Zelko

At left: The 2008 Houston Culinary Awards winners. The event was held at Mockingbird Bistro.

OUTSTANDING WINE SERVICE
1997 Rotisserie for Beef & Bird (closed)
1998 Cafe Annie
1999 Brennan's
2000 Pappas Bros. Steakhouse
2001 Mark's American Cuisine
2002 Scott's Cellar (closed)
2003 Fleming's Prime Steakhouse
2004 Vic and Anthony's
2005 Ibiza
2006 Cafe Rabelais
2007 Catalan

PASTRY CHEF
1999 Marilyn Descours
2000 Emmy Vest
2001 Sara Brook
2002 Susan Molzan
2003 Ruben Ortega
2004 Thierry Tellier
2005 Pam Manovich
2006 Lisa Biggerstaff
2007 Rebecca Masson

BAR SERVICE
1999 La Griglia
2000 Mercury Room
2001 Brennan's
2002 Pappas Bros. Steakhouse
2003 Downing Street Ltd.
2004 The Sam [Bar] (now A+)
2005 Uptown Sushi
2006 Bar Annie
2007 Hugo's

SERVICE PERSON OF THE YEAR
1999 Tom Jensen
2000 Tino Escobedo
2001 Pino Sanchez
2002 Armando Rivera
2003 Maeve Pesquera
2004 Chris Shepherd
2005 Isidro Neri
2006 Bill Floyd
2007 Shepard Ross

CATERER OF THE YEAR
1999 Jackson & Co.
2000 A Fare Extraordinaire
2001 Ruth Meric Catering
2002 Susan Mayfield Catering
2003 Abuso Catering Co.
2004 The Stone Kitchen
2005 Elizabeth Swift Catering
2006 Jim Manning Catered Affairs
2007 Goode Co. Catering

BEST INTERIOR DESIGN
1999 Américas
2000 Masraff's
2001 Zula
2002 Pesce
2003 Artista
2004 Bank Jean-Georges (closed)
2005 Bistro Moderne
2006 Glass Wall
2007 *17

BEST NEW RESTAURANT
1999 Tony Ruppe's (closed)
2000 Masraff's
2001 Pesce
2002 Mockingbird Bistro
2003 Hugo's
2004 Bank Jean-Georges (closed)
2005 Noé
2006 Glass Wall
2007 Reef

"LEGENDS" HONOREES
1999 Sonny Look
2000 John Mariani
2001 Peg Lee
2002 Ann Criswell
2003 John and Lindy Rydman
2004 Jackson Hicks
2005 Schiller Del Grande Restaurant Group
2006 Alex Brennan-Martin
2007 Michael Cordúa

Houston: It's affordable, fresh, diverse and tasty. A third location is scheduled to open on Washington Avenue in the second half of 2008.

> **2005 LEXINGTON**
> east of S. Shepherd
> **713-524-9877**
> www.lexingtongrille.com
> **MAP** E7

LEXINGTON GRILLE

Judging by the caliber of cars that queue up for valet parking every weekday for lunch and dinner, the Lexington Grille probably sees more than its fair share of black American Express cards. It's not the pricing that brings so many well-heeled sophisticates in as it is the unbeatable level of service and quality of food. The American/Continental menu may not ignite fireworks in the culinary world, but it's hardly stodgy and, better yet, always well prepared. And with owner Hossein Shajarat working the dining room, he makes it clear that the printed menu is just a starting point. "What do you feel like eating today?" is his question to every table. A little piece of fish? A nice veal chop? Keep the fat grams low? You got it. This is a straightforward, no-gimmicks spot — a grown-up's restaurant. Don't miss an opportunity to dine outside.

LITTLE HIP'S DINER

Trying to put a defining finger on this incongruous small-town cafe along hot-and-happening Washington Avenue may not do it justice or point out its limitations. Imagine dropping in several times a month on your cousin and his

> **1809 WASHINGTON**
> between Houston Ave. and Sawyer
> **713-861-4411**
> **MAP** E6

wife in Lockhart and you get an idea of what's going on here. This is simple food, country food, theme-less food. From spaghetti to barbecue, catfish to Tex-Mex food, it's a country home, only you get a menu to order a week's worth of dishes. And sometimes as happens, your cousin's wife just isn't on. But they are still family and you love them. As for the name, the consensus is it doesn't stand for a little hip as in a little "with it." It means not fat yet. (Just kidding.)

> **6690 SOUTHWEST FWY.**, just west of Hillcroft
> **713-783-2754**
> www.londonsizzler.com
> **MAP** C7

LONDON SIZZLER

Surprisingly, this is *not* the place to go if you want an overcooked English breakfast. In fact, London Sizzler is one of the city's brightest and freshest spots for South Asian cuisine and a treat for diners who are partial to the style of

Indian cuisine popular in the United Kingdom. The food here is a delightful play on what you would expect at an Indian restaurant. The vegetable *samosas* are a deliciously light start to a meal, the garlic *naan* is perfect for nibbling and dipping, and the *rogan josh* is one of many outstanding entrees where subtle flavors will have you coming back again. Not to be missed are the kebabs, of which the restaurant is understandably proud, and — bring your appetite — the London Sizzler plate, a splendid array of tandoori, kebab and masala-style meats, poultry and seafood. The Sizzler's fresh, non-sludgy *saag paneer* is possibly the best in Houston.

LULING CITY MARKET

With The Galleria and nearby Post Oak Boulevard shopkeepers selling everything from French ties to Italian luggage, as well as who knows what from every other part of the globe, could it dare leave out Texas barbecue? One would think. But, just a few blocks away from Houston's shopping mecca, this is where Luling City Market put its boots into the international ring. And while many might scoff at its almost-Galleria-area location, fans insist that the proof is in the good smoked sausage, plus an excellent mustardy sauce in bottles on the tables that have won this pit almost a cult following. Toss in the post-oak-smoked ribs, the exemplary brisket, the chicken, the turkey and all the sides one could shake a Kate Spade bag at, and, well, it's a winning performance for this knock-off of the Luling, Texas, original. Okay, it's not for those who insist on driving to some Hill Country town for good barbecue. But at the price of gasoline these days, is it really worth a $100-plus investment to eat a link of sausage with cole slaw and beans? We think Houston's Luling City Market is a more-than-adequate substitute. Note: The owners have recently opened a second location called Luling Bar-B-Q and Bar in Midtown at 138 W. Gray, 713-520-6400.

4726 RICHMOND just inside Loop 610
713-871-1903
www.lulingcitymarket.com
MAP D7

2414 SOUTHWEST FWY.
between Greenbriar and Kirby, and other locations
713-522-4419
www.lupetortilla.com
MAP E7

LUPE TORTILLA'S

Here we are with Houston's version of the Hillary Clinton platter. A lot of folks just love this place. A lot of folks say not-nice things. Unlike its original location still in operation out on the Katy Freeway at Highway 6, this location inside The Loop had more of a reputation for bossing its customers around than it did for its food — which is really too bad, because the basic Tex-Mex food made people happy. Fortunately, this location has gotten back to doing more than just a decent job with its Tex-Mex fare and having fun doing it. There's always a big emphasis on families — indicated by a sandbox for the kids to play in (you get to keep what's in their shoes) and even a kiddie bar to order soft drinks. Once you get a table — and the wait is often an hour or more — try any of the unpretentious, almost peasanty tacos, flautas, enchiladas, burritos, chiles rellenos and chalupas. Don't expect any trendy Mexican dishes. And don't get impatient. It brings out some of the bossy stuff.

LYNDON'S PIT BAR-B-Q

5320 HOLLISTER
between Pinemont and Hwy. 290
713-690-2112
MAP C4

We like a place where the owner is an actual human who interacts with diners, and that's just one good thing about Lyndon's. Yup, that's *the* Lyndon Maeker in the baseball cap and apron, carrying with him the delicious aroma of smoked meat. He runs the place with his sons Matt and Mark, and they have recently (2008) moved into new, expanded quarters. Bye-bye strip center, hello freestanding building with plentiful parking and more room for state-of-the-art smokers. And space to stretch out and enjoy some mighty fine barbecue, fork-tender and flavored to the bone. We love the barbecued chicken and sliced beef and appreciate that the chopped beef sandwich isn't pre-doused in sauce — you add the desired (warmed) amount at the fixin's bar. Lyndon's also serves some of the best fried catfish in town, and the huge onion rings just make us happy. Hill Country casual atmosphere with booths, tables and a long community picnic table. Just follow the sign at the entrance that says, "BBQ this way."

LYNN'S STEAKHOUSE

For 23 years, people from all over the Houston area, and the country for that matter, have had a beef or two with this understated steakhouse in West Houston. That's because since opening in 1985, the place has been consistently

955 DAIRY ASHFORD
south of I-10
281-870-0807
www.lynnssteakhouse.com
MAP B6

named among the best steakhouses in the city. Try the New York strip, brushed with salted butter and seared on a 1,600-degree grill to give it a savory crust. Worthy side dishes include fat onion rings, rich spinach casserole and steamy-soft baked potatoes wrapped in gold foil. The award-winning wine list is unusually deep: Cabernet Sauvignon is king and usually found in verticals of at least five deep. The decor hints of the restaurant's age. The couple who operate Lynn's also have the nearby Cafe Benedicte on Memorial.

MADRAS PAVILION

3910 KIRBY between Richmond and Hwy. 59
713-521-2617
www.madraspavilion.us
MAP E7

16260 KENSINGTON just west of the intersection of Hwy. 6 and Hwy. 59, Sugar Land
281-491-3672
MAP A9

A small chain of Indian vegetarian restaurants with locations here and other Texas cities, these are popular for a quick and wholesome lunch. At the Kirby location, which also happens to be kosher (the Sugar Land location is not), a fascinating crowd passes through for the daily lunchtime steamtable. The offerings change regularly, and on any given day might include soup, *channa masala* (with chickpeas), *palak paneer* (homemade cottage cheese cubes cooked with seasoned spinach), *medhu vada* (rather bland unsweet doughnut, good for mopping up sauces), fried veggie cutlets, vegetable *korma* (simmered in coconut cream), filled samosas and much more. An enormous cooked-to-order *dosa* (kind of like a crêpe) is included in the lunch buffet price. We think this is the best veggie Indian buffet in town, as the food is kept fresh and replenished often. At night, order from the menu.

MAGNOLIA BAR & GRILL

6000 RICHMOND at Fountain View
713-781-6207
www.magnolia-grill.com
MAP D7

Years before Cajun food became the culinary rage and celebrity chefs began to gussy it up, Magnolia Bar & Grill set up shop on an out-of-the-way corner serving the real thing. In fact, about the only thing that wasn't South Louisiana about the place was that the restaurant building was in Houston. Not a lot has changed since then, and people who love the real deal still gather here. A gracious plantation setting, complete with shutters and slow-turning ceiling fans, makes this Louisiana outpost an enduring favorite for heady etouffée, excellent soups and po'boys. Make the trip on Sunday for a stupendous Cajun brunch buffet and, during crawfish season, for huge crawfish boils. These days there's also a lively music scene. Check the website for a calendar.

MAI'S RESTAURANT

> **3403 MILAM** between Elgin and Alabama
> **713-520-7684**
> www.maisrestauranttx.com
> **MAP** E6

Just south of downtown, Houston's oldest Vietnamese restaurant (it opened in 1978) has a rabidly loyal following who don't mind the downscale setting, hit-or-miss service or occasional language confusion. They come for the exuberantly spicy cooking, some of Houston's hottest and most authentic, which even

Recommended
HAUTE TAMALES

The pre-Colombian days of ingenious cooks using whatever could be scavenged to make tamales — frog, wild boar, eggs and even bees — are past, but creativity lives on. Once considered holiday celebration food, tamales possess a special cachet in Houston. Unwrap these fragrant masa parcels from their steaming cocoons and take in a taste of the ancient world.

BERRYHILL BAJA GRILL, 2639 Revere, 713-526-8080, *and other locations*. Spinach tamales are rich and fluffy, folded with a smidgen of cheese and dotted with crunchy corn kernels. A dewy, thick blanket of sweet masa reminiscent of Southern cornbread coddles the fillings. Dip into the warm ground-chile gravy.

DOÑA TERE TAMALES, 8331 Beechnut, 713-270-8501, *and* 13238 Bellaire Blvd., 832-328-0761. This very little place is famous for its very large Mexico City-style tamales. Order no more than half the number you usually do. Be sure to order the salsa verde, too. Sweet tamales, too.

EL TIEMPO, 3130 Richmond, 713-807-1600, *and other locations*. Craving a pork tamale big-time? Chow down on these, served bursting from the cornhusk and packed with shredded meat, all covered in mild chili gravy and melty cheese.

GOODE CO. TEXAS SEAFOOD, 2621 Westpark, 713-523-7154, *and* 10211 Katy Fwy., 713-464-7933. Spicy whole shrimp- and crab-stuffed tamales are luxurious with a tomato-olive salsa. Wrapped in silky banana leaves tied with a bow, Goode's are sea-fresh, innovative and moist.

HUGO'S, 1602 Westheimer, 713-524-7744. Red snapper-stuffed tamales are beautifully presented, bundled up in supple green banana leaves. Thick masa dough unveils an interior moist with snowy chunks of snapper; spoon on the warm tomato salsa.

TEXAS TAMALE COMPANY, 3340 Fountain View, 713-953-1181. Pleasantly spicy, albeit petite, finely ground beef-stuffed tamales boast a familiar bang of cumin and cayenne inside a sturdy shell. Tomatilla, pico de gallo and fiery red salsas are *fabulosas*.

after all these years hasn't been too corrupted by Americanization. The cold spring rolls are overstuffed with vermicelli noodles, shrimp, pork, sprouts and lemongrass and are almost a meal in themselves. You may also enjoy rice and shredded pork served with egg cake (much like egg foo young), the Vietnamese equivalent of fajitas that you wrap in rice paper, a steaming bowl of *pho*, the vermicelli bowls known as *bun* or *lau ca*, a fish soup served in a huge hot pot. The iced coffee is grand, and there are many Chinese dishes on the lengthy menu, too. Note to the bar crowd and night shift: Mai's is open late, to 3 a.m. on weekdays and 4 a.m. on the weekend.

MAK CHIN'S

If anyone is planning a little party for a cross-section of the United Nations, this may be the place to have cater it. Defining itself as "Nuvo Asian," it claims to serve food reflecting the dishes of Malaysia, Singapore and other British, French and Dutch colonies as well as China, India, Vietnam, Indonesia and Thailand. Other than that, it's pretty basic. Actually, Mak Chin's, which is under the direction of chef David Yeo, has a growing fan base for its take on a lot of traditional dishes for which the ante has been upped with both imagination and globalization of flavors. Management recently did away with the original fast-casual counter-service concept to go full service (though not without a flurry of service complaints). The decor is very attractive, sleek and contemporary. If the bar reflects all the peoples and places the menu claims to, one thing everyone has in common is a good cocktail choice.

1511 SHEPHERD between Washington and I-10
713-861-9888
www.makchins.com
MAP E6

MAMA'S CAFE

From older locals to hangover-afflicted bar scene-makers, the clientele of this popular roadhouse create a profile of this unimpressed hot spot. Some places fight to be trendy. Mama's just stays that way and ignores it. It looks and feels like a well-used country cafe, something most people get to observe while waiting in line Sunday morning to get a seat at one of the booths or tables. The breakfast menu includes Mexican-style migas, biscuits and sausage gravy, eggs, grits, pancakes and cinnamon coffee. Sit and read the papers — no one will bother you. Lunch and dinner menus include burgers, chicken-fried steak, daily specials and our favorite, the messy and delicious bean burger. Yes, you'll sleep alone, but it's worth it.

6019 WESTHEIMER between Fountain View and S. Voss
713-266-8514
www.mamascafe.net
MAP C7

MARIA SELMA

> **1617 RICHMOND**
> between Mandell and Dunlavy
> **713-528-4920**
> www.mariaselma.com
> **MAP** E7

This restaurant from Joseph Varon (Maria Selma is his mother) and Rene Hidalgo is a bit different from the typical Houston Tex-Mex cafe. The Mexico City-style menu includes weekend breakfasts of *chilaquiles, huaraches* and huevos rancheros, as well as a generous lunch/dinner slate of *sopas* (soups), *tortas* (sandwiches), enchiladas and seafood. Yes, there are chips and salsa, but the chips are thicker and rougher than you find at most Tex-Mex cafes in town. (We like them.) There's *mole* on the menu, a crab-stuffed avocado and some tropical touches, such as pineapple grilled with the roasted pork. The recently constructed *palapa* makes dining out on the patio as pleasant as can be. There's also an extensive tequila collection.

MARINI'S EMPANADA HOUSE

> **3522 S. MASON** just north of Westheimer Parkway, Katy
> **281-391-4273**
> www.theoriginalmarinisempanadahouse.com
> **MAP** West of A7
>
> **10001 WESTHEIMER** between S. Gessner and Beltway 8
> **713-266-2729**
> **MAP** C6

The 1970s Montrose empanada house, which burned down in 1985, has had several incarnations since then, sometimes combined with a bakery, but always moving steadily west, it seems. The Marini family opened this cute little cafe in Katy in 2004 and more recently looked east again to open a 2007 offshoot in Carillon Center. Both spots are beloved for their savory and sweet Argentine turnovers. Among the favorites are beef gaucho (spiced ground beef, hard-boiled egg, olive and onions), Hot Tia Maria (chopped brisket, onions, jalapeño and tomato sauce), *fugazetta* (sautéed onions and cheese) and various mixed-cheese fillings. At dessert, any containing bananas are delicious, or try the chocolate or sweet potato. The friendly staff is happy to help you choose a tasty variety and will carefully label your box so, when you get home, you'll know which empanada is which.

MARK'S AMERICAN CUISINE

Even curmudgeons who disagree with the food writers (who wholeheartedly love this restaurant) should visit Mark's, if only for its most peculiar location among the tattoo parlors and junque shops and its

1658 WESTHEIMER
east of Dunlavy
713-523-3800
www.marks1658.com
MAP E6

outstanding decor. Mark's is located in a former church, and rather than try to decorate that fact out of sight, chef/owner Mark Cox and wife Lisa have done a splendid job of incorporating the theme throughout. There's dining in the choir loft and even a post-church addition given over to the architecture and subsequently called the Cloister. Outstanding

---

RECIPE **CHURRASCO WITH CHIMICHURRI SAUCE**

Churrascos, 2055 Westheimer, 713-527-8300, and 9705 Westheimer, 713-952-1988

This is the Latin American beef dish that launched restaurateur/chef Michael Cordúa's restaurant empire.

For the churrasco: Trim away all visible fat and gristle from a fresh beef tenderloin. Cut out a four-inch portion from the center. Make a half-turn with center-cut portion to bring a cut end parallel to cutting board. With a sharp knife held parallel to cutting board, starting from one side, carve it in a jelly-roll fashion to "roll out" the steak. When cut, it should be a rectangular piece of meat, about a quarter-inch thick.

Salt and pepper to taste, baste with Chimichurri Sauce (recipe below), and grill on a very hot fire to desired degree of doneness. (Note: A slow fire will dry the churrasco because it is extremely low in fat content.) Serve with extra Chimichurri Sauce on the side. Serves 2 to 4.

Chimichurri Sauce
3 bunches curly parsley, chopped
6 Tbsp. finely chopped fresh garlic
2 cups extra virgin olive oil
1 cup white vinegar
salt & pepper to taste

METHOD: Combine all ingredients in a food processor to make a thick sauce. Let sit at least 2 hours before serving. Excellent on all grilled meats, especially the churrasco, or as a dip for plantain chips and veggies. Makes 3 cups.

service (from the wait staff, not the preacher) never misses a beat, although the woman who takes reservations could be more welcoming on the phone. Mark's New American menu never bores, is never allowed to get old and dazzles with the most surprising off-the-wall dishes. It's completely seasonal, built on meat, game, seafood and fowl. Yes, the dining room is a tad noisy, but that's as much from conversation as the spontaneous *"Hallelujah" Chorus* some diners can't refrain from singing over their plates.

MASRAFF'S

1025 S. POST OAK LANE between San Felipe and Memorial
713-355-1975
www.masraffs.com
MAP D6

Looks can deceive. Pulling up to this welcoming stone lodge-like restaurant, it doesn't appear all that big — but inside it can feel cavernous. (In fact, if it's coziness you're after, ask for the Vintage Room just off the entry.) Father-and-son owners Tony and Russell Masraff have made good use of the space, however, creating an attractive bar and main dining area, lit by colorful Murano glass fixtures. Service usually adds further warmth, and at almost any given time, one will see Russell working the room to make sure all is in order. Seafood of all kinds is treated well here, although the seared foie gras with pears is an equally good catch, and this is one of the few restaurants in town where you can order steak tartare. Note: Tony makes his own delicious strawberry preserves and orange marmalade, which are sold in jars.

MASSA'S

Years ago, an indignant guest at a nearby hotel complained quite forcefully about the name of this restaurant, mistaking it for a throwback to the Jim Crow era. The truth, as she was informed before enjoying a meal there, is it's a family name that has a restaurant history going back to 1944 Galveston. Plus anyone who knows its hard-working owners, brothers Michael and Joseph Massa, knows this place wants to do nothing

1160 SMITH at Dallas
713-650-0837
www.massas.com
MAP F6

1331 LAMAR between Caroline and Austin
713-655-9100
MAP F6

more than please. There's nothing flashy at these two sibling restaurants, but traditional Gulf Coast cuisine, including gumbo and crabmeat dishes, and pastas are done well, consistently and with a heap of tradition. The restaurant is nicely decorated just to the point of being comfortable for a workday lunch and still hold its head up for a pre-theater dinner.

MAX'S WINE DIVE

4720 WASHINGTON
at Shepherd
713-880-8737
www.maxswinedive.com
MAP E6

Critics of this way-funky joint love its name — especially the *dive* word. The owners consider it a good marketing tool. The fact is, this popular wine bar/diner was created to turn everything on its head. A good deal of the menu follows a "tongue in chic" approach, using top-shelf ingredients and first-rate cooking skills to revise and even reinvent some standard dishes. A classic Philly cheesesteak, for example, is transformed into something quite different by substituting osso buco and black truffle cheese for the usual ingredients. A sloppy joe gets an extreme makeover with the addition of a Peking duck confit, and good ol' macaroni and cheese is made with *cavatappi* pasta slathered in Gruyère and black truffle fondue. Even when the menu is not being openly revisionist, it indulges in a good deal of wink-wink, nudge-nudge posturing with dishes like Three Big Balls (think meatloaf globes) and the Big Ass Brownie. As the name suggests, Max's Wine Dive takes its wine seriously. The proprietors are also the owners of the three Tasting Room wine bars, and you'd be hard pressed to find a wine list in town that's any more inviting. Service is as unpredictable as the menu, especially when it's crowded, and the noise level means one has to shout.

Given the limited indoor seating, guests often enjoy their wine on the sidewalk at Max's Wine Dive.

McCORMICK & SCHMICK'S

There's a big tip of the Stetson to this Portland, Oregon-based chain for coming to Texas and acknowledging Lone Star pride. Stained-glass mockingbird and bluebonnets greet arriving diners, and throughout the enormous

1151 UPTOWN PARK BLVD.
at Post Oak Blvd.
713-840-7900
www.mccormickandschmicks.com
MAP D6

restaurant — and it is huge — are subtle and tasteful emblems of the state tucked around everywhere. And for such a large place located on the edge of Uptown Park, there are an imaginative number of private booths (Irish bar-style "snugs") and hideaways that can make every party seem private. Of course the true pearl in this handsome oyster is the seafood — most of it done moderately well. And speaking of oysters, if you love them, you're in the right place. M&S sells more varieties of raw oysters, harvested in the cold waters of the northern Pacific and Atlantic, than any other Houston restaurant. (We're partial to the tiny, deep-cupped Kumamoto and coppery-tasting Malpeque.) A second location is scheduled to open in West Houston.

MERIDA

2509 NAVIGATION
east of S. Jensen
713-227-0260
MAP F6

It's kind of a left-handed compliment, but some of Merida's biggest fans are people who didn't want to fight the crowds at the original Ninfa's down the street and stopped in. That they keep coming back is the real compliment. Distinctly unglamorous, it's hugely popular with barrio neighbors, university students and savvy Houstonians who come for the hearty Tex-Mex and Yucatan specialties (Merida is the capital and largest city in the Mexican state of Yucatan). In addition to traditional favorites (chicken mole, *menudo*, shrimp *queso flameado*), Merida features great breakfasts and what many regard as the best bean soup on earth. If you can order only one thing, however, make it the combination platter that includes a *panucho* (meat-stuffed corn tortilla), an empanada, a *salvut* (corn tortilla topped with roast pork), black beans, guacamole and a *taco de cochinita pibil*, the Yucatan-style marinated, shredded roast pork, along with plenty of snappy pickled onions.

MEZZANOTTE

Located in Cypress smack in the middle of a strip mall. Enticed yet? Locals will snort and tell you to get over it and try this fun and imaginative Italian restaurant for the surprise you deserve. A great

13215 GRANT at Louetta, Cypress
832-717-7870
www.mezzanotteristorante.com
MAP A2

(red) atmosphere, elegant decor and live entertainment are a few of the things that will catch you off guard once you're in the door. The food could well be the other. Excellent quail, well-prepared pastas and a variety of Italian-style beef and lamb dishes please area families.

MI LUNA

2441 UNIVERSITY BLVD. between Kirby and Morningside, and other locations
713-520-5025
www.mi-luna.com
MAP E7

The city's first full-fledged tapas restaurant was a hit from early on, but expansion efforts into the 'burbs has had a mixed reception. Still, this Rice Village restaurant remains popular, especially among university students and young singles. It boasts okay food at a reasonable cost, an adventurous menu and, most critical, a happening social scene. Order any number of the traditional Spanish dishes, both *frías y calientes* (cold and hot), such as a plate of Spanish ham with manchego cheese, marinated octopus in sherry vinaigrette and Spanish potato omelet. There's a nice selection of Spanish wines as well as domestic, not to mention a well-stocked bar. Watch for specials, such as paella night every Tuesday. There's even an occasional flamenco dance lesson. Stay off the tables.

MIA BELLA

320 MAIN at Preston, and other locations
713-237-0505
www.miabellatrattoria.com
MAP F6

Located in the historic Kiam Building downtown (the building that once housed Houston's first department store), Youssef Nafaa's original Italian restaurant has an extraordinary urban feel. Imagine gazing through tall, near century-old arched windows as Metro's modern light rail zips by outside. Having survived the construction of that rail line as well as Tropical Storm Allison, Mia Bella does a brisk lunch business as well as an admirable dinner crowd. Not only are the prices reasonable, but Nafaa's "Italian with a Twist" concept juices up the menu. Sunday brunch is fun, especially when the weather permits and there's seating outside. The small chain is now in an expansion mode.

MINGALONE ITALIAN BAR & GRILL

540 TEXAS between Smith and Bagby
713-223-0088
www.mingalone.com
MAP F6

One of the original tenants of the Bayou Place complex in the downtown theater district, this Mediterranean/Italian restaurant opened with a few hiccups. Fortunately, in the years since, it has found its stride. That stride hits a march tempo with downtown theatergoers who have found the restaurant's proximity to so many venues, pleasant surroundings and ability to get them out the door in time makes for a pleasant evening. Pastas reign supreme here, but most dishes hold their own. Sitting outside on the grand terrace in the evening, when folks are scurrying to make the curtain at the nearby Wortham, Alley, Jones Hall and Hobby Center, makes one feel downright cosmopolitan.

Personal Favorites
WHERE ONE POLITICO EATS

By Anne Clutterbuck

As a Houston City Council member, I have the opportunity to experience all parts of the city. But I find that my favorite restaurants are in or near District C in Southwest Houston. Here are some of my favorite picks:

CAFE RABELAIS, *2442 Times, 713-520-8841.* Located in the heart of the Rice Village, Cafe Rabelais is the place to go for fantastic traditional French food in a cozy, fresh, comfortable setting. I love the escargot and the *entrecôte* (ribeye) with fresh shallots.

GRAVITAS, *807 Taft, 713-522-0995.* A quick five-minute drive from City Hall Annex, Gravitas is a refreshing and dynamic place to have a lunch meeting and discuss how to improve services in our great city. I suggest the cheese tortellini, and the spinach salad is a must- try. They also have a lounge area with a bar food menu and a small outdoor seating area.

NEW YORK BAGEL & COFFEE SHOP, *9720 Hillcroft, 713-723-5879.* A great spot to meet with a neighbor or friend in the southwest part of Houston, NY Coffee Shop and the adjacent bagel factory serve up bagels made in the great New York City tradition. I love the "everything" bagel with lox and the diner cheeseburger.

RAVEN GRILL, *1916 Bissonnet, 713-521-2027.* A District C neighborhood eatery, Raven Grill offers a relaxed atmosphere where you can have lunch and discuss business, read city financial reports or take the whole family out for dinner. The brown paper placed atop white tablecloths allows for doodling, which always makes contemplating the menu more fun. Some of my favorite menu picks are the onion rings and the Caesar salad with grilled shrimp.

TACO MILAGRO, *2555 Kirby, 713-522-1999.* Along Westheimer, Taco Milagro offers up one of my favorite salads in Houston, #81 (with guacamole and grilled shrimp). It also features a happy hour and patio seating in a casual atmosphere where great sangria is served.

Anne Clutterbuck is a second-term Houston City Council member.

MINT CAFE

2800 SAGE at W. Alabama
713-622-3434
www.mintcafehouston.com
MAP D7

From the name, one might wonder if it refers to a very expensive meal or that the iced tea is a specialty. Truth is, neither. The Galleria-area cafe is a trim little Mediterranean and Lebanese addition to the local dining scene, and it seems to attract quite a number of people from that part of the world. The decor is a minimalist design employing warm tones with clean-lined dark chairs, tables, a half-dozen low banquettes. The effect is both cool and comfortable, but doesn't invite lingering. Each meal is prefaced by pita chips and a bowl of tapenade-like spread. Food presentation is nicer and hipper than most Middle Eastern restaurants, though the menu offers no surprises: Shawarmas, gyros and kabobs seemed to be on practically every table during our recent visit. There's counter-service for lunch, table service in the evening.

MISSION BURRITOS

This Houston original actually serves a darn good taco, but isn't that like going to a steakhouse and wanting their vegetarian platter? Burritos rule at this offbeat chow-down place. While there are currently four locations (the newest one is in Rice Village), the Alabama location is especially inviting with its wide veranda and spreading live oak. The idea behind the concept is start with an oversized tortilla and start filling it with your choice of beans, rice, meats and sauces. If you're the indecisive type, don't go at lunch when the lines need to move. And if you're the can't-say-no kind of person, ask them to put your choices in a bowl so you can fill your own tortilla when you sit down. It's filling food for a good price, and kids are delighted by the small toys that stand in for claim checks for your order. The place is franchising, so it will be interesting to see if the offshoots hold up to the original.

2245 W. ALABAMA between Greenbriar and Kirby, and other locations
713-529-0535
www.missionburritos.com
MAP E7

MIYAKO

3910 KIRBY between Richmond and Hwy. 59, and other locations
713-520-9797
www.miyakosushibar.com
MAP E7

With the fans this chain has found in Houston along with the ever-growing popularity of sushi, this Japanese favorite is reproducing like, well, guppies. Raw-fish lovers pack the place, and while Miyako's regular prices are quite reasonable, there is a daily happy hour of particularly well-priced rolls. Other favorites, especially for those who like their food a little less swimming, include the shrimp tempura dinner, vegetarian sushi rolls and the miso soup. Critics say crowds and service sometimes makes them crabby.

MO MONG

1201 WESTHEIMER
between Montrose and Commonwealth
713-524-5664
MAP E6

Tucked away in the back corner of a large parking lot, Mo Mong looks like a place that would have a special following, and so it does. Foodies agree this is not the place to go for the city's best Vietnamese dining — there's much better to be had in the Little Saigon area south of downtown, as well as in the Chinatown in Southwest Houston — but then they still show up here regularly and wolf down the fried oysters with the wasabi sauce. Actually it's a small space with an urban vibe, cool and steely. Speaking of steel: It's not uncommon to find people with metal things attached to noses, lips, tongues and ears, and in summer when clothing gets lighter, this list gets longer. Eating is upstairs, while downstairs is a bar and tiny garden.

MOCKINGBIRD BISTRO WINE BAR

1985 WELCH at McDuffie, east of Shepherd
713-533-0200
www.mockingbirdbistro.com
MAP E6

Named for the state bird of Texas, Mockingbird serves Texas Provençal cuisine that has foodies flocking. Think "country-French-meets-American-market," Texas ingredients with a French bistro accent. Some say sophisticated comfort food, we say delicious. Standouts are killer calamari with two dipping sauces, Texas 1015 onion soup with Gruyère crouton, Kobe beef burger with foie gras and truffled frites, and warm bittersweet chocolate torte. Heck, they even have a root beer float. The interior is quirky, with gothic touches from a previous tenant, but very comfy and welcoming. (Longtime Houstonians might recognize the chandeliers from the famous long-gone Sonny Look's Sir-Loin Inn and the antique bar from Joske's downtown.) The room is downright sexy at night. Does the staff ever forget a face? We think not, as diners are

Native Houstonian John Sheely's Mockingbird Bistro is a Gourmet *magazine "neighborhood gem."*

always welcomed like old friends. Every staffer seems to know the menu *and* the wine list very well. Great monthly wine dinners, by the way. Though Mick Jagger dined at table 41, we think table 14 is best, and it is a diner favorite. However, it has standing Friday night reservations by regulars.

> **5701 MAIN** between Binz and Hermann Park, in Hotel ZaZa
> **713-526-1991**
> www.monarchrestauranthouston.com
> **MAP** E7

MONARCH

Everyone has been taught not to bring up religion or politics in a social gathering, and it may be time to add Hotel ZaZa and its Monarch restaurant to that list. Everyone seems to have a strong opinion about this new/old Houston stalwart (it's the old aristocratic, if shopworn, Warwick, utterly remade into a trendy new W-style boutique hotel) and its restaurant. Older Houstonians have balked at embracing the new wowie-zowie design elements such as easy chairs upholstered in zebra stripes, a prom-dressed mannequin suspended in a cage over a mini-lagoon and closed-circuit-TV coverage of fashion shows endlessly looping behind the front desk. On the other hand, young scene-makers seem drawn here like bees to a glass of strawberry soda. We've seen patrons flat-out screaming at the reservations clerks, and one woman is still fuming after asking to sit in the restaurant's private nook area and being told it was only for important people. Once everyone simmers down, however, most agree it's the service that sets them off. Maybe because the Dallas-based owners adhere to a different service approach than populist Houston enjoys. The restaurant's food actually ranges from average to great (unfortunately, that could be the same dish ordered on two nights). There's definitely talent in chef Bradley Manchester's kitchen, though, because when the food is good, it's superb, including the grilled wild salmon that is among the best we've ever eaten. We also liked the Thai lobster bisque and the pork chop with walnut-apple risotto. The restaurant is very attractive, all sexed up and rich, like the rest of the hotel. When your restaurant tab arrives, for example, it's in a velvet-lined silver box with a crown etched into the lid.

MONUMENT INN

This destination restaurant is kind a throwback to the typical Gulf Coast restaurant of the 1960s, but with its spectacular second-floor views of the Houston Ship Channel, Battleship Texas and San Jacinto Battleground, are you

> **4406 BATTLEGROUND RD.**
> north of Hwy. 225, in San Jacinto State Park, La Porte
> **281-479-1521**
> www.monumentinn.com
> **MAP** East of I6

really there to be culinarily challenged? Lunch or dinner here is like a field trip into Houston history. When a fire destroyed the original La Porte fixture a few years ago, Ann and Bob Laws rebuilt the restaurant and carried on. The kitchen emphasizes seafood, much of it fried, but the fact is, it does a good job. This is a fun spot to take out-of-towners for a taste of Texas history.

MORTON'S OF CHICAGO

5000 WESTHEIMER
at Post Oak Blvd.
(upstairs)
713-629-1946
www.mortons.com
MAP D6

1001 MCKINNEY
at Main
713-659-3700
MAP F6

Some people consider this fine chain restaurant Houston's stealth steak house. Although the Westheimer location has been here across the street from The Galleria for nearly a dozen years, many Houstonians still express surprise to learn there's a Morton's in town. Unlike some of the other steakhouses, this one doesn't get a lot of attention. But, considering it's within walking distance of a half-dozen large hotels and its national reputation, it doesn't hurt for business whatsoever. If you have ever been to a Morton's anywhere, the drill here will be familiar, with meat and live lobster shown tableside, a dining room decorated with Leroy Neiman prints and photographs of celebrities, and an open kitchen. There are no surprises on the menu, excepting the prices, of course — it's quite expensive. But the quality of the meat and vegetable side dishes is excellent. The downtown location opened about two years ago.

NAM

Buried in a strip center in southwest Houston, this enduring, slightly Americanized Vietnamese restaurant is a favorite in the area. Come here for cool and delicious spring rolls (called garden rolls here), as well as the tiny, crisp fried

2727 FONDREN just
south of Westheimer
713-789-6688
www.namcuisine.com
MAP C7

egg rolls served on a platter heaped with lettuce, mint and cilantro. Excellent seafood dishes, such as the whole fish marinated with lemongrass and chiles, then charbroiled. Food presentation is grander than at many Vietnamese spots: Steamed rice is packed into a mold so that a human mask looks up from your plate. If it's disconcerting, whack it with a spoon. A large aquarium, stocked with huge, fan-tailed goldfish, is perennially popular with children, and the wait staff is exceedingly hospitable.

ONLINE ORDERING
www.chefsproduce.com

COMMITTED TO SERVICE AND QUALITY

Houston (713) 643-9420
Dallas (214) 688-9930

NAM GANG

1411 GESSNER
north of Long Point
713-467-8801
MAP C5

Fans of this Korean restaurant praise its authenticity, especially some of the soups (goat, for one) and the do-it-yourself hibachi-grilled meats. Critics kind of agree. One said she's come to understand Korean restaurants are not known for good service, and this one pushed it to the extreme. We think that's a misunderstanding of Korean reserve. If you let the waitress know you're a newbie, she will be happy to help you grill the meat, deftly snipping the *kalbi* (beef shortribs) and *bulgogi* (ribeye) with her scissors. But there is a definite language barrier here, so don't expect chitchat while she's doing it. Adventurous eaters will enjoy all the many small side dishes that come with an order for barbecue (other choices for grilling include chicken, squid, shrimp and offal), and your meal ends with a rice porridge-like soup. While the place rarely seems crowded, it does seem to attract both Koreans and novices on a regular basis. Don't go for the ambiance, however. The neon lighting is a bit bright and you'll smell like grilled meat and kimchee until your next shower.

NELORE CHURRASCARIA

4412 MONTROSE just south of Richmond
713-395-1050
www.nelorechurrascaria.com
MAP E7

If you've been to other fixed-price Brazilian rodizio or churrascaria restaurants in Houston or elsewhere, then you know pretty much what to expect here. The difference is Nelore (named for Brazil's most famous breed of cattle) is smaller and feels more homey than the big places in town, such as Fogo de Chao and Fuegovivo Churrascaria. It's set in a Montrose bungalow, which means there are fewer tables and chairs, as well as a smaller, more modest salad/vegetable bar. The meat — several cuts of beef, plus lamb, pork, chicken and sausage — is brought to you by "gauchos" bearing swords. They will stop at your table to slice off as much as you like, and you eat until stuffed. As at the other churrascarias, meat quality varies sword by sword. Sometimes a piece of meat is juicy, rare, salty and delicious; the next may be too overcooked to your liking. (It's okay to pass and wait for the next sword.) Nelore will always have a place in our heart for the evening it sent us home with a bag of little cheesy popovers for breakfast the next morning.

NEW YORK BAGEL & COFFEE SHOP

Of course, we should all be over that by now, but isn't naming anything in Texas using the words "New York" just asking for it? Does

> **9720 HILLCROFT**
> south of S. Braeswood
> **713-723-8650**
> **MAP** C8

anyone want to venture a guess the immediate snide comment that's made every time service isn't up to par? Fortunately, this bustling, clean and efficiently run coffeeshop does such a good job, it has slipped by regional differences. The lengthy menu is filled with all-American breakfast items, including that diner favorite, corned beef hash. The bagel bakery is just next door with an interconnecting doorway, which means that all 15 or more kinds of bagels are always available and always fresh. If you're having eggs, don't hesitate to ask for an "everything bagel," toasted or not. Speaking of eggs, NYB&CS has some great short-order cooks, and they

Recommended
MY, OH MY, IT'S PECAN PIE!

***"You might give some serious thought to thanking your lucky stars you're in Texas,"* notes restaurateur Jim Goode on his wooden pie crates.** If you like pecans, you're in luck, because there is no climate better suited for growing pecans than Texas. But no two pecan pies are alike. When the pies of Texas are upon you, pick up from one of these pie emporiums.

DESSERT GALLERY, *3200 Kirby, 713-522-9999, and other locations.* On the weekends, slices are glorious, served with vanilla ice cream à la mode. Dark and rich with whole eggs and brown sugar, this beauty is packed with toasty pecans and encased in a thick, flaky, real-butter crust. The distinct filling is nothing short of nutty decadence.

GOODE CO. TEXAS BARBECUE, *5109 Kirby, 713-522-2530, and 8911 Katy Fwy., 713-464-1901.* The Texas pecan pie is just as legendary as the barbecue here. Somehow the tanned buttery pie crust tastes better than homemade: crackling, moist and toothy. The filling, with generous toasty pecan halves, is a wholesome brown sugar dream — a sweet one!

HOUSE OF PIES, *3112 Kirby, 713-528-3816, and 6142 Westheimer, 713-782-1290.* Okay, so the shortening crust has a manufactured appearance, but it's light and tasty. Karo-vanilla-flavored filling is gooey but not too sweet, and the crisp pecan halves are fresh and plentiful. Always works in a pinch. For something different, try the Texas pecan fudge pie heated, à la mode.

RUSTIKA CAFE & BAKERY, *3237 Southwest Fwy., 713-665-6226.* Darling individual pecan tarts with fluted crusts let you indulge any time of the year. Rustika's are pudgy and decadent with Mexican vanilla and brown sugar flavor; crispy pecans float on top. Custom-order whole pecan pies.

make some of the best home fries in town. The potatoes come with fried onions and, if you ask the server in a nice way, she will get it for you extra crisp. There is something for everyone here, provided they are not a heart patient. Smoked fish? Most of it comes direct from Brooklyn. You can order lox (regular or Nova), chubs, sable, kippered salmon and whitefish salad. There are also baked salmon, pickled herring and gefilte fish. Or how about a hot pastrami sandwich or corned beef? These aren't enormous like some New York delis serve, but they are wonderful on seeded rye and big enough for any human being. The matzoh ball soup is also incredible. If you note a gregarious guy kissing ladies and schmoozing with the men, that's co-owner Eddie Gavrila.

NIDDA THAI

1226 WESTHEIMER at Commonwealth
713-522-8895
MAP E6

Thai food lovers all but put on short skirts and grab pom-poms when Nidda Thai is mentioned. There are probably critics somewhere, but none willing to take on the people who can't seem to say enough good things about this place. The food does back them up, especially the many curries, dumplings and fish dishes. The coconut soup is also a notch above, and the famous Tiger Cries (a chile-fired beef salad) is still on the menu after all these years, presumably a paean to the space's original 1980s Thai restaurant, Renu's. There's nothing about the decor to lure one in — it's a plain and unremarkable dining room — so the food has to do it. Parking out front in this strip center may put you in close proximity to the Erotic Cabaret next door, so if that bothers you, make a big show of entering the restaurant.

NIELSEN'S DELICATESSEN

The first Danish-accented Nielsen's opened in Highland Village nearly 60 years ago, back when Highland Village would allow such a thing in. Within hours of flipping on the light, the first batch of homemade mayonnaise was whipped up, and success was assured. (Remember when mayo wasn't a four-letter word?) The flagship Nielsen's is now on Richmond and is a little ratty looking, but it's still making its own mayo and still pleasing generation after

4500 RICHMOND east of Weslayan
713-963-8005
MAP D7

26830 I-45 NORTH #B south of Woodlands Parkway, Spring
281-363-3354
MAP North of E1

generation of deli lovers. Some customers even buy the mayonnaise plain to take home and fold into their own salads. The much-loved Ellen Nielsen Andersen passed away in early 2008, but her family carries on the Nielsen's tradition. Try the corned beef-on-rye sandwich with its homemade liver paste and deviled eggs sold in little paper cups. Have some of the legendary potato salad, too. Perch on one of the barstools to eat in or, better, take your food out. Arrive early or late to avoid the lunch mob. Good brownies and cheesecake, too.

NIKO NIKO'S

2520 MONTROSE
between Westheimer and Fairview
713-528-0966
www.nikonikos.com
MAP E6

No one has to look for the sign on this popular fast-casual spot (although it isn't an easy sign to miss). You can't avoid the traffic slowing while drivers turn into the huge new parking lot at this ever-improving, ever-expanding Greek favorite. With its famous gyros, hamburger-stuffed cabbage rolls, stuffed grape leaves and Greek meatballs, the place is always bustling and the tables seem to be full both inside and out. The setting isn't much, but it's got a ringside seat for watching the crowds head to the nearby bars on Pacific Street any Friday or Saturday night. Even the low-tech decor is regarded fondly by fans of this Greek greasy spoon. We admire owner Dimitrios Fetokakis, who has taken over maintenance of the median strip in front of his restaurant and led the charge for reclaiming and revitalizing the boulevard. What we don't like: high prices for the privilege of fetching our food and eating from a paper plate with plastic cutlery.

NINFA'S

Freddy Krueger is less of an urban legend than Ninfa Laurenzo's funky *original* location on Navigation. Freddy's not nearly as popular, either. It isn't so much about the food, although there are the fans who will swear it's still the best Tex-Mex anywhere. It was this perennially popular hole-in-the-wall on the east side of downtown that greatly helped popularize Tex-Mex in the area — even nationally — and then grew to a fairly large local chain before being sold off. There's still a warming authentic, coming-home feel here, once you've worked your way through the Mercedes, BMWs and Jaguars in the parking lot and the patient line at the door (insiders know whom to call to reserve a

2704 NAVIGATION
east of S. Jensen, and other locations
713-228-1175
www.mamaninfas.com
MAP F6

table). Fajitas, which reach their apex in Houston, and the margaritas are probably the best-known attractions, but nearly everything makes this Houston original worthy of a visit. New owners recently took over and renovated (the bathrooms have been redone — thank you!), but they promise to keep the menu the way we love it. It can't be a good feeling knowing thousands of Ninfa's lovers are waiting for one wrong move.

> **2817 W. DALLAS** between Montrose and Waugh
> **713-522-5120**
> www.ninos-vincents.com
> **MAP** E6

NINO'S

To this day, the staff occasionally comes across a diner who remembers renting an apartment upstairs when this family restaurant opened 30 years ago in what is now the bar area. Owners Vincent and Mary Mandola tell how they used to stand at nights in an empty restaurant watching for approaching headlights on Dallas. Not so today. The renters are no more. The restaurant is the entire first floor with private dining rooms upstairs, and the place is rarely not full. The family subsequently opened Vincent's next door, Grappino's out back and went ahead and purchased the rest of the block for parking. Beautifully landscaped, the compound is like a little Italian village near downtown. Often overlooked by the *trendetti* these days, Nino's is one of Houston's best-loved Italian restaurants. The menu keeps abreast of current thinking, too, with excellent pastas, seafood and white beans with fragrant homemade sausage. A not-so-secret secret: While Nino's has its fans and Vincent's has its, one may stand ground in Nino's and still order a lusty roast chicken hot from the Vincent's rotisserie next door.

NIPPON

Right in the heart of eclectic Montrose, where parking is at a premium, take note, is a full-service sushi restaurant that has been drawing area residents since it opened many years ago. From the outside, it looks more like a coffeehouse, but once through its doors there's a plush dining room, awash in shades of mauve and purple. It's as untrendy as it can be, but we like the quiet old-fashioned (some might say quaint) space. It's the polar opposite of Zake, Ra Sushi, Uptown Sushi and the other big, noisy Japanese ports of call. Nippon is owned by Japanese, and you can tell. The TV in the bar is

> **4464 MONTROSE** between Richmond and Hwy. 59
> **713-523-3939**
> **MAP** E7

quietly tuned to a Japanese channel, and duos of Japanese businessmen and couples quietly converse. The prices are gentle, too. On a recent visit three of us ate until we could eat no more, and we were surprised and gratified by the reasonable figure written on our tab. You may also go raw outside on the patio. Parking? It's in the back.

6395 WOODWAY
between Fountain View and Voss, and other locations, including Nit Noi Cafes

713-789-1711
www.nitnoithai.com

MAP C6

NIT NOI THAI

"Nit noi" means "a little bit," and Thai food fans pack Alice Vongvisith's Nit Noi restaurants and cafes, which are now scattered around the city. *Mee krob* (crispy noodles with sweet-sour sauce), fried rice, noodle dishes and soup are all good. Try the *tom yum goong* (spicy and sour shrimp soup), seafood-filled "sea rolls" and *patt thai korat* (flat rice noodles stir-fried with chicken, pork or shrimp and vegetables). The food is more Americanized and the various locations are a little shinier and more upscale than the typical Thai restaurant. The longtime Village location has been closed to make room for new construction.

NOÉ

Chef Robert Gadsby abruptly departed the Omni Houston Hotel's Noé in 2007, obviously giving them his middle one when he did. His middle name, that is, which is Noé. The question is what will happen to this intellectually exciting dining venue with the old chef's name? Gadsby is off at a new restaurant (Soma, on Washington) while the hotel seems to be holding the status quo. (As we go to press with this book, its chef webpage is "under construction.") Stay tuned for the next installment. We doubt it will be called Noé.

4 RIVERWAY at Woodway, in the Omni Houston Hotel

713-871-8177
www.noerestaurant.com

MAP D6

Chefs come and go at the Omni Houston Hotel, but the food is always bold.

NOODLE HOUSE 88

9889 BELLAIRE BLVD.
just east of Beltway 8
713-771-8909
www.noodlehouse88.com
MAP A7

Located in one of the newer Asian shopping centers that are sprouting along Bellaire Boulevard, this is the spot for Chinese-Indonesian cooking. New to Indonesian food? Visit the Noodle House 88 website where, at least, you can view photos of the dishes to get you started. Some of the food is familiar if you like other Asian cuisines, including satay (chicken, beef and pork), fried wonton and steamed or pan-fried dumplings. The Indonesians are famous for their fried chicken, too, and the birds served here are tiny and young. There are also plenty of less-familiar foods that adventurous diners will want to try, especially the many seafood specialties. Two of Indonesia's best-known dishes — *gado-gado* (a mixed-vegetable salad with peanut dressing) and rich slow-cooked beef *rendang* — are here. Alas, we thought the *gado-gado* was a coarse and lazy disappointment compared to other versions we've enjoyed. Note: Bring cash; no credit cards accepted.

NORTH CHINA

North China is in West Houston. Fans call it the best-kept secret in the Memorial area and the best unknown Chinese restaurant in Houston. Would West China have worked better as a name? Truth be told, this

879 FROSTWOOD at Kingsride, west of Gessner
713-464-6774
www.houstonnorthchina.com
MAP C6

family-run Mandarin gem, now more than 30 years old, is an earnest, caring little spot with a surprisingly nice decor and, even more surprisingly, decent choice of wines. Service is a joy. Can't find what you want on the menu? If the kitchen isn't slammed, the chef will often take requests. Twice-cooked pork, lemon chicken, sizzling rice soup, Mandarin green beans and steamed or pan-fried pork dumplings are faves.

OCEAN PALACE

11215 BELLAIRE BLVD.
west of Wilcrest
281-988-8898
www.oceanpalacerest.com
MAP B7

Set in Houston's "New" Chinatown, this bowling alley-sized dim sum parlor is *not* palatial in design. However, it is comfortable enough, and you'll be happy here Saturday or Sunday morning as the carts loaded with dozens of tiny dishes are wheeled by for your inspection. Other times, order Cantonese fare from the menu. The place is huge, and on the weekends it's always packed with extended Chinese families. The lagoon and fountains out front won't do much for your appetite. The water has the murk and color of laundry pre-soak, and there's often trash floating. Inside, you may think you're in Hong Kong. This is a bit of an out-of-Houston experience ... *in* Houston.

> **5061 WESTHEIMER**
> between Post Oak Blvd. and McCue, in The Galleria
> **832-487-8862**
> www.theoceanaire.com
> **MAP** D6

THE OCEANAIRE SEAFOOD ROOM

This plush dining room feels like that of an elegant ocean liner circa 1940. But don't worry, casual Galleria shoppers in shorts won't be turned away and will feel right at home with the after-work suits and trendy daters. Though large (with two floors), the space has plenty of private nooks for canoodling over a chilled seafood platter. This is a Minnesota-based chain, but it has done a great job making it feel local with an abundance of Gulf seafood on chef Trevor White's daily menu, which changes depending on fresh catches. The raw bar at the entrance is great for happy hour, a quick meal or a first-stop on the way to the table. The oyster list usually features a half-dozen or more, from both the East and West Coasts. Sometimes you'll find littleneck clams, too. We can't think of a more splendid holiday treat than meeting an old friend at the Oceanaire for oysters and Champagne. The bloody Marys are more than generous, too.

OLIVETTE

Once you hit the grounds of The Houstonian, you know you're in for a treat. Lush landscaping with winding trails, an enchanting entrance and a smiling staff make arrival as special as the meal. The dining room's decorative theme is "totally Tuscan." Rustic tables

> **111 N. POST OAK LANE**
> between Woodway and Memorial, in The Houstonian
> **713-685-6713**
> www.houstonian.com
> **MAP** D6

and comfy seating invite diners to linger and enjoy the view, either of the open kitchen or the forested landscape beyond the windows. The menu is modern American with a solid dose of Mediterranean touches. If you haven't already tried it, order the Southwest Caesar Salad, a gazillion-time winner of the annual Caesar Salad Competition held every year in October. It's dotted with black beans, corn, *pepitas* (toasted pumpkin seeds) and cotija cheese. We also love the butternut squash soup with spiked cranberries and, after, the malted-milk ice cream profiteroles with sugared almonds. Add an after-dinner drink to your tab and carry it to the stunning hotel lobby to sip by the impressive stone fireplace.

OPEN CITY BISTRO

2416 BRAZOS north of McGowen (front door faces Bagby)
713-522-0118
www.ochouston.com
MAP E6

Houston newcomers Tamer and Nadine Aly named this spot after a Roberto Rossellini movie, but one step onto the rooftop bar and dining area will make you unapologetic for your ignorance of classic cinema. Open City boasts one of Houston's most spectacular views of downtown. There is also a downstairs dining room and patio. The menu is comfort food with a kick, and the Gruyère Mac & Cheese is the best. The chicken-fried chicken and the lamb sliders are tops, too. On Bloody Mary Saturdays there's a whole salad bar's worth of calamari, bacon, vegetables, anchovies and more to add to a prepaid bloody Mary. As far as we're concerned, that constitutes lunch. Service can be hit or miss, and the average age on weekends will make anyone over 35 claim a senior discount. Did we mention the Pop Rocks martinis.

OTILIA'S

7710 LONG POINT between Antoine and Wirt
713-681-7203
www.otilias.com
MAP D5

Set in a former fast-food drive-in (surely you recognize the Whataburger A-frame), this Spring Branch-area Mexican is explicit about its heritage: no Tex-Mex! Come here for family-style interior Mexican cooking, served by a waitstaff that is also sort of "family-style" — you can't tell if they like you or hate you. Oh well, nothing a margarita can't cure. Speaking of cures, chase away that hangover with a *michelada* — beer over ice with *mucho limón*. We like the seafood, *mole* and fresh lemonade. Also popular are the *posole* (hominy stew) and *chilaquiles*; less popular are the recent renovations and expansion that some say dull-down the place. Closed Mondays.

OTTO'S BARBECUE & HAMBURGERS

5502 MEMORIAL between Detering and Westcott, and other locations
713-864-2573
MAP E6

We don't know whether the original Memorial Drive location of Otto's will still be open by the time you read this. The owners announced early in 2008 that the property had been sold and Otto's would be bulldozed to make room for a new development. (As is the case with Ninfa's, only the original location seems to count in anyone's discussion of this much-beloved, old-style Houston institution.) However, as we go to press, Otto's is still smoking meats and hand-pressing burgers for the long-time regulars who, famously, include President George Bush senior. But here's the truth: The food is not very good here and — who knows? — maybe never was. The brisket is so-so, and the barbecue sauce and side dishes are all too sweet and dull. The burgers are decent, but the fries, sadly, are not. But even if the quality of the food never seemed to live up to Otto's mythology, the place has always counted on being included in any discussion of "real" Houston food. We hope Otto's ends its days with myth intact.

OUISIE'S TABLE

3939 SAN FELIPE
west of Willowick
713-528-2264
www.ouisiestable.com
MAP D6

Elouise Adams Jones, aka Ouisie, is a local pioneer among women chefs, having opened her first Ouisie's Table in 1973 on Sunset Blvd. The current location opened in 1995 and has pretty much ruled the roost among Southern and Gulf Coast restaurants in the region. But don't think Southern means "set." The menu has never stopped evolving, and the main dining room still has an enormous blackboard where the proprietress can add a host of daily specials. Brandied oysters, shrimp and cheese grits, seafood crêpes and "Pan-Roasted Chicken with Running Gear" are all favorites. So is the raw oyster martini with the cheese-stuffed olive. Open seven days, the restaurant stays busy, and lunches can be packed. Parking is a little hazardous if you choose not to valet.

A stylish, airy dining room is the setting for soulful Southern cooking at Ouisie's Table.

PALAZZO'S TRATTORIA

We knew there was something to this place when every holiday party we went to served take-away "Palazzo Pans" of piping hot pastas and darn good salads. This is not cutting-edge Italian, just good, solid dishes that fill the tummy, tickling a few taste buds along the way. John and Stassa

2300 WESTHEIMER
between S. Shepherd and Kirby, and other locations
713-522-6777
www.palazzoscafe.com
MAP D6

Recommended
OLD-FASHIONED TEXAS EATS

It's hard to define "a Texas-style restaurant," since Texas has so many different styles. How similar is the Texas that is hot, steamy, Cajun-accented Beaumont to the Texas represented by, say, Amarillo or El Paso or Harlingen? We've pulled together a dozen spots that represent a variety of Texases. It's a little walk down memory lane, a little cross-taste of the many kinds of foods and restaurants that we love in the Lone Star State.

ARMADILLO PALACE, *5015 Kirby, 713-526-9700.* We have several honky-tonks on this list, and this is the newest one, a Texana-crammed shrine to the Lone Star State. It's from Jim Goode, famous for his barbecue, pecan pie and much more (see Goode Co. Texas Seafood, below). Note the whiskey bar, live-music schedule (sign up for email notification), dominoes and pool tables. Step outside to the patio where, on any given day, there may be crawfish boiling, brisket smoking or fajitas sizzling.

GILHOOLEY'S, *222 9th St., San Leon, 281-339-3813.* First rule here: Kids are not allowed. You can safely assume this is a place for adults — the clientele sometimes runs a little bikerish — and it's a throwback to another time. (Last time we visited, customers were still puffing on cigarettes.) Second rule: You can't leave without ordering the wood-roasted oysters. Not all the food is great here, but these oysters, which are dressed with garlic butter and grated parmesan, then grilled in their shells over wood, are unlike anything we've had in Houston. Worth the drive.

GOODE CO. TEXAS SEAFOOD, *2121 Westpark, 713-523-7154.* Entering this railroad-car restaurant is like stepping back into a Port Aransas restaurant circa 1950. The fish, shrimp and oysters are fresh as can be and cooked with a deft hand. We recommend the mesquite-grilled catfish, oyster po'boy and *campechana extra* (a Mexican-style shrimp and crab cocktail). There's a second location at 10211 Katy Fwy., 713-464-7933.

JAX GRILL, *1613 Shepherd, 713-861-5529.* Representing the eastern part of the state with its regular Friday-night Zydeco party, this mesquite-grilled spot is famous for its smoky burgers on toasted buns, a chewy T-bone, fried oyster po'boy and gumbo. There's a second location at 6510 S. Rice Ave., 713-668-3606.

LANKFORD GROCERY & MARKET, *88 Dennis, 713-522-9555.* This is the real thing, an old-style Texas cafe and ice house, just five minutes from downtown, that still serves cheeseburgers the way you should remember them. It has breakfast and daily specials, too (e.g. chicken and dumplings, chicken-fried steak and enchiladas), but it's the old-style burgers and cold Shiner Bock that will call you back. Think *Greater Tuna*.

MAMA'S CAFE, *6019 Westheimer, 713-266-8514.* It's the bean burger with a side of fries and rings that we love here. But sometimes after church on Sunday, we cannot deny ourselves migas or pancakes or pork chop and eggs. Whatever time of day, funky booths and

Moore's original Palazzo's at 2620 Briar Ridge has been a popular spot near The Galleria for some time. At the bigger, fancier Westheimer version, look for Tuscan-inspired decor, a renovated kitchen and a patio garden. The menu includes grilled portobello mushroom in balsamic vinegar, crabcakes topped with Dijon beurre blanc, veal, seafood, pasta and pizzas. The restaurants have a great neighborhood feel, with lots of regulars, and are a safe choice when dining with kids. Delivery and catering available.

old stuff tacked up on the walls will lull you into a well-greased serenity.

RIO RANCH, *9999 Westheimer, in the Westchase Hilton, 713-952-5000.* Recently renovated, this hotel restaurant does a fine job of evoking a gentler time, with the rocking chairs and handsome fieldstone and wood outfitting. It's always Sunday dinner here: buttermilk fried chicken breast, ranchero ribeye, cornbread dressing and mesquite-grilled skewered shrimp.

SWINGING DOOR, *3818 FM 359, Richmond, 281-342-4758.* Established in 1973 by Steve and Ward Onstad, the original Swinging Door seated just 12. After a fire the following year, it was rebuilt and expanded. Its true claim to fame came in 1979, when the restaurant won the barbecue cook-off at the Houston Livestock Show and Rodeo. Today it's still family owned. Its meats are smoked over pecan wood, and there's great C&W dancing.

SYLVIA'S ENCHILADA KITCHEN, *12637 Westheimer, 281-679-8300.* Sylvia's proudly represents South Texas in this round-up. You'll think this is a typical Tex-Mex restaurant. But look again at the collection of enchiladas. There are always at least 16 varieties, including Crystal City (spinach with tomatillo sauce), McAllen (chicken) and King Ranch (fajita enchiladas with chile gravy).

TASTE OF TEXAS, *10505 Katy Fwy., 713-932-6901.* The restaurant wears its state pride on its sleeve — er, walls. The place is stuffed with Texas artifacts, so full of history that hundreds of 4th graders get a tour (and lunch) here every year. It's big and it's busy, but the wait staff is notably good natured. We'll not soon forget the sight of three Asian businessmen, wearing bibs, tucking into steaks as big as their briefcases.

THIS IS IT!, *207 W. Gray, 713-659-1608.* A modest steam-table restaurant, this is old-style East Texas dining, with such home-cooked faves as chicken and dumplings, ribs, meatloaf, beans and ham hocks, and smothered pork chops, plus long-cooked vegetables, biscuits and cornbread. The ladies who dish it up usually know what you'll like and how much you should have.

WUNSCHE BROS. CAFE & SALOON, *103 Midway, Old Town Spring, 281-350-1902.* German sausage sandwiches, squash casserole, great burgers and a few edible curiosities — sauerkraut balls, anyone? — make this century-old saloon the town's best-known draw. It has live music and legendary desserts, too, including peach cobbler and chocolate whiskey cake.

THE PALM

6100 WESTHEIMER
between Fountain View and S. Voss

713-977-2544
www.thepalm.com

MAP C7

A mention of this retro steakhouse to a friend elicited a "blue hair alert" response, but the dining room is dotted with diners of all ages, especially those with company cards (or at least daddy's card). Houston's local outpost of the New York chain resembles the original, with caricatures on the walls, huge filet mignons, lobsters the size of poodles and real New York-style cheesecake. Only the pleasant waiters give away that this is Texas, not Manhattan. The service is more professional than your standard eatery, even when you are dining at lunch to snag a bargain: $20-$22 for salad, entree and dessert. Niiiice. The 837 Club gives frequent-diner awards points. Clog enough arteries and get a free meal!

PANG TAI'S STIR FRY BISTRO

10811 WESTHEIMER
at Wilcrest

713-975-7821

MAP D6

Pang Tai's is an ambitious homage to the cuisines of the Far East. With attention to detail, the eatery gives Houstonians an opportunity to enjoy many Asian flavors, all under one roof. You'll find a full sushi bar, a menu of cooked items that run the gamut from traditional Vietnamese favorites to Indonesian- and Hunan-inspired creations, and the namesake stir-fry bar where diners can create their own dish with ingredients they select from the "vegetable market." Definitely something for everyone. We like the Cha Cha Shrimp and Bora Bora Salmon (is there an echo in here?). The dining room is stylish and welcoming, with a stunning 42-by-8-foot reflection pool stretching down the center. Daily happy hour.

PAPPADEAUX SEAFOOD KITCHEN

2410 RICHMOND east of Kirby, and other locations

713-527-9137
www.pappadeaux.com

MAP E7

Where do you geaux for seafood? Countless locals reply, "Pappadeaux," proving loyalty to the Pappas restaurant empire. This concept is the so-called Cajun branch of the line-up, and if you like themed restaurants, then you'll probably enjoy the place. The seafood is fresh and portions are huge, but we like our Cajun shacks to be a little less staged and a little more authentic. On the plus side, the staff is accommodating, but the wait for a table can be brutal and the noise level deafening. Success has its drawbacks. Overall, you will go away satisfied if not wowed.

PAPPAS BAR-B-Q

1217 PIERCE at San Jacinto, and other locations
713-659-1245
www.pappasbbq.com
MAP F6

Pappas serves Texas-style barbecue, and that means lean and juicy slow-smoked meats that aren't drowned in sweet sauce. This downtown location has siblings scattered about town, but is considered a flagship of sorts. Look for the huge cow on the roof. Peruse the large menu, then step up to the counter and place your order, cafeteria-style. This is neither the best or worst barbecue in town, but there are standout items: It's famous for its enormous chopped beef-filled Idaho bakers the size of footballs and, when consumed, coma-inducing. Beef, chicken, pork and turkey are served individually or in combos with classic barbecue sides. As with all Pappas family eateries, quick service and huge portions are trademarks.

PAPPAS BROS. STEAKHOUSE

5839 WESTHEIMER at Bering
713-780-7352
www.pappasbros.com
MAP C7

Longtime Houstonians will remember this space as the Strawberry Patch. Gone are the days of diner sandwiches and salads. Hello, meat! And seafood. But as the name implies, steaks reign supreme. Cloaked in handsome dark paneling, lined with booths and splendidly decked out from top to bottom, you can almost smell the testosterone in the air. This is a great place to celebrate, woo new business or impress a date. The beef is prime, and the wine list boasts more than 500 entries. Everything is served and priced a la carte, which is a good news/bad news scenario. On the positive, you can order anything you like; on the negative, the check total very quickly reaches stratospheric levels. The functioning retro phones at each booth are a whimsical touch.

PAPPAS SEAFOOD HOUSE

3001 S. SHEPHERD at W. Alabama, and other locations
713-522-4595
www.pappasseafood.com
MAP E7

What do Greeks know about Gulf Coast seafood? A lot, apparently. Fried calamari, stuffed flounder and all kinds of oysters and shrimp have made this link in the Pappas' chain of restaurants a hit with big appetites. Pappas brags about "portions as big as the ocean," and it ain't joking. It's a little obscene, to be honest. If you choose not to share, then take leftovers home for a late-night snack or next-day lunch. Softshell crab is a must-try in season (heaven with an ice cold beer), and the huge Greek salad for two will feed a family. Finish with the cheesecake, if you are still vertical.

PAPPASITO'S CANTINA

6445 RICHMOND
at Hillcroft, and other locations

713-784-5253
www.pappasitos.com

MAP C7

If sensory overload is your bag, this is the place for you. Hundreds of people talking at peak level over "background" music, walls crammed with every type of item imaginable, and, all around you, the aroma of Tex-Mex from passing trays. It's a lot to take in, but the more Pappasito's there are, the more people seem to love them. So brace yourself for the noise (watch your waitress strain to read your lips), circus-like atmosphere and, during busy times, a long wait for a table. It helps that the indefatigable young service staff always seem to be peppy, happy to make sure you have a good time. The chips and salsa are some of our favorites — always warm and fresh, and all-you-can-devour. In the Pappas tradition, the portions are huge. Fajitas come mounded on a sizzling platter the size of a manhole cover and so sizzling hot that you get a complimentary facial steam on the side. For the indecisive, there is a good selection of combo plates, and the lunch menu offers slightly smaller portions at slightly lower prices. The bill can stack up quickly, but you should have plenty of food for a doggie bag.

PAPPY'S CAFE

Every neighborhood should have a multi-purpose restaurant the family can fall into at the end of a day that has been stretched long by sports, music lessons, Scouts and/or a tutorial. For affluent Memorial and Spring

9041 KATY FWY.
east of Campbell

713-827-1811

MAP C6

Branch families, Pappy's is it. There's a full bar (but lousy margaritas, we're sorry to report) for the 'rents and delicious milkshakes for the kids. The menu includes chicken-strip baskets (our favorite order — ask for both gravy and honey-mustard dressing), salads, chicken-fried steak, grilled salmon and so on. Sometimes the place seems to not be as snappy as it once was — the service staff can be discombobulated, and the kitchen is profoundly uneven — but honestly, it's always been like that. It just depends on who's working and cooking. Even so, there are days when the babyback ribs call your name and nothing sounds so good as one of the two-fisted burgers. Added family attraction: Near the back entrance are some alluring games (if you're about 10 years old) that suck up quarters by the handful.

RECIPE **SEAFOOD GUMBO**

Goode Co. Texas Seafood, 2621 Westpark, 713-523-7154, and 10211 Katy Fwy., 713-464-7933

Gumbo has been one of the biggest hits on the menu at Goode Co. Texas Seafood since it opened its doors in 1986. "On a cold day, it just doesn't get any better than a big ol' bowl of gumbo with lots of hot toasty garlic bread," says Levi Goode, son of founder Jim Goode.

Adapted for the home cook
1 cup vegetable oil
1 cup all-purpose flour
2 cups chopped celery
4 cups chopped onions
2 cups chopped bell peppers
¼ cup chopped garlic
1 Tbsp. chopped fresh thyme
8 dried bay leaves
1 cup tomato paste
1 tsp. cayenne pepper
1½ gallons fresh seafood stock
1 lb. crab claw meat
1 lb. (36-42 count) shrimp, boiled and peeled
2 dozen lightly sautéed oysters
salt to taste
boiled white rice
gumbo filé (for garnish)
green onions, sliced (for garnish)

METHOD: Heat oil in a large saucepot over medium-high heat until hot but not smoking. Whisk in the flour gradually. Cook for 20 minutes or until the roux is the color of peanut butter, whisking rapidly. Add the celery, onions and bell peppers. Cook for 10 to 20 minutes or until the vegetables are tender; the roux will cool slightly as the vegetables are added and darken as the vegetables release their natural sugars. Stir in the garlic, thyme, bay leaves, tomato paste and cayenne pepper. Cook for 5 to 10 minutes or until heated through, stirring occasionally. Add the seafood stock. Bring to a boil and reduce the heat to medium. Simmer for 5 to 10 minutes, skimming the surface. Add the crab, shrimp and oysters. Taste and add salt, if needed. Discard the bay leaves. Divide cooked rice among bowls, ladle gumbo over the rice, and garnish with filé and green onions. Serves 8 to 12.

PASHA

2325 UNIVERSITY BLVD. between Greenbriar and Morningside
713-592-0020
www.epasha.com
MAP E7

We love Houston for its diversity of restaurants, and this is a prime example. Not every city boasts several Turkish-Mediterranean eateries, as we do. This one is nestled in a lovely old house, where you'll find colorful Turkish woven pieces and a requisite hookah in the waiting area, and sexy pomegranate walls give diners a warm hug. There's an extensive offering of appetizers, entrees, kebabs, seafood, Turkish sandwiches — the menu goes on and on. Can't decide? Hone in on the specialties section, or ask owner Mustafa Ozsoy for a recommendation. He believes several of his dishes — like the salmon-stuffed grilled grape leaves, *arnavut cigeri* (fried beef liver) and lamb sauté — are unique in the Houston area. Try a *gazoz* (Turkish soda) or a glass of Turkish wine for a further bit of Turkish delight.

PATRENELLA'S/CORLEONE'S

813 JACKSON HILL one block south of Washington
713-863-8223
www.patrenellas.net
MAP E6

Located in a 1938 house built by owner Sammy Patrenella's father, this home-style Italian restaurant has been going through some growing pains of late. The neighborhood has gone decidedly younger and upscale, and Washington Avenue's boom is just a block away. Stepping into the flux is chef Ryan Hildebrand, who has introduced a new menu (to the howls of old regulars) and added some other changes, including Sunday brunch in Corleone's. The result has been a lower average age in the dining room and a choice of Italian-inspired dishes that push the envelope a bit. The greatest gem of this quaint 16-year-old restaurant, though, is the one-acre garden that sits just outside the back door. There's a whole lot of that garden coming into the kitchen. Also out the back door is Corleone's, a late-night, small-bites dining room and bar that burned in 2007 but recently reopened. Service can be awkward with some on the waitstaff totally confused by what's new on the menu. Change is never easy.

PATU

2420 RICE BLVD. between Kirby and Morningside
713-528-6998
MAP E7

This small and narrow, shoebox-like cafe (the space used to be an alley) presents one of Rice Village's most intriguing storefronts, looking both exotic and Berkeley-esque at the same time. There is nothing fancy about the decor (no, the bric-a-brac by the door isn't for sale) but the food is fresh and tasty and, therefore, the main focus. Come here for chicken satay, *mee krob*, lime beef salad (we dream about it for days after) and fresh seafood and duck. Steamed rice comes in a large silver-metal soup terrine — this humble side item never had it so good. A daily lunch buffet isn't huge but has plenty to offer for vegetarians and meat eaters alike and is easy on the wallet. The size of the room tends to make you feel like you should talk in a library voice, which is hard to do when you hit the peppers hard.

PAULIE'S

1834 WESTHEIMER at Driscoll
713-807-7271
www.pauliesrestaurant.com
MAP E6

2617 HOLCOMBE at Kirby
713-660-7057
MAP E7

Paulie's is the kind of restaurant you want in your neighborhood — comfortable and casual, good food at reasonable prices. Founded by Kathy and Bernard Petronella, it is named for Kathy's son, Paulie, who is now grown-up Paul and running the show. While the restaurant serves terrific sandwiches (we love the Shrimp BLT and pork tenderloin with Cajun mustard) and salads (the Big Salad really is big), it also has a great dinner menu of pastas and satisfying entrees. Nice boutique Italian wine list and beer selection, and the walls feature rotating local art. Definitely save room for dessert — Paulie's has tasty, whimsically iced cut-out cookies, plus other cookies and brownies. Our pet peeve: Diners who snag tables before placing their order, sometimes leaving those who have picked up their meal no place to sup. The Holcombe location has a great patio.

PERBACCO

This could be one of Houston's best-kept dining secrets. Owner Vittorio Preteroti, a native of Capri, creates dishes that are lighter and more interesting than might be expected from the fairly modest setting. Kudos for having white tablecloths. Excepting the *ragù* and one other sauce, everything is cooked to order, and the food exhibits Neapolitan soul adapted to local tastes. Here you can experience how satisfying a simple pasta dish with a salad can be. And regulars know there are always great off-the-menu items available. Good choice for a low-key meal before a performance at one of the many performing arts venues nearby.

700 MILAM at Capitol, in the Pennzoil Towers
713-224-2422
MAP F6

PERRY'S STEAKHOUSE & GRILLE

> **2115 TOWN SQUARE PLACE** southeast of the intersection of Hwy. 59 and Hwy. 6, Sugar Land, and other locations
> **281-565-2727**
> www.perrysrestaurants.com
> **MAP** A9

This is one good-looking restaurant. And in a suburb filled with mid-range chains, it's nice to have a, well, nice place to go. Chris Perry's first steakhouse opened in Clear Lake, and with this cross-town location he has improved the original concept. The dry-aged steaks go through a three-step process: caramelizing with signature spices, chargrilling to trap natural juices and finishing with garlic butter. Sounds kind of like a spa day for your steak. For oenophiles, there are climate-controlled wine lockers in which to store your collection and social hour for sampling. Tableside chateaubriand and flambéed crêpes Suzette are a retro touch. Live music Wednesday through Saturday evenings. Sunday brunch is popular with the after-church crowd, who are all dressed up and want someplace to go.

PESCE

Perched (get it?) close to River Oaks, Montrose and West U, this seafood swankienda is a feast for the eyes *and* tastebuds. The homegrown white-tablecloth seafood restaurant is known for its center-of-the-action, sexy raw bar and zippy bar area, where singles, couples and expense account spenders pack in like sardines to watch and be a part of the scene. Once seated, there is a lot of *pesce* (fish) and some "not pesce" (to quote the menu) from which to choose. Watch for the jaw-dropping stacked-seafood Pesce Tower being delivered throughout the room. Executive chef Mark Holley's smile is as wide and welcoming as the seafood is fresh. His seafood martini is legendary and has spawned countless knock-offs around town.

> **3029 KIRBY** at W. Alabama
> **713-522-4858**
> www.pescehouston.com
> **MAP** E6

PHO DANH

> **11209 BELLAIRE BLVD.** west of Wilcrest, in Hong Kong City Mall, and other locations
> **281-879-9940**
> **MAP** A8

This bare-bones spot is an easy find. Once you're inside the mall, turn west and walk clear to the end. When you can go no farther, you're there. In a mall where half the storefronts are restaurants, Pho Danh is usually packed. It's clean, well-lit and inviting, and the staff is highly efficient. They should be: All they serve is *pho*. All *pho*, all the time.

Many foodies believe it's the best *pho* in town. That is high praise indeed, since Houston has more restaurants dedicated to the traditional Vietnamese soup than does any other city in the country. The basis for any good *pho* is its broth, and here it is rich, beefy and complex. Your choice of sundry meats (e.g. brisket, flank steak, beef tendon, meatballs) or offal is generously added. The soup arrives accompanied by a platter of herbs (mint, giant basil leaves and sawleaf) that are amazingly bountiful, plus a mountain of crisp bean sprouts, sliced onions, sliced fresh jalapeños and quartered limes. The sauces, chopsticks and napkins are on the table. Note: Besides beef *pho*, you can also have chicken, pork and shrimp *pho*.) Order a Vietnamese iced coffee to drink. Don't be surprised if you have to wait for a table to clear; it'll only be a couple minutes.

PHOENICIA DELI

12116 WESTHEIMER
west of Kirkwood
281-558-0416
MAP B6

Bring your appetite to this crowded counter-service eatery for lunch and early dinner (it closes at 8 p.m.). Vertical rotisseries yielding moist slices of beef and chicken are set behind the deli counter that is stocked with alluring dips, soups, flaky sweet pastries and Persian candies, all of which will put you in a Middle Eastern state of mind. Simply mention Phoenicia's chicken shawarma and mouths begin to water like those of Pavlovian dogs — this is the menu standout. The service can be a tad tough on newcomers — you have to stand in line, and it moves slowly — but hang in there. Also yummy are the hummus, falafel, tabouli, babaganoush and stuffed grape leaves. As for taking it with you: You can grab imported Armenian and Lebanese foods to go. Believe it or not, this is the small place that spawned the huge Phoenicia grocery store across the street.

PIATTO

The last name of Piatto chef/owner John Marion Carrabba might ring a bell, as he is a cousin in this first family of Italian restaurateurs in Houston. If you can make it to the hard-to-find Galleria location, reward yourself with the must-have asparagus appetizer — lightly breaded and fried asparagus topped with jumbo lump crabmeat, lemon juice and butter. Follow with one of the many perfectly grilled items (meat and seafood), pastas or pizzas. Family namesake dishes dot the menu.

1925 W. ALABAMA
east of Post Oak Blvd.
713-871-9722
www.piattoristorante.com
MAP D7

11693 WESTHEIMER
at Royal Oaks Club Dr.
281-759-7500
MAP B7

Portions are generous and the flavors spot-on. There is a definite buzz in the dining rooms, but it is more bubbly than bothersome. Nice wine list, and monthly wine dinners are enjoyable.

PICO'S MEX-MEX

5941 BELLAIRE BLVD.
west of Chimney Rock
713-662-8383
www.picos.net
MAP D7

The name says is all — this is Mexican food, not Tex-Mex — and Arnaldo Richard's eatery has been a foodie favorite for almost a quarter-century. Don't think run-of-the-mill taco salads and chalupas; think *mole*, chicken cooked in banana leaves and stuffed poblano peppers, real lick-the-fork, interior Mexican stuff. The margaritas are potent and plentiful and best enjoyed under the outdoor *palapa* (as close to a Mexican getaway you can get after a grueling, midweek workday). The atmosphere is casual and very kid-friendly, especially Mondays and Tuesdays, which are kids' days with 99-cent children's plates. The breakfast menu is served daily from 9 a.m. to 3 p.m., including *menudo*, which the menu boasts as the "breakfast of champions." Ay yay yay!

PIZZITOLA'S BAR-B-CUE

1703 SHEPHERD
just south of I-10
713-227-2283
MAP E6

What, you think an Italian can't make decent barbecue? Fuhgeddaboudit! Some locals think this is one of the town's best ... and sometimes we agree. On one visit, the meat was perfect; the next time it was drier than we prefer. But overall the hickory-smoked brisket is yummy. We took a tip from another local food writer and ordered "inside top" where the meat is moist and well-charred. Barbecued chicken with tasty sweet sauce, white bread and pickles is the favored lunch for many of the working crowd that comes here every day about noon. Ribs have fairly high finger-lickability factor. Friendly atmosphere.

PK'S BLUE WATER GRILL

6401 WOODWAY, STE. 105 one block east of S. Voss
713-339-3663
www.pkbluewatergrill.com
MAP C6

PK's is owned by Pat Kiley, a veteran of Goode Co. Texas Seafood, who opened this restaurant as an homage to his favorite food. In addition to mesquite-grilled and blackened fish and shellfish, you'll also find great gumbo, sizzling steaks, seafood salads and some of the best po'boys in town. The dining room has an ocean-going theme — deep-sea blue, with accents of chrome and silver. A 255-gallon tropical aquarium welcomes diners at the door. Black-aproned waiters are knowledgeable about both the menu and the finer points of good service. Great patio with ample shade and cooling fans, and lively bar area with live piano Wednesday through Saturday nights and during Sunday brunch. Definitely family friendly.

Recommended
CAJUN PO'BOYS DE LA MER

In N'awlins, everyone claims to have the best oyster po'boy. Not as easy in the Big H as it is in the Big Easy. We set sail to net the most authentic, the biggest and jazziest with the freshest Gulf seafood. Here's the pick of pearls in our sea of possibilities.

JIMMY G'S, *307 N. Sam Houston Pkwy. East, 281-931-7654.* A dozen snappy cornmeal-battered and Creole-spiced oysters, always hot from the fryer, float on this nicely griddled French roll moistened with spicy tartar sauce. The balanced ratio of fresh lettuce mix, thinly sliced purple onion and tomato make it dressed to thrill.

DANTON'S GULF COAST SEAFOOD KITCHEN, *4611 Montrose, 713-807-8885.* Details matter. And this dressed oyster po'boy is perfection, from the precisely fried juicy oysters (piled on and plump) to the toasty French roll slathered with an addictive garlicky remoulade that rocks. Order vinegary Daddy Pete's coleslaw alongside, instead of fries.

PAPPADEAUX, *2410 Richmond, 713-527-9137, and other locations.* The monstrous succulent shrimp and oyster combo is magically greaseless and loaded with seafood. A parmesan-dusted bun, mounds of finely shredded lettuce and spicy remoulade make this memorable. Fried catfish and crawfish also available.

RAGIN CAJUN, *9600 Westheimer, 832-251-7171, and other locations.* Folks flock to this Houston-born tradition for seasonal crawfish but note the almost 20 (!) choices of po'boy, including softshell crab, fried catfish and boudin. The fried oyster po'boy is fresh but no frills, moistened with mayo and ketchup. Doctor it up with fresh lemon and Tabasco.

TONY MANDOLA'S GULF COAST KITCHEN, *1962 W. Gray, 713-528-3474.* This pricey New Orleans po' boy is stacked with fried oysters wearing a gloriously crunchy-coarse cornmeal jacket on a grilled French bun. Note: The tartar sauce is timid, so add piquant "coon ass coleslaw." Oysters Damian, starring the same signature fried oysters crowned with pico de gallo, are divine. (See the recipe for oysters Damian on page 195.)

POLONIA

1900 BLALOCK at Campbell
713-464-9900
www.poloniarestaurant.com
MAP C5

Pierogi, bigos, golabki, oh my! The Polish cuisine here is quite hearty and somewhat unique for Houston, which has just a handful of Central European restaurants. The requisite *pierogies* (stuffed dumplings) are tasty, the borscht is very good, as are most of the offerings such as *bigos* (a stew with sauerkraut and *kielbasa*), *golabki* (stuffed cabbage), the pork and chicken entrees, and the roast duck that sometimes appears as a special. The must-have dish is *golonka*, the braised pork shank. Order a glass of Polish draft beer to wash it down. Polonia is a white-tablecloth, family-run restaurant that is quaint and friendly. A small Polish food store is nearly adjacent to the restaurant, where you can purchase deli items, imported packaged goods and that Polish flag apron you have always wanted.

POLO'S SIGNATURE

3800 SOUTHWEST FWY. just west of Timmons
713-626-8100
www.polossignature.com
MAP D7

Located in the shadows of the behemoth Lakewood Church, Polo's has an almost-heavenly location. A strip mall location without a strip mall feel, it has an inviting design with great lighting, nice warm earth tones and cushy carpet. This is a new (2007) and swanky spot, with a French-American fusion menu. We've heard mixed reviews on the kitchen's efforts but our *My Table* reviewer singled out goat cheese and lamb enchiladas and wild mushroom soup for praise, as well as the saffron-scented Chilean sea bass roasted with fennel and an entree of "caramelized" Gulf shrimp.

POST OAK GRILL

1415 S. POST OAK LANE north of San Felipe, and other locations
713-993-9966
www.postoakgrill.com
MAP D6

With so many restaurants to choose from, POG often slips our mind when making meal plans. However, this tucked-away spot near the Galleria area offers a nice choice for a meal with affable service. The business folks that pack in at lunch probably don't know what a romantic dinner spot the restaurant is, and vice versa for evening patrons. The dinner lighting makes everyone look good. The menu is American with a Mexican accent and features everything from pastas to seafood to steaks. The "first impressions" (appetizer) list is extensive and, with several ordered, makes for a nice tapas-ish meal with a selection from the decent wine list. Happy hour features live piano, and you can also tap your toes to live music during dinner Thursday to Saturday at the original Post Oak location.

PREGO

Most diners here are regulars, with favorite tables and servers, greeted with a friendly "welcome back," which creates Prego's neighborhood atmosphere. You'll be a regular, too, once you taste dishes like corn flour-crusted oysters with pancetta and chive sauce, arugula-radicchio salad with grilled portobello, oranges, peppered goat cheese and apple-walnut vinaigrette, and the (world's?) best lasagna, with layers of house-made noodles, veal meatballs, mozzarella, tomato sauce and pesto. The kitchen, which is open to the dining room, excels with seafood and pasta, and Sunday brunch with live jazz guitar is a treat. (Chef/owner John Watt often steps from the kitchen to join in on guitar.) It's tough, but try to save room for dessert. We love the casual elegance of this trattoria, as well as Watt's dedication to "promoting the marriage and enjoyment of wine and food in the dining ritual." Prego has Houston's most hidden private room — you have to walk through the kitchen to find it — and one of the city's handsomest wooden antique bars.

Prego's antique bar is a beauty.

2520 AMHERST just east of Kirby

713-529-2420

www.prego-houston.com

MAP E7

PRONTO CUCININO

One of Houston's most famous restaurant families entered the fast-casual dining market a few years ago and found its latest niche. Pronto Cucinino opened on Montrose offering many of the most popular dishes from Vincent Mandola's other three full-service restaurants (including Nino's) but without the formality. That includes building a brick oven rotisserie in Pronto for those beloved fire-roasted chickens. Diners order appetizers, salads and entrees at a counter, and waiters bring the food to the table. (Watching the chorus of plump birds turning and spitting while you stand at the counter will either

1401 MONTROSE between W. Gray and W. Dallas

713-528-8646

MAP E6

3191 HOLCOMBE at Buffalo Speedway

713-592-8646

MAP E7

make you hungrier or contemplate Dante.) Recently, a second location opened near the Medical Center, and at least two more are in the works in other parts of town. Curbside service is available for takeout orders — just call ahead from your car.

QIN DYNASTY

5115 BUFFALO SPEEDWAY at Westpark
713-660-8386
MAP D7

Given its shopping center location, we expected this to be a pedestrian Chinese eatery. However, we were knocked out by the opulent setting, featuring reproductions of Chinese archaeological finds. Of course, you can't eat those things, so we're happy to report that the kitchen also impresses — Szechwan spicy dumplings, spicy green beans, pork with slender bamboo shoot, Hunan shrimp — with cooking that is definitely cranked up a notch. Sometimes, tag-team service causes minor delays and confusion, but the waitstaff are friendly nonetheless.

QUATTRO

With a location in the Four Seasons, Quattro *has* to be good, right? Overall, yes, though sometimes a dish falls short, which smarts, given the price tag. The hotel and its restaurant used to anchor this east side of downtown, but many competitors have moved in — The Grove is newly opened just across the street, for example — and there isn't as much buzz coming from Quattro's dining room as we would like. It hurts, too, that there's been a revolving door of chefs in recent years. (We hope current executive chef Andrea Ossala stays awhile. He's the first Italian-born chef to run Quattro, and early reviews are promising.) The service is always warm and solicitous, and the attractive décor is surprisingly sensuous. The beaded metal curtains add a fun sparkle to the room, which has a splendid view. The menu is seasonal Italian, so check back often. For grazing at the bar, there is an excellent antipasti spread with more than 20 choices.

1300 LAMAR at San Jacinto, in the Four Seasons Hotel
713-650-1300
www.fourseasons.com/houston
MAP F6

RA SUSHI

3908 WESTHEIMER west of Weslayan/Willowick
713-621-5800
www.rasushi.com
MAP D7

The Houston version of Ra Sushi — the first in Texas — is drop-dead gorgeous, occupying a second-floor site (above the West Elm furnishings shop), and you can either take an elevator up or vogue and pose your

Chew softly and carry a big fork.

my table

THE ONLY MAGAZINE DEVOTED ENTIRELY TO DINING OUT IN HOUSTON.

AT BETTER NEWSSTANDS OR BY SUBSCRIPTION.

FOR A FREE SAMPLE ISSUE, VISIT WWW.MY-TABLE.COM.

way up a wide flight of stairs. The place does great business and on weekend nights, when a DJ holds forth, it's so packed you can hardly move your chopsticks. What's the appeal? Perhaps the single most informative thing we can tell you about Ra Sushi is this: Go to the website and click on Merchandise. In addition to the typical array of T-shirts and ball caps emblazoned with the corporate logo, you'll also find ... official Ra Sushi red thong underwear. As for the, *ahem*, menu — the choices are not limited to sushi concoctions. The usual suspects in the noodle, tempura and teriyaki categories are also available. Of course, the food here seems somewhat of an afterthought. It's the nominal reason to come, but the real appeal is the scene. A lot of cool people come here because a lot of cool people come here. Illuminated with dozens of red globe lights, the place is very striking and very large, with half of it designated as the Flying Fish Lounge, filled with high-top tables where you can still be served food but drinks like the Tokyo Tower (plum wine, vodka, peach schnapps), Tsunami Punch (Southern Comfort, sake, vodka) and Screaming Ninja (Jägermeister and sake) are the prime attractions. A second Ra Sushi is opening in the Memorial City area in late 2008.

RAGIN' CAJUN

4302 RICHMOND
between Weslayan and Loop 610, and other locations
713-623-6321
www.ragin-cajun.com
MAP D7

Bayou City dwellers have long satisfied their craving for Cajun cuisine at the Ragin' Cajun. Both Texas and Louisiana paraphernalia decorate everything, and ULaLa and LSU yearbooks are collected in stacks. The TVs are always tuned to a game, and LSU and Tulane alumni naturally congregate at all locations to celebrate Mardi Gras, fall football and March Madness. Many insist that the best crawfish in town are at the Cajun, where two people can quickly go through four pounds of "mudbugs," and the potatoes and corn are plentiful. Be prepared to sit at long tables and make new friends, as you'll be forced to sit in close proximity to others from March to late May during crawfish season. Other menu favorites include crab gumbo, po'boys, muffalettas, hot boudin, crawfish pie and red beans and rice. This is a perfect place to bring people visiting from up North who want some local color but aren't interested in Tex-Mex. Put on a bib and get funky, *cher*.

RAINBOW LODGE

One of Houston's most remarkable restaurant settings, the Rainbow Lodge recently relocated from its Buffalo Bayou location after 29 years to a cozy 100-year-old log cabin (formerly home to La Tour d'Argent)

2011 ELLA BLVD. at East TC Jester
713-861-8666
www.rainbow-lodge.com
MAP E5

on an acre of grounds on the White Oak Bayou. Owner Donnette Hansen's newly planted citrus orchard is barely starting to fill in, and the deck and railings have not yet weathered, but it's easy to see the care and thought that's been invested in this property. Have a cocktail at the astonishing bar, a virtual tableau from *A River Runs Through It*. The fly-fishing theme is not unique to Houston, but where else would you find such a glorious, almost-tropical setting hard on an urban river? There's an emphasis on Texas wild game in the kitchen that suits the ambiance perfectly. The Wild Game Sampling allows diners to try venison, elk, rabbit and boar, but those with less adventurous palates will be satisfied by the selection of beef, chicken and seafood as well. Don't miss the signature duck gumbo as a starter. The Rainbow Lodge has long had an outstanding wine list, too.

RATTAN PAN-ASIAN BISTRO

1396 ELDRIDGE
north of Briar Forest
281-556-9888
www.rattanbistro.com
MAP A6

Rattan hopscotches through several Asian countries including Vietnam, Thailand and Japan before landing in the suburbs of west Houston. Ron Chen, former owner of Sinh Sinh on Bellaire, opened this trendy new spot that looks like a multicolored pagoda in 2007. Standout dishes include Asian chicken salad, seared tuna teriyaki, Vietnamese garlic beef, sushi (like the Bistro Roll) and a satay sampler. While lunch is fast-casual, dinner is full service. Rattan also has an Italian Enomatic wine-dispensing system, which replaces the air in opened bottles with argon gas, a technique that preserves the condition of the wine for fresh by-the-glass servings. Consequently, there are more high-end wines by the glass than one would typically expect. Nice patio, too.

RAVEN GRILL

1916 BISSONNET
between Woodhead and Hazard
713-521-2027
www.theravengrill.com
MAP E7

Native Houstonians Rob and Sara Cromie opened Raven Grill, named after nearby Poe Elementary and the writer's famous poem, in 1998. This cozy restaurant has since become a favorite spot in the neighborhood. The kitchen grills most of its meat and fish entrees over a green mesquite fire, which adds extra flavor. Many menu items also tend towards a Southwestern flair and are more home-style than haute. Daily

Mesquite wood adds a Texas flavor to grilled items at Raven Grill

specials — Sunday's chicken-fried steak, Monday's roast chicken, etc. — and reasonable prices keep regulars coming back. The shady outdoor patio is very pleasant, as is the waitstaff. You might even spot the restaurant's pet chicken wandering around. If you have to wait for a table, a cocktail at the bar is a gentle way to pass a little time. It's no wonder *My Table* columnist Mr. Anon once called Raven Grill "the best damn restaurant in Houston." The Cromies expanded a few years ago with sandwich shop Picnic right next door.

11322-C WESTHEIMER
just west of Wilcrest
281-293-0426
www.redbasilthai.com
MAP D6

RED BASIL

This contemporary Thai bistro opened in 2007 and has become a regular stop for foodies on the west side. Creative and eye-catching — almost excessively so — are the buzzwords here, with satay served in a spray formation jutting out of half an orange and a chive flower placed here and there for added flair. The traditional Thai dishes achieve delicious authenticity and the fusion dishes such as the salmon spring roll, stuffed with salmon, jicama and cilantro, almost demand to be tasted. Build your own lunch special by choosing from the vegetarian, meat or seafood selections of starter and entree, which start at $6.99 for the veg option, plus salad or soup. We especially like the various curries (the menu lists eight) that may be ordered veggie or with tofu or protein.

REEF

Chef Bryan Caswell and front-of-the-house guy Bill Floyd (both formerly with Bank at the Hotel Icon, both past winners of Houston Culinary Awards from *My Table* magazine) have teamed up for this global seafood place on the south side of

2600 TRAVIS at McGowen
713-526-8282
www.reefhouston.com
MAP E6

downtown across from a Cadillac dealership. Much has been made of Caswell's love of fishing, and the menu is an ever-changing tribute to that passion: snapper carpaccio, roasted grouper, crispy skin snapper and "naked" ribeye with brown butter gnocchi (for the beef lovers). Scrolling down the menu, you see a simple, straightforward formula played out again and again — escolar with braised collard greens, triple tail and an artichoke stew, amberjack (or mako) and asparagus with orange mustard, a seafood "hot pot" served with fingerling potatoes. Our *My Table* reviewer noted, "If you like first-rate fish expertly prepared and paired with some atypical but rewarding side orders, Reef simply has more choices than any other establishment in town." Also of note is Reef's well-priced wine list, with scores of tempting choices, especially whites. For cocktails and lighter fare, try Reef's 3rd Bar where sliders (i.e. mini-burgers) and a raw bar are the draw. At first glance, the large, open dining room may provoke a note of alarm among those who recognize the acoustic ingredients for noise ricocheting painfully off bare walls, concrete floors and outsized panels of window glass. And it *is* intense, so take that into consideration when booking a table.

4814 ALMEDA between Blodgett and Southmore
713-520-7171
www.thereggaehut.com
MAP E7

REGGAE HUT

This is Houston's best-known place for Jamaican food. In recent years, the quality of the food had taken a nosedive. But then the restaurant was rescued by the guys who run Breakfast Klub, and it's back in good form. Order at the counter, then find a seat. Your food will be brought to your table. The menu is small — just five entrees, five appetizers and that's about it. The patties (beef, chicken or vegetable) are okay — the crust flaky and yellow with turmeric — if not quite dazzling. The entrees, though, are excellent. We especially recommend the oxtails and curry goat, both tender and well seasoned. Jerk chicken (Jamaica's take on barbecued chicken) is deeply smoky, with an alluring aroma and flavor of allspice. All entrees are served with rice and peas that are great for soaking up sauce and a veggie medley.

THE REMINGTON

Within the deep red walls of The Remington at the St. Regis Hotel, waiters who seem to glide rather than walk serve up New American cuisine that has an international accent: Thai poached shrimp salad, tandoori roasted chicken salad, tortilla soup (long a favorite here), marinated duck quesadilla and five-spice braised short ribs, for example. The setting is richly handsome; you can sense the privilege when you pull up to the valet stand. It's just something about grand hotels that inspires fabulous restaurant service. This is no exception.

1919 BRIAR OAKS LANE at San Felipe, in the St. Regis Hotel
713-840-7600
www.theremingtonrestaurant.com
MAP D6

The light-drenched Remington dining room invites a long, leisurely lunch.

We've had more special meals — graduation dinners, birthday dinners, etc. — at the St. Regis than anywhere in Houston, and it's the food *and* the solicitous service that keeps us coming back. The adjacent Remington Bar is a dark, clubby setting (as opposed to the restaurant's sun-drenched space). Come here for cocktails, live music, dancing and a light bar menu.

RICKSHAW FAR EAST BISTRO

2810 WESTHEIMER
west of Kirby
713-942-7272
www.rickshawbambu.com
MAP E6

Rickshaw shares the same feel for beats and eats as sushi restaurant Zake, but is a little more date-night and a little less date-and-mate. Still, it's a sexy place to have a late evening meal, as the booths are great for parties of four, offering some intimacy. Calling ahead is suggested — the place can get crowded at night. We don't usually order specialty drinks, but we can't help it at Rickshaw. Bambu, the bar and lounge in the restaurant, has some really sultry concoctions, such as the Rickshaw Punch, Green Dragon and the Pineapple Upside Down Cake. Hungry? Ask for the *My Table* roll that was created a couple years ago — it's not on the menu — and don't be surprised when you see vegan sushi available. Often times, even if it isn't too busy, service can be tediously slow, so bring some good gossip to share and order everything at once.

RIO RANCH

9999 WESTHEIMER
between Gessner and Beltway 8, in the Westchase Hilton
713-952-5000
www.rioranch.com
MAP B7

Fronting the Westchase Hilton, this is a hotel restaurant with some major differences, such as a pedigree that can trace its heritage to local celebrity chef Robert Del Grande. This was his take on the perennial Texas ranch-house theme, and it's a handsome setting. Del Grande associate and longtime Rio Ranch chef San Hemwattakit, a native of Thailand, has created many dishes that seem practically iconic for East Texas, among them chicken breast stuffed with andouille sausage, homemade onion rings with spicy catsup, a "knife and fork" burger with green chiles and skewers of bacon-wrapped shrimp, mushrooms, onions and jalapeños served with pico de gallo. Chicken enchiladas with green sauce and special shrimp salsa will also make you happy. The laid-back setting and an appealing buffet (with omelet and waffle stations) make this a top-notch brunching spot on Sundays.

Recommended
GREAT GREEK SALAD

Funny thing: When you order a Greek salad in Greece, traditionally you won't get any lettuce. Adding romaine or iceberg is an American adaptation — one that we expect and love — especially during Houston's summer, when salad keeps you cool as a cucumber.

ALEXANDER THE GREAT GREEK, *3055 Sage, 713-622-2778.* Meaty anchovies, red cabbage, capers, fresh parsley and a yogurt-based dressing make this marvelously Mediterranean. Request grilled shrimp on top for an awesome entree salad.

DEMERIS, *2911 S. Shepherd, 713-529-7326, and other locations.* Surprise: The Greek Demeris family — yep, known for barbecue — has been dishing up a groovy Greek salad since 1964. It's all here: sweet red peppers, juicy pepperoncinis, tomatoes, purple onions, cucumber, bricks of sharp feta and homemade vinaigrette packed with oregano and pepper. Did we mention it's huge?

FADI'S, *8383 Westheimer, 713-523-0666, and other locations.* Pile on this lean healthful salad to accompany the outstanding wood-fired pita bread, slow-cooked meats and fresh vegetables. If you like crunchy romaine and purple onions, you'll ravish this Greek glossed *au naturel*: simply olive oil and red wine vinegar.

NIKO NIKO'S, *2520 Montrose, 713-528-1308.* This classic salad is dressed for success, due to its homemade vinaigrette balanced with quality olive oil, aged red wine vinegar and cleansing oregano. The massive slab of briny feta, kalamata olives and crisp slices of onion, green pepper and cucumber up the ante.

YIA YIA MARY'S, *4747 San Felipe, 713-840-8665.* Red wine vinaigrette floods this bounteous salad trimmed with triangles of sharp feta, juicy kalamata olives, crunchy peppers and pita bread. (Add grilled lamb, chicken or shrimp if ravenous.) Restaurant cousin **PAPPADEAUX SEAFOOD KITCHEN** (*2410 Richmond, 713-527-9137, and other locations*) serves a fabulous lemony Greek salad prepared tableside. Yet another Pappas cousin, **PAPPAS BURGER** (*5815 Westheimer, 713-975-6082, and other locations*) also serves a doozy of a Greek salad.

RIOJA SPANISH TAPAS

11920 WESTHEIMER at Kirkwood
281-531-5569
www.riojarestaurant.com
MAP A8

Famous for its paella — Luis Acosta and chef Ignacio Forseca won the Houston Polo Club's International Paella Festival even before the restaurant's official opening in 2004 — the kitchen sends out the classic rice dish loaded with seafood, chicken and house-made chorizo. (Note: Individual paella is not made to order; rather, Rioja makes it fresh several times an evening in large pans and ladles some out for each person.) Hot and cold tapas and an all-Spanish wine list add to an authentic meal, which is served in a cozy pub on one side or the more elegant dining room. Service is highly praised for being so friendly and is happy to help you navigate the Spanish menu. Recommended dishes include fried calamari served with ali-oli on the side, seared Portuguese sardines (for fish lovers only), piquillo peppers stuffed with codfish and fried black Spanish sausage. Many of the ingredients such as olives and sardines are imported from Spain and can even be bought by the pound. Live Spanish guitar, too, and sometimes salsa and dancing.

Chef Ignacio Fonseca and Luis Acosta operate Rioja, a Spanish restaurant on the west side.

RISTORANTE CAVOUR

1080 UPTOWN PARK BLVD. north of San Felipe, in Hotel Granduca
713-418-1000
MAP D6

Since Hotel Granduca opened its doors in 2007, it has prided itself on impeccable service and exquisite Italian interiors. Recently it debuted a tiny jewel-box of a dining room under the direction of executive chef David Denis, who has the much-praised Le Mistral out on the West Side. Denis is not cooking here himself, but he designed the menu and trained Claudia Guimond, who had six years at Le Mistral and is the chef de cuisine of Ristorante Cavour. At lunch, there are soups, risotto, salads, sandwiches and entree plates (try the roasted shrimp with white beans); dinner skips the sandwiches and adds gnocchi, polenta and more *secondi* plates of seafood and meat. Prices are commensurate with the setting.

ROMANO'S FLYING PIZZA

Almost anyone will tell you that Romano's is the only place in Houston to get real pizza — thin crust New York-style, that is. Pizza debates can get

1528 W. GRAY
between Waugh and Dunlavy
713-526-1182
MAP E6

14520 MEMORIAL
just east of Dairy Ashford
281-589-7000
MAP A6

intense but there's no arguing that the owners have the right credentials, hailing from Ozone Park in Queens. The restaurant is constantly bustling with native New Yorkers who tout the pizza for having a perfect crust- to-sauce ratio. Other entrees such as lasagna, calzone, subs, baked ziti and ravioli are solid, and the marinara sauce also has many fans. Romano's doesn't deliver but take-out is available. Service is at the counter, but peak weekend hours mean it might be hard to snag a table.

ROUGE

When Rouge first opened in 2003, our *My Table* reviewer wrote, "It's evident that Rouge is the most promising and pleasing new restaurant on the Houston scene since Aries and Artista." The stunning French-American kitchen under the direction of chef Edel Gonçalves had diners wobbly with pleasure. Then it all came apart as the chef left and management of the restaurant passed through several hands. Rouge stayed open, but no one spoke of the restaurant any longer except to ask, "Whatever happened to …?" Then, in mid-2008, the place made a splashy comeback, via Thomas and Debi Rucker. They installed Octavio Madgril in the kitchen, made over the upstairs private-event area into a supper club and reinvigorated the wine list. We can't predict how well the re-released Rouge will work, but everyone seems to be making a grand effort. A tasting dinner at the time this book goes to press included foie gras served with the thinnest slices of mango, grilled salmon with aioli dill cream, grilled duck breast and vegetable-filled cannelloni topped with *sugo rosa* sauce. We're hopeful.

812 WESTHEIMER
just east of Montrose
713-520-7955
www.rougehouston.com
MAP E6

2503 S. GESSNER
north of Westheimer
713-782-1180
www.rudilechners.com
MAP D6

RUDI LECHNER'S

This comfortable neighborhood spot offers terrific American and German-Austrian food, including — drum roll, please — the city's best *Wiener schnitzel*, which is rushed crisp and golden from the fryer, served with a mound of sauerkraut or red cabbage and Austrian potatoes. Other menu favorites include curry wurst, stuffed cabbage rolls, goulash, sauerbraten and roasted pork shank. Deal of the week is Wednesday evening 6:30 to 9 when the restaurant offers the German sampler buffet for $14.95 per person. A special selection of desserts including *Kaiserschmarr'n* (the emperor's pancakes) and Salzburger *Nockerl* (a meringue dessert) need to be ordered 24 hours in advance, but we always order Lechner's alcohol-laced *Kaffee Gute Nacht*, or "Coffee Good Night." The food is half the fun. Every Wednesday

---

RECIPE **MOM'S CHOCOLATE CAKE**

Benjy's, 2424 Dunstan, 713-522-7602

According to owner Benjy Levit, "This recipe comes from a cookbook my mom received as a wedding gift. The cookbook was assembled by her then-married friends to help teach her, as she had no idea how to cook. It's been the centerpiece of family get-togethers for almost 60 years. Mom bakes approximately 15 of these cakes each week for the restaurant."

2 sticks margarine
1 cup water
6 Tbsp. cocoa
2 eggs
2 cups sugar
1 tsp. baking soda
½ tsp. salt
1 tsp. vanilla extract
2 cups flour
½ cup buttermilk

METHOD: Preheat oven to 350 degrees. In a saucepot, bring margarine, water and cocoa to a boil; remove from heat and set aside. In a bowl, beat eggs with electric mixer. Add sugar, baking soda, salt and vanilla and mix again. Add flour and buttermilk a little at a time until incorporated. Pour in chocolate mixture and mix well. Pour batter into a 9 x 12-inch rectangular pan that you have greased with one of the margarine wrappers and bake for about 25 minutes. Check so that you don't overbake. Frosting (recipe follows) should be made while cake is baking. Remove cake from oven and frost immediately while cake is hot.

Frosting
1 stick butter
6 Tbsp. cocoa
6 Tbsp. milk

1 lb. powdered sugar
1 Tbsp. vanilla extract
1 cup chopped pecans

METHOD: Melt butter. Add cocoa and milk. Place in mixer bowl. Add powdered sugar and vanilla and mix well. Sprinkle in pecans and stir.

through Saturday night a live polka band get diners in the mood with a 13-foot Swiss Alphorn and a tuned set of cowbells. During the real Oktoberfest, mid-September to end of October, the restaurant really cranks it up with its "Come Loosen the Lederhosen" promotion. Note: If it's a quiet meal that you desire, the hostess will put you up in a back room away from the Oktoberfest ruckus.

RUGGLES GRILL

903 WESTHEIMER
just east of Montrose
713-524-3839
www.rugglesgrill.com
MAP E6

5115 WESTHEIMER
near McCue, in The Galleria
713-963-8067
MAP D6

This trendy Montrose favorite became so popular in the 1990s and people had to wait so long to have their reservations honored that one might say fame is the root of its faltering reputation. Still, enough people flock to the original Ruggles so as to make a half-hour wait, even with a reservation, not unusual. The energy level in this remodeled house is high and can get noisy at times, especially on Sunday with the jazz brunch. Meals come in hefty portions and the Southwestern/American food is seasoned robustly. Parking is valet only and can be a headache. Chef-owner Bruce Molzan extended his reach with Ruggles 5115 in The Galleria several years ago, setting up shop in the tony Saks Fifth Avenue department store. The Ruggles Cafe Bakery in Rice Village is another offshoot.

RUTH'S CHRIS STEAKHOUSE

This New Orleans-spawned chain, named for and once run by the late Ruth Fertel, has long been a favorite spot for the local oil industry. It weathered the 1980s oil bust and still serves up old-style beef, which arrives on a sizzling tray — hold up your napkin to protect your clothes. Be sure to

6213 RICHMOND
between Fountain View and Hillcroft
713-789-2333
www.ruthchris.com
MAP C7

try the classic rich steakhouse side dishes: Creamed spinach, au gratin potatoes and the like must be ordered separately. At the end of the meal, try the bread pudding for another classic taste. Houston's "oil field trash" (the restaurant's moniker, not ours) may miss the old company signs that once decorated this place, however: The restaurant had a makeover a few years ago and is now as elegant as any spot in town. Likewise, the prices are comparable to other upscale Houston restaurants. Note: After Hurricane Katrina, Ruth's Chris — so long associated with New Orleans — moved its corporate headquarters to Orlando, Fla.

SAFFRON

2006 LEXINGTON
just east of S. Shepherd
713-522-3562
www.saffronhouston.com
MAP E7

Saffron's interiors are so totally Casbah that we flashed-back to a real trip to Morocco (sans the mickey-laden drink). Adjacent to Mia Bella, this romantic spot from Youssef Nafaa celebrates his Moroccan roots. You'll feel like a sultan in the whimsical dining room, especially the tucked-away semi-private nooks. Go for the floor-seating on puffy cushions around low tables for a fun change from the usual dining-table routine. Cocktails are a tad expensive, but definitely set the mood, as can the *b'stilla* (a phyllo-wrapped pie with chicken and nuts, dusted with powdered sugar), couscous and the classic stew-like *tagines*. If you are one of the brave few who enjoy offal, there's an interesting "Moroccan Delicacy Pie" you should order. Of course, there's belly dancing (for better or worse), and the staff is friendly, except for a maître d', who was more boorish than Moorish. Great place for groups.

SAGE

2221 W. ALABAMA just west of Greenbriar
713-526-6242
www.sagerestauranthouston.com
MAP E7

When we visited this space previously, it was a garden shop, so the name of this new (early 2008) eatery fits. Self-proclaimed as "the home of European cuisine" — no shrinking flowers here (though the china pattern is Desert Rose) — at just a few months old, it has some refining to do. The bar is seductive and very French, and the dining room is nice, sort of homemade and almost quaint. Kudos for having white tablecloths, though. The menu has a nice variety without being overwhelming — pan-seared scallops, risotto of sweet garden peas, asparagus, artichokes and baby spinach, ravioli and lamb chops — and we like that side dishes are portioned for two. Overall, the menu we sampled was mostly cold-weather foods in a warm-weather season, but this could change ... or so we hope. Inexpensive sparkling wine by the glass (which we liked) is served in clunky glasses (which we didn't). Service isn't the most refined, but the staff try hard and make you feel very welcome.

SAIGON PAGOLAC

This Vietnamese restaurant is one of the best in town in terms of a

> **9600 BELLAIRE BLVD.** just east of Corporate, in Dynasty Plaza
> **713-988-6106**
> **MAP** D6

quality-to-value ratio, particularly at lunch. The kitchen sends out a wide range of specialties like char-grilled pork over rice noodles, eggrolls, *pho* and lots of seafood dishes. What Saigon Pagolac is famous for, however, is the traditional *Bo 7 Mon*, or Seven Courses of Beef. It's a nice treat if you like meat, and we do. Have the whole table order this Vietnamese celebration of red meat. We also like the so-called Vietnamese fajitas (beef you roll in rice wrappers), and here you cook-your-own — interactive and tasty. Minor drawback: The smell permeates your clothes, which isn't so good if you have an afternoon business meeting. Lest we forget, vegetarian options are also available. The service can seem brusque, but maybe it's a cultural thing. Finish with a Vietnamese iced coffee.

SAWADEE

Just as with Mexican food, Houstonians are loyal to their fave Thai eateries. Many used to call Sawadee the best Thai in town, but changes in the kitchen have some wondering. The place is neat and tidy, with mahogany wood accents and Thai trinkets, and the staff wears warm smiles, but it feels a bit past its prime. On the menu you will find all the Thai standards, and some of the worst menu photos we have seen — grainy black and white shots that are barely distinguishable, especially under the odd blue lamps that light the room. The lunch menu is quite extensive and a tad more on the Chinese side. Among dishes we most recently sampled were the glass noodles with pork and lime beef salad. Both were missing that Thai touch of spice. The iced tea was pungent and delicious, however. This is far from being the best Thai in town anymore, but it will do in a pinch.

> **6719 WESLAYAN** at Bellaire Blvd.
> **713-666-7872**
> **MAP** D7

SHADE

The word "shade" conjures a happy feeling, one of shelter and comfort, so is a befitting name for this neighborhood favorite. Chef/owner Claire Smith (she previously had Daily Review Cafe) and husband Russell Murrell transformed a scruffy antiques 'n' coffee space into a highly evolved urbane dining room. The minimalist bar is ideal for a cocktail or casual meal (a treat

> **250 W. 19TH** just west of Yale
> **713-863-7500**
> www.shadeheights.com
> **MAP** E5

after trolling the nearby shopping strip), and the large windows give a NYC bistro feel and great views of Heights passers-by. Do we like the menu or the service better? Tough call. We recommend the fried green tomatoes, grilled feta-stuffed ground lamb with salad-mint pesto over greens, pulled pork tostadas and pecan-brown butter tart with buttermilk ice cream. The menu is seasonal, so check back often. Very nice wine list at reasonable prices, which allows for experimentation. Sometimes parking is a challenge but don't let that keep you away.

SHAWARMA KING

3121 HILLCROFT between Westheimer and Richmond
713-784-8882
www.shawarmakingonline.com
MAP C7

Shawarma King's pita-wrapped sandwiches are delicious, especially the chicken and beef versions, which feature slices of moist and savory meat that has been slowly roasted then put to bed inside a large piece of fresh pita bread along with shredded lettuce, tomato, pickles and tahini. All the usual Mideastern deli suspects are here — hummus, babaganoush, tabouli, stuffed grape leaves, spinach pies in phyllo, falafel and *kibbe* (minced meat and bulgur) — but the friendliness of the owner gives this modest shop an edge. Over the lunch hour, the wait can be a little longer than you might like, but it's worth it. Long live the king!

SICHUAN CUISINE

Don't come here for the décor. This is your basic dining hall, starkly decorated with slightly ragged pages listing dishes in Chinese that probably aren't on the English menu and that we don't doubt for a second are even more delicious

9114 BELLAIRE BLVD. between Gessner and Ranchester
713-771-6868
MAP C7

than anything we might order. But do come here for the terrific and terrifically hot food, including crispy chicken with three chiles (a mound of boneless chicken bites fried along with an equal amount of red chiles and Szechwan peppercorns). Or order the smoked tea duck, which manages to be simultaneously spicy, juicy and smoky, a duck-lover's dream. The Dong Po Pork Elbow is actually a long-braised pork shank, tender and juicy, rich and fatty, pretty much everything one wants from pork, happily resting in a small pond of rich brown sauce. We also recommend the blazing hot *ma po tofu* (tofu with spicy minced meat) the nearly incendiary Szechwan pickle cabbage, the steamed mini soup buns and the dan dan noodles with peanut sesame sauce.

SIMPOSIO

8401 WESTHEIMER at Dunvale
713-532-0550
www.simposioristorante.com
MAP C7

This former hot spot (an *Esquire* "Best New Restaurant" pick when it opened in 1997) has gone through some changes — new location, new owner, new chef — but one thing is the same: serious Italian food. The appealing and sometimes complex flavors remain from the past, and the execution is nearly as good. There can be *risotto al tartufo*, fresh fettuccine in a Bolognese-style *ragù*, breaded and grilled calamari, fresh pasta stuffed with fish and served in a lemon-scented, light cream sauce, and rare, thinly sliced steak. These are complemented with a respectable Italian-heavy wine list. The dining room is attractive and stately, but often seems too quiet, which is a plus if you actually want to converse with your dining companions. Late-night revelers can dine after-hours in the lounge. *Mangia!*

SKYLINE BAR & GRILL

1600 LAMAR at Crawford, in the Hilton Americas
713-577-6139
www.hilton.com
MAP F6

For sheer suck-in-your-breath drama, this restaurant atop Houston's largest hotel has no competition. The city is spilled out in panoramic views below Skyline's 24th floor perch like an armful of jewels. The space is contemporary, with blue and silver touches, and can be as romantic (start with a Love Potion cocktail) or as festive as you like. The bar serves nice cocktails (at a predictably "high" tariff, given the view). So snag a table by the window and let the city do all the work to impress first-timers and out-of-towners. The kitchen has a Mediterranean accent — Spain meets Italy meets France and so on. We wish there were more choices, but we did like the house special corn soup, scallops, spice-rubbed pork tenderloin with lentil ragout and Texas goat cheese-stuffed chicken. The newly opened Discovery Green park is across the street and makes for a nice couple's stroll before or after dinner. Late night lounge service.

SMITH & WOLLENSKY

4007 WESTHEIMER at Drexel
713-621-7555
www.smithandwollensky.com
MAP D7

This is one of several East Coast steak chains to open a Houston outpost. Why? We aren't sure, especially if you don't bring your "A game." We more often hear S&W recommended for drinks than dining, as the steaks often fail to impress. Yes, the valets are often crazy busy, but it's mostly bar patrons, who come for the generous martinis. If you do decide to dine, head to the second floor and order the famous two-pound crackling pork shank, a plate of pig that *USA Today* once named its #1 Dish of the Year. (It's clearly not an entree for the dainty.) We like the good wedge salad and impressive shellfish bouquet, and the truffled macaroni and cheese is nice and portioned for two. The wine list is all-American (literally) with some 600 selections, and a glass of vino on the large balcony can be a real treat if you get there before the loud "bar sceners."

SOMA

4820 WASHINGTON
between Shepherd and Durham
713-861-2726
MAP E6

Chef Robert Gadsby is cooking like a gladiator at this sizzling spot on Washington Avenue. It's a sushi bar, yes, but more. It feels like a swanky Los Angeles lounge, with soaring ceilings, cool red glass-pipe hanging lamps and throbbing techno music. It's from Yun Cheng and the Azuma folks, so the sushi is good, if perhaps a little mayonnaise-dominated for our taste. When we visited in early 2008, the side patio was still being built out and the menu was labeled "draft," but that didn't take anything away from Gadsby's kitchen skills. Although menu descriptions can be a little cryptic, the French-Asian tidbits (yes, servings are small) that turn up on your table will delight you. We recommend the hamachi slicked with mustard sauce, a strange little seafood cup that presented one creamy nubbin of fish and shellfish after another, and curried braised beef that will haunt your dreams. Want to go all the way? The chef offers a multi-course *omakase* tasting menu. The place has been discovered by the under-30 kids, so go early in the evening or try lunch.

SORRENTO

The area around Sorrento is a United Nations "food court" — Japanese, Indian, Tex-Mex, Mediterranean British and more. Sorrento is a solid pick for somewhat Americanized Italian food. Abbas Hussein (veteran of Michelangelo's) and Pedro Castro (once with Aldo's) created an elegant escape in this rather generic strip center. Dark woods, hand-painted murals, warm lighting and well-appointed tables set the stage. If you get sticker shock easily, don't say we didn't warn you. But salads are always well dressed, duck prosciutto with figs is fab, fried calamari is perfect and the open-face lasagna is delicious, as are the grilled items we have sampled. The bar is the size of a postage stamp, neighbored by a melodic piano. Good service.

415 WESTHEIMER
between Taft and Montrose
713-527-0609
www.sorrentohouston.com
MAP E6

507 WESTHEIMER
between Taft and Montrose
713-524-1000
www.sovinowines.com
MAP E6

SO'VINO BISTRO & WINE BAR

Veteran restaurateur Manfred Jachmich (Ruggles, Post Oak Grill, etc.) and partner Elizabeth Abraham have put together a tony place where the focus is sharply on wine, especially those from the

Recommended
GREEN WITH ENVY

For those of us who don't do goopy Tex-Mex enchiladas submerged in a dark swamp of chile gravy and clogged with yellow cheese interiors, there is a brilliant alternative: *enchiladas verdes*. Stylish and sassy, this enchilada doesn't like to be smothered to death or dress in drab colors. Grab a fork and go green.

CHUY'S, *2706 Westheimer, 713-524-1700.* If the "911 Hot Plate" enchiladas featuring devilishly spicy green chile sauce are too hot to handle, tuck into the super-meaty white-chicken enchiladas with a citrusy-smooth tomatillo-avocado sauce topped with diced avocado and pico de gallo. Elvis would be proud.

LA GUADALUPANA BAKERY & CAFE, *2100 Dunlavy, 713-522-2301.* Puebla-style bundles of joy are stuffed with shredded chicken and ladled with a spicy, thick green tomatilla sauce that pops with flavor. Crumbles of *queso fresco*, avocado slices, leafy cilantro, lettuce shreds and sweet onions garnish the top. ¡Delicioso!

MARIA SELMA, *1617 Richmond, 713-528-4920.* You'll say: *I can't believe I ate the whole thing.* These *enchiladas verdes* bulging with moist white chicken are ladled with a tangy garlic-touched tomatilla sauce that tastes lovingly homemade. Farmer's cheese, cilantro and chopped onions crown this generous dish.

PICO'S MEX-MEX, *5941 Bellaire Blvd., 713-662-8383.* Cheese lovers dig these chicken *enchiladas verdes* smeared with mild tomatilla sauce, swaddled in a plush blanket of yellow and white Monterey jack cheeses and topped with sour cream. Note to the lean and mean: The seafood enchiladas are an opulent treat with less cheese.

SYLVIA'S ENCHILADA KITCHEN, *12637 Westheimer, 281-679-8300.* Homemade everything, starting with the soft fresh tortillas, makes Sylvia's Crystal City enchiladas stuffed with toothy sautéed spinach really shine. Limey-tart *verde* sauce and a careful gilding of cheese will keep you light on your toes.

TEOTIHUACAN, *1511 Airline, 713-426-4420, and other locations.* Here's your hangover cure: two fluffy corn tortillas filled with chicken fajita pieces and topped with chunky and piquant *salsa verde*. On top, expect a slather of sour cream, a mound of Monterey jack and onion sprinkles. Oh yes, and the mandatory dribble of grease.

southern hemisphere (hence the name, So'Vino). A good-looking bar area, with back lighting that shows off sparkling upside-down hanging wine glasses flanked by black glass straight-up vintage bottles, the place has a distinctive New York lounge feel to it. There are 13 bubblies to choose from — and paired with truffle-oiled popcorn, you've got ambrosia. The list of wines goes ever on, and the addition of sweet dessert wines from Australia — Tokay and Muscat — finishes a tour nicely. The kitchen puts out some tasty morsels; try the beet and goat cheese salad, shrimp and grits, Shiraz-braised short ribs or thin-crust pizza. There is some beer and designer water for the un-wined in your party, and making reservations is a good idea. Open for dinner only Monday through Saturday.

4701 N. MAIN at Airline
713-869-1706
www.spanish-flowers.com
MAP E5

SPANISH FLOWERS

If there's one thing Houstonians agree on, it's a shared love of Mexican food. However, you can easily ignite a lively debate as to where to find the best Mexican or Tex-Mex food. Open since 1979, Spanish Flowers has many devotees, especially breakfast fans who can indulge any time at this all-nighter (except for the late Tuesday-night closure when it's cleaned). We love to sit outside on the patio among the flowering plants with a plate of green chicken enchiladas, the piled-high *tostadas de carnitas* or fajita tacos — or chicken *mole* when we want something more filling. Mary Bernal's restaurant is known for its freshly made tortillas served by the strolling waitress with tongs at your table, and all entrees come with a complimentary cup of soup that is *delicioso*, as well as fresh fruit for dessert. The decor used to be strictly truck stop, but the whole place had a makeover a few years ago and it's now very nice. In fact, in this part of town, it is an eye-catching "flower" among some very dreary restaurants. It also boasts one of the best juke-boxes in town.

SPANISH VILLAGE

Where do old Christmas lights go to die? Spanish Village, that's where. They add a happy sparkle to the place, as do the made-with-fresh-lime margaritas. (But

4720 ALMEDA at Blodgett
713-523-2861
www.spanishvillagerestaurant.com
MAP E7

don't come here just to drink. There's no bar area, and they won't serve drinks without food.) The décor is kitschy and well-worn from generations of happy diners crossing the threshold. Locals like to take out-of-towners to this sentimental favorite for a taste of "the real

Houston." There is much here to like — try the chile relleno, pork *carnitas* or special enchiladas. What's Southern-fried spring chicken with fries and buttered rolls doing on the menu? And grated cheese as an ($3) appetizer? Just go and kick back. It's a beloved local dive. Design note: The broken-tile tables were a fixture here long before Williams-Sonoma catalogs began featuring them.

1600 LAMAR at Crawford, in the Hilton Americas
713-577-8325
www.spencersforsteakandchops.com
MAP F6

SPENCER'S FOR STEAKS & CHOPS

Located in the massive Hilton Americas near the George R. Brown Convention Center and Toyota Center in downtown, you'll find a wide variety of diners here — conventioneers, vacationers, sports figures, touring musicians as well as locals before a concert. The dining room is ritzy and a tad modern, and the lighting isn't always as mood-settingly dim as we prefer in our steakhouses (the better for disguising prices). But the crabcakes are more crab than cake, and dry-aged steaks are sizzling hot (especially the porterhouse) but look so sad alone on the plate. For a side, try the Idaho baker, prepared tableside, or garlic skin-on smashed potatoes. Resist the temptation to manhandle and strip clean the double-cut lamb chops bones. Lunch menu has lighter items. After dinner, head to the roof for an amazing view and one last drink in the Skyline Bar & Grill.

STAR PIZZA

Houston's most popular upscale pizza joint offers everything from calzone to lasagna, but it's the pizza — and most particularly Joe's Pizza, a spinach-and-garlic favorite — that has secured its fame. This sturdy pie, made on a grainy whole-wheat crust with a sweet rich flavor (beer is added) or common white crust, is strictly knife-and-fork material. We also recommend the goat cheese appetizer, which has minimal nutritional value and is completely doused in herbs and olive oil. The two locations can be noisy, so be prepared for the aural onslaught. Surprisingly, home delivery can sometimes be faster than table service in the restaurant itself. Added bonus: When you call for delivery, they remember what

2111 NORFOLK just west of S. Shepherd, north of Hwy. 59
713-523-0800
www.starpizza.net
MAP E7

77 HARVARD at Washington
713-869-1241
MAP E6

you ordered last time — you're in the computer — in case you forgot what it was you enjoyed so much.

STELIO'S

5215 RICHMOND at Sage
713-622-2625
MAP E7

This is going to sound crazy, but our favorite Greek food in Houston is served up in a service station. Since 2006 when it opened, the word about Stelio's has been crackling through the foodie community. Now it's true that Stelio's does have a couple of drawbacks. There are only a few tables on the sidewalk outside the restaurant, but, on the plus side, they do all offer a lovely view of the gas pumps. (Clearly, most orders are to go.) Everything is good, but we're partial to the gyros — slightly crispy pieces of meat mixed with soft tender slices. Try also the *tiropetes* (cheese pie) and *spanakopita* (spinach pie); both are light, flaky and tasty. On the combo plate, the *pastichio* (sort of like baked ziti with ground beef, spices and a rich custardy, cheesy layer on top) and moussaka were delicious. The *keftedes* (meatballs) and stuffed grape leaves are both splendid, too. Word is that a real sit-down restaurant is on the drawing board for the Stelio's folks. Tip: On one or two Saturdays a month, owner Stelios Bouboudakias roasts a whole pig, goat and lamb. Call ahead for exact time and dates.

STRIP HOUSE

1200 MCKINNEY at San Jacinto, in the Park Shops Mall
713-659-6000
www.theglaziergroup.com
MAP F6

If you don't mind nekkid burlesque stars (via photos) looking over your shoulder while you dine, then head downtown to Strip House for a mighty fine steak in a setting that challenges you *not* to whisper "bordello." The interiors play on the double-entendre inherent in the name with a luscious, all-red interior enhanced with rosy lighting and those cheeky (*ahem*) photos. Slip into a leather banquette and enjoy a crisp-edged, double-cut strip steak, veal T-bone, lamb and more — it's all about flesh here. Sides include truffled cream spinach and goose fat potatoes. For starters we love the presentation of the warm garlic bread with gorgonzola fondue — rectangular "logs" of buttery garlic bread stacked Jenga-style and drizzled with blue cheese — pow! Nice wine selection.

SULLIVAN'S STEAKHOUSE

This 1940s-style chophouse is named for John L. Sullivan, the 19th-century bare-knuckle heavyweight boxer, which explains the name of

> **4608 WESTHEIMER** at Westcreek, just inside Loop 610
> **713-961-0333**
> www.sullivanssteakhouse.com
> **MAP** D7

the adjacent Ringside jazz and cigar lounge. The place has the ideal steakhouse trifecta of steaks, martinis and jazz. You can dine at Ringside — nice bar menu — but it is best for cocktails and carousing. (Check the website for the music calendar.) The main dining room is handsome and spacious. The majority of patrons fall into the late 20- and 30-something range, so it's a bit of a "starter steakhouse," but don't let that keep you away. It makes for a less-pretentious-than-most steakhouse. Steaks are well-prepared, as is seafood, and a soufflé makes for a nice ending. Cigar lovers — there is a fully stocked humidor waiting just for you.

SUSHI JIN

> **14670 MEMORIAL** just west of Dairy Ashford
> **281-493-2932**
> **MAP** A6

Sushi Jin is tucked into the corner of an unassuming strip center near Memorial Athletic Club. Don't let the modest exterior fool you. Sushi Jin is run by Japanese, and the reason for coming here is the spectacularly fresh sushi. What else would you expect from a restaurant owner who also owns Prime Sales and Trading Ltd., a seafood wholesaler that flies fish in from Japan and elsewhere? Sushi Jin has four Japanese sushi chefs, with chef Katsuhiro Uotani at the helm. The chefs or your server will be happy to recommend "what's good today," and we suggest you follow their advice. On our most recent visit, the Canadian salmon alone was worth the trip. Pale orange flesh marbled with creamy stripes of fat created a rich melt-in-your-mouth experience. Yes, we ordered more. The chopped scallop sushi was almost as good. The spider roll and spicy Cajun roll (okay, you won't find this one in Tokyo) are good, too, but save the Cajun roll for last — it's spicy enough to overpower every subtle flavor in the place. Sushi Jin has a full bar and several private dining areas that host everything from gaggles of middle-school girls celebrating birthdays to groups of businessmen from Tokyo closing business deals.

SUSHI KING

> **3401 KIRBY** at Richmond
> **713-528-8998**
> www.sushiking.us
> **MAP** E7

Keeper and Christine Lin opened this spot a few years ago where Floridita Seafood Grill previously cut fish. The owners call it a Continental-style Japanese restaurant, which we take to mean that cooked dishes share equal billing with sushi and sashimi. Whatever. It's the only attractive storefront in an otherwise scruffy strip center. The best thing we sampled: Asian tartar, a tower built of fried wonton skins with fresh tuna, avocado and seasonings. Our favorite specialty roll is the Cowboy Roll, which marries spicy salmon or tuna with blackened beef. Service sometimes seems unpolished, but the spicy ponzu sauce is the best we've had — perfect for dipping your edamame. Live piano music is a draw, too. Easy parking.

12637 WESTHEIMER just west of Dairy Ashford
281-679-8300
www.sylviasenchiladakitchen.com
MAP A7

SYLVIA'S ENCHILADA KITCHEN

As the name implies, enchiladas rule the menu at this way-outside-the-Loop eatery. Chef/owner Sylvia Casares-Copeland uses the phrase "enchiladas to drive for," and most of the time we are pleased we made the trek. Chips and (warm) salsa are good, and with 18 varieties of individually rolled and cooked enchiladas to choose from, there is something for everyone. We especially like the *sarita* (with squash and corn) and Crystal City (spinach, named for the Texas town that is the spinach capital), but skip the chile rellenos (that batter is weird). At dessert, opt for the chocolate-cinnamon *tres leches*. There is a patio for outdoor dining. Inside, the walls can go day-glo bright on a sunny day, and the owner's collection of mini tea sets are a quirky-yet-personal touch. Note: Casares-Copeland teaches fajita and tamale-making in the restaurant. Check the website for class schedule.

T'AFIA

T'afia ("TA-fee-ah") is 100 percent Texas, and that's fantastically refreshing. Renowned chef Monica Pope builds her menu around what local ranchers and farmers raise, even some area wines. That explains the name, a derivative of "ratafia,"

3701 TRAVIS one block north of Alabama
713-524-6922
www.tafia.com
MAP E6

Creole wine made with seasonal produce. Pope, who cut her culinary teeth as a teenager at Cafe Annie, closed the upscale Boulevard Bistrot in 2004 to open T'afia in a transitional Midtown neighborhood. What we considered risky a few years back is a popular and culinary success today. The dining room is a study in almost monk-like asceticism. Blank brick walls. Concrete floor. Industrial ceiling. Po-mo acrylic tables. And that's about it. All the better to concentrate on the

Monica Pope of T'afia is the only female Texas chef to be named a "Top 10 Best Chef" by Food & Wine *magazine.*

remarkable food, no doubt. Since the menu's ever-changing, it's impractical to start rattling off must-have dishes. For example, one evening you might find an antelope chop in a perfectly reduced red wine sauce, but who knows when or if that will gallop by again? With T'afia, each visit is a roll of the dice, but the odds are you'll find something to catch your fancy. When offered, order the Texas quail or buffalo ribeye rubbed with local coffee and a down-home side, such as the sinfully rich mac'n'cheese. FYI: A tasting menu and seasonal plates are offered, too. It's worth an early visit to T'afia for cocktails and killer lounge food that's free Tuesday through Thursday. Open evenings only, except for a prix-fixe lunch on Fridays. This is also the site for the Saturday morning Midtown Farmers Market.

TACO MILAGRO RESTAURANT & BEACH BAR

2555 KIRBY at Westheimer, and other locations
713-522-1999
www.taco-milagro.com
MAP E6

The Mexican food at this trendy fast-casual restaurant is mostly average, save a good soft chicken taco, fish taco and a quesadilla or two. But Taco Milagro seems to have become more of a margarita joint than a culinary destination. Which makes us wonder, Is Taco Milagro the redheaded stepchild within the Schiller Del Grande Restaurant Group, an organization famous for the groundbreaking Cafe Annie, Cafe Express and The Grove? What else should we think of a restaurant that touts "party pics" on its website? Still, the salsa bar serves up several excellent varieties to which you may help yourself, the chips are free and the margaritas are strong. This is no secret, of course. The oversized street-side patio is packed on warm weekdays, lazy Sunday afternoons and late summer nights. Inside, expect a lot of noise and stick with the tacos and quesadillas, unless you have had one too many margaritas to care. Two notes: The bar is famous for its tequila selection of 150-plus bottles. And, surprisingly perhaps, Taco Milagro turns out a darn good hamburger that stuffs chorizo and green chiles in the beef patties.

TACOS A GO-GO

3704 MAIN just north of Alabama
713-807-8226
www.tacosagogo.com
MAP E6

You have to respect, if not love, a taco joint that serves breakfast all day, stays open until 2 a.m. Friday and Saturday nights, and doesn't price anything over $6.99. You also have to know what kind of taco joint Tacos a Go-Go is. You get the food to go because the tacos are to die-for but the ambiance isn't. Read the sign, right? It doesn't say Tacos a Stay-Stay. Plus, it's mighty convenient that the always-friendly staff will deliver an order to the Continental Club next door — if they aren't too busy. We spoke to an employee recently over the din of cooks taco-making up a storm, and he said the most popular items are, of course, the tacos (pick a tortilla: corn, flour, whole wheat or crispy). He suggested a first-timer order an egg taco and a chicken or beef one. Vegetarians, don't run off. There is a veggie taco, he said, that "makes me forget I like meat."

TASTE OF TEXAS

10505 KATY FWY. between Gessner and Beltway 8
713-932-6901
www.tasteoftexas.com
MAP B6

Don't count on the "boys' club" ambiance of upscale steakhouses. This beefy joint opts for a casual country feel, including vaulted ceilings and a salad bar. Wife-and-husband co-owners Nina and Edd Hendee also step out of the box by offering complete meals with each cut of meat, mostly including a salad, bread and a side. That's a relief in the land of $12 sides. No-cow-for-me diners aren't forgotten, either: There's a grilled-veggie plate, as well as Texas pecan-crusted chicken breast stuffed with goat cheese, grilled onions and roasted pecans. What started as a mom-and-pop steakhouse in 1977 has turned into an enormous Texas trading post with mail-order steaks, gift boxes, memorabilia mugs and even a newsletter.

TEALA'S

3210 W. DALLAS west of Waugh
713-520-9292
www.tealas.com
MAP E6

Your almost-certain wait can be mollified with fresh, fruit-flavored margaritas (don't miss the mango) sipped in a warm, wood-lined bar area. If the aroma wafting from diners' dishes has your tummy growling, grab your drink and relax on the welcoming deck. (Yes, it's a little odd that the owner of Thai Pepper opened a Mexican restaurant, but the website explains it by noting both regions are by the sea and use similar spices.) Teala's concentrates on coastal Yucatan dishes, and when ordering, you should too. Don't pass on the *cochinita pibil* with cucumber salad or the chicken in a peanut *mole* sauce. These off-the-beaten-menu dishes outshine the Tex-Mex staples (fajitas, burritos and such) you'll find. It's no wonder Teala's is a neighborhood fave of River Oaksters and nearby denizens.

> **1511 AIRLINE** just north of N. Main, and other locations
> **713-426-4420**
> **MAP** E5

TEOTIHUACÁN

We were first introduced to Teotihuacán by chef/restaurateur Claire Smith, who eats here when she isn't running the kitchen at Shade. The name is a mouthful, but leave room for the delectable and amazingly affordable food at this casual Mexican comfort spot. The exterior is hot pink and hard to miss. Inside doesn't cool off, either, with spicy salsa and steaming chargrilled meats. Whether you choose the chicken, quail, beef or all of the above, the grill is the way to go. Teotihuacán is known for its fresh corn tortillas — it's love from the queen, co-owner Silvia Galvan, who made tortillas at Ninfa's for years. Breakfast scores, too. Servings here are large and so are the crowds. But despite it all, service is quick and friendly.

TEX CHICK

You probably can't guess from the name what kind of restaurant this is. Surprise: It's Puerto Rican. Actually, this teeny place, which has just four tables — and that's crowding it — is so small it hardly can be described as a

> **712 FAIRVIEW** east of Montrose
> **713-528-4708**
> **MAP** E6

restaurant. It's more like eating in your grandmother's kitchen. You're sitting here and the cooks are right there, just an arm's length away. The food is very hearty, of course (just like grandma's) and has a devoted following. Diners want to keep this little gem their own little secret, but they couldn't hide something so good. *Houston Press* awarded Tex Chick "Best Plantains" in 2006 for the shock-to-the-heart *mofongo* (a fried ball of plantains with garlic and pork rind) and "Best Mom and Pop" a few years back. Pop is Teodoro Gonzalez, and Mom is his wife, Carmen. Together they're building up quite a fan club for their *pastel-arroz habichuelo* (similar to tamales), *arroz con granduras* (white rice and pigeon peas) and *carne guisada* (beef stew). To drink, grab a non-alcoholic Malta Goya from the cooler. The Gonzalezes once made some mean burgers and onion rings, but Teodoro said there's hardly time for that now.

RECIPE: BACON-WRAPPED TEXAS QUAIL WITH TOMATILLO-CILANTRO SAUCE

Mark's American Cuisine, 1658 Westheimer, 713-523-3800

The simple flavors of the applewood bacon and quail pair very well with the cool flavor of the tomatillo sauce in this dish. Chef/owner Mark Cox wanted to create "an upscale, rustic, Texas-style comfort food-type dish that was versatile, perfect for a light lunch or a dinner appetizer."

Preparing the quail
1 portobello mushroom, gills scraped
salt (either kosher or sea salt) & pepper
4 semi-boneless quail
1 jalapeño, sliced in thin strips lengthwise (can be omitted or substituted with another chile)
4 sundried tomato halves, sliced thin
1 package applewood-smoked bacon
4 Tbsp. grapeseed oil
1 Tbsp. unsalted butter
Tomatillo-Cilantro Sauce (recipe below)

METHOD: Season mushrooms with salt and pepper and grill or sauté mushrooms, depending on preference, until cooked through. Slice into long strips, about ¼-inch wide, that are as long as the quail lengthwise. Trim quail of legs and wings, open the cavity and season with salt and pepper. Stuff each quail with one slice of portobello, a sliver of jalapeño and one of the sliced sun-dried tomatoes. Place sheet of plastic wrap on counter and then place bacon slices on top of it so that one slice slightly overlaps the other and they run up and down the counter. Once all placed, trim so that it is the correct length to wrap the quail once with about a ½-inch overlap. Place one of the stuffed quail perpendicular across the bacon at the bottom end. Using the plastic wrap for assistance, roll the bacon around the quail, then wrap securely in the plastic and set aside. Quail can be prepared in advance and refrigerated until ready to use.

When ready to cook, heat oil in large non-stick skillet over medium-high heat. Remove plastic from quail and place quail in skillet starting with seam-side down. Add butter and brown quail on all sides (being

THAI PEPPER

2049 W. ALABAMA
just east of S. Shepherd
713-520-8225
www.tealas.com
MAP E6

People often say good Thai is difficult to find in Houston. But that's not quite true. *Consistently* good Thai is hard to find in Houston. Thai Pepper is no different. Order four dishes here, and you're bound to find one or two fantastic and the others average. Every so often, a dish slips to subpar. The menu is what you expect from Thai food toned down in America. Standouts include the spring roll appetizer, coconut-milky chicken soup from which the aroma of lemongrass tickles your nose and an outstanding *pad Thai* with rice noodles, shrimp, bean curd and bits of egg. The noodles, curries, lime salads and soups are prepared to your preferred degree of spice. While the food quality may bounce around, most people agree there's one thing consistent about the restaurant: good service. The dark intimate setting might strike you as romantic. Curious about the website address? Owner Teal Anomaiprasert also owns Teala's, the Mexican restaurant.

---

sure to end back on the seam side), getting a nice golden color to bacon. Baste quail frequently with butter from the pan. Place quail in a 350-degree oven for 5 to 7 minutes to finish cooking through. Remove from pan and drain.

Assembly: Spoon room-temperature sauce onto plate. Slice hot quail into five or six rings and place in a line down the middle of the sauce so they slightly overlap one another. Serve immediately. Serves 4.

Tomatillo-Cilantro Sauce
2 Tbsp. grapeseed oil
2 cloves fresh garlic, minced
1 medium shallot, finely diced
5 large tomatillos, husks removed then quartered
3 cups low-sodium chicken stock
1 large bunch cilantro, leaves only
1 serrano pepper (optional)

METHOD: Heat oil in medium saucepot over medium-low heat. Add garlic and shallots and cook until tender and translucent. Add tomatillos and stock; bring to boil and then simmer till tomatillos are tender, about 5 minutes. Remove from heat and chill in an ice bath. Once chilled, pour into blender, add cilantro and pepper and puree until smooth. Sauce can be made the day before and refrigerated.

THAI SPICE

5117 KELVIN at Dunstan, and other locations, including Thai Spice Express and Thai Space Buffet
713-522-5100
www.thaispice.com
MAP E7

The original Thai Spice is a must-eat for its "treetop" balcony, which certainly trumps the somewhat-kitsch, art-filled dining room. The flavors feel westernized for Americans' freshman palates, even though the restaurant launched in 1996 to bring traditional Thai food to Houston. A manager recently told us the offshoots of cornerstone Thai Spice (Thai Spice Buffet I and II, Thai Spice Express and Thai Spice Asian Cuisine) are franchised with different owners, so be aware. The kitchen here serves many vegetarian items and seafood that's usually quite good. Thai Spice knows locals love a good spring roll and offers four "seasonal" varieties: spring, summer, autumn and winter (the last includes mushrooms, onions and cream cheese). The wine list lacks, but that's standard for most Texas Thai restaurants, and some friends complain the service does too. Still, Thai Spice is a favorite for many in the Rice University area, especially at lunchtime.

THAI STICKS

4319 MONTROSE near Richmond
713-529-4500
www.thaistickshouston.com
MAP E7

Most everything at Thai Sticks is done a little better than at many of its competitors, but the prices are higher, too. The contemporary setting replaced Monica Pope's Boulevard Bistrot, and maybe some of that chef's talents stuck around. We love the curvy hostess stand studded with smooth black river rocks, as well as the clear soup set off with a single wonton-like dumpling. Thai royal court cooking is spoken in the beautiful plating (e.g. carrots carved into roses) and a more inventive menu than most Thai in town. Take the tamarind mahi mahi topped with grilled scallops, roast duck with vegetables or the lamb chops in a rich brown sauce. Live on the fringe and try *prik khing* with pork or a curry. The *massaman* curry, with its hit of tamarind, is particularly nice with chicken. Thai Sticks is a partnership between Yanee Sornchai Greenwood from Thailand and Mary Varcados from Greece. We still don't understand the name.

THELMA'S BAR-B-QUE

It's a barbecue place, so you probably aren't expecting much in the way of décor. That's good, because Thelma's is even less than you expect in terms of interior design. This place is a total dive — there's just no other

> **1020 LIVE OAK**
> at Lamar
> **713-228-2262**
> **MAP** F6

way to say it — in a desolate no-man's-land east of the George R. Brown Convention Center. Yet, it's a beloved joint that barbecue fans revel in taking friends to. We find the smoked meats and sausage delicious, but the sauce and sides rather over-sugared. (Who knew potato salad and cole slaw could be too sweet?) But, and here's what you have to know, the very best thing at Thelma's is the fried catfish. It's the most delicious we've ever eaten — smokin' hot from the fryer with a well-seasoned cornmeal crust and tenderest sweet fish. Service? It's as sweet as the sweetened iced tea. The last time we were in, the whole restaurant was led in a "Happy Birthday" song to one of the guests. So leave your coat and tie in the car, and relax. Warning: Don't even try to place an order while talking on your cell phone. The counter ladies don't like it, and you may get the boot, cowboy.

THIS IS IT!

A move up the street to a larger and spiffier new location a couple years back did not dull the soul of this soul-food institution: It's still food to soothe and nourish, with a steam table that includes meatloaf, yams, braised oxtails, chitlins, barbecued ribs and biscuits.

> **207 GRAY** west of Bagby
> **713-659-1608**
> www.thisisithouston.com
> **MAP** E6

If you are interested in learning more about African-American food, this is the perfect starting point. Since the booming redevelopment of Midtown, This Is It! has recently found itself in a trendy neighborhood. It used to be something of a destination, but now clumps of pedestrians pass by day and night, as they go from bar to bar. The $9.95 dinner includes your choice of one entree and three veggies. But after having your sweet self some fried catfish with collard greens and cornbread, you'd pay twice that and still say you got a deal. The late Mattie and Frank Jones started This Is It! in 1959, and now their grandson and his family are running the show. All you need to see is the overflow of appetites willing to wait in too-long, after-church-on-Sunday lines to know you're at the right place.

TILA'S RESTAURANTE AND BAR

> **1111 S. SHEPHERD**
> just south of W. Dallas
> **713-522-7654**
> www.tilas.com
> **MAP** E6

Stick a restaurant on an odd-shaped island of real estate on the edge of high-dollar River Oaks. Add a Mexican kitchen, plant-screened patio and cozy Mexican-art-filled dining room. This is itty-bitty Tila's. Be sure to bring a few bucks to tip the valet because you'll have to park in his domain. But once inside the golden-lit, quirky joint, it's easy to forget those few bucks. Strong margaritas made with a choice of more than 60 tequilas also help. We like it that they are made straight up and served in individual carafes. And we love the bucket of warm tortilla chips and plantain chips that arrive at the table with both green and red salsa. Service can be erratic, but is usually welcoming and attentive. The menu is unpredictable in a more consistent way. Shake up your taste buds with brie and pear quesadillas or roasted corn with herbed butter as an appetizer. If that's enough eating outside the box, opt for more traditional staples that Tila's offers, such as enchiladas, delicious Mexican Caesar salad and chiles rellenos. Still feeling frisky? Hit the *chilaquiles* for dinner. It's owner Tila Hidalgo Leach's take on a Mexican casserole of chicken, cheese, sour cream, corn tortillas and the kitchen sink.

3600 W. ALABAMA
between Buffalo Speedway and Weslayan
713-622-4224
www.tinyboxwoods.com
MAP E7

TINY BOXWOOD'S ESPRESSO BAR AND CAFE

In this instance weird has worked, at least with River Oaks' ladies who lunch. A cafe squeezed into the design center of chi-chi landscapers Thompson + Hanson serves up an ungimmicky but fairly creative breakfast and lunch. The handsome, cool interior lends an expansive feel to the place. And although it's "Tiny," the chalkboard menu is over-sized. The food is girly with a French twist. *Le "tiny" dejeuner* is just that, little, *sans* bacon, *sans* pancakes, *sans* hash browns. (Why couldn't we figure out how French women stay thin?) Typical salads (such as Cobb and Provençal) and a couple of soups play with thin-crust pizza and more interesting sandwiches, like the Frenchman: crispy wheat bread layered with sliced prosciutto, goat cheese, tomato and homemade basil pesto. We'll take that Frenchman home!

Tiny Boxwood's stylish touches let the chic clientele know they aren't eating in an abandoned nursery stockroom.

TIO PEPE

5213 CEDAR near N. 5th St. off Bissonnet, Bellaire
713-667-4409
MAP D7

The scent of garlic dances at this Spanish restaurant in Bellaire, but as much as we love those pungent cloves, it's a bit over the top, especially at lunch. Dinner is your better bet here, and coworkers will thank you, too. With the sun down and Barcelona on your mind, order great standards of Spain: *tapas* to start, gazpacho, paella, *sopa de ajo* (garlic soup) and a Catalonian fish soup called *zarzuela de mariscos*. Indulge in house-made sangria (white and red) or sip from a decent wine list. Strolling guitarists can't help but make you smile, and suddenly the day wears off. It gets tight on Wednesday nights when flamenco dancers wind up the small restaurant. Bonus: The spaghetti Bolognese sauce is an unexpected treasure.

TOMMY'S SEAFOOD STEAKHOUSE

11660 WESTHEIMER between Wilcrest and Kirkwood
281-679-1112
www.tommys.com
MAP E6

2555 BAY AREA BLVD. just north of Space Center Blvd.
281-480-2221
MAP Southeast of I9

Tommy's, long a Bay Area fixture, set up shop on Houston's Westside a few years ago. The menu here is similar to the original, meaning meat is king, seafood is queen and Cajun flavors provide the spice. After basic steaks, choose from creative dishes like pork tenderloin stuffed with wild rice, roasted pecans and andouille sausage or a 14-ounce ribeye with a Creole sauce. An array of fish is available, cooked as you like and paired with your choice of sauce, such as Pontchartrain, meunière, Oscar and fresh mango. Otherwise, the menu is fairly predictable. There's live music several nights a week (see the website for schedule), but performers sometimes start later than scheduled.

TONY MANDOLA'S GULF COAST KITCHEN

1962 W. GRAY between Dunlavy and Shepherd
713-528-3474
www.tonymandolas.com
MAP E6

Y'all pony up to a little Nawlins' in the heart of River Oaks, where blackened snapper sizzles in lime butter and crawfish ravioli dance in your mouth. The kitchen manages a seamless blending of Southern-Italian, Creole, Cajun, Mexican and native Gulf Coast influences to create wonderful seafood dishes that are representative of the Houston area. Find gumbo on the menu just above *sopa Tomas* (shrimp soup with pico de gallo and avocado) and *cioppino*, an Italian-style bouillabaisse. The seafood is always fresh, and the preparations are dependable, often piquant and usually hearty. If you can only order one thing, make it oysters Damian: Tender fried oysters are tucked back into their shells and topped with pico de gallo. (See our recipe for oysters Damian on page 195.)

TONY'S

> **3755 RICHMOND**
> at Timmons
> **713-622-6778**
> www.tonyshouston.com
> **MAP** D7

Velvety, fresh and delicately stuffed pastas, tender veal and impeccable seafood are just some of Tony's attractions, not to mention the always excellent service, award-winning wine selection and intriguing setting outfitted with *important* art. The kitchen is a little French, a little Italian, rather like what you might find along the Riviera. The printed menu is surprisingly short but offers to honor any dietary requests. Which makes it limitless, right? Owner Tony Vallone knows how to cosset the rich, the famous and the powerful and has decades of experience doing exactly that. This is the spot for a complete surrender: the best food, the best wines and best service. After 30-plus years on Post Oak Blvd., Tony Vallone moved his namesake restaurant in 2005 to this Greenway Plaza site where Maxim's once stood, spending a reputed $5 million on renovations. With its fresher-feeling dining room (designed by Shafik Rifaat) and shorter menu, it's all been edited and cropped, although the feeling of luxury is still here. Tony's procures the finest ingredients, and chef Olivier Ciesielski translates them into magnificent creations. The menu includes a trio of wasabi-crusted fish, roasted chicken carved tableside, sautéed flounder, braised lamb shank, even an *akaushi* hamburger with hand-cut fries. This is a big-deal restaurant. Tune up your credit card and come celebrate.

TOOKIE'S

Come for the locally famous onion rings and fall in love with the burgers at this Texas burger house near Clear Lake. Tookie's has been a popular stop near the Kemah Boardwalk since 1975, and there's good reason. Charred beef patties

> **1202 BAYPORT BLVD.**
> near Hwy. 146 and NASA Rd. 1, Seabrook
> **281-474-3444**
> **MAP** East of I9

anchor a straightforward hamburger that makes you appreciate simplicity. "The Squealer," which adds ground bacon to the beef patty, is the menu favorite, but the bean burger has its followers, too. Tasty burgers, yes, but they're thin. If you're on empty, order double meat between the buns for only a little more. Wash it down with cherry Coke and feel like a kid again.

TREEBEARDS

315 TRAVIS on Market Square, and other locations
713-228-2622
www.treebeards.com
MAP F6

If Treebeards ever left, downtown just might go with it. And what a shame it'd be to lose Louisiana food of the most remarkable kind — earthy gumbos, red beans and rice with chunks of sausage, duck gumbo, jambalaya and sinfully dirty rice. This lunch-only staple started in 1978 between a peep-show arcade and a rowdy bar, back when Houstonians went downtown only if they had to. It has since flourished into four downtown locations. Lunch is served cafeteria-style and built upon daily specials like étouffée-topped blackened catfish and pot roast. Grab the full deal (an entree and two sides) for cheap or three sides for even cheaper. As one wag observed, the only good thing about jury duty is eating at Treebeards.

TREVÍSIO

6550 BERTNER (top floor) at Moursound in the Texas Medical Center
713-749-0400
www.trevisiorestaurant.com
MAP E7

You're immediately intrigued by the 64-foot exterior waterfall that pours down the parking garage upon which Trevisio is perched. Ride the elevator to the top floor to find a large rambling space with a spectacular view of the Med Center on one side and several adjoining private rooms (for when the pharmaceutical company reps come calling). Chef Jon Buchanan's contemporary kitchen rolls out fresh, light Italian fare, such as sautéed shrimp with pancetta and griddled polenta in a spicy *bianco* sauce. Pasta dishes have flare, like the *perciatelli* with roasted fingerling potatoes, green beans and pesto, and meats are all dressed up like the *vitello*, sautéed veal slices with prosciutto, garlic-sage sauce, asparagus and truffled potato ravioli. There have been complaints of spotty service, though we have never experienced anything less than perfectly fine service. This is the first fine-dining restaurant in the Med Center for many years, and our *My Table* reviewer called the menu "assured and flavorful, innovative without being fussy." The only thing it lacks: Enough customers to fill its elegant space. So go.

TRIPLE A

2526 AIRLINE inside Loop 610
713-861-3422
MAP E5

Next to the popular Canino's produce market, this old-fashioned Southern-style diner has a standard menu that includes eggs, breakfast meats, toast and biscuits, as well as meatloaf and chicken-fried steaks. The service is usually friendly, and the 1942-era setting will have you spouting "when-I-was-a-kid" memories. Predictable menu? Maybe. But sometimes routine and comfort are just what you're hungry for. When you've finished here, stop next door to do your week's fresh-food shopping.

TRULUCK'S

5350 WESTHEIMER
between Sage and Yorktown
713-783-7270
www.trulucks.com
MAP C7

Here's a chain dressed as a local restaurant, but we let Truluck's slide for its sweetly delicious (we could eat 100) Florida stone crab claws. If you only know local blue crabs, these claws are quite a treat. Order them as an entree, or add four claws to anything for a pretty price of $18.95. And there's always all-you-can-eat-claws on Monday. The ocean is a goldmine for Truluck's, and the menu dances with seafood: flounder Pontchartrain (parmesan-crusted Atlantic flounder with rice, shrimp, crawfish tails and spicy Creole sauce piquant), shrimp and grits, grilled halibut, miso-glazed Chilean sea bass and jalapeño salmon (grilled Scottish salmon topped with blue crab, Gulf shrimp and the restaurant's signature jalapeño béarnaise sauce). Landlubbers can have steak and chops. The local Truluck's traded a cozy-diner location in 2007 for this upscale, over-the-top spot close to The Galleria. Certain appetizers are half-price during the cocktail hour (4 to 7 p.m.) Monday through Friday. Outstanding wine list, too.

UPTOWN SUSHI

Savvy restaurateur Donald Chang (who also has Blue Fin) successfully applied his knack for luring the young and beautiful to Uptown Sushi, a cosmopolitan Asian-fusion newcomer that opened in 2003. Cocktails are tasty — the restaurant won *My Table*'s 2005 Houston Culinary Award for Best Bar Service — the sushi is fresh and the scene is a real draw. Techno beats bounce as fabulously dressed and yet-to-see-a-wrinkle hipsters circulate through the LA-inspired interior. The dining area is slightly tiered so that the sushi bar becomes a theater-in-the-round, and it has a supper-club crowd that parties late. We once arrived at 10:30 p.m., and the valet stand still jumped and a team of five sushi chefs could hardly catch up to the orders that poured in. There are a number of specialty rolls on offer in which the chefs combine a hodgepodge of flavors and textures with surprising success. The Lickety Split roll — "our most popular," affirmed the waiter — tops tuna, crawfish, cucumber and sprouts with spicy tuna

1131-14 UPTOWN PARK BLVD. north of San Felipe
713-871-1200
www.uptown-sushi.com
MAP D6

(sashimi grade mixed with red pepper sauce, sesame oil and sesame seeds, rice wine and sugar), yellowtail, salmon and avocado. A variation called the Scuba Diver adds similar toppings to soft-shell crab. The rolls are sizable, so don't order too much too soon. It's fascinating to watch the chopping and rolling. But fellow diners are the real performers here.

VAN LOC

3010 MILAM between Elgin and McGowen
713-528-6441
www.vanlocrestaurant.com
MAP E6

At the edge of Houston's shabby Little Saigon in Midtown is Van Loc, where the reliable, affordable and authentic Vietnamese fare excuses cold-shoulder service and a lackluster environment that is brown and very tired. The

Recommended
UPSCALE BURGERS

Down and dirty burgers have a revered place in the dining-out world. But sometimes one longs for real plates and a well-made cocktail to wash it down. When that mood strikes, here are five choice spots.

CAFE ANNIE, *1728 Post Oak Blvd., 713-840-1111.* The Cafe Annie hamburger with cheddar is available during lunch and in Bar Annie at night. This burger lives up to the Cafe Annie standard with a juicy, amazingly flavorful, freshly ground chuck patty between plush buns.

GRAVITAS, *807 Taft, 713-522-0995.* The grilled Gravitas cheeseburger features exemplary buns from its Kraftsmen partner that perfectly complement the excellent beef. Nicely finished with tomato relish and your choice of cheese.

MAX'S WINE DIVE, *4720 Washington, 713-880-8737.* The Kobe beef burger is made with pedigreed American *wagyu* beef from East Texas' Yama Farms. The decadence is compounded with gooey Brillat-Savarin cheese, in-house pickled jalapeños, ripe tomato and Bibb lettuce on Kraftsmen brioche buns.

MOCKINGBIRD BISTRO, *1985 Welch, 713-533-0200.* The American Kobe beef burger is an amazingly rich burger, topped, if you wish, with stinky and lovely Stilton cheese. Or be completely hedonistic and add a thick slice of Hudson Valley foie gras. Truffled fries on the side, of course.

RAVEN GRILL, 1*916 Bissonnet, 713-521-2027.* Who can resist a fluffy toasted onion roll stacked with a moist, perfectly charred beef patty, pungent red onions, tomato and buttery sautéed onions? Add avocado, smoky poblano strips, bacon or Swiss if you must take it over the top.

owners say "van loc" means lots of luck in Vietnamese, and you'll need it to get through the extensive menu. Thankfully, many dishes, if not all, are under $12, and most are quite good, if not fantastic. But we'll save you the trouble with a few suggestions. For starters, Van Loc makes summer rolls with ideal texture, and they perfectly cook vermicelli in a soup of shrimp and pork. Don't miss the barbecued pork, clay-pot catfish, whole fried fish and the *bo luc lac* (steak with lettuce and tomato). Meatless feasters should try the tofu fried with chile peppers, garlic and scallions.

2401 FONDREN
north of Westheimer
713-782-3888
www.vargosonline.com
MAP D7

VARGO'S

You come for the scenery, not the food. You come for lush gardens, not low prices. Vargo's, which sits on some eight acres of land with a private lake, is a landmark in the Memorial area and a choice spot for countless weddings, bar mitzvahs and private receptions of all stripes. Sit outside and geese or peacocks will beg for handouts, and you won't feel bad giving them a nibble or two. The American-Continental cuisine is very average and unduly overpriced. Keep reminding yourself that you're paying for Vargo's environment, not its cuisine. Alas, the tree that once grew straight through the dining room has been cut down. FYI: If you want breakfast food for brunch, skip Vargo's, where the Sunday menu reads more like dinner.

VIC & ANTHONY'S

Downtown Houston's first major-league steakhouse, located across the street from Minute Maid Park, is the crown jewel of the diverse Landry's Restaurants, Inc. Before its April 2003 debut, much was made of the fact that Landry's CEO Tilman Fertitta traveled the country with father Vic and cousin Anthony, sampling steakhouses and taking notes. The result of their road trip is this beautiful two-story Craftsman-style setting with fine wood, gorgeous wrought ironwork and oversized stained-

1510 TEXAS at LaBranch
713-228-1111
www.vicandanthonys.com
MAP F6

If you prefer dining rooms with a wow factor, make sure Vic & Anthony's is on your list.

glass chandeliers. The brief menu reads like a steakhouse all-star round-up: iceberg wedge with crumbled Roquefort, crabcakes, oysters Rockefeller, creamed spinach, mountains of gossamer onion rings, Prime cuts of beef and the best mashed potatoes in town. There's also an unexpected Italian accent on the menu, as evidenced by the veal chop Milanese and shrimp scampi served with angelhair marinara. From the get-go, this steakhouse was conceived to impress, and its award-winning wine list is nothing short of awesome. It offers breadth and vintage depth along with 26 offerings by the glass, almost 40 half-bottles and numerous large-format bottles. You may have to cash in a certificate of deposit to afford dinner, but the food, wine and ambiance are worth it. If you arrive without a reservation, snag a seat at the counter that runs alongside the sleek stainless-steel display kitchen.

VIENG THAI

6929 LONG POINT
between Silber and Antoine
713-688-9910
MAP D5

The Spring Branch strip-center location is drab, but the kitchen dishes up fantastic Thai food, rivaling some of our favorites, including Nidda Thai and Kanomwan. Order anything and, not to be trite, you won't go wrong, from *tom ka gai* (coconut milk soup) to the beef *panang* curry to *pad sar-tor*, which is shrimp sautéed in chili paste with *sar-tor* (also called "stink beans"). Try the *som tam*, a green papaya salad that includes chiles, palm sugar and tiny dried shrimp. Unlike most local Thai restaurants, Vieng Thai doesn't water down its true cuisine for American palates — the proof is its reputation for funky Thai sausages. Still, we can't have our cake and eat it, too (shucks!). Service is flat, and the atmosphere is bland. This is not a "romantic evening" restaurant but a place to go for darn good food.

VIETOPIA

The restaurant is an Asian utopia for many West U denizens who come here for the lush, yet charming, setting, kind staff and reliable entrees. The food has been called "soft-around-the-edges" Vietnamese

5176 BUFFALO SPEEDWAY at Westpark
713-664-7303
www.4anyorder.com/vietopia
MAP E7

cuisine, and the menu does occasionally veer into other food styles — French, Italian, Chinese — with things like risotto and crab fingers. Let's just say Vietopia's food is creatively true to its culture. If you want to avoid the pricey seafood and specialty items at dinner, stop in for lunch specials.

VINCENT'S

2817 W. DALLAS
between Montrose and Waugh
713-528-4313
www.ninosvincents.com
MAP E6

The best roasted chicken (seasoned with lemon and garlic and pure *amore*) and some of the top mashed potatoes in Texas at an Italian restaurant? Yep. And that's only the beginning at this younger brother to Nino's. After more than two decades of treating Houston, Vincent Mandola's menu has long since moved beyond pizzas and pastas (yet, these dishes are lovely here, too) and today leans on what can only be called home-cooking in any language. The Veal Vincent speaks for itself, and a starter of carpaccio will seduce. The service is always dependable, and the surroundings are comfortable. Enjoy a glass of *vino* in the courtyard that Vincent's and Nino's share — evidence that a little sibling rivalry doesn't beat brotherly love.

VOICE

220 MAIN at Prairie, in the Hotel Icon
713-224-4266
www.hotelicon.com
MAP F6

Let's begin with the name of this newcomer, which opened in April 2008. Management explains it is meant to give a "voice" to the Houston idiom and play up Houston's culinary traditions, including South Texas, Gulf Coast and neighborhood farmers' markets. The dining room itself is breathtaking. You probably won't recognize the space that once was Bank. It's been overhauled and given a contemporary edge, including an octagonal walnut bar with cowhide-backed barstools. (The heavy velvet decor was so-o-o 2004.) And the food? Executive chef Michael Kramer works in all the hot-button foods and cooking methods. We loved the lobster slider (and feel like a scrooge pointing out the lobster is not really a part of the Gulf Coast idiom), the *sous-vide*-cooked venison, a gorgeous piece of striped bass on parsnip purée and a shot glass of seasonal butternut-squash "cappuccino" with curry foam. The desserts, which will tickle your imagination, are by pastry chef Charles Allen. The drink menu will touch you as well. This is one of downtown's most remarkable restaurants.

Many of Voice's dishes look as elegant as they taste.

WAZA SUSHI & ROBATA GRILL

6927 FM 1960 WEST
just east of Cutten
281-580-8858
MAP C2

Waza has become a haven for Northside foodies and a sushi ambassador to those who said they'd never eat raw fish. It gracefully weds fantastically fresh sushi and innovative rolls (try the shaggy dog — avocado, shrimp tempura, eel sauce, spicy mayonnaise, all topped with crab) to kitchen-prepared foods, like a Hot Rock Kobe Beef and robatas (chargrilled skewers). Local diners say the service is spot-on, even when the restaurant is packed. The dramatic interior is modern and sleek, but surprisingly relaxed, with the soft murmur of waterfalls along the walls. The Zen wanes on weekend nights when the hum of young hipsters streams through Waza, making a seat and, sometimes, your sanity hard to find. If noise bothers you, got at non-peak times, if they exist any more.

WILLIE G'S

1605 POST OAK BLVD.
north of San Felipe
713-840-7190
www.williegs.com
MAP D6

Rebuilt even better than before after a fire a few years ago, this local seafood house is all Houston, with more than three decades in the Galleria area. Seated in the upscale ocean liner-like dining room, you'll find the menu to be fairly typical of higher-end fish joints. But the fish is fresh and a perk is a dozen types from which to choose. Top your choice with a special sauce (e.g. étouffée, avocado lump crab, Creole, Pontchartrain or Opelousas) for $6.50 more. A favorite is the blackened snapper Pontchartrain. Other dishes include shrimp remoulade, crabcakes, Cobb salad, iceberg wedge with blue cheese and soft-shell crabs. The service is solicitous, there's a decent wine list and the energy is high, as are the prices. Willie G's is a good safety call for seafood, but in the restaurant-dense area of The Galleria, it has some stout competition.

WUNSCHE BROS. CAFE

103 MIDWAY at W. Hardy, Spring
281-350-1902
www.wunschebroscafe.com
MAP E1

The oldest building in Spring, a wood-frame 1902 tavern, was given new life several years ago when Brenda and Scott Mitchell first transformed it into a burger joint. (They subsequently sold the restaurant to co-owner Sherry Sinisi.) This is a honky-tonk that offers musical entertainment in the evenings, but also serves excellent fried foods — try the sausage crumb salad served with homemade beer bread — and some healthful items, too, such as grilled chicken salad. At least once you should sample the sausage sauerkraut balls, a Wunsche Bros. original that the menu describes as "hot gooey combo sauerkraut, sausage and cheese, golden deep fried." The Wunsche burger, a half-pounder with all the fixin's, is probably what keeps this place in business. Wunsche Bros. is just as famous for its chocolate whiskey cake. This is the perfect place to stop after a few hours shopping the surrounding Old Town Spring shops (antiques, Christmas decorations, clothing boutiques, toys and such). Expect a wait, especially at lunch on the weekends, and plan your appetite accordingly. Live entertainment in the evenings; check the website for music schedule.

YAO RESTAURANT & BAR

9755 WESTHEIMER at Gessner
832-251-2588
www.yaorestaurant.com
MAP C7

It seems owning a restaurant raises your celebrity status, and the man-giant round-baller Yao Ming is there. Not that the 7-foot-6-inch Houston Rockets player needs it. Ming opened this sports bar-cum-Chinese restaurant along with his parents, Yao Zhiyuan and Fang Fengdi, near the Westchase Churrascos. The tables and chairs are oversized (one must make room for NBA pals), and plenty of big screens feed nonstop sports action. The menu, designed by George Phou, who founded Fu's Garden restaurants, is unoriginal at best, with specialties ranging from Mongolian beef to Szechuan shrimp. Even the Yao flavored shrimp is nothing but lightly battered and fried shrimp with a brown sauce. Yet, diners find the food consistently good and the service gracious. Yao has to be doing something right. He's opening another eponymous restaurant downtown, reportedly by the end of 2008, although an employee told us that construction is behind schedule.

YATRA BRASSERIE

This trendy Indian restaurant — we wouldn't really call it a brasserie — belies the notion that downtown eateries live or die by lunch alone. Yatra's space spills into the Butterfly High cocktail lounge next door and Bar Bollywood nightclub in the basement, creating a Bermuda triangle of food and drink that the owners (who also have a place in London) hope will keep you there the whole evening. Since replacing Laidback Manor in this location in 2006, Yatra has served up traditional

706 MAIN at Capitol
713-224-6700
www.yatrabrasserie.com
MAP F6

Brit-Indian favorites such as tandoori shrimp and lamp chops, chicken tikka masala and Goan shrimp curry. The chefs send out healthful low-carb alternatives and several vegetarian choices as well. The kitchen has also experimented with a sort of Indian-Texan fusion of dishes, such as "Los Burritos," which have various fillings (e.g. *seekh kebab*, chicken *kadai*) wrapped in flatbread and served with chutney. If you just want a light bite with drinks, there are several appetizers of note, including chile chicken wings and *keema* (ground lamb) empanadas.

Yatra's menu has something for Indian cuisine connoisseurs and "newbies" alike.

YILDIZLAR

3419 KIRBY at Richmond
713-524-7735
MAP E7

In a city rich with ethnic restaurants of every style, this small rundown counter-service spot holds its own, dealing in kabobs, falafel, gyros, babaganoush, hummus and such. The real star at Yildizlar is the chicken shawarma sandwich. If you can't commit, order the combination plate with bites of 10 different foods. Have a unique experience and sip some of the rose water, but expect a mild perfume taste that lasts for hours. If you hanker for something a little sweeter, try a pastry. Advice: Get your order to go. This place is grim, and the food in the glass-fronted displays sometimes actually seems to be moldering before your eyes. Plus, with the constant din from a TV in the corner, you may as well be dining at a frat house.

YUM YUM CHA

Welcome to a different dim sum experience. Flipbooks with color photos of the tiny offerings replace the traditional dim sum parlor's pushcarts. The advantage is that you order what you like and don't have to wait for a cart to wend its way through the crowd and find you. (On the other hand, service is very slow here, so don't plan to order in stages. Your subsequent orders will go to the end of the line.) This is technically the only Inner Loop restaurant that specializes

2435 TIMES between Morningside and Kelvin
713-527-8455
MAP E7

in dim sum, and the food doesn't disappoint. Is it the best dim sum in the city? No. But it's good, and many West U neighbors visit weekly to indulge in the 50-plus regular menu items and additional daily chalkboard specials. Favorites include shrimp-and-chive dumplings, turnip cake, steamed buns, sticky rice with sweet sausage and chicken, and the various potstickers. Show-off eaters will find more esoteric choices, too, including chicken feet and beef stomach with black bean sauce. Really, it's hard to go wrong. And did we mention it's BYOB at dinner (except Sunday)? Note: The tiny restaurant's AC can't keep up, so avoid weekend afternoons in the summer, when the place is jammed and everyone is sweaty.

ZABAK'S

5901 WESTHEIMER
at Fountain View
713-977-7676
MAP C7

We asked co-owner Peter Zabak (he runs Zabak's with sister Sandra and brother Donald) what the heck was in the falafel that makes it so good. Garbanzo beans, jalapeños, onions and a blend of spices — but he didn't specify what spices — are ground together, formed into flattened patties, deep fried and served warm inside a pita or alone with sides. Wow! Whatever they're doing, the result is addictive. This is some of the best falafel we've had in Houston. The Zabak siblings opened their minimalist little cafe in 2006, following in the footsteps of their parents, an Israeli couple who operated Mama's Po'boy on Hillcroft for 26 years, Peter said. Already, Zabak's has garnered a couple "best of" awards in the local media. The Greek chicken salad is another favorite, alongside tabouli, chicken Caesar pita sandwich and Mediterranean pizza. Diners (including us) always remark on the hospitality here. Sandra has been known to greet customers at the door, give a quick tour and tell the family's restaurant history. The siblings make it a point to remember first names. It may become difficult as their falafel's reputation spreads and the number of falafel addicts grows.

ZAKE SUSHI LOUNGE

Zake might just offer the best happy-hour specials when it comes to the South Shepherd stretch, mainly because sushi is on the happy-hour menu, too (weekdays only, last call is at 7 p.m.). People race here after work to score cheap deals on

2946 S. SHEPHERD
at W. Alabama
713-526-6888
www.zakerestaurant.com
MAP E7

Sapporo, Kirin, vodka tonics, spicy tuna rolls and novelty rolls. For the friend who doesn't like sushi, have no fear: Zake offers a well-rounded menu of cooked items too. Sushi newbies should try the Chicken

Crunch roll — crispy fried chicken and tuna, so it really does "taste like chicken." Be prepared for a younger crowd. The bar fills up with singles out on the prowl, and this is the first stop of the night for many 20- and 30-somethings who are living large. Around 9 p.m. the music gets louder, and so does the crowd. As a DJ spins and the lights are lowered, mixing-and-mingling becomes a competitive sport.

ZIGGY'S HEALTHY GRILL

2202 W. ALABAMA at Greenbriar
713-527-8588
www.ziggyshealthygrill.com
MAP E7

302 FAIRVIEW at Taft
832-519-0476
MAP E6

Don't let the name lull you — or put you off — there's plenty on the menu here that's not particularly healthful, including three kinds of French fries (sweet potato fries, we love you), Ziggyritas and shortbread cookies with a spicy zest. But the use of "healthy" does make us feel better about ourselves, and in fact, Ziggy's allows you to indulge without busting the calorie counter. Opt for the buffalo or ostrich burger, vegetable lasagne or spicy garlic turkey pizza with low-fat mozzarella on focaccia crust. The hummus is good, and it comes with baked whole-wheat chips. We are also fond of the Tex-Mex dishes, such quesadillas and enchiladas. Breakfast offers choices for both the healthful and the indulgent, and there are happy-hour specials every day 3 to 6 p.m. (A Ziggy snack comes free with any drink from the bar.) Free WiFi and doggy biscuits for your furry friend. Woof it down!

ZYDECO LOUISIANA DINER

Taking a cue from Treebeards, this Louisiana-accented cafeteria dishes up all the down-home favorites, including fried oyster po'boys, meat-and-three steam-table specials (e.g. stuffed pork chops, jambalaya, chicken fricassee, chicken and sausage Creole),

1119 PEASE at San Jacinto
713-759-2001
www.zydecodiner.net
MAP F6

gumbo, and oysters and shrimp every which way. The ramshackle setting seems to season the food, which doesn't need much of a touch-up because it's usually served just right, ya'll. The crawfish étouffée is one of the city's best versions (tender tails, spicy gravy), and the smothered pork chops and fried chicken aren't too shabby either. The sides cannot be upstaged by the main dishes because they stand alone: moist cornbread, smoky black-eyed peas, *maque choux* (Cajun-style smothered corn), stewed okra and garlic-mashed potatoes that you hope will never end.

indexes

INDEX BY CUISINE TYPE

- American (New)
- American (Traditional)
- Argentinean
- Asian/Eclectic
- Barbecue
- Belgian
- Bosnian
- Brazilian
- British/Irish
- Burgers
- Cajun/Creole
- Chinese
- Continental
- Cuban
- Deli
- Diner
- Eclectic
- Ethiopian
- French
- German
- Greek
- Guatemalan
- Health Food
- Indian
- Indonesian
- Italian
- Jamaican
- Japanese
- Jewish
- Korean
- Latin American
- Lebanese
- Mexican
- Middle Eastern
- Moroccan
- Pakistani
- Persian
- Pizza
- Polish
- Puerto Rican
- Salvadoran
- Sandwich Shop
- Seafood
- Southern/Soul Food
- Southwestern
- Spanish
- Steakhouse
- Swiss
- Tex-Mex
- Thai
- Turkish
- Vietnamese

INDEX BY BUSINESS TYPE

- Bakery
- Brewery
- Butcher
- Chocolate & Candy
- Coffeehouse
- Dessert
- Dive
- Ethnic Market
- Farmers' Market
- Fishmonger
- Gelato/Ice Cream
- Grocery Store
- Hotel Bar
- Neighborhood Bar
- Pub
- Restaurant Bar
- Retail Wine & Spirits
- Specialty Market
- Sports Bar
- Teahouse
- Upscale Bar
- Wine Bar
- Winery

INDEX BY SPECIAL FEATURES

- Bistro
- Breakfast
- Dramatic Interior
- Great Service
- Hotel Dining
- Ladies Who Lunch
- Outdoor Dining
- Romantic Setting
- Veggie-Friendly
- View
- Wild Game
- Wine List of Note

ALPHABETICAL INDEX

INDEX BY CUISINE TYPE

Many establishments do not fit neatly into a single category. You'll find some restaurants and shops are listed in two or even three spots.

AMERICAN (NEW)
*17
Artista
Backstreet Cafe
Benjy's
Bistro Lancaster
Black Walnut Cafe
Cafe Extraordinaire
Cava Bistro
Cullen's Upscale American
Daily Review Cafe
Farrago
Glass Wall
Gravitas
Jabour's Fine Dining
Laurier Cafe
Mark's American Cuisine
Masraff's
Mockingbird Bistro
Monarch
Olivette
Polo's Signature
Post Oak Grill
Rainbow Lodge
Shade
T'afia
Tony's
Voice

AMERICAN (TRADITIONAL)
Ashland House
Barbecue Inn
Barnaby's Cafe
Beaver's Ice House
The Buffalo Grille
Cleburne Cafeteria
Dosey Doe Coffee
Empire Cafe
Gilhooley's
Hard Rock Cafe
James Coney Island
Jasper's
Jax Grill
King Biscuit Patio Cafe
Lankford Grocery & Market
Lexington Grille
Monument Inn
Raven Grill
The Remington

Ruggles Grill
Vargo's

ARGENTINEAN
Marini's Empanada House

ASIAN/ECLECTIC
Bamboo House
Cafe 101
Lemongrass Cafe
Mak Chin's
Pang Tai's Stir Fry Bistro
Rattan Pan-Asian Bistro

BARBECUE
Goode Co. Texas Bar-B-Que
Luling City Market
Lyndon's Pit Bar-B-Q
Otto's Barbecue & Hamburgers
Pappas Bar-B-Q
Pizzitola's Bar-B-Cue
Thelma's Bar-B-Que

BELGIAN
Cafe Montrose

BOSNIAN
Cafe Pita+

BRAZILIAN
Fogo De Chao
Fuegovivo Churrascaria
Nelore Churrascaria

BRITISH/IRISH
Black Labrador Pub
Bull & Bear Tavern & Eatery
Brian O'Neill's Irish Pub & Restaurant
Feast
Kenneally's Irish Pub
McGonigel's Mucky Duck
Red Lion Pub

BURGERS
Becks Prime
Christian's Tailgate Bar & Grill

Dry Creek Cafe
Goode Co. Taqueria & Hamburgers
Hard Rock Cafe
The Lake House Waterside Cafe
Lankford Grocery & Market
Pete's Fine Meats
Someburger
Tookie's
Wunsche Bros. Cafe & Saloon

CAJUN/CREOLE
BB's
Brennan's of Houston
Danton's Gulf Coast Seafood Kitchen
Jimmy G's Cajun Seafood Restaurant
Jimmy Wilson's Seafood & Chop House
Magnolia Bar & Grill
Pappadeaux Seafood Kitchen
Ragin Cajun
Tony Mandola's Gulf Coast Kitchen
Treebeards
Willie G's
Zydeco

CHINESE
Cafe Le Jadeite
China View
Fung's Kitchen Seafood Restaurant
Gigi's Asian Bistro & Dumpling Bar
Kam's Fine Chinese Cuisine
North China
Ocean Palace
Qin Dynasty
Sichuan Cuisine
Yao Restaurant & Bar
Yum Yum Cha

CONTINENTAL
The Brownstone
Charivari

La Colombe d'Or
Lexington Grille
Masraff's
Sage
Tony's
Vargo's

CUBAN
Cafe Piquet
El Meson
Latina Cafe

DELI
Brown Bag Deli
Kahn's Delicatessen
Kenny & Ziggy's
Nielsen's Delicatessen

DINER
59 Diner
Avalon Drug Co. & Diner
Fountain View Cafe
Harry's
House of Pies
Little Hip's Diner
Mama's Cafe
Pappy's Cafe
Triple-A Restaurant

ECLECTIC
Alamo Drafthouse
Aquarium Restaurant
Baba Yega
Be-Wiched Bistro
Cafe Benedicte
Cafe Express
Cafe Extraordinaire
Charivari
Courses
Cullen's Upscale American
Dharma Cafe
Eric's Restaurant
Feast
Gilhooley's
Goode's Armadillo Palace
Grand Lux Cafe
Hard Rock Cafe
Hollywood Vietnamese & Chinese
Hungry's Cafe and Bistro
La Vista
Max's Wine Dive
Open City Bistro
Paulie's
Quattro

The Remington
Ristorante Cavour
Sage
Skyline Bar & Grill
So'Vino Bistro & Wine Bar
T'afia
Tiny Boxwood's Espresso Bar and Cafe

ETHIOPIAN
Addisaba

FRENCH
Au Petit Paris
Aura
Bistro Calais
Bistro Don Camillo
Bistro Le Cep
Bistro Provence
Brassiere Max & Julie
Cafe Rabelais
Chez Nous
La Colombe d'Or
La Madeleine
Le Mistral
Rouge

GERMAN
Charivari
Rudi Lechner's

GREEK
Alexander the Great Greek
Niko Niko's
Stelio's

GUATEMALAN
El Pueblito Place

HEALTH FOOD
A Moveable Feast
Field of Greens
Hobbit Cafe
Sandy's Produce Market
Whole Foods Market
Ziggy's Healthy Grill

INDIAN
Bombay Brasserie
Indika
Khyber North Indian Grill
Kiran's
London Sizzler
Madras Pavilion
Yatra Brasserie

INDONESIAN
Noodle House 88

ITALIAN
Amerigo's Grille
Amici
Andrea Ristorante Italiano
Antica Osteria
Arcodoro Ristorante Italiano
Arturo's Uptown Italiano
Bice
Brio Tuscan Grill
Carmelo's
Carrabba's Italian Grill
Ciro's Italian Grill
Collina's Italian Cafe
Corelli's
Crapitto's
Da Marco
Damian's Cucina Italiana
D'Amico's Italian Market Cafe
Divino
Frenchie's
Grappino di Nino
Grotto
Josephine's
La Griglia
La Strada
La Trattoria
La Vista
Mezzanotte
Mia Bella
Mingalone Italian Bar & Grill
Nino's
Palazzo's Trattoria
Patrenella's/Corleone's
Perbacco
Piatto
Prego
Pronto Cucinino
Simposio
Sorrento
Trevísio
Vincent's

JAMAICAN
Reggae Hut

JAPANESE
Azuma/Azumi
Blue Fish House
Japaneiro's Sushi Bistro & Latin Grill

Kaneyama
Kenzo Sushi Bistro
Kobe
Kubo's Sushi Bar and Grill
Miyako
Nippon
RA Sushi
Rickshaw Far East Bistro
Soma
Sushi Jin
Sushi King
Uptown Sushi
Waza Sushi & Robata Grill
Zake Sushi Lounge

JEWISH
Kenny & Ziggy's
New York Bagel & Coffee Shop
Three Brothers Bakery

KOREAN
Nam Gang
Super H Mart

LATIN AMERICAN
Amazon Grill
Américas
Artista
Churrascos
Inka
Japaneiro's Sushi Bistro & Latin Grill
Julia's Bistro

LEBANESE
Cafe Lili

MEXICAN
100% Taquito
Armandos
Doña Tere Tamales
El Rey Taqueria
Gorditas Aguascalientes
Hugo's
La Guadalupana Bakery & Cafe
La Tapatia Taqueria
Maria Selma
Merida
Otilia's
Pico's Mex-Mex
Rustika Cafe and Bakery
Spanish Flowers
Teala's
Teotihuacan

Tila's Restaurante & Bar

MIDDLE EASTERN
Aladdin
Fadi's Mediterranean Grill
Mint Cafe
Phoenicia Deli
Yildizlar
Zabak's

MOROCCAN
Saffron

PAKISTANI
Himalaya

PERSIAN
Darband Shishkabob
Kasra Persian Grill

PIZZA
Candelari's Pizzeria
Dolce Vita Pizzeria Enoteca
Late Night Pie
Romano's Flying Pizza
Star Pizza

POLISH
Polonia

PUERTO RICAN
Isla Coqui
Tex Chick

SALVADORAN
El Pupusodromo

SANDWICH SHOP
Carter & Cooley
Cricket's Creamery & Caffe
Dessert Gallery
Epicure Bakery
French Gourmet Bakery
French Riviera Bakery & Cafe
Kraftsmen Baking
Panera Bread Bakery Cafe
Picnic
Ruggles Cafe Bakery
Shawarma King

SEAFOOD
Aquarium Restaurant
Captain Benny's Half Shell Oyster Bar
Crawfish & Beignets

Danton's Gulf Coast Seafood Kitchen
Denis' Seafood House
Goode Co. Texas Seafood
Jimmy G's Cajun Seafood
Jimmy Wilson's
Joyce's Seafood & Steaks
Massa's
McCormick & Schmick's
Oceanaire Seafood Room
Pappadeaux Seafood Kitchen
Pappas Seafood House
Pesce
PK's Blue Water Grill
Reef
Tony Mandola's Gulf Coast Kitchen
Truluck's
Willie G's

SOUTHERN/SOUL FOOD
Barbecue Inn
Beaver's Ice House
Breakfast Klub
Frenchy's Chicken
Ouisie's Table
This Is It!

SOUTHWESTERN
The Burning Pear
Cafe Annie
The Grove
Rio Ranch
Ruggles Grill

SPANISH
Catalan Food and Wine
Ibiza
Mi Luna
Rioja
Tio Pepe

STEAKHOUSE
Brenner's
Capital Grille
Del Frisco's
Fleming's Prime Steakhouse
Frank's Chop House
Killen's Steakhouse
Kirby's Prime Steakhouse
Lynn's Steakhouse
Morton's of Chicago
The Palm
Pappas Bros. Steakhouse
Perry's Steakhouse & Grille

Ruth's Chris Steakhouse
Smith & Wollensky
Spencer's for Steaks & Chops
Strip House
Sullivan's Steakhouse
Taste of Texas
Tommy's Seafood Steakhouse
Vic & Anthony's

SWISS
Thierry Andre Tellier Cafe & Pastry Shop

TEX-MEX
Berryhill Baja Grill
Cadillac Bar
Cantina Laredo
Chuy's Comida Deluxe
Doneraki
El Tiempo
Escalante's
Gringo's Mexican Kitchen
Guadalajara Bar and Grill
Irma's
La Mexicana
Last Concert Cafe
Lupe Tortilla's
Mission Burritos

Ninfa's
Pappasito's Cantina
Spanish Village
Sylvia's Enchilada Kitchen
Taco Milagro
Tacos a Go-Go

THAI
Kanomwan
Khun Kay Thai-American Cafe
Nidda Thai
Nit Noi Thai
Patu
Red Basil
Sawadee
Thai Pepper
Thai Spice
Thai Sticks
Vieng Thai

TURKISH
Empire Turkish Grill
Istanbul Grill
Pasha

VIETNAMESE
Kim Son
Les Givral's Kahve

Cafe Adobe is famous for its slushy Meltdown Margarita.

Mai's Restaurant
Mo Mong
Nam
Pho Danh
Saigon Pagolac
Van Loc
Vietopia

INDEX BY BUSINESS TYPE

The following establishments are not restaurants in the strict sense of the word. However, many of them do serve meals.

BAKERY
The Acadian Bakers
Arandas Bakery
Croissant Brioche
Dacapo's Pastry Cafe
Droubi's Bakery & Deli
Epicure Bakery
French Gourmet Bakery
French Riviera Bakery & Cafe
Kolache Factory
La Guadalupana Bakery & Cafe
La Madeleine
La Victoria Bakery
Le Petit Paris Bakery
Panera Bread Bakery Cafe
Pie in the Sky
Rao's Bakery
Ruggles Cafe Bakery

Rustika Cafe and Bakery
Stone Mill Bakers
Thierry Andre Tellier Cafe & Pastry Shop
Three Brothers Bakery

BREWERY
Saint Arnold Brewing Company

BUTCHER
El Tiempo Market
Hebert's Specialty Meats
Jerusalem Halal Meat Market
La Boucherie
La Michoacana Meat Market
Omaha Steaks, Inc.
Pete's Fine Meats

CHOCOLATE & CANDY
Candylicious
Chocolat du Monde
Chocolata Cocoa Bar
The Chocolate Bar
Kegg's Candies
Raindrop Chocolate

COFFEEHOUSE
Antidote Coffee
Brasil
Catalina Coffee
The Coffee Groundz
The Daily Grind
Dosey Doe Coffee
Empire Cafe
Inversion Coffee House
Java Java
Mojo Risin'

Notsuoh
Stir-It-Up Coffeehouse
Waldo's Coffee House

DESSERT
Acadian Bakers
Chocolat du Monde
Chocolata Cocoa Bar
The Chocolate Bar
The Cookie Jar Bakery
Cupcake Cafe
Dacapo's Pastry Cafe
Dessert Gallery
Edible Arrangements
Epicure Bakery
House of Pies
Juice Box
Kolache Factory
La Madeleine
La Victoria Bakery
Ooh La La
Pie in the Sky
Sugarbaby's
Thierry Andre Tellier Cafe & Pastry Shop
Who Made the Cake?

DIVE
Cecil's Tavern
Griff's Shenanigans Cafe & Bar
Kay's Lounge
Roll-N Saloon
Under the Volcano
West Alabama Ice House

ETHNIC MARKET
Asia Market & Convenience
Balkan Market
Droubi's Bakery & Deli
El Tiempo Market
Fiesta Mart
Golden Foods Supermarket
Hong Kong Food Market
India Grocers
Jerusalem Halal Meat Market
La Michoacana Meat Market
Mi Tienda
Nippon Daido
Nundini Food Market
Phoenicia Specialty Foods
Russian General Store
Super H Mart
Super Jordan Imported Food & Bakery
Super Vanak International

FARMERS' MARKET
See sidebars on pages 28 and 43
Airline Farmers Market
Canino Produce Market
Farmers Marketing Association

FISHMONGER
Airline Seafood Mart
Connie's Seafood Market
Crawfish & Beignets
Louisiana Foods

GELATO/ICE CREAM
Amy's Ice Cream
Chocolata Cocoa Bar
The Chocolate Bar
Gelato Blu
Hank's Ice Cream Parlor
La Palatera
Moo Hive Honey Ice Cream
Nundini Food Market
Sorbetto's

GROCERY STORE
Belden's
Central Market
Fiesta Mart
Golden Foods Supermarket
Hong Kong Food Market
Kroger Signature
Mi Tienda
Rice Epicurean Market
Super H Mart
Whole Foods Market

HOTEL BAR
Bistro Bar – Lancaster Hotel
Four Seasons Hotel Lobby Bar
Hilton Americas – Lobby Bar
The Houstonian – The Bar
Inn at the Ballpark – Atrium Bar & Lounge
La Colombe d'Or – The Bar
The Magnolia Bar
The Remington Bar
Rio Ranch Bar

NEIGHBORHOOD BAR
Absinthe Brasserie
Avant Garden
Blanco's Bar & Grill
The Boom Boom Room
Byzantio Cafe & Bar
Christian's Tailgate Bar & Grill
Deco
The Flat
Front Porch Pub
The Ginger Man
Hans' Village Bier and Vino Haus
The Harp
The Hideaway
Kelvin Arms
La Carafe
Lola's
Mugsy's
Notsuoh
The Social Lounge & Patio Bar
T.K. Bitterman's
Warren's Inn

PUB
Baker Street Pub & Grill
Black Labrador Pub
Black Swan Pub
Brewery Tap
Brian O'Neill's Irish Pub & Restaurant
The Bull and Bear Tavern and Eatery
Downing Street Pub
Firkin & Phoenix
Front Porch Pub
Griff's Shenanigans Cafe & Bar
Kenneally's Irish Pub
McElroy's Irish Pub
McGonigel's Mucky Duck
Red Lion Pub
Richmond Arms
Rudyard's British Pub
Shay McElroy's Irish Pub
The Stag's Head Pub

RESTAURANT BAR
Bar Annie
Capital Grille Bar
Cézanne
Grappino di Nino
The Lounge at Benjy's

RETAIL WINE & SPIRITS
Christopher's Wine Warehouse
D'Vine Wine of Texas

Houston Wine Merchant
Leibman's Wine & Fine Foods
Richard's Liquors & Fine Wines
Salud! Winery
Sonoma Retail Wine Bar & Boutique
Spec's Wines, Spirits & Finer Foods
The Tasting Room
Taverna Winery & Restaurant
Vine Wine Room
Vineyard on the Square
Vino 100
The Wine Bucket Boutique & Bar

SPECIALTY MARKET
Fredlyn Nut Company
Hebert's Specialty Meats
House of Coffee Beans
Houston Pecan Company
Kho Bo
La Boucherie
Leibman's Wine & Fine Foods
McCain's Market
Nippon Daido
Penzey's Spices
Sandy's Produce Market
Spec's Wines, Spirits & Finer Foods

SPORTS BAR
Fox Sports Grill
Live Sports Cafe

TEAHOUSE
The Path of Tea
Té House of Tea

UPSCALE BAR
Belvedere
The Cotton Exchange Bar & Lounge
Marfreless
Mosaic
Sambuca
Scott Gertner's Sky Bar
The Tree House
Zimm's Martini & Wine Bar

WINE BAR
13 Celsius
Cork Cafe
The Corkscrew
Cova
D'Vine Wine of Texas
Oporto Cafe
Salud! Winery
Sonoma Retail Wine Bar & Boutique
The Tasting Room
Taverna Winery & Restaurant
Vine Wine Room
Vineyard on the Square
Vino 100
The Wine Bucket Boutique & Bar
Zimm's Martini & Wine Bar

WINERY
Haak Vineyards and Winery

INDEX BY SPECIAL FEATURES

These lists of special features are not exhaustive. Rather, we've spotlighted the restaurants and cafes we think do the *best* job in each category.

BISTRO
Backstreet Cafe
Be-Wiched Bistro
Bistro Calais
Bistro Don Camillo
Bistro Lancaster
Bistro Le Cep
Bistro Provence
Cafe Montrose
Cafe Rabelais
Cava Bistro
Gravitas
Julia's Bistro
Laurier Cafe
Le Mistral
Mockingbird Bistro
Raven Grill

BREAKFAST
in addition to bakeries, etc.
59 Diner
Avalon Drug Co. & Diner
Barnaby's Cafe
Black Walnut Cafe
Brasil
Breakfast Klub
The Buffalo Grille
El Pupusodromo
El Rey Taqueria
Empire Cafe
Fountain View Cafe
Goode Co. Taqueria & Hamburgers
Gorditas Aguascalientes
Irma's
Java Java
Katz's Deli
Kenny & Ziggy's
Kraftsmen Baking
La Madeleine
La Mexicana
Lankford Grocery & Market
Mama's Cafe
Maria Selma
New York Bagel & Coffee Shop
Pico's Mex-Mex
Triple-A Restaurant

DRAMATIC INTERIOR
*17
Américas
Aquarium Restaurant
Arcodoro Ristorante Italiano
Armandos
Artista
Bice
Brennan's of Houston
Brenner's (Birdsall location)
Brio Tuscan Grill
The Brownstone
Cafe Annie
Cafe Le Jadeite
Capital Grille
Catalan Food and Wine
Da Marco
Fleming's Prime Steakhouse
Gigi's Asian Bistro & Dumpling Bar
Glass Wall
Goode's Armadillo Palace

Grand Lux Cafe
Gravitas
The Grove
Hugo's
Jasper's
La Colombe d'Or
Mark's American Cuisine
Masraff's
Oceanaire Seafood Room
Ouisie's Table
Pappas Bros. Steakhouse
Perry's Steakhouse & Grille
Pesce
Quattro
RA Sushi
Rainbow Lodge
The Remington
Shade
Skyline Bar & Grill
Smith & Wollensky
Soma
Strip House
Sullivan's Steakhouse
Tony's
Trevísio
Truluck's
Uptown Sushi
Vic & Anthony's
Voice

GREAT SERVICE
*17
Américas
Amerigo's Grille
Backstreet Cafe
Bistro Provence
Brenner's
Brennan's
Cafe Annie
Capital Grille
Chez Nous
Churrascos
Da Marco
Del Frisco's Double Eagle Steakhouse
Fleming's Prime Steakhouse
Glass Wall
Kiran's
Laurier Cafe
Lynn's Steakhouse
Mark's American Cuisine
Masraff's
Mockingbird Bistro
Morton's of Chicago
Oceanaire Seafood Room
The Palm
Pappas Bros. Steakhouse
Perry's Steakhouse & Grille
Pesce
Prego
Quattro
Rainbow Lodge
Reef
The Remington
Ruth's Chris Steakhouse
Shade
Strip House
Sullivan's Steakhouse
Taste of Texas
Tony's
Truluck's
Vic & Anthony's

HOTEL DINING
*17 (Alden Hotel)
Bistro Lancaster (Lancaster Hotel)
Burning Pear (Sugar Land Marriott)
La Colombe d'Or (La Colombe d'Or)
Monarch (Hotel ZaZa)
Noé (Omni Houston Hotel)
Quattro (The Four Seasons Hotel)
The Remington (St. Regis)
Rio Ranch (Westchase Hilton)
Skyline Bar & Grill (Hilton Americas)
Spencer's for Steaks & Chops (Hilton Americas)
Voice (Hotel Icon)

LADIES WHO LUNCH
*17
Amici
Aura
Backstreet Cafe
Benjy's
Be-Wiched Bistro
Brennan's of Houston
Cafe Express
Cafe Extraordinaire
Grotto
La Griglia
Laurier Cafe
Masraff's
Mockingbird Bistro
Monarch
Ouisie's Table
Paulie's
Raven Grill
Ristorante Cavour
Ruggles Grill
Shade
Tiny Boxwood's Espresso Bar and Cafe
Tony's

OUTDOOR DINING
Our favorite patios
Amazon Grill
Américas
Arcodoro Ristorante Italiano
Artista
Arturo's Uptown Italiano
Baba Yega
Backstreet Cafe
Becks Prime
Black Labrador
Brasil
Brennan's of Houston
Cafe Express
Chuy's Comida Deluxe
Crapitto's
Daily Review Cafe
D'Amico's Italian Market Cafe
El Pueblito Place
El Tiempo
Empire Cafe
Farrago
Feast
Grappino di Nino
Grotto
The Grove
Hugo's
Ibiza
Indika
Jasper's
Jax Grill
Kraftsmen Baking
La Griglia
La Madeleine
La Mexicana
Maria Selma
Marini's Empanada House
Mingalone Italian Bar & Grill
Mission Burritos
Monarch
Niko Niko's
Ninfa's (Navigation location)
Open City Bistro
Otilia's

Ouisie's Table
Palazzo's Trattoria
Pico's Mex-Mex
Pronto Cucinino
Raven Grill
Red Lion Pub
Sage
Sambuca
Spanish Flowers
Taco Milagro
Teala's
Tila's Restaurante & Bar

ROMANTIC SETTING
*17
Antica Osteria
Artista
Brennan's of Houston
Brenner's (Birdsall location)
Cafe Annie
Cafe Le Jadeite
Churrascos
Da Marco
La Colombe d'Or
Mark's American Cuisine
Rainbow Lodge
Tony's
Vic & Anthony's

VEGGIE-FRIENDLY
A Moveable Feast
Aladdin
Baba Yega
Backstreet Cafe
Benjy's
Daily Review Cafe
Dharma Cafe
Fadi's Mediterranean Grill
Field of Greens
Hobbit Cafe
Indika
London Sizzler
Madras Pavilion
Mission Burritos
Mockingbird Bistro
Ouisie's Table
Ruggles Grill
Sandy's Produce Market
T'afia
Zabak's
Ziggy's Healthy Grill

VIEW
Dramatic vistas
Américas (The Woodlands)
Artista

Brenner's (Birdsall location)
Del Frisco's Double Eagle
   Steakhouse
The Grove
Monarch
Open City Bistro
Rainbow Lodge
Skyline Bar & Grill
Trevísio
Vargo's

WILD GAME
in season
*17
Amerigo's Grille
Arcodoro Ristorante
   Italiano
Beaver's Ice House
Bistro Calais
Bistro Le Cep
Brassiere Max & Julie
Brennan's of Houston
Brenner's
The Burning Pear
Cafe Annie
Catalan Food and Wine
Charivari
Chez Nous
Cullen's Upscale American
   Grill
Da Marco
Feast
Glass Wall
Gravitas
The Grove
Ibiza
La Colombe d'Or
La Vista
Mark's American Cuisine
Masraff's
Mockingbird Bistro
Monarch
Noé
Quattro
Rainbow Lodge
The Remington
Shade
T'afia
Vic & Anthony's
Voice

WINE LIST OF NOTE
Well-chosen, well-written
*17
Américas
Amerigo's Grille

Arcodoro Ristorante
   Italiano
Backstreet Cafe
Benjy's
Brassiere Max & Julie
Brennan's of Houston
Brenner's
Brio Tuscan Grill
Cafe Annie
Cafe Rabelais
Capital Grille
Catalan Food and Wine
Chez Nous
Da Marco
Del Frisco's Double Eagle
   Steakhouse
Dolce Vita Pizzeria Enoteca
El Meson
Fleming's Prime Steakhouse
Glass Wall
The Grove
Hugo's
Ibiza
Kiran's
Laurier Cafe
Le Mistral
Lynn's Steakhouse
Mark's American Cuisine
Masraff's
Max's Wine Dive
Mockingbird Bistro
Morton's of Chicago
Pappas Bros. Steakhouse
Perry's Steakhouse & Grille
Pesce
Prego
Quattro
Rainbow Lodge
Reef
The Remington
Rioja
Shade
Smith & Wollensky
So'Vino Bistro & Wine Bar
Strip House
Sullivan's Steakhouse
Taste of Texas
Tony's
Truluck's
Vic & Anthony's

ALPHABETICAL INDEX

*17 139
13 Celsius 83
59 Diner 139
100% Taquito 139

A Moveable Feast. 140, 192
A+ 83, 91
Absinthe Brasserie 83
Acadian Bakers, The 19
Acqua Lounge 84
Addisaba 141
Airline Farmers Market 19
Airline Seafood Mart 19, 41
Aladdin 141
Alamo Drafthouse 20
Alexander the Great Greek. 142, 299
Amazing Cake Supplies 71
Amazon Grill. 142
Américas 143
Amerigo's Grille. 143
Amici. 144
Amy's Ice Cream 20
Andrea Ristorante Italiano. 144
Antica Osteria 146
Antidote Coffee. 21
Aquarium Restaurant. 146, 212
Arandas Bakery 21
Arcodoro Ristorante Italiano . . 147, 154, 216
Armandos 148
Art Institute of Houston 63
Artista 140, 148, 173
Arturo's Uptown Italiano 149
Ashland House 150
Asia Market & Convenience 22
Atkinson Farms 43
Au Petit Paris 150
Aura 150
Avalon Drug Co. & Diner. 152
Avant Garden 84
Azuma/Azumi 152

Baba Yega 153
Backstreet Cafe 153, 154
Baker Street Pub & Grill 85
Baker's Ribs 206
Balkan Market 22
Bamboo House 156
Bar Annie 85, 91
Barbecue Inn 156, 241
Barnaby's Cafe 156
Bayou City Farmers' Market 28, 43
Bayou City Seafood 'N Pasta 209
BBQ Pits by Klose 37

BB's 157
Beaujolais Wine and Food Festival 24
Beaver's Ice House 113, 157
Becks Prime 157
Beirne, Maynard & Parsons, LLP 23
Belden's 25
Bellaire Broiler Burger 159
Belvedere. 85
Benihana 212
Benjy's . . . . 158, 302 (recipe)
Bergner and Johnson 33
Bering's 66
Berryhill Baja Grill 158, 254
Be-Wiched Bistro 160
Bice 160
Big Mama's Homecookin' 179
Bistro Bar 86, 91
Bistro Calais 160
Bistro Don Camillo 161
Bistro Lancaster 161
Bistro Le Cep 162
Bistro Provence 162
Black Labrador Pub 86, 104, 140
Black Swan Pub 87
Black Walnut Cafe 163
Blanco's Bar & Grill 88
Blue Fish House 163
Bombay Brasserie 165
Boom Boom Room, The 88
Boondoggles Pub 113
Brasil 25
Brassiere Max & Julie 165
Breakfast Klub 166, 179
Brennan's of Houston . . . .
. . . . 62, 154, 167, 244 (recipe)
Brenner's 167
Brewery Tap 88
Brian O'Neill's Irish Pub & Restaurant . . . 89
Brio Tuscan Grill 168
Brown Bag Deli 168
Brownstone, The 169
Bubba's Texas Burger Shack 159
Buffalo Grille, The 169
Buffalo Hardware 66
Bull and Bear Tavern and Eatery, The . . . 89
Burning Pear, The 170
Burns Bar BQ 206
Byzantio Cafe & Bar 89

Cadillac Bar 170
Caesar Salad Competition 24
Cafe 101 171
Cafe Adobe 97

At the Oceanaire Seafood Room, the oyster menu changes daily.

Cafe Annie .... 97, 171, 236 (recipe), 327
Cafe at the J. 145
Cafe Benedicte. 172
Cafe Express 172, 192
Cafe Extraordinaire 172
Cafe Le Jadeite. 174
Cafe Lili 174
Cafe Montrose. 174
Cafe Piquet 175
Cafe Pita+ 175
Cafe Rabelais. 176, 262
Cafe Red Onion 176
Candelari's Pizzeria 177, 216
Candylicious 26
Canino's Produce Market. 21, 26
Cantina Laredo 177
Capital Grille. 178
Capital Grille Bar, The. 90
Captain Benny's Half Shell Oyster Bar. . .
 . . . . 178, 227
Carlos Beer Garden 130
Carmelo's. 178
Carol's at Cat Spring 49
Carrabba's Italian Grill. 180
Carter & Cooley 180
Catalan Food and Wine. 180
Catalina Coffee 27
Cava Bistro 140, 181
Cecil's Tavern. 90
Central City Co-op 29
Central Market 21, 27, 71, 125
Cezanne. 92
Chantal Cookware. 66
Charivari 182
Chefs' Produce. 267
Chez Nous. 182
China View 182
Chmielewski's Blueberry Farm. 36
Chocolat du Monde 30
Chocolata Cocoa Bar. 30
Chocolate Bar, The 31
Christian's Tailgate Bar & Grill . . . 92, 159
Christopher's Wine Warehouse 92
Churrascos . . . . 183, 257 (recipe)
Chuy's Comida Deluxe 184, 212, 309
Ciro's Italian Grill 184
Cleburne Cafeteria. 184
Coffee Groundz, The 31
Collina's Italian Cafe 121, 186
Connie's Seafood Market. 32
Conrad N. Hilton College of Hotel and
 Restaurant Management, The 63
Cookie Jar Bakery, The 32
Corelli's 121, 186
Corinthian, The. 33
Cork Cafe 93
Corkscrew, The 93, 125
Cotton Exchange Bar & Lounge, The. . . .
 . . . . 91, 94
Courses 186
Cova 95
Crapitto's 187
Crawfish & Beignets 34
Creekside Farmers Market 29
Cricket's Creamery & Caffe. 187
Croissant Brioche 34
Culinary Institute LeNotre 63
Cullen's Upscale American Grill. 187
Cupcake Cafe 34
Cuts of Color 43

Da Marco 188
Dacapo's Pastry Cafe 36
Daily Grind, The. 36
Daily Review Cafe 173, 189
Damian's Cucina Italiana. 189
D'Amico's Italian Market Cafe. 188
Danton's Gulf Coast Seafood Kitchen . . . .
 . . . . 190, 227, 289
Darband Shishkabob 190
Deco 95
Del Frisco's Double Eagle Steakhouse . . . 190
Demeris. 299
Denis' Seafood House 193
Dessert Gallery. . 36, 205 (recipe), 213, 269
Dharma Cafe. 193
Discovery Green 33
Divino. 194
Dolce Vita Pizzeria Enoteca. 192, 216
Doña Tere Tamales 38, 254
Doneraki 196
Dosey Doe Coffee 38
Downing Street Pub 91, 95
Droubi's Bakery & Deli. 38
Dry Creek Cafe 196
D'Vine Wine of Texas 96, 125

E&B Orchards 46
Edible Arrangements 39
Einstein Bros. Bagels 53
El Meson........................ 196
El Pueblito Place 196
El Pupusodromo 197
El Rey Taqueria 197, 231
El Tiempo 198, 254
El Tiempo Market................. 39
Embossed Graphics of Texas 33
Empire Cafe 40
Empire Turkish Grill 198
Epicure Bakery 40
Eric's Restaurant 199
Escalante's 199
Events 33
Events Company, The 33

Fadi's Mediterranean Grill . . . 192, 201, 299
Farmers Market Association......... 17
Farrago 201
Feast 202
Field of Greens 202
Fiesta Mart 21, 40
Finer Event, A 33
Firkin & Phoenix, The.............. 96
Flat, The 98
Fleming's Prime Steakhouse......... 202
Floyd's Cajun Seafood House 209
Flying Saucer.................... 113
Fogo De Chao................... 203
Fountain View Cafe............... 203
Four Seasons Hotel Lobby Bar....... 98
Fox Sports Grill 98, 116
Frank's Chop House 204
Fredlyn Nut Company 42
French Gourmet Bakery 42
French Riviera Bakery & Cafe 44
Frenchie's...................... 204
Frenchy's Chicken 204, 241
Front Porch Pub 99, 113, 116
Fuegovivo Churrascaria 206
Fung's Kitchen.......... 185, 207, 212

Garcia, Arthur.................... 33
Gator Pit....................... 37
Gelato Blu...................... 44
Generations Tea Room 60
Gigi's Asian Bistro & Dumpling Bar . . . 207
Gilhooley's 208, 278
Ginger Man, The............. 99, 113
Glass Wall 208
Golden Foods Supermarket 44
Goode Co. Hall of Flame 37
Goode Co. Taqueria & Hamburgers .....
.... 166, 209

Goode Co. Texas Bar-B-Que ....
.... 192, 210, 269
Goode Co. Texas Seafood ....
..... 210, 227, 254, 278, 283 (recipe)
Goode's Armadillo Palace....... 102, 278
Gorditas Aguascalientes.... 166, 210, 231
Grand Lux Cafe................... 211
Grand Wine and Food Affair......... 24
Grappino di Nino 102, 173
Gravitas.................. 211, 262, 327
Greater Houston Convention & Visitors
  Bureau............ inside front cover
Gremillion Gallery.................. 33
Griff's Shenanigans Cafe & Bar 102
Gringo's Mexican Kitchen 213
Grotto 214
Grove, The...................... 214
Guadalajara Bar and Grill 215
Guava Lamp 100
Gulf Coast Entertainment........... 33
Gundermann's Peachland Farms 43

Haak Vineyards and Winery 103
Hand, Phyllis 33
Hank's Ice Cream Parlor 45
Hans' Village Bier and Vino Haus 113
Hard Rock Cafe............. 212, 215
Harp, The 104
Harry's........................ 216
Hattermann's Poultry Farms 43
Hebert's Specialty Meats 45
Henderson's Chicken Shack......... 241
Hickory Hollow 212
Hideaway, The.................. 105
Hilltop Herb Farm Restaurant........ 49
Hilton Americas – Lobby Bar 105
Himalaya...................... 217
Hobbit Cafe 217
Hollywood Vietnamese & Chinese .....
.... 200, 218
Hong Kong Food Market 41, 46
Hot Bagel Shop................... 53
House of Coffee Beans.............. 47
House of Pies.............. 48, 200, 269
Houston Community College Central . . . 63
Houston Downtown Management District
.... back cover flap
Houston Farmers' Market 28
Houston Pecan Company 48, 71
Houston Wine Merchant........... 106
Houstonian – The Bar, The 91, 106
Hugo's . . 87 (recipe), 97, 154, 173, 218, 254
Hungry's Cafe and Bistro........... 219

Ibiza 219
Ikea.......................... 213

In Bloom 33
India Grocers 48
Indika 220
Inka South American Cuisine 221
Inn at Dos Brisas 49
Inn at the Ballpark – Atrium Bar & Lounge
 107
In-N-Out 100
Inversion Coffee House 50
Irma's 221
Isla Coqui 222
Istanbul Grill 222

Jabour's Fine Dining 222
James Coney Island 224
Japaneiro's Sushi Bistro & Latin Grill . . . 224
Jarro Cafe 166
Jasper's 224
Java Java 50
Jax Grill 225, 278
Jerusalem Halal Meat Market 50
Jimmy G's Cajun Seafood Restaurant . . . .
 . . . . 225, 289
Jimmy Wilson's Seafood & Chop House . . 226
Jones Hall 33
Josephine's 226
Joyce's Seafood & Steaks 228
JR's Bar and Grill 100
Juice Box 51
Julia's Bistro 228

Kahn's Delicatessen 229
Kam's Fine Chinese Cuisine 229
Kaneyama 229
Kanomwan 230
Karr Limousine 33
Kasra Persian Grill 230
Katy Farmer's Market 29
Katz Coffee 43
Katz's Deli 200
Kay's Lounge 107
Kegg's Candies 51
Kelvin Arms 107, 113
Kenneally's Irish Pub 104, 108, 216
Kenny & Ziggy's 145, 231
Kenzo Sushi Bistro 232
Kho Bo 51
Khun Kay Thai-American Cafe 232
Khyber North Indian Grill 233
Killen's Steakhouse 233
Kim Son 154, 185, 234
King Biscuit Patio Cafe 234
King's Orchards, The 36
Kiran's 60, 235
Kirby's Prime Steakhouse 237
Kobain 116

Kobe 238
Kolache Factory 52
Kraftsmen Baking 52, 140
Kroger Signature 53
Kubo's Sushi Bar and Grill 238
KUHF-88.7 Houston Public Radio 57

La Boucherie 54
La Carafe 108, 140
La Colombe d'Or 140, 239
La Colombe d'Or – The Bar 110
La Griglia 239
La Guadalupana Bakery & Cafe . . . 240, 309
La Madeleine 54
La Mexicana 240
La Michoacana Meat Market 54
La Palatera 56
La Strada 240
La Tapatia Taqueria 242
La Trattoria 242
La Victoria Bakery 56
La Vista 121, 242
L'Aglio 62, 66
Lake House Waterside Cafe, The 243
L'Alliance Francais de Houston 125
Lance's Turtle Club 130
Lankford Grocery & Market . . 159, 243, 278
Last Concert Cafe 245
Late Night Pie 245
Latina Cafe 245
Laurier Cafe 246
Le Leed's Cooking School 62
Le Mistral 154, 246
Le Petit Paris Bakery 56
Leibman's Wine & Fine Foods 58
Lemongrass Cafe 247
Les Givral's Kahve 247
Lexington Grille 250
Linen House 33
Little Hip's Diner 250
Live Sports Cafe 110
Lola's 111
London Sizzler 250
Lopez's Restaurant 212
Louisiana Foods 41, 58
Lounge at Benjy's, The 111
Luby's Cafeterias 212
Lucio's BYOB & Grill 121
Luling City Market 206, 251
Lupe Tortilla's 212, 251
Lyndon's Pit Bar-B-Q 252
Lynn's Steakhouse 252

Madras Pavilion 145, 253
Magnolia Bar & Grill 209, 253
Magnolia Bar, The 111

Mai's Restaurant 200, 254
Mak Chin's 255
Mama's Cafe 255, 278
Mardi Gras Grill 209
Marfreless 112
Maria Selma 166, 256, 309
Marini's Empanada House. 256
Mark's American Cuisine. . 256, 318 (recipe)
Masraff's 258
Massa's. 258
Matt Family Orchards 36
Max's Wine Dive 241, 259, 327
McCain's Market 58
McCormick & Schmick's. 227, 259
McElroy's Irish Pub 112
McGonigel's Mucky Duck . . . 104, 113, 114
Merida. 260
Messina Hof 49
Mexico's Deli Tortas and Tacos 231
Mezzanotte 260
Mi Luna 261
Mi Tienda 59
Mia Bella. 261
Midtown Farmers Market 29
Mingalone Italian Bar & Grill 261
Mint Cafe 263
Mission Burritos 192, 263
Miyako 263
Mo Mong 264
Mockingbird Bistro Wine Bar . . . .
. . . . 109 (recipe), 264, 327
Mojo Risin' 60
Molina's Mexican Restaurant 212
Monarch 173, 265
Monkey Bar. 130
Monument Inn 265
Moo Hive Honey Ice Cream 61
Morton's of Chicago 266
Mosaic. 114
Mugsy's 115

Nam 266
Nam Gang. 268
Nassau Bay Farmer's Market 29
Nelore Churrascaria. 268
New Golden Palace Restaurant 185
New York Bagel & Coffee Shop. . . . .
. . . . 53, 145, 262, 268
Nidda Thai 270
Nielsen's Delicatessen. 270
Niko Niko's 271, 299
Ninfa's. . . . . 55 (recipe), 97, 271
Nino's 272
Nippon 272
Nippon Daido 61
Nit Noi Thai 273

Noah's Ark Bar & Grill 130
Noé 273
Noodle House 88 274
North China 274
Notsuoh 115
Nundini Food Market. 61

Ocean Palace 185, 274
Oceanaire Seafood Room, The. . . 227, 275
Olde World Farms. 43
Olivette 275
Omaha Steaks, Inc. 64
Ooh La La 64
Open City Bistro 276
Oporto Cafe 115
Original Greek Festival, The 24
Otilia's 276
Otto's Barbecue & Hamburgers. 276
Ouisie's Table . . . . . 164 (recipe), 173, 276
Outriggers 131

Palazzo's Trattoria. 276
Palm, The 280
Palmer Packaging Supplies. 71
Panera Bread Bakery Cafe 65
Pang Tai's Stir Fry Bistro 280
Pappadeaux Seafood Kitchen. . . . .
. . . . 280, 289, 299
Pappas Bar-B-Q. 281
Pappas Bros. Steakhouse 281
Pappas Burger 299
Pappas Seafood House. 281
Pappasito's Cantina 282
Pappy's Cafe 282
Parador, The 33
Party Cloths. 33
Pasha 284
Path of Tea, The. 56, 65, 71
Patrenella's/Corleone's 284
Patu. 284
Paulie's. 285
Penzey's Spices 65
Perbacco 285
Perry's Steakhouse & Grille 286
Pesce . . . . 151 (recipe), 227, 286
Pete's Fine Meats 67, 159
Pho Danh 286
Phoenicia Deli. 287
Phoenicia Specialty Foods 68
Piatto 287
Picnic 68, 192
Pico's Mex-Mex 288, 309
Pie in the Sky. 69
Pitts and Spits 37
Pizzitola's Bar-B-Cue 206, 288
PK's Blue Water Grill. 288

Polonia 290
Polo's Signature 290
Post Oak Grill 290
Prego........................... 291
Pronto Cucinino 291
Pub Fiction 116

Qin Dynasty 292
Quattro 155, 292

RA Sushi 292
Ragin Cajun 209, 289, 294
Rainbow Lodge.... 155, 223 (recipe), 294
Raindrop Chocolate 69
Rao's Bakery 70
Rattan Pan-Asian Bistro............ 295
Raven Grill 155, 262, 295, 327
Red Basil 296
Red Lion Pub 104, 113, 116
Reef .... 35 (recipe), 296
Reggae Hut 297
Remington Bar, The 91, 117
Remington, The................... 297
Rice Epicurean Cooking School....... 62
Rice Epicurean Market 70
Rice, Harry 33
Rice University, Susanne M. Glasscock
    School of Continuing Studies 125
Richard's Liquors & Fine Wines 117
Richmond Arms 113, 118
Rickshaw Far East Bistro 297
Rio Ranch 155, 279, 297
Rio Ranch Bar.................... 118
Rioja........................... 300
Ripcord, The 101
Ristorante Cavour 300
Rodeo Uncorked! Roundup and Best Bites
    Competition.................. 25
Roll-N Saloon 120
Romano's Flying Pizza 300
Rouge 301
Royers Round Top................. 49
Rudi Lechner's 301
Rudyard's British Pub 120
Ruggles Cafe Bakery 70
Ruggles Grill 303
Russian General Store 72
Rustika Cafe & Bakery 72, 269
Ruth's Chris Steakhouse............ 303

Saba's.......................... 145
Sacher, Karen 33
Saffron......................... 304
Sage............................ 304
Saigon Pagolac................... 304
Saint Arnold Brewing Company 122

Salud! Winery 123, 125
Sambuca 123
Sandy's Produce Market............ 72
Santa Fe Bar and Patio............. 100
Sawadee........................ 305
Scott Gertner's Sky Bar & Grille 124
Serenitea Tea Room 60
Shade................... 155, 305
Shawarma King.................. 306
Shay McElroy's Irish Pub 124
Sichuan Cuisine................... 306
Simposio 307
Skeeter's........................ 212
Skyline Bar & Grill 307
Smith & Wollensky 307
Social Lounge & Patio Bar, The...... 124
Soma........................... 308
Someburger..................... 159
Sonoma Retail Wine Bar & Boutique ....
    .... 125, 126
Sorbetto's........................ 73
Sorrento........................ 308
SOS Taste of the Nation 25
South Beach the Nightclub 101
Sovereign Services 33
So'Vino Bistro & Wine Bar 309
Spanish Flowers.............. 200, 310
Spanish Village 97, 241, 310
Spec's Wines, Spirits & Finer Foods... 126
Spencer's for Steaks & Chops........ 311
Stag's Head Pub, The 113, 127
Star Pizza.................. 216, 311
Starbucks
    at Willowbrook................. 76
    Ella and 43rd 77
    Highland Village................ 76
    I-45............................ 77
    Kingwood...................... 77
    Montrose 76
    River Oaks 76
    Spring......................... 77
    Westheimer and Post Oak........ 77
State Bar & Lounge, The............ 91
Stelio's......................... 312
Stir-It-Up Coffeehouse 73
Stone Mill Bakers 74
Strip House...................... 312
Sugarbaby's 74
Sullivan's Steakhouse 312
Super H Mart 75
Super Jordan Imported Food & Bakery... 75
Super Pita 145
Super Vanak International Food 75
Sur La Table................. 63, 66
Sushi Jin 313
Sushi King....................... 313

The Backstreet Cafe patio, at night.

Suzie's Grill 145
Swinging Door 279
Sylvia's Enchilada Kitchen . . . 279, 309, 314

T.K. Bitterman's. 128
Taco Milagro 262, 315
Tacos a Go-Go 316
T'afia. 314
Tan Tan 200
Taqueria Arandas. 231
Taste of Texas. 279, 316
Tasting Room, The 127
Tavern 116
Taverna Winery & Restaurant 128
Té House of Tea. 60, 78
Tea with Charles Marcel 52
Teala's 316
Teotihuacan. 166, 309, 317
Tex Chick 317
Texas Orchards 36
Texas Pit Crafters. 37
Texas Tamale Company 254
Thai Pepper 319
Thai Spice 320
Thai Sticks. 320
Thelma's Bar-B-Que. 206, 320
Thierry Andre Tellier Cafe & Pastry Shop . . 78
This Is It! 179, 279, 321
Three Brothers Bakery 53, 78, 145
Tila's Restaurante & Bar 155, 321
Tiny Boxwood's Espresso Bar and Cafe . . 322
Tio Pepe 323
Tommy's Seafood Steakhouse. 323
Tony Mandola's Gulf Coast Kitchen . . . . .
. . . . 195 (recipe), 289, 323
Tony's 324

Tony's Bar Supply 67
Tookie's 324
Tree House, The 129
Treebeards 325
Trevísio 325
Triple-A Restaurant 325
Truluck's 326

Under the Volcano. 129
University of Houston Continuing
    Education 125
Uptown Sushi 326

Van Loc 327
Vargo's 328
Vic & Anthony's 328
Vieng Thai 329
Vietnam Restaurant. 121
Vietopia. 329
Vincent's 330
Vine Wine Room 131
Vineyard on the Square 125, 132
Vino 100 132
Voice 330

Waldo's Coffee House 79
Warren's Inn 132
Waza Sushi & Robata Grill 331
Wells Fargo 119
West Alabama Ice House 133
Who Made the Cake? 79
Whole Foods Market. 21, 41, 79
Williams Sonoma 67
Willie G's. 331
Wine Bucket Boutique & Bar, The . . . 134
Wood Duck Farms 43
Words & Food. 43
Wortham Center Onstage 33
Wunsche Bros. Cafe & Saloon. . . 279, 331

Yao Restaurant & Bar 332
Yatra Brasserie 332
Yia Yia Mary's Greek Kitchen 299
Yildizlar. 333
Yo' Mama's Soul Food 179
Yum Yum Cha 121, 185, 333

Zabak's 334
Zake Sushi Lounge 334
Ziggy's Healthy Grill 335
Zimm's Martini & Wine Bar 134
Zydeco. 335